AF699270

Inflation and Pensions

Other publications of the
PENSION RESEARCH COUNCIL:

Fundamentals of Private Pensions—*Dan M. McGill*
Concepts of Actuarial Soundness in Pension Plans—*Dorrance C. Bronson*
Social Aspects of Retirement—*Otto Pollak*
Positive Experiences in Retirement—*Otto Pollak*
Ensuring Medical Care for the Aged—*Mortimer Spiegelman*
Legal Protection of Private Pension Expectations—*Edwin W. Patterson*
Legal Status of Employee Benefit Rights under Private Pension Plans—*Benjamin Aaron*
Decision and Influence Processes in Private Pension Plans—*James E. McNulty, Jr.*
Fulfilling Pension Expectations—*Dan M. McGill*
Collectively Bargained Multi-Employer Pension Plans—*Joseph J. Melone*
Actuarial Aspects of Pension Security—*William F. Marples*
Status of Funding under Private Pension Plans—*Frank L. Griffin, Jr.*, and *Charles L. Trowbridge* (out of print)
Guaranty Fund for Private Pension Obligations—*Dan M. McGill*
Preservation of Pension Benefit Rights—*Dan M. McGill*
Retirement Systems for Public Employees—*Thomas P. Bleakney*
Employer Guarantee of Pension Benefits—*Dan M. McGill*
Reciprocity among Private Multiemployer Pension Plans—*Maurice E. McDonald*
A New Look at Accounting for Pension Costs—*William D. Hall and David L. Landsittel*
Social Security and Private Pension Plans: Competitive or Complementary?—*Dan M. McGill* (ed.)
Pension Mathematics—*Howard E. Winklevoss*
Indexation of Pension and Other Benefits—*Robert J. Myers*
Joint Trust Pension Plans—*Daniel F. McGinn*
Financing the Civil Service Retirement System—*Dan M. McGill* (ed.)
Continuing Care Retirement Communities—*Howard E. Winklevoss* and *Alwyn V. Powell*
Social Investing—*Dan M. McGill* (ed.)
Employer Accounting for Pensions—*E. L. Hicks and C. L. Trowbridge*
Pensions, Economics and Public Policy—*Richard A. Ippolito*
Fundamentals of Private Pensions—*Dan M. McGill*
Search for a National Retirement Income Policy—*Jack L. VanDerhei*

HD
7105.35
.U6
W33
1987

SOLOMON R. BAKER LIBRARY
BENTLEY COLLEGE

Inflation and Pensions

Susan M. Wachter
Associate Professor of Finance
The Wharton School
The University of Pennsylvania

1987

Published for the
Pension Research Council
Wharton School
University of Pennsylvania
by

RICHARD D. IRWIN, INC.
Homewood, Illinois 60430

© 1987 by the
Pension Research Council
Wharton School
University of Pennsylvania

All Rights Reserved

This book was set in Melior by Compset Inc.
The editors were Karen Smith and Jean Roberts.
The production manager was Bette Ittersagen.
The Maple/Vail Book Publishing Group was the printer and binder.

ISBN 0-256-05957-8
Library of Congress Catalog Card No. 87–80744

Printed in the United States of America

1 2 3 4 5 6 7 8 9 0 MP 4 3 2 1 0 9 8 7

PENSION RESEARCH COUNCIL

Chairman and Research Director

Dan M. McGill, Chairman, Insurance Department, Wharton School

Associate Research Director

Jack L. VanDerhei, *Assistant Professor of Insurance,* Wharton School

J. Vance Anderson, *Counsel for Employee Relations,* Mobil Oil Corp., New York City

Kenneth Blaylock, *President,* American Federation of Government Employees, Washington, D.C.

Zvi Bodie, *Associate Professor of Finance and Economics,* Boston University

George W. Cowles, *Senior Vice President,* Bankers Trust Company, New York City

Charles D. Ellis, *Partner,* Greenwich Associates, Greenwich, Connecticut

Michael Gordon, *Partner,* Mittelman and Gordon, Washington, D.C.

Donald S. Grubbs, Jr., F.S.A., *Consulting Actuary,* George B. Buck Consulting Actuaries, Washington, D.C.

Ronald E. Keller, *Senior Vice President,* Bankers Life Company, Des Moines

Raymond C. Lauver, *Member of the Board,* Financial Accounting Standards Board, Stamford

Alicia H. Munnell, *Senior Vice President and Director of Research,* Federal Reserve Bank of Boston

Roger F. Murray, *Emeritus Professor of Banking,* Columbia University, Wolfeboro, New Hampshire

Robert J. Myers, F.S.A., *International Consultant on Social Security,* Silver Spring, Maryland

George J. Pantos, Esq., Vedder, Price, Kaufman, Kammholz & Day, Washington, D.C.

Samuel H. Preston, *Director,* Population Studies Center, University of Pennsylvania, Philadelphia

James E. Pesando, *Professor of Economics,* University of Toronto

Jerry S. Rosenbloom, *Professor of Insurance,* Wharton School, Philadelphia

Sylvester Schieber, *Director of Research and Information Center,* The Wyatt Company, Washington, D.C.

Marc M. Twinney, *Manager of Pension Department,* Ford Motor Company, Dearborn, Michigan

L. Edwin Wang, *President,* Board of Pensions of Lutheran Church in America, Minneapolis

Randolph W. Westerfield, *Professor of Finance,* Wharton School, Philadelphia

Howard E. Winklevoss, *Vice President,* Johnson & Higgins, New York City

Howard Young, F.S.A., *Special Consultant to the President,* United Auto Workers, Detroit

PURPOSE OF THE COUNCIL

The Pension Research Council was formed in 1952 to undertake academic research into those institutional arrangements designed to provide financial resources for secure and dignified old age. It seeks to broaden public understanding of these complex arrangements through basic research into their social, economic, legal, actuarial, and financial foundations. While generally geared to the long view of the pension institution, projects undertaken by the Council are always relevant to real life concerns and frequently focus on issues under current debate. The Council does not speak with one voice and espouses no particular point of view. The members do share a general desire to encourage and strengthen private-sector approaches to old-age economic security, while recognizing the essential role of social security and other income-maintenance programs in the public sector.

PREFACE

This monograph analyzes inflation's impact on pensions. Its purpose is to further an understanding of the causes of inflation, inflation's impact on pensions, and alternative public policy responses. Thus, the monograph is written to be accessible to the noneconomist reader. Where the issues are unavoidably difficult, technical appendixes are added with nontechnical summaries provided in the text.

The monograph is divided into four parts. Part One reviews the causes of inflation, its measurement, the process of indexation, and the extent of indexation of retirement benefits. Part Two analyzes the impact of inflation on capital markets and the implications for the indexation of pensions. Part Three focuses on the fundamental factors that influence the demand for savings and pensions, and how these are affected by inflation. Part Four discusses public policy issues and concludes with a summary of inflation's impact on pensions and alternative public policy responses.

Each of these parts begins with the basic economic theory and empirical evidence so that readers will be able to form their own understanding of the underlying theoretical issues and the extent to which the available evidence supports the theory.

Given the substantial lack of data, much remains unknown about inflation's impact on pensions, especially in the two critical areas of whether individuals rationally plan their retirement savings and whether they recognize inflation's negative impact on the real value of their nominal pensions. Nonetheless, on the basis of economic theory and the available evidence, this study comes to five major conclusions.

First, to prevent inflation's erosion of the real value of nominal pensions, variable annuity pensions can be designed to provide an inflation-hedging income stream; the cost to employees, however, would substantially exceed the cost of nominal pensions. Second, fully indexed private pensions are not economically feasible. Third, with moderate inflation and with a large proportion of the average retiree's preretirement income replaced by indexed Social Security and Medicare benefits, costlier inflation-hedging pensions may be neither freely chosen nor socially optimal. Fourth, increased longevity and possible future Social Security and Medicare benefit decreases, if combined with renewed double-digit inflation, may make some form of private pension indexation necessary, in spite of its cost, to assure the public policy goal of retirement income security. Fifth, these additional costs can be avoided if inflation is controlled by appropriate monetary policy.

This monograph could not have been written without the continuing advice and support of the truly exemplary advisory committee established by the Pension Research Council at the Wharton School. The members were Robert A. Brown, Arthur W. Frank, Jr., A. Gilbert Heebner, G. David Hurd, P. Michael Laub, Adrian Lee, Barry L. Shemin, Michael Sproule, Keith Stevenson, James Swenson, Dr. Howard E. Winklevoss, and Dr. Dan M. McGill. In addition, the author is indebted to Dr. Alicia Munnell, Dr. Jeffrey Jaffe, Dr. Zvi Bodie, Dr. James Pesando, and Dr. Robert J. Myers for their comments and the insight of their scholarly work, and also to the many researchers who are too numerous to list here but whose studies are cited throughout. Conclusions and errors of omission and commission are the sole responsibility of the author.

The author gratefully acknowledges the funding of this monograph by a grant from the Pension Research Council at the Wharton School of the University of Pennsylvania.

Susan M. Wachter

CONTENTS

PART ONE

Causes, Measurement, and Indexation of Inflation

This part reviews the causes of inflation, its measurement, the process of indexation, and the indexation of pensions to inflation. Chapter 1 analyzes the causes of inflation. Long-run inflation results from an ongoing excess supply of money that drives down the value of money relative to the value of goods and services. In the short run, supply and demand shocks can cause inflation, without money supply expansion. Supply shocks decrease real output growth, rendering a previously nonexpansionary money supply excessive. The result is a one-time price level increase. Demand shocks increase the real interest rate, which decreases the demand for money balances, again rendering a previously nonexpansionary money supply excessive. While such factors can be responsible for a one-period increase in the price level or the inflation rate, inflation cannot persist without money supply expansion.

The measurement and indexation of inflation are discussed in Chapter 2. Inflation is defined as "neutral" if it is caused by a fully anticipated, neutrally distributed increase in the money supply that has no real effects; its measurement is easy; and "indexing" occurs automatically—all payments adjust by the anticipated inflation rate. But real world inflation is not neutral; it is accompanied by real effects, especially in capital markets. In the short run, money-demand and supply-shock causes of inflation are accompanied by changes in relative prices, output levels, and real interest rates. A change in the anticipated rate of growth of the money supply also has real effects, because the resulting inflation differs from the previously anticipated inflation rate embodied in contracts.

Measurement of nonneutral inflation poses difficult and, to some extent, unsolvable theoretical and technical problems. More critically, there is no technically feasible way to index contracts to neutralize the effects of inflation. While indexation of pensions and other contracts can neutralize the effects of money-shock inflation, indexation worsens the effects of inflation caused by supply shocks. In particular, indexation exacerbates the output slowdowns that are correlated with supply-shock inflation. Nonetheless, monetary contracts that are fixed in nominal terms, and especially long-term contracts such as pensions, are vulnerable to inflation. Thus, even though residual effects remain, partial forms of indexing of long-term contracts may prove helpful if there is substantial uncertainty over future inflation rates.

Chapter 3 surveys the existing extent of indexation of retirement benefits in private and public sector plans in the United States and briefly reviews pension indexation in other countries.

Causes of Inflation

1

Excessive Growth in the Money Supply as a Cause of Inflation

The Long Run

Inflation in the long run is a monetary phenomenon. To indicate the role of the money supply in the long run with a simplified example, assume that the economy is at full employment, producing a given amount of real national income or, equivalently, output, measured as real gross national product, GNP. Also, assume a given money supply. With real full-employment output and money supply unchanged, there is no inflation. If the money supply grows and real output stays the same, inflation results. More dollars are used to purchase the same real output so that prices are bid up and each dollar buys less. The increase in the money supply, if it occurs only once, bids up the price level for a one-time positive inflation rate. If the money supply increase occurs every year, ongoing or long-run inflation results.

A familiar monetarist statement of the relationship of inflation to the money supply is known as the quantity theory equation:

$$MV = PY \tag{1.1}$$

where money supply is indicated by M, the price level by P, real output (or income) by Y, and the income velocity of money by V.

The quantity theory equation does no more than define the term V, the income velocity of money, as equal to $\frac{PY}{M}$. As a definition, it is always true.

The quantity theory equation can also be expressed in first difference form, as follows:

$$\dot{P} = \dot{M} - \dot{Y} + \dot{V} \tag{1.2}$$

where dot superscripts indicate percentage rates of change.[1] Again, this is an identity that must always hold since, by definition, $\dot{V} = \dot{P} + \dot{Y} - \dot{M}$. Without additional assumptions, there can be no presumption as to direction of causality among the four variables.

However, economic theory converts Equation 1.2 into a hypothesis about the long-run relationship between inflation and money supply growth. This is accomplished by assuming that, in the long run, the rate of growth of real output and velocity are independently determined and not affected by the growth rate of the money supply. Thus, in the quantity theory equation, it is the inflation rate that adjusts to the given rate of growth of the money supply, determined by monetary authorities.[2] In the long run, changes in the money supply growth rate, $\dot{M}$, have no impact on $\dot{V}$ and $\dot{Y}$, which are at their long-run equilibrium levels, but rather cause one-for-one changes in the inflation rate, $\dot{P}$.[3] The long-run equilibrium rate of growth of real output is $\dot{Y}_f$, subscripted to indicate that $\dot{Y}_f$ may be greater or less than the actual rate of growth of real output $\dot{Y}$. Assuming unchanged velocity, inflation results if the rate of growth of the money supply exceeds $\dot{Y}_f$. Hence, given the rate of growth of real output and velocity, it is an excessive supply of money that propels the price level upward and creates inflation.[4]

The monetarist policy implication, embodied in the quantity theory equation, is that in the long run, monetary authorities can reduce inflation by limiting the money supply growth rate. Moreover, monetary authorities can achieve long-run price stability by equating the money supply growth rate, $\dot{M}$, to the long-run growth rate in real potential (full-employment) output, $\dot{Y}_f$, with an adjustment for long-run trends in velocity when necessary.

The Short Run

Monetarists acknowledge, however, that it is not possible for monetary authorities to eliminate short-run fluctuations in the price level or inflation rate by controlling the rate of monetary expansion.

First, in the short run, inflation can be caused by several factors other than overexpansion of the money supply. Increases in aggregate demand for goods and services raise interest rates. Higher interest rates raise the cost of holding money and increase $\dot{V}$, the income velocity of money. The result is demand-pull inflation. Declines in $\dot{Y}_f$ also translate into increased $\dot{P}$, unless monetary authorities foresee the changes in $\dot{Y}_f$ in sufficient time to decrease $\dot{M}$. In addition, excess demand bids up prices in commodity sectors with flexible prices and, with inflexible prices elsewhere in the economy, the overall price level will rise, temporarily. These nonmonetary causes of inflation are discussed further below.

Second, in the short run, decreases in monetary expansion do not result in equivalent decreases in inflation. Because of lags in price and wage adjustments, the short-run impact of money supply changes falls on velocity and output and not on prices. Thus, in the short run, unlike in the long run, the rate of growth of velocity and real income are not given and are not independent of the money supply growth rate; the assumption that causality goes directly from money supply expansion to one-for-one changes in the inflation rate does not hold. Rather, in the short run, the rate of money supply growth influences rates of output and velocity so that a given decrease in the money supply expansion rate does not result immediately in an equivalent decrease in the inflation rate.

The Pervasiveness of Lags in Price and Wage Adjustments. Especially troublesome for the ability of monetary policy to achieve price stability is the positive short-run relationship between money supply growth rates and real income growth rates. A contractionary monetary policy will decrease real income before it decreases inflation, and an expansionary monetary policy will increase real income before it increases inflation. Lags may create a political bias toward increasing price levels and inflation rates over time.

The initial impact of money on real income rather than prices occurs because prices and wages are not fully adjustable. Both formal and informal price and wage contracts are pervasive. With contractual markets, prices and wages are set for some predetermined period when the contract is to be renegotiated.[5] The rationales for implicit and explicit contracts include, first, the saving in the cost of renegotiating the terms of the contract continuously, and second, risk-sharing.

Lags occur in all markets except for the few true, mostly commodity-based, auction markets. The traditional example of lags is the labor union which bargains with a firm to set a three-year contract. Although the contract allows for wage increases each year of the contract, the size of each increase is predetermined. A change in the inflation rate does not result in a wage change until the contract period is over. At the point when contracts are negotiated, the wage level and the rate of wage increases are influenced by past inflation and expectations of future inflation, as well as by immediate market conditions.

The fixed contract is only the proverbial tip of the iceberg. Most firms, whether or not they are unionized, follow a wage pattern in which wages do not respond immediately to market conditions. The rationale is inherent in the desire for an ongoing relationship between firms and their work forces. This arises because jobs, largely as a result of on-the-job training, tend to be highly specific to a given firm. As a consequence, these jobs do not have a direct demand and supply component in the external labor market. Rather, the jobs are part of the internal labor market of the firm, interconnected through a series of promotion ladders. Once workers are promoted, they receive a wage higher than the one they could receive by quitting and starting at the entry level of a new firm. As a result, workers are not always "in the market" and need not always receive market-clearing wages. What is important is the long-run wage received. Because wages need not be continuously recontracted and because frequent wage and price changes are costly (besides the physical costs, lacking an auction to set prices, information must be processed), implicit as well as explicit wage contracts exist. Since these contractual wages are determined for the period of the contract, they will lag any changes in the expectation of future inflation.

Similar examples are easy to find in the product markets, and especially in capital markets. As Chapter 3 will discuss, business puts fixed investment in place for the long term. To minimize risk, it is desirable to finance long-term investment with funds whose costs are contractually fixed for the long term. Variable rate long-term financing is an option, but, as we will see, this exposes the firm to additional risk.

The importance of implicit and explicit contracts is that they create an inertia in the price- and wage-setting process. Due to these institutional factors, prices and wages do not adjust rapidly to market pressures. Rather, they are heavily influenced by past inflation rates and expectations of future inflation.

Role of Lags in Creating a Short-Run Phillips Curve. To understand the implications of price and wage rigidity for the political-economic causes of inflation, it is useful to focus on the aggregate demand for and supply of goods and services, rather than on the demand for and supply of money.

An excessive supply of money is equivalent to an excessive aggregate demand for goods and services, including financial assets.[6] Thus, the scenario of an inflation caused by too great an increase in the money supply can also be described in terms of what happens in the markets for goods and services.

As monetary authorities inject more money into the economy than people originally intended or expected to hold, individuals attempt to reduce their money holdings by purchasing more goods, services, or financial assets. Thus, an excessive increase in the money supply is reflected in an excessive aggregate demand for all goods and services and for financial assets. The prices of financial assets rise in response to the greater demand which is equivalent to a decline in their interest rates. This increases the demand for investment goods and consumer durables and contributes to the excessive aggregate demand for goods and services.

In the contractual sector, firms produce greater output because of the increased demand and because, temporarily, their costs of production have not been bid up. Firms operate at higher than normal capacity during booms. They fire fewer workers and hire more. Before prices fully adjust, output temporarily expands beyond the full-employment level. Some prices, especially those set in auction markets, respond immediately to excess aggregate demand. The money supply increase is reflected in an increase in both output growth and prices. Thus, an increase in real output growth is associated with an increase in inflation.

However, overfull-capacity output levels cannot be sustained. Eventually the increased money supply bids up wages and the prices of all goods and services. In equilibrium, the increase in the rate of money supply expansion leads only to an increase in the price level.[7] Real GNP drops back to the full-employment level. Only nominal GNP (i.e., real GNP expressed in current prices) is increased.

With the higher price level and nominal GNP, the new higher money supply is now demanded and is no longer excessive. Because money supply is no longer excessive, there is no longer excess aggregate demand in the market for goods, services, or financial assets. Sales, output, and employment return to normal levels, as do interest rates. Real output, relative prices, and interest rates are unchanged by the money supply increase. Only the price level has increased.

Thus, eventually, the direction of causality from money supply increases to price increases implied in the quantity theory equation does hold. In the short run, however, money supply increases initially result in real income growth and employment increases. The lack of an immediate adjustment in prices and wages allows the unemployment rate and real income growth rate to differ in the short run from their long-run equilibrium levels. Their inverse variance with unanticipated inflation generates what is known as a short-run Phillips curve.[8]

The Phillips curve can be stated in equation form, as follows:

$$\dot{P} = f(\dot{Y} - \dot{Y}_f, \dot{P}_e) \quad \textbf{(1.3)}$$

In the short run, inflation ($\dot{P}$) is a positive function of (1) the gap between actual and full-employment output growth ($\dot{Y} - \dot{Y}_f$) and (2) inflationary expectations ($\dot{P}_e$). In the long run, $\dot{Y}$ equals $\dot{Y}_f$; and inflation, $\dot{P}$, equals $\dot{P}_e$, the expected and equilibrium inflation rate, at the given excessive money supply growth rate.

To illustrate the workings of short-run and long-run Phillips curves, assume zero excess aggregate demand and no inflationary expectations. The short-run Phillips curve, illustrated as SS' in Figure 1–1, crosses the zero inflation rate at U_e, the nonaccelerating inflation rate of unemployment (NAIRU), which is con-

FIGURE 1–1
Short- and Long-Run Phillips Curves

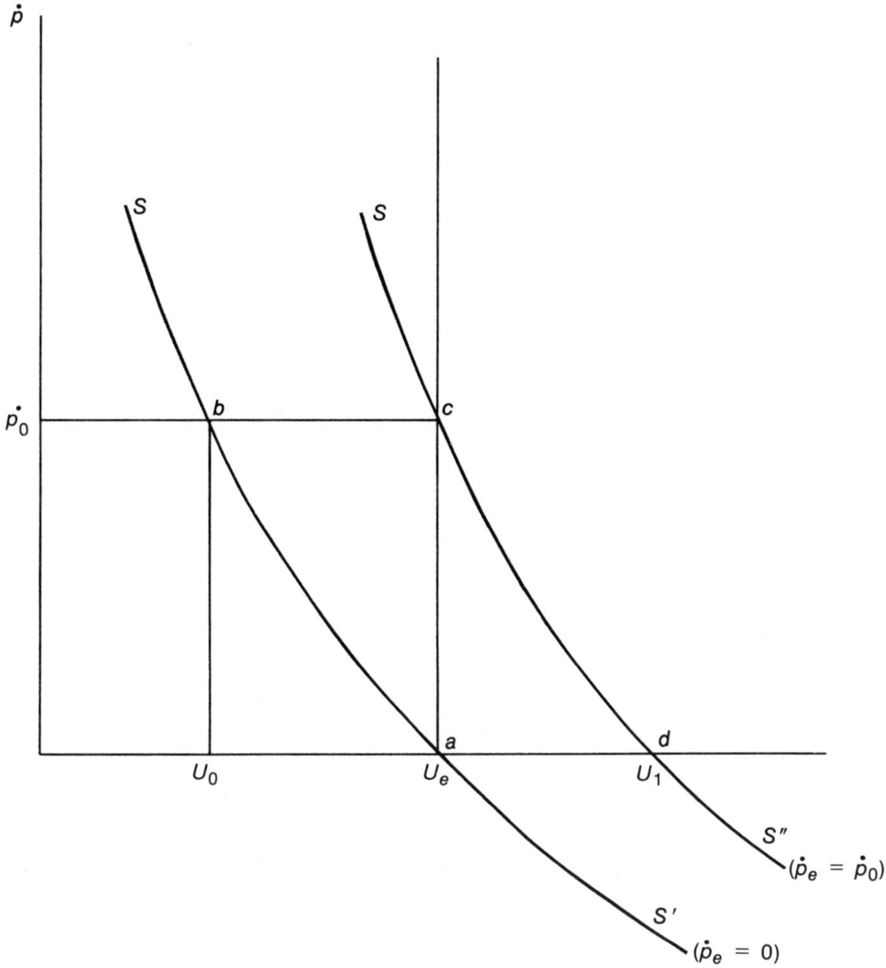

sistent with $\dot{Y}_f$. NAIRU is, by definition, the unemployment rate at which the price level or the inflation rate does not change (because there is no excess aggregate demand). It is also termed the *natural* rate of unemployment. Over time, prices and wages adjust downward in sectors with greater than equilibrium unemployment and rise in sectors with vacancies.[9] Inflation is zero at NAIRU (assuming no inflationary expectations, i.e., with the expected inflation rate, $\dot{P}_e$, equal to zero) because the amount of downward wage pressure due to frictional unemployment is balanced by an equal amount of upward wage pressure due to vacancies.[10]

In this setting, if the government expands aggregate demand with a one-time excessive increase in $\dot{M}$, the positive rate of price and wage increase in sectors with vacancies rises further, and declines in wages and prices in sectors with unemployment lessens. Since some contracts are coming due, the net effect is that some inflation (less than proportionate to $\dot{M}$) is observed in both contractual and auction markets. But the price and wage changes do not clear all markets, since some contracts have not come due. The increase in aggregate demand also results in an increase in output and a decline in unemployment in these sectors.

In Figure 1–1, there is a movement along SS' from point a to point b where U_0 is less than U_e and where the inflation rate, $\dot{P}_0$, is greater than zero. Wages and prices eventually fully adjust upwards in all sectors until at the new higher price and wage levels there is no excess aggregate demand for goods, and vacancies again balance unemployment. At this point, the economy returns to U_e and zero inflation.[11]

With inflation persisting at $\dot{P}_0$ for some time (due to a continuation of the expansionary rate of growth of money supply, $\dot{M}_0$), inflationary expectations will eventually equal the actual inflation rate, $\dot{P}_0$. With all firms expecting $\dot{P}_0$, they will set their wages and prices so that $\dot{P}_0$ results, with no excess aggregate demand and with unemployment equal to U_e. The short-run Phillips curve, in Figure 1–1, shifts up to SS'' so that inflation continues at the expected rate, $\dot{P}_0$ (with $\dot{M}$ equal to $\dot{M}_0$), even without overfull employment. The economy is at point c, with unemployment at the natural rate, U_e, and with inflation and inflationary expectations equal to $\dot{P}_0$. Thus, as stated in the natural rate hypothesis, the economy deviates from the natural rate of unemployment, U_e, only in the short run.

To maintain U below U_e (for example, at U_0) necessitates persistent rises in the actual inflation rate, in inflationary expectations, and in unanticipated money supply growth. At unemployment rates to the left of U_e, actual inflation is always greater than expected inflation. The result magnifies inflationary expectations, causing the short-run Phillips curve to continue to shift upward. While unemployment can be lowered beneath U_e in the short run at the cost of increased inflation, in the long run unemployment returns to U_e, with increased inflation and an increased expected inflation rate. The shifting short-run Phillips curves trace out a vertical long-run Phillips curve at U_e. Thus, the Phillips curve Equation 1.3 indicates that at long-run equilibrium (with money supply expansion just sufficient to support expected inflation, $\dot{P}_e$, plus full-employment income growth, $\dot{Y}_f$) inflation equals expected inflation, $\dot{P}_e$. In the long run, the natural rate hypothesis prevails. It is not possible to trade off higher inflation for lower unemployment. In the long run, the Phillips curve is vertical.

Conversely, in the short run, monetary deceleration results in temporarily higher unemployment (and lower output growth), although eventually proportional disinflation results. This is shown in Figure 1–1 as a movement from point *c* to point *d*, where unemployment is U_1 and inflation is $\dot{P}_0$. If noninflationary growth of the money supply is maintained, inflationary expectations will eventually dissipate, and the Phillips curve will shift back to SS', where because inflationary expectations are zero, full employment is consistent with price stability. Again, the long-run Phillips curve is vertical. Zero inflation is consistent with full employment, after inflationary expectations subside and all contracts are renegotiated.

There is an additional mechanism which can explain both the existence of a short-run trade-off and a long-run vertical Phillips curve. In this case, the mechanism that allows unemployment to vary in the short run is the transitory deviation between the expected and actual inflation rates. A crucial role is played by the inflationary expectations held by workers looking for jobs or suppliers of services in general; the view is that these suppliers (including workers as suppliers of labor) are fooled by the inflation. While they can easily see that their wages are rising during an inflation, it is more difficult for them to judge that the overall wage or price level is rising as well. Hence, workers, for example, believe that their relative or real wages are rising, and this encourages them to accept employment that they would not otherwise accept. This "fooling" of workers leads to the observation that falling unemployment is correlated with above-average rates of inflation (in other words, with actual inflation greater than perceived inflation).[12]

A problem with this analysis is that it seems unlikely that the costs of gathering information about the present are so high that workers' perceptions are likely to stray far from the actual events. The expectational and nominal contract models both provide an explanation for the distinction between the short- and long-run Phillips curves of Figure 1–1. However, the latter seems more consistent with the data.

A more extreme neoclassical position is put forth in some rational expectation models. In these models, excessive growth in the money supply translates into price rises immediately. Thus, there will be no deviation from U_e or from the vertical Phillips curve at any time. That is, firms and laborers are fully aware that the increase in demand for the firm's product is due to an increase in demand for all output so that the increased aggregate demand bids up input prices immediately to such an extent that it does not pay to increase output. Thus, any actions on the part of monetary authorities are fully anticipated and cannot, even in the short run, have any real effects.

To the extent that economic actors either do not fully anticipate the eventual inflationary impact of the growth of money supply or cannot continuously adjust contractually determined wages and prices to new information, monetary authorities do have an impact on output in the short run. The evidence, cited below, indicates that short-run changes in the money supply do have real effects. The long-run result, however, is only higher inflation.

In sum, if the monetarist equations held for the short and long run, control over inflation could be easily accomplished through the money supply. Unfortunately, inflation does not respond immediately, in full, to changes in the money supply growth rate. Decreased monetary expansion decelerates inflation, but only at the cost of a short-run output slowdown. Conversely, increased monetary expansion accelerates inflation, but also yields a short-run output growth spurt. The possibility of manipulating short-run real growth and employment rates, and the political incentives to do so, may make it difficult to adhere to rates of monetary growth consistent with price stability.

In addition, as noted above, the monetarist equations do not hold for the short run because nonmonetary factors, such as autonomous aggregate demand increases, aggregate supply decreases, and relative price increases in commodity sectors, can accelerate short-run inflation without an expansion of money supply growth rates. Short-run inflationary spurts of nonmonetary origin will be transformed into long-run increases in inflation if monetary authorities respond with an expansion of the money supply growth rate.

Nonmonetary causes of short-run inflationary spurts and the incentives for monetary authorities to accelerate money supply growth to accommodate short-run inflationary pressures, with a resulting increase in long-run inflation, are discussed in the next section.

Once monetary policy supports continuing inflation, individuals formulate expectations of future inflation. Not only does inflation become anticipated but the expected rate of future inflation may become more uncertain. A later section of this chapter examines the formulation of inflationary expectations and the concepts of anticipated, unanticipated, and uncertain inflation. The chapter ends with a summary of the political-economic factors that can cause an increase in both the anticipated rate of inflation and inflation uncertainty.

The Interaction of Monetary and Nonmonetary Causes of Inflation

Demand-Pull versus Supply-Shock Inflation

Demand-Pull Inflation. In the short run, demand-pull inflation may be caused by either monetary or nonmonetary factors. In terms of Equation 1.2, a rise in $\dot{M}$ or in $\dot{V}$ can induce increased $\dot{P}$. Nonmonetary inflation occurs through a rise in $\dot{V}$.

Nonmonetary inflation can be caused by an excessive increase in private or government spending, funded by an increase in private or government debt. The increased debt raises the interest rate and $\dot{V}$.

For example, increased government spending can result in inflation, without an increase in the money supply, because the increased government debt raises interest rates. Additional government bonds cannot be sold to the market except at a lower price (i.e., at an increased interest rate). Similarly, a tax decrease, with constant government spending, must be financed with increased government debt which, as before, raises interest rates.

In addition, off-budget federal loans, loan guarantees, or local government borrowing can contribute to excessive aggregate demand. Generally, any autonomous upward shift in public or private investment or consumption spending can cause increased aggregate demand and interest rates.[13]

In terms of Equation 1.2, it is the interest rate increase and consequent velocity rise which cause inflation. The higher interest rate decreases the demand for money, which allows an increase in the price level (and a short-run increase in the inflation rate). The higher interest rate encourages the holdings of smaller real money balances, so that the given money supply is consistent with a higher nominal income and price level.[14]

There are two critical differences in the results of monetary- ($\dot{M}$) and of a nonmonetary- ($\dot{V}$) caused excessive increase in aggregate demand. First, a nonmonetary expansion in the absence of accompanying money supply growth increases debt and interest rates, while an increase in the money supply initially decreases interest rates. Second, as discussed below, the inflation rate increase produced by a nonmonetary demand shock cannot continue without a money supply increase. The long-run effect of expansionary fiscal policy on inflation depends only on monetary policy.

Supply-Shock Inflation. As Equation 1.2 indicates, inflation occurs when the rate of growth of the money supply is expanded by monetary authorities at a pace that exceeds the given full-employment rate of growth of real output. This equation also indicates that there will be inflation if, given the rate of growth of money supply, there is a decline in the potential growth rate of real output. Monetary authorities may be pursuing a previously noninflationary monetary policy with money supply growth equal to expected growth in potential real output, when an unanticipated output slowdown renders their policy inflationary. Such an unanticipated decline has been termed a *supply shock*. Because the supply shock is not anticipated in advance of its occurrence, the money supply increase that has already been scheduled and implemented is too large to maintain price stability.

If supply-shock inflation were accompanied by across-the-board output declines, its effects would be indistinguishable from demand-pull inflation due to monetary expansion. $\dot{P}$ would rise simply because $\dot{M}$ is too large relative to $\dot{Y}$, which is consistent with monetarist Equation 1.2

In fact, supply-shock inflation is generally caused by exogenous output declines in specific sectors, and the result is relative price increases in the affected sectors, along with overall inflationary pressures. Moreover, as a result of the pressure of relative price shifts, the direction of causality embodied in Equation 1.2 may be reversed. Instead of too high $\dot{M}$ relative to $\dot{Y}$ causing higher $\dot{P}$, price rises may occur without any of these changes. The rise in $\dot{P}$ may then cause an endogenous rise in $\dot{V}$ and decline in $\dot{Y}$.

This reverse causality occurs because of sectoral bottlenecks, together with price adjustment lags elsewhere in the economy. With a given money supply and a given level of aggregate demand, prices elsewhere should decline eventually, so that relative prices adjust with the overall price level unchanged. However, prices elsewhere in the economy do not immediately decline because they are set by formal and informal contracts. Thus, the overall price level, or inflation rate, rises. In addition, at the higher price level, the given money supply is in greater demand so that interest rates rise. Due to higher interest rates, spending (aggregate demand) may decrease. As a result, output may decline not only in the offending sectors but throughout the economy. It is the lack of price flexibility elsewhere in the economy that causes the price level rise and the endogenous real output slowdown. There may also be an exogenous output slowdown due to supply shocks in specific sectors. The association of output slowdowns (whether exogenous or endogenous) with an acceleration of inflation has been popularly termed *stagflation*.

Three forms of supply-shock inflation can cause stagflation. The first is cost-push (or wage-push) inflation, which raises inflation rates, in the short run, through the use of monopoly (or union) power. The exertion of monopoly (or union) power creates an artificial scarcity and bids up prices (or wages). Prime recent examples are the OPEC-caused inflationary spurts of 1973–74 and 1979. The result of the energy price rises was an exogenous and an endogenous decline in the rate of real output growth, together with worldwide inflation.

A second form, which can be termed *structural inflation*, results through relatively high excess demand pushing prices up in those sectors where prices react quickly (e.g., agricultural and raw materials) at the same time that excess supply in slowly reacting sectors (e.g., manufacturing and services) does not provide a balancing price decline. In this case, it is possible for the price level or inflation rate to increase without any exogenous output slowdown. The distribution of aggregate demand may change so that there is excess demand in some sectors and excess supply in others. If excess demand occurs in those sectors with rapidly adjusting prices, with excess supply in sectors with slowly adjusting prices, the overall price level increases. This causes an excess demand for liquidity and higher interest rates which decrease aggregate demand. The result is a temporary endogenous output decline that reverses when prices in the excess supply sectors adjust downwards.[15] Excess demand in agriculture, due to unusual weather patterns, contributed to the 1973–75 worldwide inflation spurt which was led by food prices (as well as by oil prices).

A third form of supply-shock inflation operates through an exchange rate devaluation. As an economy's balance of payments worsens (because the economy's goods are less competitive, i.e., less in demand), there will be an excess supply of the country's currency. This causes a decline in the exchange rate (e.g., in the value of the dollar in terms of the amount of other currencies that can be purchased with the dollar). But with a lower exchange rate, the prices of internationally traded goods (both imports and exports) and their substitutes rise, in terms of the domestic currency. Because prices in the noninternationally traded goods and services sector of the economy are not likely to fall immediately, upward pressure on the overall price level results. Once again the exogenous rise in the price level is accompanied by an exogenous output slowdown (due to the decrease in competitiveness) and possibly an endogenous output decline as well due to higher interest rates with a fixed money supply growth rate.

In the past, sharp balance of payment swings are unlikely to have been an important factor in the U.S. inflation, due to imports' and exports' small share of total output. This source of supply-shock inflation will grow in importance as the U.S. economy becomes more open. In particular, the U.S. economy's recent increased reliance on foreign capital inflows creates a new area of vulnerability. Decreased confidence in the U.S. economy's real growth and monetary stability relative to that of other economies could cause a capital outflow with a resultant supply-shock inflation.

Nonmonetary Factors and a Passive Money Supply

For nonmonetary demand-pull or supply-shock factors to result in ongoing inflation, an increase in money supply growth must ratify price rises. An accommodative monetary policy is not required for short-run inflation spurts but is necessary if the short-run spurts are to result in ongoing higher inflation rates. If monetary authorities do "accommodate" inflation by adjusting the money supply upwards, the money supply is determined by the price level rather than the reverse. The money supply is said to be endogenously or passively determined. The following discussion describes the necessity and tendency for money supply increases to ratify nonmonetary inflation.

Without an expansion in money supply growth rates, short-run inflation caused by expansionary fiscal policy results in higher real interest rates and a crowding out of private investments as borrowing costs rise.[16] The greater the deficit financing, necessitated by the expansionary fiscal policy, the more real interest rates will rise. If monetary authorities keep the money supply constant in spite of the increased deficit and interest rates, the one-period price level increase would be permanent, with a permanently higher real interest rate. The higher real interest rate encourages the holdings of smaller real money balances so that the given money supply is consistent with a higher nominal income and price level.

It must be emphasized that the resulting one-shot decrease in the demand for money allows a one-shot increase in the price level, not ongoing inflation at a higher rate. Ongoing inflation in the absence of a money supply increase requires a continuous increase in velocity and in the rate of growth of the real interest rate. This scenario is unlikely because the initial nonmonetary factor—in this case the increase in the deficit as a percentage of GNP—which raises the inflation rate in the period in which it occurs, is not likely to recur annually. If the underlying increase in the deficit as a percentage of GNP did recur annually, the ever-higher real interest rates would cause ever-worsening dislocations in the private economy (especially in the consumer durable, private investment, and local government investment sectors) along with price level increases.

Except under the unlikely circumstances noted, if monetary authorities did not increase the money supply, the price level would remain higher than otherwise, but inflation would not continue. If monetary authorities do respond and passively increase the money supply, inflation is ratified and persists as long as the higher rate of monetary expansion continues. There is a political incentive to increase the rate of monetary expansion because by doing so it is possible to temporarily lower interest rates. The decline is temporary because, as discussed below, interest rates increase with augmented inflationary expectations. Thus, although monetary authorities may attempt to reduce interest rates by increasing the money supply, they can do so successfully only in the short run. In the long run, inflation and interest rates rise.

The long-run inflationary effects of supply shocks also depend on the response of monetary policy.[17] Supply shocks may lower the economy's potential real output growth rate. If the rate of money supply growth is not reduced by the same amount, inflation results. In the short run, this is unavoidable. The initial unanticipated price level (or inflation) rise is not controllable beforehand; however, the long-run rate of price increase depends on whether money supply growth is adjusted downward in response to the decline in potential output growth. It is not the decline in potential output growth that results in ongoing inflation; rather it is the adjusted upward rate of monetary growth.

The factors that cause supply shocks may lower potential output growth rates for a number of years, as did the 1973–74 and 1979 OPEC shocks. Yet recognizing the economy's lowered growth potential may be difficult. Moreover, the supply shock will place political pressure on monetary authorities to raise rather than to reduce the rate of monetary expansion to mitigate output slowdowns and increased interest rates. If the central bank has a low tolerance for unemployment, high interest rates, and recessions, such shocks will be ratified, and the price and wage increases will persist.

Empirical evidence supports the role of nonmonetary factors in temporary increases in the inflation rate, as indicated by the literature review in Appendix 1.A to this chapter. There is, however, no empirical support for an increase in the long-run inflation rate without a corresponding increase in the long-run rate of monetary expansion. Inflation can be triggered or temporarily worsened by nonmonetary demand or supply shocks, but persistent inflation results from excessive money supply.

Anticipated, Unanticipated, and Uncertain Inflation

Inflationary Expectations and the Anticipated Inflation Rate

If monetary authorities expand the money supply either actively or passively in response to inflationary shocks, eventually inflationary expectations will become embedded in the price system. After some years of above-zero inflation, individuals expect price increases to continue in the future. These expectations then become self-fulfilling, and they themselves lead to ongoing actual inflation. Workers expect prices to rise and therefore demand higher wages. Firms expect costs to rise and therefore demand higher prices. Lenders and borrowers adjust the nominal interest rate that they require and are willing to pay to reflect their expectations of future inflation. All prices, wages, and interest rates rise in response to expectations of inflation.[18]

Thus, inflationary expectations are likely to have an independent impact on inflation. Yet it is difficult to judge the extent of this impact since inflationary expectations are not observed. In the absence of frequent, good surveys of inflationary expectations, their formation must be modeled. Adaptive and rational expectations are two competing models of expectation formation.

The hypothesis of adaptive expectations, introduced by Cagan,[19] asserts that individuals formulate their expectations of future inflation based on their experience of past inflation. More precisely, the theory postulates that individuals examine how well their forecasts predict actual inflation and revise their future forecasts by some fraction of their past error. For example, if 4 percent inflation is forecasted and actual inflation is 8 percent, individuals might revise their expectations upward by 50 percent of their error to a forecast of 6 percent inflation in the following periods.[20]

Adaptive expectations are backward looking. They do not allow individuals to adjust expectations in the light of new information about the future, except if the new information has already affected past actual inflation rates. In particular, if inflation is continuously increasing, individuals with adaptive expectations will always underestimate inflation.

The hypothesis of rational expectations postulates that individuals do not make systematic forecasting errors. Because there is uncertainty and information is incomplete, individuals do not have perfect foresight. However, they use information on how past variables influenced inflation and on the likely future values of these variables to formulate expectations. Thus, new information, along with information on past inflation, is incorporated into expectations. Their ability to use this information is such that, although individuals will make forecasting errors, the mathematical expected value of their errors will be zero. This implies that the actual inflation rate in period t is the best estimate of the inflation rate individuals expected in period t.

Tests of the two competing hypotheses, strictly interpreted, in the moderately inflationary post–world war U.S. economy, lend more support to the adaptive expectation than to the rational expectation hypothesis.[21] However, there is evidence that individuals do use expectations of likely future events, to some extent, in formulating price expectations.[22] Moreover, studies of expectation formation in the United States find that the process has changed over the decades. A study by Benjamin Klein[23] indicates that the experience of ever-increasing money supply growth rates and inflation that began in the 1960s and extended into the 1970s seems to have induced individuals in the 1970s to emphasize recent experience in formulating their expectations of future inflation. Thus, the evidence of these studies is consistent with the view that individuals gradually acquire knowledge of the workings of the system. In general, the empirical evidence seems to support a broad interpretation of a rational expectations model in which adaptive expectations still play a role due to the costs of information gathering.

Unanticipated and Uncertain Inflation

If actual inflation always equals the anticipated inflation rate, under either adaptive or rational expectations, individuals will come to expect the anticipated inflation rate with a probability of one, as illustrated in Figure 1–2a. The variance of the expected inflation rate $\sigma_{\dot{P}_e}$, equals zero. Under these circumstances, there is no uncertainty over future expected inflation rates. In reality, however, the issue is not whether a particular inflation rate is certain or not, but how much uncertainty there is.

Given unanticipated inflation, individuals' expectations of future inflation will take the form of probability distributions, as shown in Figure 1–2b. Each individual can be thought of as formulating a probability distribution of the expected inflation rate for all future periods. The best estimate of expected inflation is then the mean of the probability distribution. The greater the range or variance of the distribution, the greater is the uncertainty ($\sigma_{\dot{P}_e}$) over the future expected inflation rate. For example, an individual may estimate that inflation will be 5 percent in the following period, with only a 10 percent chance that inflation will be less than 4 percent or greater than 6 percent. Alternatively, the individual may be more uncertain about the outlook for inflation and, while maintaining 5 percent as the most likely inflation rate, believe that there is a 50 percent chance that inflation will be less than 4 percent or greater than 6 percent.[24] As long as the probability distribution is not a single point, as in Figure 1–2a, there is inflation uncertainty. Figure 1–2c illustrates greater uncertainty over future expected inflation rates than does 1–2b.[25]

With increased long-term inflation uncertainty, individuals shorten the duration of long-term contracts to lessen the chance of their distortion by the deviation of actual from anticipated inflation. The shortening of long-term contracts which occurred in the 1970s in the United States[26] is consistent with an increase in long-term inflation uncertainty.

FIGURE 1–2
Certain and Uncertain Inflation

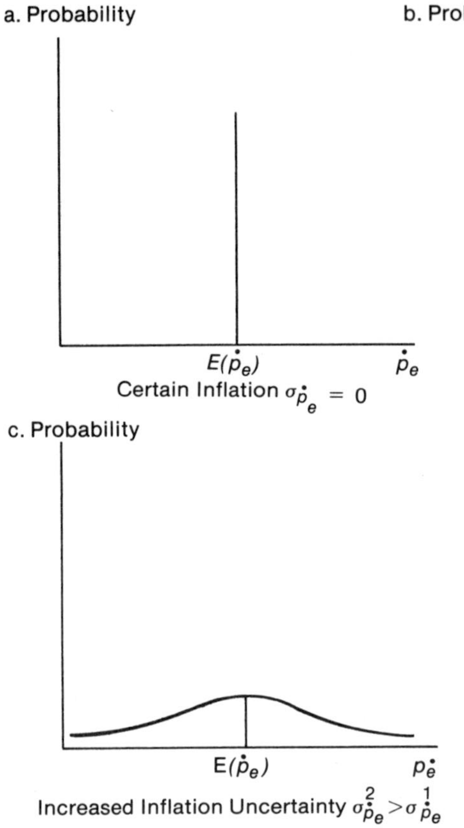

Neutral Inflation

Neutral inflation results when the factors that cause inflation only raise the price level, that is, when these factors have no impact on real output or relative prices. Total output and output in each sector remain unchanged by the causes of inflation, as do relative prices. The only change is in the overall price level.

Inflation must be anticipated to be neutral. When inflation is anticipated, no excessive aggregate demand or excess demand in any sector becomes apparent. The growing demand for money equals the growing supply of money, and the aggregate demand

FIGURE 1–3
The Impact of Neutral Inflation on Sector i's Price, p_i, and on Quantity, q_i

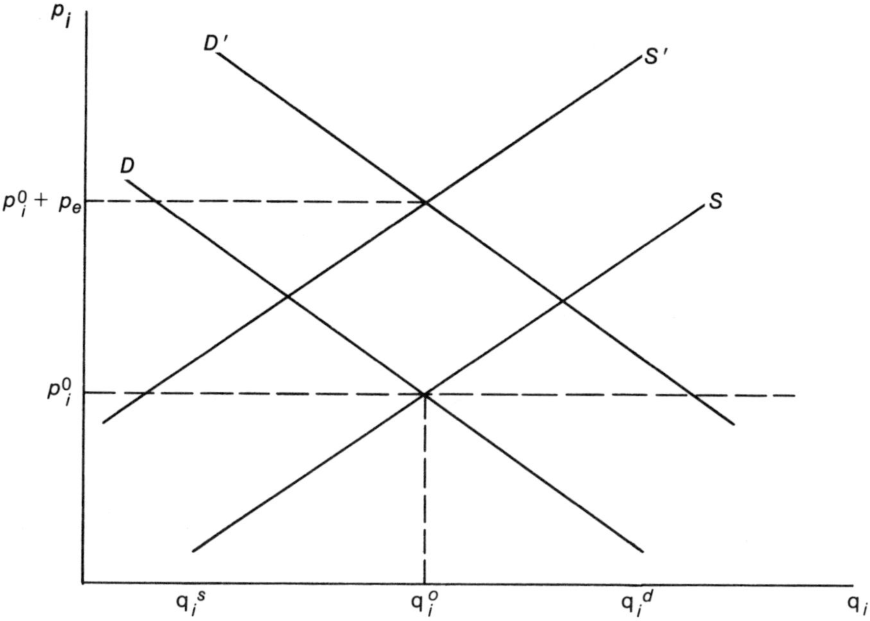

for goods equals the aggregate supply at the increasing prices. Contracts can be set to include the anticipated inflation rate, and since actual inflation will equal anticipated inflation, contractually set prices and wages will not be distorted by misguessing the anticipated inflation rate.

If inflation is anticipated (and if several other conditions to be discussed are fulfilled), inflation shifts up demand and supply curves in each sector by the anticipated inflation rate, $\dot{p}_e$, as illustrated in Figure 1–3, and neither relative prices nor output levels are affected. Money supply growth then has no impact on sector i's, equilibrium output, $\dot{q}_i$, and raises sector i's price, p_i, by precisely the anticipated inflation rate, $\dot{p}_e$, for all sectors. As a result, inflation is said to be neutral.

Inflation that is caused by supply shocks or nonmonetary demand shocks cannot be neutral. Under supply-shock inflation, real supply conditions change. Nonmonetary demand-pull inflation is accompanied by raised interest rates which change the composition of GNP and relative prices. Only inflation that is monetary in origin can be neutral and then only under specific limited conditions. Inflation, caused by unanticipated increases in the money supply, is not neutral because it lowers interest rates and increases output in sectors with contracts. Thus, short-run inflation that is caused by either money or real shocks is not neutral.

If inflation is caused by anticipated increases in the money supply, it need not be associated with greater money or real shocks than in the absence of inflation. Sustained inflation must be caused by money supply increases rather than real shocks. Moreover, in the long run, according to both rational and adaptive expectation theories, serially correlated money supply increases, which are required for long-run inflation, will be anticipated. Thus, long-run inflation may be neutral.

Inflation, caused by anticipated increases in the money supply, is neutral if several other conditions are met. First, the money supply must be distributed in a neutral fashion.[27] It is obvious that if the increased money supply were distributed only to vegetarians, say, the price of meat would deteriorate relative to other food. But neutral distribution involves another issue as well. As shown by Mundell[28], there is a potential negative effect of higher rates of inflation on real interest rates. As the quantity theory equation indicates, higher inflation makes it more costly to hold monetary balances. This will affect the form in which individuals wish to hold their savings, motivating increased real investment and less cash holdings. The result of greater investment is lowered real interest rates as projects with lower returns on the margin are undertaken. This result holds unless the additional money supply is distributed to currency holders "neutrally," that is, in proportion to their holdings so that the real value of monetary balances is unchanged.

Second, inflation cannot be neutral if it results in increased uncertainty. Even if current inflation is anticipated, increased uncertainty over future monetary policy may affect individuals' probability distributions of future expected inflation. Higher rates of anticipated inflation may be accompanied by greater uncertainty over future expected inflation rates. Thus, future inflation must be anticipated with the same degree of certainty for neutrality.

In sum, neutral inflation requires (1) inflation that is due to an increase in the money supply, (2) money supply increases that are distributed "neutrally," (3) money supply increases that are anticipated before negotiations of any current contracts, and (4) unchanged probability distributions of expected future inflation.[29]

The following chapter discusses the indexation of contracts to an inflation measure as a response to unanticipated and uncertain inflation. If inflation were always due to (unanticipated but neutrally distributed) money shocks, it could be neutralized by indexation.[30] Indexation can effectively neutralize such inflation because relative prices in equilibrium are unchanged. Only the price level changes in equilibrium, and indexation speeds that change. However, indexation will worsen the relative price distortions that are correlated with other sources of inflation. Most critically, indexation blocks the necessary relative price changes[31] that supply shocks require and exacerbates output slowdowns. Thus, the indexation that is required to deal with unanticipated and uncertain inflation, resulting from money shocks, is harmful when dealing with supply-shock inflation. The possibility that supply-shock inflation will occur precludes the use of indexation to neutralize inflation due to money shocks, and, without indexation, even money-shock inflation will have real effects.[32]

Political Economic Causes and Effects of Inflation

Political Economic Causes of Inflation: A Summary

In the post–World War II period, there has been a worldwide secular increase in price levels and, until the 1980s, in inflation rates as well. Chronic inflation could not have occurred without money supply increases. But the money supply need not have increased over time. Thus, the question of the causes of chronic inflation must be answered by another question: What have been the causes of the increases in the money supply? The causes may not be merely economic but may involve political factors as well.

Part of the explanation for the pervasive worldwide increase in prices in the post–World War II period may lie in the interaction of price and wage adjustment lags with the short-run decision-making horizon of politically influenced monetary and fiscal authorities.

First, because of the existence of lags in the wage and price adjustment process, the supply-shock causes of inflation in the 1970s increased the inflation rate and decreased output growth. Political pressure was then placed on monetary authorities to ratify the price rises and mitigate the unemployment and output declines. In part, the increase in money supply growth in the United States in the 1970s may be attributed to this. In general, although supply shocks may be randomly distributed, the monetary response to these shocks may not be. If positive supply-side shocks decrease inflation and increase output, there is likely to be no political pressure to lower money supply growth. The result is a politically induced upward bias to the inflation rate.

The second source of upward bias derives from the incentive for politicians to overheat the economy to attain higher output and lower unemployment. The result is the frequency of pre-election tax cuts, spending programs and money supply acceleration, and what has become known as the political cycle. There is econometric evidence of a political cycle in the past in the U.S. economy, which is consistent with an attempt to create boom conditions to coincide with political elections.[33]

Third, price and wage adjustment lags can interact with misperception of the economy's growth potential to create accelerating inflation over time. It is technically difficult to forecast real growth potential, and it may be politically difficult to accept growth limits lower than those of the past. If monetary and fiscal authorities act as if the economy has greater growth potential than it actually does, the overly optimistic growth targets will be partially met in the short run. Only in the long run will the misjudgment become fully apparent when prices rise more and output less than expected. By that point, the inflationary damage has been done. In the period of declining economic growth potential in the 1970s, the Congressional Budget Office and the President's Council of Economic Advisors persistently overestimated the productivity growth rates.[34] This is perhaps to be expected in a period of abnormally low growth potential.

As a result of an increase in inflation, uncertainty over future inflation may also increase over time. With each upward twist of the inflationary spiral, the range of the probability distribution of expected inflation is likely to increase because a zero inflation rate remains a possibility and because increasing inflation indicates the propensity of monetary authorities to future inflationary increases in the money supply.

A corrective contractionary monetary policy may not decrease inflation uncertainty, except with time. Paradoxically, the intermediate effect may be a decrease in actual inflation together with increased inflation uncertainty, since the probability of low future inflation rates may now be higher, without a corresponding decrease in the probability of high future inflation. After a period of chronic inflation, the reduction of inflation uncertainty requires time. The reduction of inflation itself requires time and the political willingness to accept a period of slowed growth or economic decline. Moreover, price stability, once achieved, can be maintained only if monetary authorities do not accelerate money growth to achieve temporary output gains.

Uncertain Inflation and Slowed Productivity Growth

By definition, neutral inflation has no real effects. However, real world inflation is unlikely to be neutral. In particular, there is evidence that increased uncertainty has accompanied the higher worldwide inflation rates in the post–World War II period through the 1970s.

The high unemployment rates of the 1970s were in part due to a relatively large unskilled youth cohort. With the aging of the population, full-employment unemployment rates have declined.[35] The slowing of productivity growth rates of the 1970s in the United States and elsewhere involved other factors as well. The OPEC-induced oil price shocks were a critical factor. In addition, part of the explanation of the decline of the 1970s lies in low capital information, due to government-required OSHA and EPA expenditures, and part lies in low capital formation per worker, due to the large youth cohort;[36] but part may lie in greater unanticipated inflation and greater inflation uncertainty.

Unanticipated and uncertain inflation may adversely affect

output potential for several reasons. First, additional time and resources must be shifted to the more frequent negotiation of contracts. Second, temporary relative price distortions will occur, missignaling resource allocation. Third, resources will shift away from those undertakings that require fixed nominal contracts for long time periods. In addition, there will be greater risk attached to those long-term contracts that are still transacted. All transactions in which nominal prices are contractually fixed become riskier due to inflation uncertainty. In particular, long-term nominal debt contracts become riskier for lenders and borrowers, and interest rates on long-term nominally fixed debt must rise to reflect increased inflation uncertainty. The result is increased risk and cost to long-term investment. Hence, investment for the long term declines.

Each of these sources of inefficiencies would be eliminated if contracts could be indexed without loss of efficiency. However, efficient indexing is not feasible as inflation is caused by both nonmonetary and monetary factors.

The move to indexation is an attempt to neutralize the effects of unanticipated and uncertain inflation, requiring an accurate measure of inflation. For reasons discussed in the following chapter, creating an index that will accurately reflect cost-of-living changes is no simple matter. Even with an accurate measure of inflation, indexation can only undo the real effects of inflation that derive from money shocks. Indexation prevents the economy from efficiently responding to real shocks since it locks in relative prices. Indexation cannot eliminate the negative effects of inflation on productivity growth.

Because greater long-term inflation uncertainty means greater risks and costs associated with long-term contracts, and because indexing is not a perfect solution to the increased uncertainty, both long-term labor contracts and long-term capital formation will become riskier and will be discouraged.[37] Sustained and uncertain inflation may result in slowed productivity growth.

Summary and Implications for Pensions

Short-run spurts in the inflation rate that do not persist may be due to unexpected decreases in output growth rates. A money supply growth rate that is not excessive with normal economic growth rates becomes inflationary with sudden declines in real output, that is, with supply shocks.

Short-run spurts of inflation may also be caused by destabilizing monetary policy, that is, by money shocks. Unexpected increases in money supply growth rates cause temporary increases in output growth rates, which are followed by declines in growth rates, and inflation. Spurts in inflation that are due to money and supply shocks cannot be neutral; they must have real effects on the economy.

Only inflation that is due to fully anticipated increases in money growth rates (anticipated before the initiation of any current contract and with no impact on uncertainty) is neutral. But the political economic explanations for inflation suggest that inflationary spurts often are associated with money and supply shocks. In addition, chronic inflation is likely to be accompanied by greater uncertainty over the course of future inflation rates as well as by greater uncertainty about the real economic outlook.

Real world inflation is not likely to be neutral. Thus, real world inflation will have effects on capital markets and, in particular, on long-run capital market instruments that are denominated in fixed-dollar terms. Defined-benefit pensions are an example of such instruments.

Inflation erodes the real purchasing power of fixed-income streams, such as pensions. Two other major impacts of inflation and increased inflation uncertainty on pensions are to raise their nominal return and risk and, therefore, expected nominal and real returns as discussed in Part Two. The owners of nominal instruments like pensions may be compensated for their decreased purchasing power and increased risk, when there is greater inflation and inflation uncertainty, by increased expected nominal and real rates of return. However, the ostensible purpose of pensions (and their tax-advantaged treatment) is to provide a secure retirement income. Pensions that are fixed in dollar terms are adequate if inflation is confined to a narrow band. High levels of persistent inflation rapidly erode the real value of a nominally fixed income stream. Thus, it would seem useful to convert nominal pensions to indexed pensions if inflation is chronic.

The sources of inflation discussed in this chapter indicate that real world inflation is not neutral. Yet only if inflation is neutral can indexation also be neutral. The following chapter discusses why indexation is not a costless solution to inflation.

APPENDIX 1.A
Empirical Evidence on Monetary versus Nonmonetary Causes of Inflation

Empirical evidence supports the hypothesized necessary role of monetary growth in sustained inflation and the possible role of both monetary and nonmonetary factors in short-run inflation.

Many studies test for the relationship of monetary growth to inflation using quantity theory and Harberger equations. They do so by regressing the inflation rate on current and past changes in the money supply, along with other variables. In the original study, Harberger[38] tests his model using Chilean data for the period 1940 to 1956. He finds first, as predicted, that a 1 percent increase in the rate of monetary expansion, *ceteris paribus*, is accompanied by a 1 percent increase in the inflation rate. Second, as predicted, a 1 percent increase in the growth of real income, *ceteris paribus*, is accompanied by a 1 percent decrease in the inflation rate. The Harberger study has been extended through 1970, and other studies have used the Harberger model with parallel results.[39]

There have also been long-term historical studies that found a strong link between money supply and price increases. For example, Milton Friedman and Anna J. Schwartz's research on the United States and United Kingdom for the period 1867–1975 finds a pervasive influence of money on prices, although with long and variable lags.[40] Their work confirms the theoretical hypothesis that increases in the money supply growth rate, above the real output growth rate, cause inflation of the same magnitude: "A sustained change of one percentage point in the rate of monetary growth ultimately produces a one percentage point change in the same direction in the rate of price change."[41] However, the full impact of money on prices depends on the full adjustment to new expected levels of money supply growth and inflation, which may take more than a decade. Friedman and

FIGURE 1–4
Growth in the Money Supply and GNP Expenditures in 25 Countries from 1969 to 1980

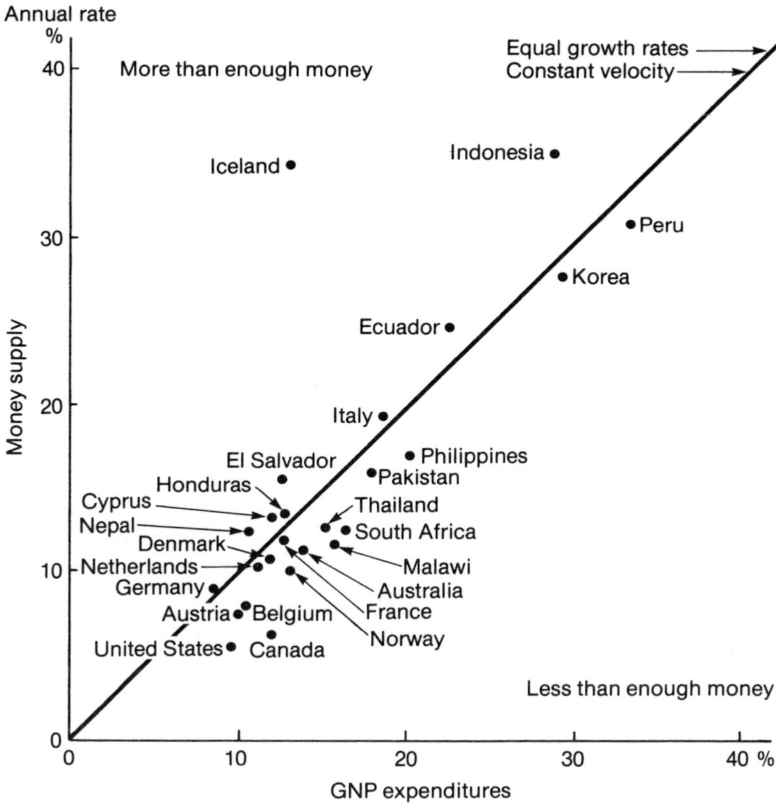

SOURCE: *International Financial Statistics* 34, no. 7, taken from Paul F. Smith, *Comparative Financial Systems* (New York: Praeger Publishers, 1982).

Schwartz also provide evidence, for the U.S. economy, of a transitory impact of money on output, as do others.[42]

Cross-section studies of inflation also show a linkage between money supply growth and inflation. Figure 1–4 shows the extent to which high money supply growth rates accompanied the unprecedented worldwide inflation, and thus, nominal GNP growth in the 1969–80 period in 73 countries.[43] The vertical axis of Figure 1–4 indicates the annual rate of money supply growth and the horizontal axis, the rate of growth of nominal GNP which combines the rate of growth of real output and prices. The points indicate the locus of money supply and nominal GNP growth rates for each country. If velocity were constant, money supply and nominal GNP growth rates would be equal, so that the points would all be on the 45° line drawn from the origin. Data problems as well as velocity changes explain the divergence that occurs. Since real GNP rates of growth for all these countries were moderate (on the average under 3 percent), the substantially positive nominal GNP growth rates reflect inflation, which has been accompanied, as the chart indicates, by substantially positive money supply growth rates.

Figure 1–4 illustrates the wide divergence of inflation across nations in the 1969–75 period. However, for most economies, this was a period of increased inflation.[44] A comprehensive survey of inflation in eight industrialized nations provides econometric evidence that this increased inflation was accompanied by increased worldwide monetary growth.[45] This survey concludes that a major cause of inflation in the early 1970s was an acceleration of U.S. monetary growth, while in the later 1970s inflation was due to the acceleration of domestic monetary growth by the individual central banks, which were reluctant, perhaps, to impose the recessionary policy necessary to reduce inflation to pre-1970 levels.[46]

Empirical studies leave no doubt that long-term inflation requires money supply growth. But they leave open the question of what initiates inflation and the money supply growth. The long history of inflation in the United States, as shown in Figure 1–5 indicates that throughout our history prices have generally increased during wars and decreased after wars. It is only in the post–World War II period (in which the Keynesian theory that government can reduce unemployment became intellectually accepted and the commitment to "full employment" became an explicit part of public policy) that the upward movement in prices continued, even in times of peace. The change in 1934 from a gold to a fiduciary monetary standard made it possible to attempt to use monetary expansion to achieve employment and output goals. Econometric evidence indicates a post–World War II political cycle, with accelerated money supply growth inducing output growth prior to elections and accelerated inflation after elections.[47]

Inflationary episodes are not all initiated by money supply in-

FIGURE 1–5
The GNP Price Deflator Index, 1867–1973 (1929 base)

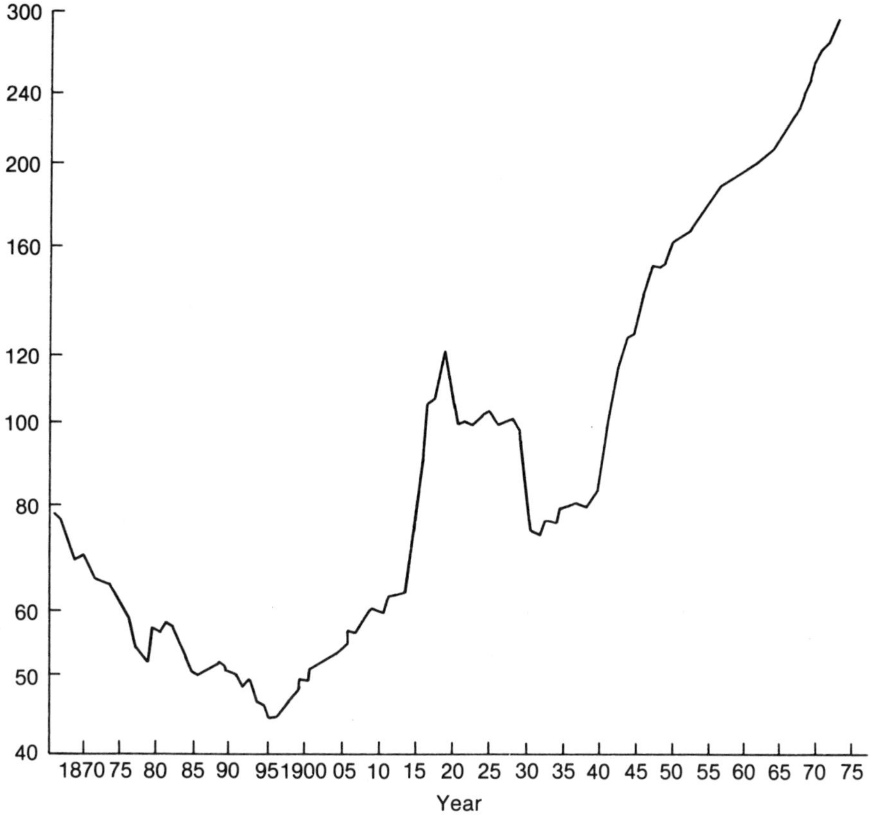

SOURCE: Taken from Robert Solow, "The Intelligent Citizen's Guide to Inflation," *Public Interest*, Winter 1975.

creases. There is also evidence that money supply increases occur in response to prior increases in the deficit or prices. Several studies attest to the role of previous deficits in inducing inflation and money supply increases in the post–World War II U.S. experience.

A study by Alan Blinder shows first that in the period 1949 to 1981 growth in the deficit helps to predict the price level and second that the deficit is, to some extent, monetized by the Federal Reserve Board's actions, more so in the post-1961 period than earlier.[48] William Dewald's study of the association between deficits and monetary growth, between 1948 and 1982, indicates that a one percentage point increase in the deficit relative to gross national product is associated with a one and one-half percentage point increase in monetary growth.[49]

In addition, there is some evidence that supply-shock factors have increased the short-run inflation rate and that monetary authorities have responded with increased growth of the money supply. Several studies have tested the influence of supply-shock factors on inflation in the United States and elsewhere. Although exogenous wage or cost increases from the unionized and governmental sector may at times be a factor in inflation, the evidence suggests that their part is small or nonevident.[50] However, other supply-shock factors, namely energy and food price increases, influenced price level movements during the 1970s in the United States.[51] Dallas S. Batten finds that, as a result of OPEC, rates of inflation increased dramatically in West Germany, Switzerland, the United Kingdom, and the United States from 1973 to 1975.[52] In addition, there is historical evidence that supply-shock factors, emanating from agriculture, have been partially responsible for initiating inflationary episodes in several Latin American economies.[53]

Quantity theory–based studies of inflation, such as Harberger's, which find a significantly negative coefficient of real income changes also confirm the role of supply shocks. Fama estimates a quantity theory equation for the United States for the 1953 through 1977 period.[54] Real activity measures are current, future, and past annual growth rates of industrial production. As predicted by theory, negative coefficients for real activity growth rates and positive coefficients for money growth rates are found. His results also show "the absence of positive simple correlations between money supply and real activity growth rates during post-1953 period."[55] This is consistent with inflation that is predominantly caused by supply shocks and aggregate demand shocks, rather than by money shocks, with monetary growth playing a (mostly) stabilizing role.

Thus, the possibility exists that some of the relationship found between money and prices in econometric studies reflects a passive response of monetary authorities to nonmonetary shocks. Christopher Sims has devised a method to determine the direction of causation between inflation and monetary growth rates.[56]

Sims finds that for the United States in the period 1947–70, inflation was caused by overexpansion of the monetary supply. More recently, Peter Berman has investigated the relationship between money supply and price changes for the United States in the period 1956 through 1977.[57] The results of this work indicate causation running from money growth to inflation through most of the period, with evidence for nonmonetary induced inflation in the period of 1973–75. Thus, the statistical evidence for the United States indicates that an active overexpansion of the money supply has been the dominant factor in inflation, although a passive overexpansion of the money supply responding to supply shock or other nonmonetary factors has also played a role. Similar tests for five Latin American economies show that inflation has been the result of both active and passive money supply increases.[58]

Notes

[1] See Arnold Harberger, "The Dynamics of Inflation in Chile," in *Measurement in Economics: Studies in Mathematical Economics in Memory of Yehuda Grunfeld*, ed. Carl Christ (Stanford, Calif.: Stanford University Press, 1963), pp. 219–50, for a good description of this model.

[2] There are, of course, serious problems involved in the measurement of the money supply. There are a number of near-substitutes to what is termed M-1 money (i.e., cash and checking accounts). The degree to which near-substitutes are included in the money supply provides differing measures of how the money supply has changed. However, we define money supply as M-1 money here and discuss measurement issues below.

[3] In the long run, market forces assure that the real output growth rate $\dot{Y}$ is equal to full-employment output growth rate, $\dot{Y}_f$. This output growth rate is determined by fundamental forces, principally, the growth rates of population and of capital and technological change. Velocity is predetermined and together with the given real income and money supply determines the current inflation rate. In the Harberger equation, velocity is a function of the cost of holding money (i.e., the nominal interest rate, which itself is predetermined by the real interest rate and the expected inflation rate). In a more general quantity theory approach, velocity may be a function of both nominal interest rates and real income, since at different levels of real income, individuals may desire to hold a greater or lesser percentage of their real income in the form of money. It is also possible that in the long run V may increase with communication advances and new technology that come with income growth; thus, $\dot{V}$ may be positive over time. In addition, it should be noted here, although it will be discussed further below, that changes in the money supply growth rate will affect velocity because changes in the inflation rate influence interest rates.

However, changes in the money supply growth rates have lasting effects only on the level of velocity. They contribute to a positive (negative) $\dot{V}$ only if money supply expansion rates accelerate (decelerate) over time in the long run, as in a hyperinflation. In the long run, neither velocity growth rates (except for the latter case) nor real output growth rates are affected by money supply growth rates. As a result, a change in the money supply growth rate leads to an equal change in the inflation rate.

[4] The rate of money supply growth will determine the rate of growth of nominal GNP. It is the response of prices to money supply growth that is behind the relationship, because real GNP growth is determined by real full-employment output.

[5] Because prices and wages are set until some future period, formulating expectations on the expected movement of the general price level and incorporating these into the contract becomes important, as discussed below.

[6] See Alain Enthoven, "Monetary Disequilibria and the Dynamics of Inflation," *The Economic Journal,* June 1956.

[7] We assume no changes in inflationary expectations. If the money supply growth is fully anticipated, before any contracts are entered into, it need not have any real effects, even in the short run. See below for a full discussion of the requirements for neutral inflation.

[8] Empirical support for such a relationship was first found by A. W. Phillips in "The Relation between Unemployment and the Rate of Change of Money Wage Rates in the United Kingdom, 1861–1957," *Economica* 25 (November 1958), pp. 283–99.

[9] This "natural" or "noninflationary" unemployment rate, U_e, is not zero. It includes structural unemployment (which occurs when a worker's productivity, and hence the wage offered, is lower than the wage at which the worker wishes to work, or in the presence of minimum wage laws, can work) and frictional unemployment (which occurs because vacancies in some sectors balance unemployment in others).

[10] Eventually, prices and wages adjust so that these markets return to equilibrium with no unemployment or vacancies. In a growing, dynamic economy, however, new disequilibrium conditions continuously arise so that there is an ongoing amount of frictional unemployment and vacancies in the economy.

[11] As the economy returns to the original equilibrium growth path, the unemployment rate may temporarily rise above and the output growth rate may temporarily fall below their equilibrium levels.

[12] See Robert E. Lucas, Jr., "Expectations and the Neutrality of Money," *Journal of Economic Theory,* April 1972. See also Thomas Sargent and Neil Wallace, "Rational Expectations and the Theory of Economic Policy," *Journal of Monetary Economics,* April 1976. Both the "fooling" and "sticky-prices" explanations for a short-run Phillips curve are consistent with rational behavior. But the latter seems to accord better with observed empirical regularities, including evidence that output fluctuations are induced by anticipated monetary movements and evidence that real wages are procyclical. See Bennett T. McCallum, "Macroeconomics after a Decade of Rational Expectations: Some Critical Issues," *Economic Review of Federal Reserve Bank of Richmond* 68 (November–December 1982), pp. 3–12.

[13] Autonomous private investment increases may occur because the productivity of investment in the underlying capital has increased, thus shifting up the demand for investment funds and putting upward pressure on interest rates. Autonomous consumption spending may increase, for example, because of underlying demographic forces which put a larger proportion of the population in the household formation years.

[14] As with expansionary monetary policy, aggregate demand increases that result from fiscal policy, or from autonomous investment or consumption increases, lead first to an increase in output and only then to an increase in prices. The increase in $\dot{V}$ (or $\dot{R}$) initially frees monetary holdings which are used to purchase more goods and services. The overfull employment that results then bids up wages and input prices throughout the economy. A rise in $\dot{V}$ initially increases $\dot{Y}$ and then $\dot{P}$.

[15] See Susan M. Wachter, *Latin American Inflation: The Structuralist-Monetarist Debate* (Lexington, Mass.: D. C. Heath, 1976), for a discussion of structural inflation.

[16] An expansion in federal expenditures, financed by borrowing from the public, can also have an indirect inflationary effect if it slows real economic growth potential. Debt financing makes it more expensive for the economy to raise private capital for investment. The lack of private capital may slow growth, and this may, as discussed below, result in excessive money supply expansion.

[17] For example, a deterioration in the terms of trade cannot in itself cause an inflationary cycle. It is the monetary accommodation to higher price levels that causes an ongoing cycle of devaluation and accelerated inflation. See Dallas S. Batten and Mack Ott, "Five Common Myths about Floating Exchange Rates," *Federal Reserve Bank of St. Louis Review* 65, no. 9 (November 1983), pp. 5–15.

[18] Individuals do not need to form expectations of future prices in a world in which prices instantaneously adjust to market disequilibria, so that markets always clear. In such an economy, all markets would be auction markets with prices adjusting continuously. There would be no need to form expectations of future prices to negotiate wage and price contracts. Continuous recontracting would occur so that future price level changes need not be anticipated.

In actuality, informal and formal price and wage contracts exist, and prices are not readjusted continuously but prevail for some time. This means that expectations of future price changes must be taken account of in setting prices and wages that are expected to continue for some time into the future. Buyers and sellers must make forecasts about the future and build these predictions into the contracts.

[19] See P. Cagan, "The Monetary Dynamics of Hyperinflation," in *Studies in the Quantity Theory of Money*, ed. M. Friedman (Chicago: University of Chicago Press, 1956).

[20] It can be shown mathematically that revision of forecasts based on past errors is equivalent to formulating expectations based on a weighted average of past inflation rates. The weights do not have to be monotonically increasing, nor do they all have to have positive signs. The adaptive expectation mechanism is consistent with a "return to normality" model of expectations formation in which individuals expect a return to a prior normal price level or infla-

tion rate. Jacob Mincer's study, "Models of Adaptive Forecasting," in *Economic Forecasts and Expectations,* ed. Jacob Mincer (New York: Columbia University Press for the National Bureau of Economic Research, 1969), indicates that unless nonautoregressive information is incorporated into the determination of the normal rate, the reduced form of return-to-normal models should perform equivalently to other autoregressive models.

A study by Shirley Almon demonstrates a mechanism to estimate the weights on past inflation rates that produce the best equation for predicting inflation. See Shirley Almon, "The Distributed Lag between Capital Appropriations and Expenditures," *Econometrica* 33 (1965), pp. 178–96. An alternative solution for the determination of weights makes their size depend on the size of the most recent forecasting error, which increases the speed of adjustment to recently observed inflation.

[21] See John D. Rea, "The Explanatory Power of Alternative Theories of Inflation and Unemployment, 1895–1979," *The Review of Economics and Statistics* 65, no. 2 (May 1983), pp. 00.

[22] A study by Kane and Malkiel of a survey of inflation expectations demonstrates that expectations are influenced by information that is not already incorporated in past price changes, thus supporting the rational expectations model. See Edward J. Kane and Burton G. Malkiel, "Autoregressive and Nonautoregressive Elements in Cross-Section Forecasts of Inflation," *Econometrica* 44 (January 1976). Kane and Malkiel find, for the United States over the survey period 1969–72, that although return to normality forecasting prevails, the forecast of the normal inflation rate shifts upward with new information on the expected values of variables that could be thought to influence inflation.

Clearly, a generalized model is needed. Relying to a large extent on information on past inflation rates may be efficient, given the costs of information gathering. Thus, a generalized model of expectation formation might include a role for adaptive expectations. In such a model, expectations would incorporate more information, as the financial costs of not doing so grow. In slower moving inflationary experiences, there is less incentive to gather information quickly. Such a model is supported by the historical evidence which shows that in experiences of hyperinflation people adjusted prices upward quickly in expectation of excessive *future* money supply growth. See Cagan, "The Monetary Dynamics of Hyperinflation."

[23] See Benjamin Klein, "The Social Costs of the Recent Inflation: The Mirage of Steady 'Anticipated' Inflation," in *Carnegie-Rochester Conference Series on Public Policy: Institutional Arrangements and the Inflation Problem,* ed. Karl Brunner and Allen H. Meltzer, vol. 3, 1976; and by the same author, "The Measurement of Long- and Short-Term Price Uncertainty: A Moving Regression Time Series Analysis," *Economic Inquiry* 16 (July 1978), pp. 438–52.

[24] There is no presumption that the same probability distribution holds for all future periods. Indeed, the mean and variance of the expected inflation rate are likely to vary with the term of the forecast.

[25] Little is known about the determinants of inflation uncertainty. Empirical evidence links higher inflation with more variable inflation. Gordon and Halpern find, in a 33 cross-country comparison, for the years 1952 to 1972, that "the correlation between the mean percentage price change and the standard deviation over the 33 countries was .9081, and significant at the .001 level." More variable inflation implies more inflation uncertainty, however, only if

individuals place more confidence in their estimates of steady inflation than in their estimates of variable inflation. An alternative explanation of why higher inflation rates might entail both greater long-run variability and greater uncertainty over the range of future inflation is based on the arguments that a zero rate remains a possibility and that the transition to higher inflation indicates the predisposition of monetary authorities to surprising increases in the rate of monetary expansion. See Myron J. Gordon and Paul J. Halpern, "Bond Share Yield Spreads under Uncertain Inflation," *American Economic Review* 66, no. 4 (September 1976), p. 564. Also see Steven A. Holland, "Does Higher Inflation Lead to More Uncertain Inflation?" *The Federal Reserve Bank of St. Louis Review* 66, no. 2 (February 1984), for a summary of the literature. Holland does not claim to know why this relationship holds, but he feels it is reasonable to argue that "an inflationary economy creates an environment in which major policy changes become more likely" (p. 18). Holland finds additional indirect evidence supportive of a positive link between higher inflation and inflation uncertainty. Using Joseph Livingston's survey of expert forecasters' inflation estimates, he shows that the standard deviation of individual inflation forecasts increases with the level of inflation.

[26] Recent empirical evidence that links increases in the worldwide level of inflation and in annual inflation variability is due in part to the unanticipated supply shocks of the 1970s which were ratified by monetary expansion. Indeed, in the United States, in the post–World War II period until the 1970s, inflation and inflation variability moved in opposing directions, with inflation increasing and the annual standard deviation of inflation decreasing. This is a reflection of the autocorrelated price level change process under the monetary standard. As described by Klein, the variability of the average inflation rate over five years increased steadily in the first decades after World War II, even as the short-run variability declined. The negative or zero autocorrelation of price level changes in the earlier gold standard period made it difficult to predict the following year's price change. However, rates of price level change over a five-year period tended to average out to zero, so that that five-year average price level change variability was relatively low and a return to price level stability predictable. In contrast, the positive correlation of the post–World War II period decreased year-to-year variability (until the 1970s); however, the ratio of long-term to short-term variability increased. See Klein, "The Social Costs of the Recent Inflation."

[27] See Don Patinkin, *Money, Interest, and Prices: An Integration of Monetary and Value Theory,* 2nd ed. (New York: Harper & Row, 1965), pp. 175–76.

[28] See below and Robert A. Mundell, "Inflation and Real Interest," *Journal of Political Economy* 71 (June 1963), pp. 280–83.

[29] Tax effects may also render an otherwise neutral increase in the money supply nonneutral, as discussed below. Here it is assumed that the tax system is also neutral.

[30] Without lags, indexation would not be necessary to neutralize money supply inflation that satisfied the other four conditions, since relative prices would not be affected by different adjustment rates. But without lags, supply-shock factors would still lead to nonneutral inflation as would demand-pull factors due to fiscal expansion.

[31] Indexation can only neutralize the effects of inflation caused by unanticipated money supply increase because only in this case are long-run relative

prices constant. Generally, the greater the relative price change brought about by the factors that cause inflation, the greater the disruptions caused by indexation.

[32] Alternatives to price indexes such as monetary indexes are considered below.

[33] See William D. Nordhaus, "The Political Business Cycle," *The Review of Economic Studies*, April 1975. In addition, an unanticipated money supply increase can decrease interest rates and allow increased government expenditures in the short run. The problem with such expansionary policies is that attempts to raise output result in higher inflation rates and then higher inflationary expectations. Any attempt to decrease inflation and inflationary expectations requires the political acceptance of a period of recession. As illustrated by the aftermath of the Federal Reserve Board's decision to lower money supply growth rates in October 1979, attempts to slow inflation result in the pain of recession before a proportional deceleration of inflation. Avoiding the pain of curtailing inflation after a period of expansionary policy assures an inflation rate that increases over time.

[34] See the *Economic Reports of the President* for the years 1974–79 for empirical evidence on this bias.

[35] See Michael L. Wachter and Susan M. Wachter, "The Fiscal Policy Dilemma: Cyclical Swings Dominated by Supply-Side Constraints," in *The Economic Consequences of Slowing Population Growth*, ed. Espenshade (New York: Academic Press, 1978), pp. 71–99.

[36] See Michael L. Wachter and Susan M. Wachter, "The Setting for a Pro-Growth Strategy," in *Removing Obstacles to Economic Growth*, ed. Michael L. Wachter and Susan M. Wachter (Philadelphia: University of Pennsylvania Press, 1984).

[37] As a result, the rate of potential output growth will decline and the natural unemployment rate may rise with increased inflation and inflation uncertainty. In contrast to the short-run negative relationship between inflation and unemployment and the hypothesized vertical long-run Phillips curve under neutral inflation, the long-run Phillips curve may be positively sloped. Richard T. Froyen and Roger N. Waud, in "Demand Variability, Supply Shocks and the Output-Inflation Tradeoff," Working Paper No. 1081, National Bureau of Economic Research, February 1983, demonstrate a negative relationship between the variability of inflation and the natural rate of output. Similarly, Michael T. Belongia, in "Money Growth Variability and GNP," *The Federal Reserve Bank of St. Louis Review*, 66, no. 4 (April 1984), indicates a negative relationship between variation in money growth and the level and growth rate of GNP.

[38] See Harberger, "The Dynamics of Inflation in Chile," pp. 219–50.

[39] See Wachter, *Latin American Inflation;* and Adolfo Diz, "Money and Prices in Argentina," in *Varieties of Monetary Experience*, ed. David Meiselman (Chicago: University of Chicago Press, 1970).

[40] See Milton Friedman and Anna J. Schwartz, *Monetary Trends in the United States and the United Kingdom: Their Relation to Income, Prices, and Interest Rates, 1867–1975* (Chicago: University of Chicago Press, 1982).

[41] Ibid., pp. 8–9.

[42] See Dallas S. Batten and Courtenay C. Stone, "Are Monetarists an Endangered Species?" *Federal Reserve Bank of St. Louis Review,* May 1983.

[43] See Paul F. Smith in "Two Ways to Finance an Inflation," unpublished manuscript, February 4, 1980.

[44] The average inflation rate among 14 industrialized economies doubled from approximately 5 to 10 percent in this period. See Robert Solow, "The Intelligent Citizen's Guide to Inflation," *Public Interest,* Winter 1975, p. 58.

[45] See Michael R. Darby, and James R. Lothian, "Introduction and Summary," in *The International Transmission of Inflation,* ed. Darby and Lothian (Chicago: University of Chicago Press, 1983).

[46] In a world of fixed exchange rates, where the dollar is used for international reserves, growth in the U.S. money supply would fuel inflation elsewhere, unless this growth were sterilized by nonreserve central banks. The evidence of Darby and Lothian, ibid., indicates that an upward trend in the U.S. monetary growth began in the latter half of the 1960s but was sterilized until the 1970s. With the abrogation of Bretton Woods and adoption of floating exchange rates in 1974, inflation was accompanied by growth in the domestic currencies. Even with floating exchange rates, attempts to "manage" the float will induce domestic monetary growth and inflation that parallels that of the United States. For evidence that this explains Canadian inflation, see Michael D. Bordo, and Ehsan U. Choudhri, "The Link between Money and Prices in an Open Economy: The Canadian Evidence from 1971 to 1980," *Federal Reserve Bank of St. Louis Review* 64, no. 7 (August/September 1982), pp. 13–23.

[47] See Nordhaus, "The Political Business Cycle," pp. 169–90.

[48] See Alan S. Blinder, "On the Monetization of Deficits," NBER Working Paper No. 1052, May 1983. Evidence of a study by R. W. Hafer, and S. E. Hein indicates that this first effect was minor in the period 1955 through 1980. See R. W. Hafer and S. E. Hein, "Evidence on the Temporal Stability of the Demand for Money Relationship in the United States," *Federal Reserve Bank of St. Louis Review,* December 1979, pp. 3–14. Also see Richard W. Lang, "The 1975–76 Federal Deficits and the Credit Market," *Federal Reserve Bank of St. Louis Review,* January 1977, pp. 9–16; and Michael J. Hamburger and Burton Zwick, "Checking Inflation in Spite of a Deficit," *Business Week,* March 23, 1981, pp. 12–15.

[49] See William G. Dewald, "Deficits and Monetary Growth," *Economic Review,* Atlanta Federal Reserve Bank 69 (January 1984), pp. 11–20. Scott E. Hein's study of the relationship between growth rates of the federal debt and money supply in the United States in the years 1955 through 1980 also finds evidence of an important link from 1955 through early 1975. See Scott E. Hein, "Deficits and Inflation," *Federal Reserve Bank of St. Louis Review* 63, no. 3 (March 1981), pp. 3–10.

[50] For evidence that cost- (or wage-) push factors have not caused inflation, see Robert J. Gordon, "World Inflation and Monetary Accommodation in Eight Countries," *Brookings Papers on Economic Activity* 2 (1977), p. 433; and James R. Barth and James T. Bennett, "Cost-Push versus Demand-Pull Inflation: Some Empirical Evidence," *Journal of Money, Credit and Banking,* August 1975, p. 397. Overall, in the post–World War II period, U.S. wages have lagged price changes. Nonetheless, recent evidence suggests that employee compensation

costs increased as a percentage of total cost and profits over the 1970s, perhaps due to increased use of COLA clauses in union contracts. (See *Economic Report of the President* (Washington, D.C.: U.S. Government Printing Office, January 1981), p. 247.)

[51] The U.S. inflationary spurt of 1973–74 was accompanied by supply shocks and structural pressures. Besides an OPEC increase in oil prices, the dollar was depreciating by 10 percent, following a similar depreciation in the preceding year. In addition, the food component and the nonfood, nonfuel crude materials component of the WPI were up by more than 25 percent. See Solow, "The Intelligent Citizen's Guide to Inflation"; and Susan M. Wachter, "The Impact of Agricultural Prices on Inflation," *Business Economics* 10, no. 4 (September 1975), pp. 84–88.

[52] See Dallas S. Batten, "Money Growth Stability and Inflation: An International Comparison," *Federal Reserve Bank of St. Louis Review* 63, no. 8 (October 1981).

[53] See Susan M. Wachter, *Latin American Inflation.*

[54] See Eugene F. Fama, "Stock Returns Real Activity, Inflation, and Money," *American Economic Review* 71, no. 4 (September 1981), pp. 545–65.

[55] Ibid., p. 551.

[56] See Christopher A. Sims, "Money, Income, and Causality," *American Economic Review,* September 1972.

[57] See Peter I. Berman, *Inflation and the Money Supply in the United States* (Lexington, Mass.: D. C. Heath, 1977). Also see Charles R. Nelson, "Inflation and Rates of Return on Common Stocks," *The Journal of Finance* 31, no. 2 (May 1976), pp. 471–87. Nelson provides evidence that on the average most, but not all, of accelerations or decelerations in inflation are undone in subsequent periods, presumably because monetary expansion does not change proportionately with the change in inflation. Ongoing inflation increases by .14 of a 1 percent unanticipated increase in the inflation rate. The evidence suggests that inflation is highly autocorrelated with a small percentage of innovations (i.e., unanticipated inflation, carried over to future inflation). This idea is consistent with a monetary policy that mostly attempts to keep inflation from increasing over time, although given positive shocks some monetary acceleration and inflation increases do occur.

[58] See Susan M. Wachter, *Latin American Inflation.*

Bibliography

ALMON, SHIRLEY. "The Distributed Lag between Capital Appropriations and Expenditures." *Econometrica* 33 (1965), pp. 178–224.

BALASSA, BELA. "Adjustment to External Shocks in Developing Economies." *Federal Reserve Bank of St. Louis Review,* October 1981.

BARTH, JAMES R., and JAMES T. BENNETT. "Cost-Push versus Demand-Pull Inflation: Some Empirical Evidence." *Journal of Money, Credit and Banking,* August 1975, pp. 391–97.

BATTEN, DALLAS S. "Inflation: The Cost-Push Myth." *Federal Reserve Bank of St. Louis Review,* June/July 1981, pp. 20–26.

_______. "Money Growth Stability and Inflation: An International Comparison." *Federal Reserve Bank of St. Louis Review,* October 1981, pp. 7–12.

BATTEN, DALLAS S., and MACK OTT. "Five Common Myths about Floating Exchange Rates." *Federal Reserve Bank of St. Louis Review* 65, no. 9 (November 1983).

BATTEN, DALLAS S., and COURTENAY G. STONE. "Are Monetarists an Endangered Species?" *Federal Reserve Bank of St. Louis Review,* May 1983.

BELONGIA, MICHAEL T. "Money Growth Variability and GNP." *Federal Reserve Bank of St. Louis Review* 66, no. 4 (April 1984), pp. 23–31.

BERMAN, PETER I. *Inflation and the Money Supply in the United States.* Lexington, Mass.: D. C. Heath, 1977.

BLACK, FISCHER. "General Equilibrium and Business Cycles." National Bureau of Economic Research, Working Paper No. 950, August 1982.

BLINDER, ALAN S. "On the Monetization of Deficits." National Bureau of Economic Research, Working Paper No. 1052, May 1983.

BORDO, MICHAEL D., and CHOUDHRI U. EHSAN. "The Link between Money and Prices in an Open Economy: The Canadian Evidence from 1971 to 1980." *The Federal Reserve Bank of St. Louis Review* 64, no. 7 (August–September 1982), pp. 13–23.

CAGAN, PHILLIP. "The Monetary Dynamics of Hyperinflation." *Studies in the Quantity Theory of Money.* Ed. Milton Friedman. Chicago: University of Chicago Press, 1956.

CARLSON, KEITH M. "Money, Inflation and Economic Growth: Some Updated Reduced Form Results and Their Implications." *Federal Reserve Bank of St. Louis Review,* April 1980, pp. 13–19.

_______. "The Lag from Money to Prices." *Federal Reserve Bank of St. Louis Review* 62, no. 8 (October 1980), pp. 3–10.

CORDEN, W. M. *Inflation, Exchange Rates, and the World Economy.* Chicago: University of Chicago Press, 1981.

COUNCIL OF ECONOMIC ADVISORS, Office of the President. *Economic Reports of the President.* Washington, D.C.: U.S. Government Printing Office, 1974–1979.

DARBY, MICHAEL R., and JAMES R. LOTHIAN. "Introduction and Summary." *The International Transmission of Inflation.* Ed. M. R. Darby and J. R. Lothian. Chicago: University of Chicago Press, 1983.

"Deficits: Their Impact on Inflation and Growth," Staff Study of the Subcommittee on Monetary and Fiscal Policy of the Joint Economic Committee, July 30, 1981.

DEWALD, WILLIAM G. "Deficits and Monetary Growth." *Economic Review of the Atlanta Federal Reserve Bank* 69 (January 1984).

DIZ, ADOLFO. "Money and Prices in Argentina." *Varieties of Monetary Experience*. Ed. David Meiselman. Chicago: University of Chicago Press, 1970.

ENTHOVEN, ALAIN. "Monetary Disequilibrium and the Dynamics of Inflation." *The Economic Journal*, June 1956.

FAMA, EUGENE F. "Stock Returns Real Activity, Inflation, and Money." *American Economic Review* 71, no. 4 (September, 1981), pp. 545–65.

FRIEDMAN, BENJAMIN. "Optimal Expectations and the Extreme Information Assumptions of Rational Expectations Macro-Models." *Journal of Monetary Economics* 5, no. 1 (January 1979), pp. 23–46.

FRIEDMAN, MILTON. "Nobel Lecture: Inflation and Unemployment." *Journal of Political Economy*, June 1977, pp. 451–72.

FRIEDMAN, MILTON, and ANNA J. SCHWARTZ. *Monetary Trends in the United States and the United Kingdom: Their Relation to Income, Prices, and Interest Rates, 1867–1975*. Chicago: University of Chicago Press, 1982.

FROYEN, RICHARD T., and ROGER N. WAUD. "Demand Variability, Supply Shocks and the Output-Inflation Tradeoff." National Bureau of Economic Research, Working Paper No. 1081, February 1983.

GORDON, ROBERT J. "World Inflation and Monetary Accommodation in Eight Countries." *Brookings Papers on Economic Activity*, 1977.

HARBERGER, ARNOLD. "The Dynamics of Inflation in Chile." *Measurement in Economics: Studies in Mathematical Economics in Memory of Yehuda Grunfeld*. Ed. Carl Christ. Stanford: Stanford University Press, 1963.

HOLLAND, STEVEN A. "Does Higher Inflation Lead to More Uncertain Inflation?" *Federal Reserve Bank of St. Louis Review* 66, no. 2 (February 1984), pp. 15–26.

KANE, EDWARD J., AND BURTON G. MALKIEL. "Autoregressive and Nonautoregressive Elements in Cross-Section Forecasts of Inflation." *Econometrica* 44 (January 1976), pp. 1–16.

KLEIN, BENJAMIN. "The Measurement of Long- and Short-Term Price Uncertainty: A Moving Regression Time Series Analysis." *Economic Inquiry*, July 1978.

———. "The Social Costs of the Recent Inflation: The Mirage of Steady 'Anticipated' Inflation." *Carnegie-Rochester Conference Series on Public Policy: Institutional Arrangements and the Inflation Problem*, Vol. 3. Ed. Brunner and Meltzer, 1976.

LAIDER, D. E. W., and J. M. PERKIN. "Inflation: A Survey." *Economic Journal* 85 (December 1975).

LAWRENCE, R. Z. "Within and between Country Variance in Inflation Rates." *Journal of Monetary Economics* 5 (January 1979), pp. 145–52.

LUCAS, ROBERT E., JR. "Expectations and the Neutrality of Money." *Journal of Economic Theory*, April 1972.

MARSTON, RICHARD C. "Real Wages and the Terms of Trade: Alternative Indexation Rules for an Open Economy." National Bureau of Economic Research, Working Paper No. 1046, December 1982.

MCCALLUM, BENNETT T. "Macroeconomics after a Decade of Rational Expectations: Some Political Issues." *Economic Review of Federal Reserve Bank of Richmond* 68 (November–December 1982).

MEISELMAN, DAVID I., and ARTHUR B. LAFFER. "Introduction-Worldwide Inflation: A Monetarist View." *The Phenomenon of Worldwide Inflation*. Washington, D.C.: American Enterprise Institute for Public Policy Research, 1975.

MINCER, JACOB. "Models of Adaptive Forecasting." *Economic Forecasts and Expectations*. Ed. Jacob Mincer. New York: Columbia University Press for the National Bureau of Economic Research, 1969.

MUNDELL, ROBERT A. "Inflation and Real Interest." *Journal of Political Economy* no. 71 (June 1963), pp. 280–83.

NORDHAUS, WILLIAM D. "The Political Business Cycle." *The Review of Economic Studies*, April 1975, pp. 169–90.

PATINKIN, DON. *Money, Interest, and Prices: An Integration of Monetary and Value Theory*. 2nd ed. New York: Harper & Row, 1965.

PHILLIPS, A. W. "The Relation between Unemployment and the Rate of Change of Money Wage Rates in the United Kingdom, 1861–1957." *Economica* 25 (November 1958).

REA, JOHN D. "The Explanatory Power of Alternative Theories of Inflation and Unemployment, 1895–1979." *The Review of Economics and Statistics* 65, no. 2 (May 1983), pp. 183–95.

SANTOMERO, ANTHONY M., and JOHN J. SEATER. "The Inflation-Unemployment Trade-Off: A Critique of the Literature." Federal Reserve Bank of Philadelphia, Research Paper No. 21, March 1977.

SARGENT, THOMAS, and NEIL WALLACE. "Rational Expectations and the

Theory of Economic Policy." *Journal of Monetary Economics,* April 1976, pp. 169–84.

SHIFFER, ZALMAN F. "Money and Inflation in Israel: The Transition of an Economy to High Inflation." *Federal Reserve Bank of St. Louis Review,* August/September 1982, pp. 28–39.

SIMS, CHRISTOPHER A. "Money, Income, and Causality." *American Economic Review,* September 1972, pp. 540–52.

SMITH, PAUL F. *Comparative Financial Systems.* New York: Praeger Publishers, 1982.

_______. "Two Ways to Finance an Inflation." Unpublished manuscript, February 4, 1980.

SOLOW, ROBERT. "The Intelligent Citizen's Guide to Inflation." *Public Interest,* Winter 1975.

"The Impact of the Federal Reserve System's Monetary Policies on the Nation's Economy (Second Report)." Staff Report of the Subcommittee on Domestic Monetary Policy of the House Committee on Banking, Finance, and Urban Affairs, December 1980.

WACHTER, MICHAEL L., and SUSAN M. WACHTER. "The Fiscal Policy Dilemma: Cyclical Swings Dominated by Supply-Side Constraints." In *The Economic Consequences of Slowing Population Growth,* ed. Epenshade. New York: Academic Press, 1978.

_______. "The Setting for a Pro-Growth Strategy." *Removing Obstacles to Economic Growth.* Ed. M. L. Wachter and S. M. Wachter. Philadelphia: University of Pennsylvania Press, 1984.

WACHTER, SUSAN, M. *Latin American Inflation: The Structuralist-Monetarist Debate.* Lexington, Mass.: D. C. Heath, 1976.

_______. "Structuralism versus Monetarism: Inflation in Chile." *Short-Term Macroeconomic Policy in Latin America.* Ed. Jere Behrman and James A. Hanson. National Bureau of Economic Research Other Conference Series, no. 14 (1979).

_______. "The Impact of Agricultural Prices on Inflation." *Business Economics* 10, no. 4 (September 1975), pp. 84–88.

2

The Measurement and Indexation of Inflation

The task of measuring inflation is conceptually simple if relative prices remain constant. If all prices increase by the same percentage, the measurement of inflation becomes trivial. An index is not necessary since the percentage change in any price will serve as an index for all price changes. However, relative price changes do occur and generally accompany inflation. Since each commodity's proportion of output varies over time with changes in relative prices, it is necessary to choose, first, the prices to include in an index and, second, the weights for these prices. Given the multitude of possible ways to measure inflation (depending on which prices are included and with what weights), the choice of an appropriate index of inflation is improved by a prior determination of the information that the index is supposed to provide.

One logical approach to the measurement of inflation is to construct an expenditure-based cost-of-living (COL) index. This index provides information on the ratio of expenditures required, by the price changes between two periods, to maintain a constant standard of living. It can be constructed as a Laspeyres index (to give the change necessary to purchase the first-period set of goods and services) or as a Paasche index (to give the change necessary to purchase the second-period set of goods and services). In either case, it includes a sample of prices of goods and services with each price weighted by its share of total consumption in the period chosen. By calculating the percentage change of total dollar expenditures necessary to maintain the consumption of the given period, an expenditure-based COL index provides information on the "average" price change since or until that period.

The consumer price index (CPI) and the gross national product deflator for personal consumption expenditures (PCE) are generally used (the CPI most frequently) as expenditure-based COL measures of inflation for indexing purposes. They differ in several respects, most importantly in their choice of a base period. The next section of this chapter discusses the formulas and data used in each index. In the section after that is an analysis of possible sources of measurement bias and a discussion of alternatives.

A later section examines the use of indexes to escalate private nominal contracts and government transfers. The search for a method to escalate nominal payment contracts to neutralize unanticipated inflation is a more recalcitrant problem than the measurement of inflation. Unanticipated inflation disturbs previously agreed on nominal contract agreements, but frequent recontracting is expensive and risky. The goal of automatic escalation of nominal contracts by a previously chosen index is the avoidance of increased contracting costs and risk. However, some increase in these will be unavoidable, except under the unrealistic circumstance of neutral inflation.

Price Indexes: How They Are Constructed

The Consumer Price Index

The Bureau of Labor Statistics (BLS) of the Department of Labor has constructed and published the CPI since 1921. The CPI is designed to measure changes in the cost of purchasing the "average" family's consumption of goods (new and used) and services. Thus, federal or state income taxes do not enter into the index; however, all sales and property taxes are included in the prices used. The CPI is a Laspeyres or fixed-weight index. The item weights are the amount spent on each item as a proportion of total family expenditures and are changed at 10- to 15-year intervals (in 1940, 1953, 1964, and most recently in 1978).[1]

The Data Used. The number of items included, the weights used, the price sampling methods, and the population coverage have undergone several revisions, most recently in 1978. The index currently includes 300 items which are weighted according to expenditures reported in the 1972–74 Consumer Expenditure Survey. Twenty thousand families were interviewed personally, and another 20,000 families completed a two-week diary reporting all expenditures. The survey was used to determine the amount each family spent on each item in the index. These amounts were then summed across families. The total amount all families spent on an item, such as milk, was then divided by all families' total expenditures to determine the weighting of the item in the CPI.

The 1972–74 survey was designed to increase the coverage of the CPI. In the past, the CPI population sample covered urban wage earners and clerical workers only. The 1972–74 survey resulted in two CPI indexes: the CPI-W measures price changes in goods consumed by urban wage earners and clerical workers; the CPI-U measures price changes in goods consumed by all urban families. The CPI-U covers approximately 80 percent of the total U.S. noninstitutional civilian population. Persons living outside urban areas, such as farm families, are excluded. The CPI-W represents about one half of the population covered by the CPI-U. Although most wage contracts and federal benefits continue to be linked to the CPI-W, the two indexes provide an almost identical measure of prices.

Prices for the market baskets consumed by the two population groups are collected in 85 urban areas (metropolitan statistical areas) from 18,000 tenants, 18,000 housing units (for property taxes), and about 24,000 establishments (e.g., grocery and department stores, hospitals, filling stations, and other types of stores and service establishments). All sales taxes are included in prices used. Prices of most goods and services are obtained by personal visits of BLS agents. Mail questionnaires are used for other items.

Under the 1978 revision, a process termed *disaggregation* was employed for selecting the detailed items to be priced. Previously, a fixed basket of about 400 specific items was priced. The current procedure gives each variety, brand, size, and the like of a fairly general category a chance of selection proportional to its importance in total sales for the general category in the particular store. Once selected at an outlet, the same item continues to be priced.

The CPI data is published monthly in both a seasonally adjusted and unadjusted form. The published CPI is broken down by broad categories (food and beverages, housing, apparel, transportation, medical care, entertainment, other goods and services), by subcategories, and by item for the United States as a whole, for the large metropolitan statistical areas (MSAs), and for regions (Northeast, North Central, South, and West). It is also cross-classified by five population classes: major metropolitan areas (more than 4,000,000 people), large metropolitan areas (1,250,000–4,000,000 people), medium metropolitan areas (385,000–1,250,000 people), small metropolitan areas (75,000,000–385,000 people), and urban areas outside of metropolitan areas (less than 75,000 people).[2]

Treatment of Housing. The homeownership component is the largest category within the CPI. The treatment of this component has been the most controversial issue involved in the calculation of the CPI. First is a brief description of the treatment that has been used to calculate the CPI-W through 1985. The new methodology is essentially the same for the CPI and the PCE and is described in a later section.

Prior to 1985, the homeownership component was divided into five elements: home purchase, contracted mortgage interest cost, property taxes, property insurance, and maintenance and repairs. The home purchase and mortgage interest weights were determined, in the same way as other CPI weights, as the amount spent by all consumers on home purchases and contracted mortgages divided by the amount spent by all families on total expenditures (as indicated by the 1972–74 survey). The home purchase figures were calculated by taking the purchase price for homes bought in the survey year, less the sale price for homes sold, plus transactions costs for purchases and sales. The mortgage interest cost was based on the amount of interest that borrowers were contractually obligated to pay during the first half of the term of their mortgage loans (assumed to be the average actual duration of the mortgages).[3]

Because of the bias inherent in the manner in which homeownership costs were calculated, the BLS in 1978 established five experimental measures of the CPI using different conceptual approaches to homeownership. As of January 1984, the CPI-U incorporated the rental equivalent experimental (x − 1) measure of housing costs, and the CPI-W also incorporated the new measure as of 1986. There have been substantial differences in the movement of price indexes incorporating x − 1 or other alternative measures of housing costs and the CPI-U and CPI-W, as traditionally measured.

To understand the likely impact of the change on the measurement of the inflation rate, it is useful to discuss the bias of the previous approach. In the past, the CPI's measurement of housing was deficient in two respects. First, the share of resident-owned housing was overestimated. Second, the measured cost of living in one's own home was biased upwards.

At the end of the period of use of the house, homes are not valueless but are sold, often at a profit, in real terms. Thus, including the entire purchase minus sales price plus half of interest costs overweights the importance of housing consumption.[4] In addition, the years of the household survey were good ones for housing with unusually strong housing construction.[5]

Empirical evidence supports the hypothesis that the approximately one-fourth homeownership weight, used in the past, was disproportionately large. In the pre-1984 CPI, homeownership costs were almost five times more important than residential rents, while homeownership is only about two and one half times as important as rental housing in the national income accounts and only about two thirds of dwelling units are owner-occupied.

While the approach used in calculating housing costs in the CPI overweighted housing, this did not in itself necessarily bias the index up or down. An upward bias occurred if the price of a house and current mortgage interest rates were increasing faster than the accurately measured cost of living in one's own home. The overweighting of these incorrect prices worsens the bias. Empirical evidence indicates that this indeed occurred in the 1970s. A theoretically correct weighting and measuring of housing costs would have resulted in a lower measured inflation rate in this period.

Obviously, owner occupants do not consume entire houses each year but rather the flow-of-services provided by the house.

Thus, a theoretically correct approach weights and measures the user costs of the flow-of-services that owner-occupied housing provides. The user cost of housing or, in general, of any consumer durable is its price multiplied by the real interest rate plus depreciation, maintenance, insurance, and taxes, less appreciation. When financed in part by a mortgage and in part by the owner's equity, the user cost of housing includes: the real mortgage interest rate multiplied by the amount of funds borrowed, the real interest rate (measured as an opportunity cost) multiplied by the equity in the house, property taxes, insurance, maintenance, and repairs. These expenditures are offset by any capital gains (net of depreciation) and savings on personal income taxes due to the favored treatment of owner-occupied housing in the tax code.

In the decade of the 1970s, housing prices and mortgage interest rates increased more than other prices. As a result, the price of the homeownership component, as historically measured, rose more rapidly than the prices of other components of the CPI. The real user cost of occupant-owned housing, however, calculated in a study by Diamond, actually steadily declined over this period from a level set at 100 in 1970 to 70.5 in 1979.[6]

The divergence between housing costs, as accurately measured in a user cost framework and as historically measured is, to a large extent, due to the interaction of inflation with the tax benefits of owner-occupied housing. Due to the progressivity of the federal income tax structure, inflation in the 1970s pushed families into higher tax brackets, while the deductibility of mortgage interest payments lowered the real interest cost of housing. In addition, even at the same tax bracket, higher inflation itself lowers real housing costs because tax laws allow the deduction of the nominal rather than the real interest rate and, with inflation, the nominal rate increases. Finally, real interest rates declined in this period. Thus, the real after-tax interest rate decreased and for some even became negative. These cost-lowering factors are not reflected in the traditional measure of housing costs. Indeed, this measure is likely to increase when accurately measured costs decline.

When the inflation rate increased in the 1970s, appreciation in the nominal and real price of housing occurred. The deductibility of higher nominal interest rates and reduced real interest rates lowered actual housing costs. As a result, individuals bought more housing and the increase in the demand for housing bid up housing prices. Appreciation then further reduced actual housing costs. The appreciation in housing prices caused the historical methodology to measure an increase in housing costs when costs were declining.[7] The extent of the possible bias and a description of the alternative indexes that the BLS has experimented with are discussed in Appendix 2.A.

The Gross National Product Deflator for Personal Consumption Expenditures

The Bureau of Economic Analysis of the Commerce Department publishes implicit price deflators. These are used in national income accounts to deflate nominal measures of output.

The gross national product (GNP) deflator is the ratio of nominal GNP in a given period to real GNP (i.e., constant dollar GNP) in that period. The gross national product is defined as the sum of the value of final goods and services produced annually in the nation's economy. Nominal GNP measures the value of output in a given period in the prices of that period, or in current dollars. Real GNP is derived by dividing the current dollar estimates by the GNP price deflator, currently based on 1972 as 100. The GNP deflator could therefore be used as a measure of inflation for the period from which the base prices for calculating real GNP are taken to the current period; the current percentage change in the GNP deflator could be used as a measure of current inflation. However, the deflator is not primarily constructed to measure inflation since it incorporates changes in weights as well as changes in prices, as described below.

The price sources used in the construction of implicit price deflators include the consumer price index, the wholesale price index, the Department of Agriculture's "Prices Paid by Farmers" series, construction cost indexes, and indexes for exports and imports published by the Department of Commerce.

The BEA publishes this index and subindexes (by sector, by major type of product, and for various expenditures groups, including personal consumption expenditures) quarterly, with a considerable time lag, rather than monthly (as is the case for the CPI). In addition, previously published data are often revised, with a lag of several years.

Personal consumption expenditures consist of the market value of purchases of newly produced goods and services (e.g., food, clothing, housing, and financial services) by individuals and nonprofit institutions. The most important indexes used for constructing the personal consumption expenditure deflator are the CPI and, to a lesser degree, the "Prices Paid by Farmers" series. The PCE does not include used goods.

Thus, the principal deflating index used to derive the PCE is the CPI discussed above. The major differences between the PCE and the CPI in the past have been (1) the weights used and the frequency of weighting changes and (2) the treatment of housing. The revised CPI-U has adopted the PCE's treatment of housing; thus, the principal remaining distinction is in the frequency of weighting changes.

In theory, the PCE deflator (and the other GNP deflators) is a Paasche index. That is, the weights used are derived from the current year's output rather than from the base year's output which is used to weight prices in constructing the CPI.[8] These weights are only used to combine aggregate groups of goods into an index; within groups, the weights used are those from the CPI. Thus, the PCE combines both fixed and variable weights. Thus, the weighting differences between the CPI and PCE are not as large in practice as in theory. The implications of these differences are considered in the following section which examines possible sources of bias in the CPI and PCE measurement of cost-of-living changes.

Critique of Existing Indexes and Alternatives

The CPI and PCE are used as expenditure-based COL indexes, that is, as though they measured the increased expenditure cost of maintaining a given standard of living (a constant level of happiness or, in economic terms, a constant level of utility). As shown in Table 2–1, in the 19-year period 1950–69, the CPI and the PCE moved together closely. In the 1970 decade, however, as seen in Table 2–2, these two indexes gave substantially different measurements of inflation. On the evidence of this divergence, there was either a systematic negative bias in the PCE and/or a positive bias in the CPI or both.

Indeed, there can be no one true measure of expenditure-based

TABLE 2–1
Alternative Measures of the Rate of Inflation, 1950–1969

Year	*CPI-W*	*PCE*
1950	1.0	2.0
1951	7.9	6.5
1952	2.2	2.3
1953	.8	1.9
1954	.5	.8
1955	−.4	.9
1956	1.5	2.0
1957	3.6	3.2
1958	2.7	2.2
1959	.8	1.9
1960	1.6	1.8
1961	1.0	1.1
1962	1.1	1.5
1963	1.2	1.5
1964	1.3	1.3
1965	1.7	1.8
1966	2.9	2.9
1967	2.9	2.5
1968	4.2	4.1
1969	5.4	4.6
Annual average	2.2	2.3

SOURCE: Wharton Econometrics Forecasting Associates Data Bank.

COL changes. Intractable theoretical and practical problems make such a measurement impossible. Only if (1) product quality were constant, (2) relative prices and tastes did not change, and (3) all people were the same, would it be possible to construct a perfect COL index of market-purchased goods and services. In addition there is the mechanical problem of measuring the price of the flow-of-services provided by durable goods. Even with the recent modification of the treatment of housing in the CPI, difficult issues remain in the pricing of housing and other durable goods.

The next four sections examine the extent to which these difficulties cause the CPI and PCE to give systematically biased estimates of expenditure-based COL increases in market-purchased goods and services. Then the following section summarizes the discussion and briefly compares the CPI and PCE to both more and less inclusive alternative measures of inflation.

TABLE 2–2
Alternative Measures of the Rate of Inflation, 1970–1983

Year	*CPI-W*	*PCE*
1970	5.9	4.5
1971	4.3	4.3
1972	3.3	3.6
1973	6.2	5.7
1974	11.0	10.1
1975	9.1	7.6
1976	5.8	5.1
1977	6.5	5.8
1978	7.6	7.0
1979	11.5	9.0
1980	13.5	10.3
1981	10.2	8.6
1982	6.0	5.8
1983*	3.8	4.0
Annual average 1970–1980	7.7	6.6
Annual average 1970–1983	7.5	6.8

*Estimated.
SOURCE: Wharton Econometrics Forecasting Associates Data Bank.

Measurement of Quality Changes

It is not clear whether imperfections in measuring quality changes bias the CPI and PCE up or down. In the absence of any attempt to adjust for quality changes, the bias presumably would be positive, since the quality level of most goods and services improves over time. However, the BLS endeavors to account for this general type of quality improvement. The price indexes utilize a linking procedure that attempts to achieve comparability between the prices of old and new products by excluding any additions to prices that are a reflection of the increased production cost of the new products.

Various analyses of the value of quality change through the estimation of so-called hedonic equations (in which prices paid are regressed against product characteristics) indicate that the BLS adjustment methods may understate quality improvements for some products and overstate them for others. In addition, for some items (e.g., existing housing) quality can deteriorate. There is evidence that this deterioration may not be properly incorporated.[9] This biases the indexes downward. Thus, although quality error may be a problem in the CPI and PCE, the sign of the sum of the errors cannot be determined. As a result, it cannot be assumed that mismeasurement of product quality biases the CPI or PCE measures of inflation in either direction. In any case, the extent of the bias is likely to be small in terms of the mismeasurement of inflation at moderate inflation rates. Paradoxically, the higher the inflation rate, the lower this bias will be as a percentage of the inflation rate. Conversely, mismeasurement of product quality will have a large percentage impact on relatively low inflation rates. Hence, at low inflation rates, it becomes more difficult to determine whether a given monetary policy is sustaining inflation or whether there is actually no inflation because of quality changes that are not measured.

In sum, we cannot know if a bias exists and whether it is significant unless further work on quality changes is undertaken. Hedonic studies of privately produced goods can be suggestive, although the mingling of demand and supply factors preclude clear-cut results. Even more crucial are studies of environmental quality and the quality of other nonpriced public goods. The issue of the inclusiveness of the CPI and PCE will be discussed in a later section. Briefly, note that the CPI and PCE are not designed to measure cost-of-living changes of all goods, private and public, although they are used as if they do measure such changes. It would not be feasible to investigate quality changes in all public goods on a regular, monthly, or even annual base. Nonetheless, studies of trends are necessary to put meaningful bounds on real income growth and inflation estimates, especially in periods when it is known that there is significant change in the quality of public goods.

Changing Relative Prices and Tastes

If all prices change proportionately, the system that is used to weight prices does not affect the measured inflation rate. In the presence of relative price changes, the decision whether to use an index with past period market weights (termed a *Laspeyres index*) or an index with current-period weights (termed a *Paasche index*) matters. Economic theory indicates that a Laspeyres index may overstate inflation relative to a true COL index, while a Paasche index may understate it. The greater the degree of relative price change, the greater is the potential positive or negative bias.[10]

The reason for these biases is that neither index takes into account consumers' substitution behavior in response to relative price changes. When prices increase at different rates, consumers have the opportunity to escape part of the burden of the price increase by buying substitutes for the goods whose prices are increasing most rapidly. A Laspeyres index ignores this possibility and, therefore, exaggerates the welfare loss from inflation. A Paasche index implicitly assumes that these substitutions entail no loss of satisfaction and hence understates the burden of inflation.

Consider the following example. Suppose a household initially spends $2 each for one pound of fish and one pound of chicken for a total of $4. In the next period, the price of fish doubles, but the price of chicken remains the same. Would expenditures have to increase by 0 percent or 50 percent (or by some intermediate percent) to keep the household at a constant level of satisfaction? The 0 percent and 50 percent represent two polar cases depending on whether the household views the two items as perfect substitutes or perfect complements. If fish and chicken are perfect substitutes to the household unit, then expenditures would not have to increase at all to keep the household at a constant level of satisfaction. The household would change its purchases to two pounds of chicken without any loss of utility. The Paasche index would record no inflation, since it is based on the second-period consumption weights, and it would be accurate. If a Laspeyres index were used, however, it would measure inflation as 50 percent, which would in this case be overestimating inflation by that amount. Only if fish and chicken were perfect complements to each other for this household would the Laspeyres measure be accurate.

In the general case, when fish and chicken are not perfect substitutes or complements to each other, inflation is correctly measured as somewhere between 0 percent and 50 percent. For example, the family may like one and three quarters pounds of chicken and one half a pound of fish as much as the original bundle. This new bundle would cost $5.50 ($1.75 \times 2 + 0.5 \times 4$). The Laspeyres index implies that it will cost $6 to make the consumer as well-off as in the base period, but in reality it will only cost \$5.50. That is, it indicates a 50 percent rate of inflation while the true rise in the COL is 37.5 percent. The Paasche approach uses the second-period weights in the second period and thus estimates that the COL was \$5.50 in that period. Using second-period weights in the first period, the Paasche approach estimates a COL of \$4.50 ($1.75 \times 2 + 0.5 \times 2$) for the first period. The COL is measured as increasing by 22.2 percent (instead of the true rate of 37.5 percent). Thus, in this case, the Laspeyres index overestimates inflation because it uses the base-year weights in both periods, while the Paasche index underestimates inflation because it uses the current-period weights in both periods.

The Paasche index establishes a lower bound on cost-of-living increases to its reference period market basket and the Laspeyres index an upper bound from its reference period basket. However, since these reference periods are not the same, we cannot even say with certainty that the true cost-of-living change is somewhere in between without knowing the individual consumer's preferences. All that we know is that one provides an upper bound and the other a lower bound on an estimate of the COL change between the different periods that they cover.[11]

Appendix 2.B reviews the evidence of empirical studies on the extent of the substitution bias. This evidence suggests the following: first, that any bias in the CPI for the 1950–70 period was perhaps low, averaging .1 percent of an index point per year; second, that the bias was somewhat worse in the 1970s than earlier, although the bias was not large enough to explain much of the large divergence between the CPI and the PCE in this period; and third, that sharp relative price changes may cause a significant bias in the years in which they occur.

An alternative to the CPI and PCE would be a Fisher's Ideal index which averages the Laspeyres and Paasche formulas.[12] This index need not more closely approximate the correct rate than others. However, for many reasonable descriptive functions of consumer behavior, this (along with other mixed-weight index formulas) has been shown to be a close approximation of the true cost-of-living index.[13]

The construction of such an index should be encouraged for several reason: First, unlike the case with either the (Paasche) PCE index or (Laspeyres) CPI index, a mixed-weight index does not have an a priori negative or positive bias. Second, additional studies on a more disaggregated level may show greater substitution possibilities and, therefore, a greater bias (although smaller relative price movements may counteract this so that the substitution bias may still be small) than the literature currently reports. Third, even if the average substitution bias over time is low, it can have a destabilizing effect on actual inflation if indexation is widespread. With indexation, short-run mismeasurement can become embodied in actual inflation. As discussed below, this may be a serious problem if supply-shock factors are the source of the inflation, because in this case even indexation to an accurately measured inflation rate lowers GNP and employment. A positive measurement error worsens this problem. Thus, it would be useful to develop alternative indexes that are less biased.

The interaction between changing tastes and the substitution bias must also be considered in evaluating the seriousness of the latter. Taste shifts complicate the construction of indexes that are designed to measure changes in the cost of a fixed standard of living, since the consumption of the same goods no longer provides the same fixed standard of living. Depending on whether preferences increase (decrease) for those goods whose prices have gone up (down), any index will overstate (understate) inflation. There is, however, no systematic reason for preferences to increase for those goods whose prices have gone up or for preferences to decrease for those goods whose prices have gone down. Thus, there is no overall tendency for overstatement (or understatement) from this source. In addition, exogenous taste changes are not likely to change substantially enough in the short run to have a significant impact on prices.

Tastes, however, may adjust in response to relative price changes in a way that does affect the degree of bias of the CPI and PCE. Tastes themselves are dependent on the experience of consuming goods. To the extent that this is true, substitutability among goods increases over time. To illustrate, sometime after a new technology is developed, the price of the product may drop rapidly. Consumers may substitute this product for others both because its price has declined and because they have become more knowledgeable about and accepting of its use. The CPI, however, will continue to weight the higher priced earlier products in the proportion of their previous use, in spite of the growing substitutability of the new product. All other things being equal, this means that the substitution bias of the CPI may increase as tastes adjust, and it provides an additional rationale for the development of an alternative to the current CPI index.

Measuring Cost-of-Living Changes for Groups with Differing Characteristics

Both the CPI and PCE measure the price level change for the general population. Because the consumption pattern of the elderly differs from that of the general population and because relative prices change, cost-of-living changes for the elderly and for the general population may differ. The theory of constructing a true measure of cost-of-living changes applies to the individual. Aggregating across individuals introduces a bias whenever consumption patterns differ. However, there is no theoretical reason for the direction of the bias to be systematically positive or negative. The direction and size of any bias must be determined empirically.

Several long-run empirical studies have been done comparing specific group indexes with general indexes. Studies that compare price indexes weighted for retired persons' consumption patterns versus the CPI indicate, for the period 1950 through 1970, no more than a 2 percent underestimate by the CPI.[14]

These studies use data from a period with comparatively stable relative prices and low inflation. In a study performed over the period 1961–82, Michael J. Boskin and Michael D. Hurd also find little difference in inflation across age groups.[15] Boskin and Hurd divide the population into a younger than 55 cohort, five year cohorts from age 55 to age 75, and an older than 75 cohort. Tables 2–3 and 2–4, taken from their study, summarize their results.

Boskin and Hurd first calculate the percentage expenditure weights of 17 commodity groups in the consumption of each cohort and, as shown in Table 2–3, find expenditure weights that vary significantly among population age groups.[16]

In spite of these differences, however, cumulative cost-of-living and annual inflation rates calculated for each group vary only slightly, as shown in Table 2–4.[17] The cumulative cost-of-

TABLE 2–3
Percent of Expenditure Shares by Age

	Rental Equivalent				
Commodity	*Less than 60*	*60–64*	*65–69*	*70–74*	*75+*
1. Food at home	14.9	16.3	16.9	17.8	20.1
2. Food away from home	5.3	4.9	4.3	3.7	3.3
3. Alcoholic beverages	1.1	.8	.8	.6	.5
4. Tobacco products	1.6	1.5	1.4	1.1	.8
5. Rented dwelling and other lodging	8.1	5.8	7.0	8.2	10.4
6. Owned dwelling, home	14.2	17.9	20.3	20.5	20.0
7. Fuel, utilities, and telephone	6.4	7.3	7.7	8.3	9.2
8. Domestic services	1.3	1.6	1.6	1.8	3.1
9. House furnishings	4.7	3.9	3.7	3.0	2.6
10. Dry cleaning and laundry	1.0	.9	.9	.9	.9
11. Clothing	7.0	5.6	5.0	4.5	3.7
12. Total transportation less (13)	20.2	17.8	15.2	14.2	8.5
13. Transportation other than auto	1.3	1.7	2.1	1.8	1.8
14. Medical care	4.9	6.9	7.3	8.3	9.8
15. Personal care	1.1	1.5	1.5	1.5	1.5
16. Recreation, reading, TV, education	6.0	4.7	3.8	3.4	2.9
17. Miscellaneous	1.0	.8	.6	.6	.9

SOURCE: Michael J. Boskin and Michael D. Hurd, "Are Inflation Rates Different for the Elderly?" NBER Working Paper No. 943, July 1982.

living differences over the years 1961–81, in the rental equivalent CPI, is less than 1 percent for all age groups. Although inflation rates differed in certain years, the maximum difference between any elderly age group and the nonelderly was less than one percentage point. The average difference was less than half of a percentage point. Thus, the findings of Boskin and Hurd are not dissimilar to those reported in the earlier studies.

In an even more detailed study, Robert T. Michael examines the disparity of group versus household specific indexes.[18] The difference that he finds between groups, however, is small compared to the dispersion within groups. He concludes that group-specific inflation escalators for wages would not eliminate the bulk of distribution effects of inflation due to differences in the prices of individual market bundles. This conclusion is rein-

TABLE 2–4
Cumulative Cost-of-Living

	Age Group						Official
Year	*Young*	*55–59*	*60–64*	*65–69*	*70–74*	*75+*	*CPI-U*
1961	90.5	90.4	90.4	90.5	90.5	90.5	89.6
1962	91.3	91.2	91.2	91.3	91.3	91.1	90.6
1963	92.5	92.4	92.4	92.5	92.5	92.5	91.7
1964	94.0	94.0	94.0	94.0	94.0	94.0	92.9
1965	95.6	95.6	95.6	95.6	95.6	95.6	94.5
1966	97.7	97.7	97.7	97.7	97.7	97.8	97.2
1967	100.0	100.0	100.0	100.0	100.0	100.0	100.0
1968	103.5	103.5	103.4	103.4	103.0	103.4	104.2
1969	107.8	107.9	107.8	107.8	107.7	107.8	109.8
1970	113.0	113.1	113.1	113.0	112.9	113.0	116.3
1971	118.1	118.2	118.2	118.2	118.1	118.2	121.3
1972	121.5	121.7	121.8	121.9	121.9	122.2	125.3
1973	128.8	129.2	129.3	129.5	129.6	130.3	133.1
1974	142.2	142.7	142.8	142.7	142.9	143.7	147.7
1975	154.1	154.8	154.9	154.7	154.9	155.8	161.2
1976	163.8	164.6	164.7	164.3	164.4	165.0	170.5
1977	174.7	175.7	175.8	175.5	175.7	176.4	181.5
1978	186.3	187.6	187.7	187.4	187.8	188.8	195.4
1979	205.0	206.5	206.5	205.8	206.3	206.8	217.4
1980	228.2	230.1	229.8	228.8	229.2	228.9	246.8
1981	250.1	252.4	252.1	251.1	251.4	250.8	272.4

SOURCE: Michael J. Boskin and Michael D. Hurd, "Are Inflation Rates Different for the Elderly?" NBER Working Paper No. 943, July 1982.

forced by his finding that observed differences among groups or types of households were not stable over time. Over the whole of the period studied, no particular groups of consumers suffered disproportionately from inflation. At the same time, constructing individualized indexes for specific population groupings would increase the accuracy of the measurement of inflation in the short run. The costs of doing so need to be analyzed and balanced against the potential gains of increased accuracy.

An additional area deserving of further research is an analysis of the variance of substitution bias among different groups. It may well be that groups differing in age or in income have greater or lesser accessibility to substitutes which would result in a nonuniform substitution bias.

The Use of Rental Equivalents to Calculate Housing Costs

The rental equivalent $X - 1$ series is an attempt to implement a flow-of-services approach to the measurement of housing costs. The BLS derives the weight for this index from the estimated rental value of all owner-occupied homes in the 1972–73 Consumer Expenditure Survey.[19] The current CPI rent index is then used to measure cost changes of homeownership.[20]

Although undoubtedly an improvement, the use of this index to impute rents to owner-occupied dwellings may have shortcomings of its own. First, the mix of housing types that are rented varies greatly from that of owner-occupied housing. Second, the rental index may be biased downwards since adjustments are not made for quality deterioration as rental units age.[21] Most importantly, the cost of identical rental and owned housing will not move together. When factors that influence the incentive to own rather than to rent change, a divergence is likely to result. An increase in the inflation rate will lower the relative price of owning versus renting because of inflation's effect on the after-tax cost of owning.

The CPI based on the $X - 1$ variant moves very closely with the fixed-weight PCE price index, as shown by their substantially equivalent measure (6.6 percent and 6.8 percent, respectively) of annual inflation in the 1970s.[22] This result is to be expected since the PCE and the CPI use the same rent index. Both may overestimate the cost of homeownership when inflation is high or increasing and underestimate the cost when inflation is low or decreasing.

Given the profound difficulties in directly measuring the cost of living in owner-occupied housing, the rental equivalent $X - 1$ series is the best currently available alternative. However, the extent of bias in the use of $X - 1$ should be investigated more thoroughly. The ideal measure of homeownership costs is the cost of the flow-of-services of renting to oneself. In principle, the flow-of-services approach should be used to calculate price movements in all durables.[23] Because neither the current CPI, nor the CPI-$X - 1$, nor the PCE provides such an index for housing or for other durables, further work in this area would be useful.

Alternatives to Expenditure-Based Cost-of-Living Indexes

The CPI and the PCE measure the change in total expenditure necessary to purchase a set of market goods and services. As such, they are broad-based expenditure measures of inflation although they exclude nonmarketed goods and services. Alternative indexes of inflation are possible and, depending on the planned use of the index, potentially more appropriate. For example, narrower indexes such as the components of the producer price index are useful for firms desiring information on prices of particular raw material inputs, especially those with volatile prices, which are important to the costs of their output. These prices, together with labor costs (largely fixed on an annual basis), determine their variable costs. Firms can announce a linkage of their list prices to the index that is closest to their major input and, thus, provide their customers with a guaranteed maximum price over a period of time. This enables customers to determine which firm provides the best competitive value, given the quality of the product. One problem is that, while the movements of such narrow indexes may be the best predictor of variable cost changes, they cannot be wholly accurate and at times will be very imperfect measures of cost change. Yet in an inflationary environment some indexation may be better than none to preserve the possibility of long-term contracts.

Similarly, wage or benefit indexation may be deemed important to protect individuals' income from inflation. The CPI is widely used for this purpose, in spite of the measurement problems described above. But as an expenditure-based COL index, it has additional limitations, especially if it is to be used to preserve a real standard of living.

The CPI and PCE are designed to measure changes in the cost of all *market* purchased goods. As such, they are constructed as market goods expenditure-based COL indexes. They do not measure changes in income from assets, taxes, or the cost of public goods and of nonmarket in-the-home production.

Thus, in theory, they are not designed to answer the question of how much income (from all sources) must be escalated to preserve a real standard of living. Construction and periodic measure of indexes to answer this question is not practical. Appendix 2.C discusses such indexes and considers what additional information would be needed for their construction.

With the exception of some partial income and intertemporal indexes, it would not be feasible to construct and track these theoretical COL indexes. They help indicate, however, the limits of the information provided by the CPI and PCE. Because these do not consider tax effects, nonmarket goods, or the existence of other sources of income (including assets), they are imperfect if used as inflation escalators to protect real income.

There are also the practical measurement difficulties that remain in the CPI and PCE expenditure-based COL indexes due to product quality changes, substitution bias, individual consumption differences, and the lack of explicit prices for the flow-of-services provided by durable goods, principally housing. The empirical evidence, discussed in Appendixes 2.A and 2.B, suggests that the large divergence between the CPI and PCE measures of inflation in the 1970s was due primarily to the CPI's past treatment of housing. Nonetheless, evidence suggests that the substitution bias and treatment of housing may still systematically bias measured inflation rates. Of the remaining price measurement problems, some are unavoidable at any cost, and some could be reduced if more money were spent on data collection. In any case, it is probably fair to say that the empirical studies do not provide evidence of large measurement biases. However, as the following indicates, even if we could develop a "near perfect" measure of inflation, achieving perfect protection against inflation is economically feasible only under unrealistic conditions.

The Indexation of Inflation

Definitions

Indexation is first the process by which private parties to a contract link payments to an inflation index or to an index that moves with inflation such as a short-term interest rate. Along with private pensions, collective bargaining contracts, long-term rental contracts, insurance policies, and debt payments may be indexed. Second, indexation is the linkage of government transfer payments or tax schedules to an inflation index. Government transfer payments that are currently indexed include Social Security, military, federal civil service and municipal retirement payments, and food stamp benefits.

The indexation process, whether private or public, can differ in (1) the index that is used; (2) the frequency of adjustment and whether adjusted at fixed time intervals, such as quarterly or annually, or at variable time intervals when movements in the index reach certain levels; (3) the mechanics of the linkage, for example, linkage between a percentage change in the index and the percentage change in payments, or a linkage between the basis points change in the index and the absolute amount of the payments; (4) degree of indexation, that is, whether payments are adjusted fully by the change in the index or as a proportion of the change; (5) limits, if any (for example, "caps" which restrict the increase in payments during a given time period or over the whole of the contract); (6) minimum changes, if any, required to initiate indexation; and (7) symmetry or asymmetry in the treatment of positive and negative changes in the index, among other features.

The BLS estimates that about one half of the U.S. population is involved in indexing arrangements of one kind or another.[24] The next two sections discuss the rationales and effects of indexing in the private and public sectors.

Indexation in the Private Sector

Indexation as a Response to Inflation Uncertainty. Uncertain inflation increases the risk of contracts set in nominal terms. For example, a three-year labor contract involves more risk when future inflation rates are unknown. If wage growth is set high in the expectation of high inflation, and if actual inflation is less than expected inflation, real wages increase more than anticipated. The increase in the prices of the firm's output is less than anticipated, so that the firm suffers a profit loss while employees suffer by being laid off. If inflation is greater than anticipated, wage growth rates will be set too low. The employer then suffers labor shortages, and employees suffer a loss of income.

Similarly, it is more difficult to determine at what interest rate to lend or borrow into the future, given uncertain inflation. Because the anticipated inflation rate is incorporated into interest rates, the borrower suffers if inflation is less than anticipated, and the lender suffers if inflation is greater than anticipated. Risk-averse borrowers and lenders alike will demand risk premiums. As a result, long-term inflation uncertainty could preclude contracts that are long term for both borrowers and lenders. An alternative is a loan contract in which the lender is committed to providing long-term funds but the borrower can repay the loan, with a penalty. In such a contract, the lender suffers if inflation is greater than anticipated, but the borrower is not at risk nor does the lender gain (except for the predetermined amount of the penalty) if inflation is less than anticipated. The borrower pays a premium to the lender for absorbing money risk and for "call" protection provided by the option of early repayment.

In general, the risk created by uncertain inflation is that real payments will be different from those anticipated and warranted by market conditions. The risk affects *all* parties engaged in contracts. In an environment where there is initially little uncertainty, the lender will be hurt by an unanticipated increase in the inflation rate, and the borrower will gain. But when past experience makes it clear that future inflation rates are uncertain, the lender will demand a premium from the borrower to lend at any nominally fixed rate to cover the increased lending risk and call protection.

Similarly, in negotiating a fixed contract, firms faced with uncertain inflation will want to protect themselves by setting wage growth rates somewhat lower than otherwise if inflation is uncertain. But wage earners also are worse off with a fixed contract under uncertain inflation since lower than anticipated real wage growth is possible. Again, the effect is that fixed-wage contracts are less attractive to both parties. In sum, uncertain inflation raises the risk and/or cost to all parties engaged in a nominal contract. Such contracts become less desirable.

There are two solutions to the risk introduced by uncertain inflation; neither is perfect. One is to shorten contracts. But this creates difficulties (1) because there is time and effort involved in renegotiating contracts and (2) because, for planning and risk-minimizing purposes, it is useful to know what future contractual obligations will be in advance. The latter is crucial in the investment decision. Undertaking long-term investments is discouraged when the costs of refinancing are unknown. If refinancing is done on a short-term basis, the need for capital may arise at a time of credit tightness which may make the investment (or the enterprise as a whole) unprofitable.

The other solution is to index contracts. Indeed, indexation arises, in private markets, in response to uncertain inflation because of the costs and risks associated with short-term contracts. For some, indexation of long-term contracts is a far better solution. First, with indexation, recontracting is unnecessary, resulting in consequent savings in time and effort. Second, indexation reduces uncertainty about future costs (to some extent) and thus aids planning and, in particular, long-term investment. Investors, for example, know that a continuing source of funds is available. They also know something about the costs of these funds—namely that they are linked to an inflation-related index.

However, indexation does not resolve all the problems of long-term contracts in a world of uncertain inflation and may create new problems. With indexation, credit risk may increase. Because inflation is correlated with real shocks, it can be risky for a firm to offer indexed bonds or to agree to link its wage payments to an index, since the prices of its products may not move with overall inflation rates. If so, the linkage of a firm's wages and/or long-term interest payments to an inflation index may cause liquidity problems.

The full linkage of contractual payments to an inflation index is an ideal mechanism to avoid the effects of uncertain inflation produced by money shocks. Such indexation is optimal, however, only if *all* inflation is caused by money shocks.[25] The difficulty is that inflation can be provoked by real (demand and supply) shocks.[26] Due to supply shocks, inflation may increase while real income and employment rates decline. If so, firms and households may find it difficult to meet indexed debt payments. As a result, default and bankruptcy rates can be expected to rise with the use of these instruments.

Nominal contracts insulate the economy from supply-shock-caused decreases in real growth rates and, thus, lower the bankruptcy rate. As indicated by the quantity theory model of inflation, a real shock, which reduces output by 1 percent below its expected level, causes the inflation rate to rise by 1 percent. For a net debtor firm with nominal contracts, payments do not increase with this rise in inflation. The result is that the firm's real contractual payments decline by the same amount as the unanticipated decline in real output growth. Because real contractual payments are reduced proportionately, profits do not decrease as much as they do with indexation.

To avoid the additional risk associated with indexation to the inflation rate, more complicated indexation rules would have to be adopted. While the specific index formula for optimal indexation would depend on the structure of the economy, Karni has shown, for a simple macroeconomic model, that payments must be linked proportionately to price level changes and to the deviation of output from its expected level.[27] Thus, if output is 10 percent below its expected output level, payments would be adjusted downwards by 10 percent. Without a downward adjustment in payments to reflect negative real shocks, the system is subject to additional "indexing" risk.[28]

A similar alternative is a "monetary index" proposed by Joel Popkin.[29] This index is designed to capture the effects of monetary inflation alone and is based on the rate of change of monetary growth. However, to avoid inflation in a growing economy, the long-run growth of real income is subtracted from the rate of monetary growth to arrive at the monetary index.

The implementation of such schemes requires agreement on the expected output level or growth rate of the economy. Information on this is not readily available, and government estimates would be widely disputed.

Indeed, monetary policymakers need to know the expected level of real output to determine the money supply that would avoid serially correlated price level changes. The optimality of adopting a policy goal of price level stability may be precisely that the economy will then provide an objective measure of the accuracy of these output estimates. If they are consistently too high, for example, positive serially correlated price level changes result. Without such a goal, there is no similar independent measure of the accuracy of the level of "expected output" that can be verified over time.

Thus, indexation is likely to be of a second-best variety, linked to inflation (or proxies such as interest rate) indexes alone, without output adjustments. But because of the increased risk with full indexing to inflation indexes, most firms that adopt indexing do so with limits. They accept some money risk to mitigate the increased vulnerability to supply shocks that comes with indexation. They also trade off the risks of these alternatives against the risks and costs of shortened contracts. The combination that a particular firm should adopt depends on how the firm's circumstances—the nature of the product and the inputs used—influence the costs and risks of the different alternatives.

In sum, the result of uncertain inflation will be the shortening of contracts as well as the implementation of various forms of indexation, although neither of these changes will entirely eliminate the increased risk and costs arising from uncertain inflation.

Private Sector Indexations' Effect on Inflation. With indexation, inflationary and deflationary pressures both affect the inflation rate more quickly. Thus, indexation accelerates inflation in periods of excessive monetary growth. But downward pressures on the inflation rate due to cutbacks in monetary growth are similarly speeded through the economy. Thus, in a recession, widespread indexation induces faster disinflation.

How much indexation affects inflation also depends on the source of the inflationary pressure. If supply shocks are the source of inflationary spurts, indexation will similarly spread the impact of these factors throughout the economy. But in this case, output is lower than otherwise with indexation, since indexation will limit necessary relative price adjustments. The decreased output increases inflationary pressures, given the rate of monetary expansion. If money supply accelerates in response to output slowdowns or, passively, in response to previous price increases, an inflationary spiral can result.[30] In general, whenever a real shock changes relative prices and decreases output growth rates, indexation blocks relative price changes and slows the real growth of the economy further and, thus, accelerates inflation further (at a given rate of monetary growth). Nonetheless, some partial indexation is desirable to minimize the risks and costs of frequent recontracting, given substantial inflation uncertainty.

Indexation in the Government Sector

Currently most government social transfer payments are indexed to the CPI. These include entitlement programs and explicit income redistribution programs, most importantly, Social Security. The federal government also indexes retirement benefits paid to its civil and military employees.

Indexation of federal income tax brackets was implemented in 1986. There is also ongoing discussion of indexing interest rates on long-term government debt. The following discusses the rationales and economic effects of the indexation of debt, income tax brackets, and social transfer payments, respectively.

Indexed Government Debt. The pros and cons of offering indexed government debt involve a number of issues. Two arguments are made in favor of indexed debt. First, in theory nominal long-term debt provides an incentive for the government to inflate the economy, since unanticipated inflation reduces the nominal debt real cost. Indexed debt provides no such incentive to inflate the economy. Second, if inflation is sufficiently uncertain, the use of indexed debt is less burdensome to the taxpayer than nominal long-term debt, since the latter has to include a risk premium to compensate for money risk (i.e., the risk that inflation will exceed the anticipated rate).

Symmetrical arguments can be made against indexed debt. First, the government supply of indexed bonds transfers the risk of uncertain inflation to the taxpayer. Second, indexed debt makes it more difficult for the government *not* to inflate the economy. With moderately uncertain inflation, these disadvantages may outweigh the benefits to the taxpayer. The following discusses these two points in more detail.

The risk to the taxpayer of offering indexed debt is that unanticipated accelerations of inflation will be correlated with depressed real income. The financial burden to the taxpayer of financing debt instruments varies with the source of inflation and with whether the debt is in indexed or nominal terms. The financial burden depends on the ratio of the real debt servicing costs to real after-tax income. The real servicing cost of *indexed* debt does not vary with inflation while the cost of nominal long-term debt varies inversely with inflation.

With an unanticipated acceleration of inflation due to monetary expansion, the real servicing cost of long-term nominal bonds declines.[31] The cost decrease occurs at the same time that real income increases, due to the positive effect of the unanticipated money supply increase on aggregate demand and real output. A decline in inflation, caused by monetary contractions, has opposite effects; the cost of long-term debt is increased at a time when taxpayers' incomes are depressed. This makes an anti-inflationary monetary policy more painful.

With nominal debt, accelerations of inflation resulting from supply shocks lead to lower real debt costs at a time of reduced income; decelerations in this case raise costs as real income increases. Under these circumstances, nominal debt reduces the tax burden, when such reductions are most helpful, and increases in the tax burden occur, when they are most affordable. Thus, nominal debt is beneficial in dealing with unavoidable supply-shock inflation and overall would be desirable, if money-shock-caused accelerations in inflation could be limited.

On the other hand, if such accelerations cannot be controlled, the use of indexed debt may become necessary, and such use further destabilizes the economy. As real income and government tax revenue growth slows with supply-shock inflation, the treasury must either increase taxes (and slow real disposable income growth more) to fund the constant real cost of indexed debt or allow the deficit to grow.[32] The latter is inflationary, the more so if increased debt is monetized. Thus, the use of indexed debt further destabilizes the economy either by decreasing already depressed incomes or by increasing already high inflation.

Because of these effects, it is harmful to have to resort to the use of indexed debt. However, the costs of nominal debt rise with inflation uncertainty. If money risk is perceived as substantial, with both intermediate and long-term debt salable only with a substantial risk premium, indexed bonds may become the least cost alternative.

An alternative to indexed debt is greater reliance on Treasury bills. Historically, these have yielded a near-zero real interest rate, and their nominal yield has closely tracked inflation rates. For indexed bonds not to be more costly to the taxpayer, their guaranteed real rate of return would have to be lower than this alternative.[33] But assuming that indexed bonds are optimal, the offering of indexed bonds would still make taxpayers worse off than in the situation where there is little inflation uncertainty, a low money risk premium, and no indexed debt.

Income Tax Indexation. With a graduated income tax, inflation raises nominal incomes and automatically increases average and marginal tax rates and the government's tax revenues. The rationale of indexed income tax brackets, implemented in 1986, is the avoidance of the resulting "tax bracket creep." Without indexation, the tax revenue bonus of inflation can provide an incentive for government officials to inflate the economy so that the higher tax revenues may be used for increased government expenditures. Indeed, the possibility of increasing revenues in this way may be one of the explanations for the increase in federal government expenditures as a percentage of GNP in the post–World War II U.S. economy. This is a potential concern because, unless the value of government expenditures exceeds that of alternative private consumption, they are inefficient.[34] Although the weight of these arguments has led Congress and the president to index tax brackets as of 1986, there has been increasing discussion of modifying this legislation. The argument against tax bracket indexation is that the graduated income tax, in the absence of indexation, serves a useful function as an automatic stabilizer. Inflation of aggregate demand origin (money or demand shocks) increases tax revenues and, if unspent, reduces the government deficit or increases the surplus. Since private disposable income is reduced, private spending decreases, and if government spending does not increase, aggregate demand is decreased. The result is lower interest rates, lower inflation, and less pressure on the Federal Reserve to monetize the debt. Inflation of supply-shock origin also is stabilized by the resulting increase in tax revenues although after-tax income declines are exacerbated.[35]

Of course, if monetary growth continues to be excessive, inflation continues. In this case, the use of nominal tax brackets as an automatic stabilizer only slows inflation in the short run, and the negative growth effects of tax bracket creep remain. Thus, maintaining nominal tax brackets for their usefulness as automatic stabilizers is effective only with monetary stability.

Government Social Transfer and Retirement Benefit Indexation. In the presence of inflation, government social transfer and retirement benefit payments must be adjusted on a more frequent basis to avoid real losses to beneficiaries due to an adjustment lag. It is convenient to have decision rules to use in making these adjustments. The only decision rule that does not lead to lower real payments is to escalate payments using an inflation index. Thus, just as in the private sector, indexation in the political sector arises out of uncertain inflation. Again, as in the private sector, indexation of government transfer payments can neutralize inflation only when inflation is due to neutral monetary expansion. Otherwise, while partial indexation will be useful, full indexation will make the economy more prone to inflation and will result in slower output growth.

Without indexation, inflation reduces real transfer payments. This decline in real transfer payments may be desirable if overall output declines. Indexation results in an agreement that did not exist before to protect real payments against inflation. Although the agreement is not a contractual obligation, the politics of the situation make it difficult to retract inflation protection once granted. This is troublesome if an increased inflation rate is accompanied by an output slowdown caused by supply-shock inflation. If supply shocks decrease real output, the nation's total expenditures must be decreased. Without a decline in real transfer payments, the full burden of the decrease will be on the private economy.

If the necessary decline in real income in the private sector is not politically acceptable, the result will be an inflationary spiral. In any case, supply-shock inflation will raise the percentage of GNP that goes to indexed entitlement benefits. If unfunded, this increases the size of the deficit relative to GNP. If funded, the expenditure increases taxes, which may be perceived as inequitable, since private disposable income may already be reduced. Further, there are likely to be negative effects on investment, due to higher interest rates, and on labor supply, due to higher tax rates.[36] Automatic full indexation will also increase the risk to the private sector since tax payments or interest rates will increase when supply shocks cause sales growth declines. In spite of these concerns, partial indexation may be desirable for all transfer payments to avoid time-consuming readjustments, and full indexation may be desirable for some transfer payments, given equity goals.

Summary

Nominal contracts are a stabilizing force in the face of economywide supply shocks. They allow those who supply inputs to the firm (and, in particular, employees) who have an interest in the long-run viability of the firm to absorb part of the profit hit of these economywide shocks, which even a well-managed firm cannot avoid. Nominal contracts will yield higher than expected real payments to the firm's suppliers when economywide positive supply shocks result in actual inflation that is less than anticipated inflation. Thus, over time, expected average remuneration is not affected by shocks, and at the same time the firm's default risk is lower.

Serially correlated inflation (with higher than expected inflation tending to be followed by another period of higher inflation) may raise the risk of long-term nominal contracts. A surprising loss in real purchasing power due to an increase in inflation is likely to be followed by a similar loss. Long-term nominal contracts, such as pensions, are particularly vulnerable to serially correlated inflation. Yet the alternative of indexing pensions is not costless. Indexation cannot distinguish between money-shock and supply-shock inflation. Only if inflation is due to money shocks will indexation be benign. Indexation to inflation precludes contracting to share the risk of economywide supply shocks. Indeed if all prices and wages in an open economy are indexed to inflation, external supply shocks, due to an initial devaluation, can lead to an ever-worsening cycle of devaluation and increased inflation.

Firms may find that the terms on which they can offer indexed contracts to suppliers are so unfavorable due to the increased risk borne by the firm's owners that suppliers prefer nominal contracts. The following chapter examines the extent to which pensions are indexed. The widespread lack of indexation may be due to a rational preference for nominal contracts. Variable rate pensions could closely track inflation if invested in inflation-hedging assets without risk to the firm, but such pensions would be more costly to recipients because of their necessarily lower real rate of return.

Part Three discusses the role of pensions in individual savings decisions. Nominal pensions, even in the face of inflation, may be rationally chosen by individuals to maximize their economic well-being. However, widespread myopia and money illusion (nonrecognition of the impact of inflation on the value of pensions) could also result in the "choice" of nominal pensions. Public policy implications of the impact of inflation on pensions are discussed in Part Four.

APPENDIX 2.A
Housing: A Flow-of-Services or an Investment Asset?

In the United States most families live in their own homes, and their homes are their major investment. Thus, resident-owned housing provides a flow-of-services that is a substitute for the services of rented housing and, at the same time, provides a means of storing wealth. In the past, the CPI ignored the durable asset aspect of housing and treated housing as though it were similar to any other good that was consumed in its entirety over the course of a year. As of January 1984, the Bureau of Labor Statistics instituted a new procedure to calculate the percentage of expenditures spent and the price of living in one's own residence. The new procedure changes the measure and weight of resident-owned housing in the all-urban CPI-U. The CPI-W is similarly adjusted as of 1986.

When the BLS originally computed the weight on home purchases, it used the purchase price of homes bought in the survey year minus the selling price of homes sold in that year plus any transactions costs associated with these purchases and sales. Resales of existing owner-occupied structures cancel out of the weight determination calculation, leaving only newly constructed homes or homes that enter the owner-occupied category for the first time (such as conversions from rental status). Thus, the entire purchase price of new housing was entered into the CPI just exactly as any other good. In addition, the homeownership weight included the first half of the contracted mortgage interest payment on these purchases. This implies that new houses are entirely consumed in the year of purchase in the same way that milk bought over the year is consumed and that half the interest payments required to finance this consumption are also consumed within the year.

Because real homeownership costs declined in the 1970s, nominal homeownership costs must have increased less rather than more than the overall index. The overweighting and mispricing of homeownership resulted in a substantial upward bias in the CPI over the decade of the 1970s.

It is the treatment of the housing component which accounts for most of the annual 1 percent difference in the CPI and the PCE measurements of inflation over the 1970s, with the Laspeyres-Paasche distinction accounting for substantially less of the observed difference. This is demonstrated by comparing the 7.6 percent average annual rate of inflation as measured by the traditional CPI, shown in Table 2–2 with the 6.8 percent average annual rate of inflation as measured by the new owners' equivalent rental index (CPI X − 1) described below, and the 6.6 percent average annual rate of change in the fixed-weight PCE over this period.[37] If the latter two measure inflation correctly, the annual 1 percent higher inflation rate measured by the CPI over this decade can be entirely attributed to the upward bias in its treatment of housing.

In addition to the upward bias, the immediate incorporation of short-run interest rate changes made the CPI far more volatile than it should be. The interest rate that represents the owner's opportunity cost or, if financed, ongoing interest costs, is not the current nominal interest rate, but rather an average of real interest rates, past and future, that have been and will be paid to finance the property.[38] Because transactions costs in the buying and selling of housing are so large, the housing market is not organized as an auction market with the frequent estimation of current costs and values and frequent buying and selling. An average of costs, especially volatile financing costs, over the long term are far more appropriate in determining long-term or "permanent" housing costs. This suggests that current interest rates are relevant to the cost of housing only to the extent that they change consumers' views on the likely long-term interest cost. As a result, the incorporation of current interest rates increased the volatility of the index, as compared to that of a true housing cost index.

Although the past approach was theoretically flawed, the implementation of the flow-of-services concept to measure housing costs presents many practical difficulties. To estimate the appreciation (or depreciation) of housing values and average real interest cost on a monthly basis is not a practical possibility. Proxies would have to be found, and there are no obvious proxies that could be used. More fundamentally, the CPI entirely excludes income taxes and the income tax deductibility of various items in calculating changes in the price of goods and services. To change this aspect of the CPI's calculation would mean that the impact of the deductibility of any item on its after-tax "price" would have to be incorporated. Again, this is unlikely to be feasible.

However, there was virtually universal agreement (even within the BLS) that the housing component was the major conceptual flaw in the CPI and that it needed to be revised. As a result, the BLS experimented with five alternative measures, denoted $X - 1$ through $X - 5$. Experimental measure $X - 1$ is a rental equivalent using CPI rent; $X - 2$ is a measure of user cost with current interest costs; $X - 3$ is a user cost measure with average interest costs; $X - 4$ and $X - 5$ are outlay measures using current interest costs and average interest costs, respectively. Of these, the BLS decided to incorporate the rental equivalent $X - 1$ index into the CPI-U in 1984 and the CPI-W in 1986. Since the CPI-W is used most frequently for indexing wages, this two-year lag was to give unions and businesses time to observe and adjust for any changes in the way the new index measures inflation as compared to the old.

The other experimental indexes are less satisfactory. The $X - 2$ series uses current interest rates to calculate the costs of old as well as new mortgages and, thus, is volatile and sensitive to the interest rate used. The $X - 3$ series uses an average interest rate, which is less volatile. However, the weighting scheme reflects the age distribution of existing mortgages and is, as a result, heavily front-loaded: 31 percent of the weight is on the first one and a half years, and 69 percent is on the first five and a half years. Thus, the $X - 2$ and $X - 3$ series have moved together, though $X - 3$ lagged behind $X - 2$. Both are more volatile than the historical homeownership component. The volatility of the $X - 2$ and $X - 3$ series raises doubt about their appropriateness as measures of housing costs. Yet the $X - 2$ and $X - 3$ methodology does closely approximate the conceptual ideal of the user-cost approach. The problem, as discussed above and noted by Blinder, is that the user-cost approach simply interpreted provides what is essentially a "spot price" view of the cost of housing.[39] The user cost approach should average interest rates to arrive at a long-term average user cost. This would provide a "permanent" cost analogue to the permanent income concept which, evidence suggests, consumers use for decisions.

The $X - 3$ and $X - 5$ series, based on outlays, lack conceptual validity. (The weights of $X - 4$ include actual expenditures made in the base period for property taxes, property insurance, maintenance, and repairs, with the weight for the mortgage interest term the same as in $X - 2$. The weights of $X - 5$ are similar to those in $X - 4$, except that $X - 5$ treats the mortgage interest cost term as in $X - 3$.) No appreciation or equity terms are included in either. Not all homeowners are represented in this measure; those who made no mortgage debt payment in the base period are excluded.

APPENDIX 2.B
Relative Price Changes and the Substitution Bias

There have been several econometric studies of the potential positive substitution bias of the CPI; they indicate that a bias existed, although it was low over the 1950–70 period.[40] For example, Steven D. Braithwait finds for the period 1948–73, an average bias of .1 percent of an index point per year. Since the CPI was set to equal 100 in 1967 and equalled 133.1 in 1973, this represents, approximately, a .1 percent annual bias in the CPI over these years.[41]

It may be that the substitution effect has been greater in the post-1973 period of greater inflation and more dramatic short-run movements in relative prices. The large difference between the change in the published PCE and a PCE with Laspeyres (1972) weights (shown in the fifth row of Table 2–5) suggests that this may be so. However, this cannot be used as evidence of an

TABLE 2–5

Comparison of Changes in PCE Deflators, 1975–1980 (percent)

Item	*1975*	*1976*	*1977*	*1978*	*1979*	*1979**				*1980**	
						First Quarter	*Second Quarter*	*Third Quarter*	*Fourth Quarter*	*First Quarter*	*Second Quarter*
Laspeyres PCE, 1972 weights†	8.2	5.1	5.9	7.1	9.6	11.0	10.3	11.3	10.5	13.8	11.1
Laspeyres PCE, chain index‡	8.2	5.1	5.9	7.0	9.2	10.4	10.0	10.6	10.1	13.0	10.9
Difference, Laspeyres 1972 weights, minus Laspeyres, chain index	0.0	0.0	0.0	0.1	0.4	0.6	0.3	0.7	0.4	0.8	0.2
Published implicit PCE deflator	8.1	5.1	5.7	6.8	8.9	10.8	9.3	9.7	9.7	12.5	10.6
Difference, Laspeyres 1972 weights, minus implicit deflator	0.1	0.0	0.2	0.3	0.7	0.2	1.0	1.6	0.8	1.3	0.5

*Seasonally adjusted data at annual rates.

†Published as the "fixed-weight" price index for personal consumption expenditures.

‡The PCE chain index uses weights from the first of the two periods being compared (for example, the index change between 1979:2 and 1979:3 uses weights from 1979:2).

SOURCES: Data for the 1975–78 period are from *Survey of Current Business* 59 (July 1979), table 8.9, p. 70; for the 1979–80 period, from *Survey of Current Business* 60 (August 1980), table 27, p. 15.

increased substitution bias in this period. Nor can the increased divergence between changes in the CPI and the PCE since 1973 be used as evidence of a stronger substitution bias. The PCE is a Paasche index, with the properties described above. Nonetheless, changes in a Paasche index do not share in the properties of a Paasche index, basically because they confound weight changes with price changes.[42]

The substitution bias can be approximated, however, by comparing a fixed-weight (Laspeyres) version of the PCE with the links of a PCE chain index. Jack E. Triplett has done this in a recent study.[43] Table 2–5 shows the relevant indexes. The first index is very similar to the CPI, since it is a fixed-weight (Laspeyres) version of the PCE,[44] using 1972 weights. The chain index is constructed by using fixed weights to compare price levels between two periods. Thus, a Laspeyres chain index would be calculated by using the market basket for period one between period two and one; between period three and two, market basket two would be used. This procedure mitigates the substitution bias (because the original market basket is not maintained beyond one period) without confounding weight changes and price changes.

Comparing the chain index to the Laspeyres fixed-weight version of the PCE, the difference (shown in the third row of Table 2–5) provides an estimate of how updating the Laspeyres weights would affect the measured rate of current inflation. The data imply that a fixed-weight index may have exaggerated the inflation rate by .4 to .5 percent of an index point in 1979 and 1980 and by .1 percent of an index point in 1978.

Data collected by Lawrence E. DeMilner indicate that the PCE chain index and Laspeyres fixed-weight version of the PCE also diverged (though by less than in 1979–80) in 1973 and 1974, and that the two indexes diverged by 2.5 percent over the years 1970–80, yielding a .25 percent annual bias, while the CPI and PCE diverged by 20 percent.[45]

These results show the following: first, that if DeMilner's results of a .25 percent bias can be compared to Braithwait's earlier estimates of a .1 percent bias, the substitution bias was somewhat worse in the 1970s than earlier; second, that relative price changes cannot explain much of the divergence between the CPI and the PCE in the 1970s; and third, that in spite of this, sharp relative price changes may have been responsible for significant substitution bias in the years in which they occurred.

APPENDIX 2.C
Theoretical COL Indexes[46]

An expenditure-based COL is constructed to answer the question: What is the change in total expenditure necessary to purchase a given set of goods and services over two periods?[47] As such it cannot perfectly protect real income.

A better alternative for this purpose would be an income-based COL index. Such an index would answer the question: What is the change in income necessary to purchase a given set of goods and services over two periods? An income-based COL index would differ from an expenditure-based COL in its inclusion of income and payroll taxes along with the sales taxes that are included in an expenditure-based COL. An income-based COL index would be useful if the index were designed to protect a worker or benefit a recipient's income from inflation, assuming that all sources of income were escalated. However, the data difficulties involved are so formidable that creating such an index is not feasible.

A second alternative to the expenditure-based COL index would be a wealth-defined index. Such an index would include assets and changed asset values. If both physical and human capital were included, this index would merely be a further broadening of the income-based COL index in a longer time frame, since income depends on physical and human capital. Thus, this COL index would answer the question: What is the change in lifetime income (or wealth) necessary to purchase a given set of goods and services under two price regimes? Although this index has considerable conceptual interest, since it gets away from one-period decision making it suffers from all the feasibility problems of the income-based index as well as additional measurement problems inherent in a multiperiod setting.

A particular version of this index which focuses on the effects of real interest rate changes on the cost of a constant real stream of income is both pertinent and feasible. If the real interest rate increases, the cost of constant real stream of income declines.

Thus, augmenting the CPI measure of inflation with a term to measure real interest rate changes would result in an intertemporal price index that could be used to measure the change in the cost of a future real income stream.[48] In particular, an intertemporal price index could be used to measure the change in the real amount of wealth needed to purchase an annuity which would provide a constant real income stream.

A third alternative can be derived once it is noted that the CPI and PCE are actually designed to answer the question of the change in cost of market-purchased goods and services. Many goods and services are not purchased. These include, for example, government services, the quality of the environment, and home production. A fixed standard of living depends on the quality and quantity of these as well. Thus, once the importance of these nonmarket goods is acknowledged, it cannot be asserted that a market expenditure-based COL answers the question of the change in expenditures required to maintain a given level of satisfaction over two periods. Such a question depends not only on what has happened to prices of market-purchased goods over the two periods, but also on what has happened to the quality and quantity of nonmarket goods. The market expenditure-based COL (and the income-based COL) actually answers the narrower question: What is the cost, at today's market prices, of a bundle of market-purchased goods and services equivalent to the bundle consumed in the base period?[49] While the answer to the broader question which includes nonmarket goods would certainly be useful to have, it involves evaluations of environmental quality, government services, and home production that are difficult to perform and time-consuming. It would be impossible to collect data to answer such a question on a timely periodic basis.

Finally, if the use to which the COL index is to be put is the maintenance of an individual's fixed living standard through escalating an income or benefit source, and the recipient receives more than one income source, a partial COL index would be more appropriate than any of the above. Such a partial income COL index might exclude certain goods and services. For example, if a retiree owns a house (thus receiving housing services in kind) and is fully insured for medical expenses, then an appropriate COL index would not include price changes in housing or medical services. A partial income COL index might also have to be adjusted by more than an expenditure-based COL index, if other sources of income were not indexed to inflation. If the partial income index were truly designed to preserve a given standard of living, income and payroll tax effects, as well as the quantity of nonmarket goods and services provided, would have to be considered in its construction. Clearly, such an index would be impossible to construct. However, less ambitious versions of a partial income index could be feasible.

Notes

[1] More precisely, the CPI compares the current and base year costs of a basket of goods of fixed composition. The CPI for a given year, t, is derived by constructing a weighted average, P_t, of prices in that year of all i items sampled where P_{it} is the price of the ith item:

$$P_t = \sum_i w_{i0} P_{it}$$

where the w_{i0} are the fixed base period (at which time $t = 0$) expenditure weights:

$$w_{i0} = \frac{P_{i0} c_{i0}}{\Sigma_i p_{i0} c_{i0}}$$

and c_{i0} is the quantity of the ith item consumed in the base period. The expenditure weights, w_{i0}, represent the percent of the total budget spent on good i in the base year.

The CPI in the base period is set equal to 100 (by dividing p_t in year 0 by itself and multiplying by 100). Thus, using 1967 as the base year, $P_{1967} = 100$. In the following years, the CPI is set equal to the current weighted average prices (P_t) divided by weighted average prices in the base period, multiplied by 100.

$$\text{CPI}_t = \frac{P_t}{P_0}(100)$$

Since the CPI index in 1968 was 102.8, the index point change (which is often used in escalator formulas) was 2.8, as was the percentage increase.

Movements of the index from one period to another are usually expressed as a percentage increase rather than as a change in index points because index point changes are affected by the level of the index in relation to the base period while percentage changes are not. For example, $\text{CPI}_{1977} = 181.5$ while $\text{CPI}_{1978} = 195.4$. The index point change was 13.9 while the percentage change was 7.7 percent [$= (195.4 - 181.5) \times 100/181.5$].

[2] This cross-classification allows MSAs that do not have specifically reported CPIs to use the appropriate population-size class to approximate a region specific index.

[3] Given low turnover rates, it was not feasible to price a fixed sample of

houses as is done for other items in the CPI. Therefore, housing price data were for average house sales financed with Federal Housing Administration insured mortgages. These prices were adjusted for metropolitan area, for the age of house, and for size. Price changes for the other homeownership elements were estimated in accord with the standard CPI technique of following the prices of a fixed set of selected items over time.

[4] Homeownership represented 24.9 percent of the 1982 CPI weighted by five parts: home purchase (10.4 percent), contractual mortgage interest cost (8.7 percent), property taxes (1.7 percent), property insurance (0.6 percent), and maintenance and repairs (3.6 percent). Only the two major components, home purchase and contractual mortgage interest costs, raised serious problems. The three other components of the homeownership index (property taxes, insurance, and maintenance) are annual expenditures and, as such, it makes sense to treat them just like any other CPI item.

[5] See Janet L. Norwood, "The Anatomy of Price Change," *Monthly Labor Review,* March 1981, p. 63.

[6] See Douglas B. Diamond, Jr., "Taxes, Inflation, Speculation and the Cost of Homeownership," *AREUEA Journal* 8 (1980).

[7] Other problems derive from the BLS use of data on sales of FHA-insured house sales. In 1973, these purchases constituted only 6 percent of the home purchase market. The chief reason for this is that the FHA mortgage ceiling was $89,500, eliminating higher-priced housing. Further, in some areas there are very few FHA transactions. These two effects may create offsetting biases. See Alan S. Blinder, "The Consumer Price Index and the Measurement of Recent Inflation," *Brookings Papers on Economic Activity* 2 (1980), p. 551.

[8] In symbols, the weighting scheme used is as follows:

$$p_t = \frac{\Sigma_i p_{it} c_{it}}{\Sigma_i p_{i0} c_{it}} = \Sigma_i w_{it} p_{it}$$

where

$$w_{it} = \frac{1}{p_{i0}} \frac{p_{i0} c_{it}}{\Sigma_i p_{i0} c_{it}}$$

are the weights, with the variables defined as above. As with the CPI, the base period PCE is set equal to 100, so that P_t at period 0 is divided by itself and multiplied by 100. The PCE for subsequent periods then is derived by dividing by P_t in the base period and multiplying by 100.

[9] See Jack E. Triplett, "The Measurement of Inflation. A Survey of Research on the Accuracy of Price Indexes," in *Analysis of Inflation,* ed. Paul H. Earl (Lexington, Mass.: Lexington Books, 1975), pp. 19–83. Also see, by the same author, "Concepts of Quality Input and Output Price Measures: A Resolution of the User-Value-Resource Cost Debate," *The U.S. National Income and Product Accounts: Selected Topics,* NBER Conference on Research in Income and Wealth, November 1980; and Robert J. Gordon, "The Consumer Price Index: Measuring Inflation and Causing It," *The Public Interest* no. 63 (Spring 1981).

[10] See Steven D. Braithwait, "The Substitution Bias of the Laspeyres Price Index: An Analysis Using Estimated Cost-of-Living Indexes," *American Economic Review* 70, no. 1 (March 1980), pp. 64–77.

[11] See Robert A. Pollak, "The Theory of the Cost-of-Living Index," BLS Working Papers, U.S. Department of Labor, Bureau of Labor Statistics, Working Paper 11, June 1971.

[12] Chain indexes also have been proposed as alternatives to the PCE and the CPI. The problem with their use is that under certain circumstances they will distort the measurement of COL changes by more than either a Laspeyres or Paasche index. A chain index is superior to these when relative price changes continue in the same direction. When relative prices fluctuate, however, the substitution bias accumulates in the chain index. See Jack E. Triplett, "Three Studies of Indexes and Indexing: A Review Essay," and studies cited therein, *Journal of Money, Credit and Banking* 15, no. 3 (August 1983).

[13] See W. Erwin Diewert, "Exact and Superlative Index Numbers," *Journal of Econometrics* 4 (May 1976), pp. 115–45.

[14] See T. S. Torda, "The Impact of Inflation on the Elderly," *Federal Reserve Bank of Cleveland Review*, October–November 1972; John P. Mackin, *Protecting Purchasing Power in Retirement* (New York: Fleet Academic Editions, 1971); and Data Resources, Inc., *Inflation and the Elderly*, Summary Report Part 1, Lexington, Mass.: Lexington Books, January 1980.

[15] See Michael J. Boskin and Michael D. Hurd, "Are Inflation Rates Different for the Elderly?" National Bureau of Economic Research, Working Paper No. 943, July 1982. They modify the traditional measurement of housing with a rental equivalent to approximate the improvement (discussed below) adopted by the BLS after January 1974. This neutralizes the impact of the mismeasurement of housing in the traditional index. Their results estimate the overstatement of inflation by the official consumer price index as 22 basis points or 10 percent, over the 10 years of their study, which is consistent with results discussed below.

[16] The "older" elderly (ages 70–74 and over age 75) spend more than the "younger" elderly (ages 60–64 and 65–69) on food at home, rental and owned dwellings, fuel and utilities, domestic services, and medical care and less on food away from home, alcoholic beverages, tobacco products, house furnishings, clothing, transportation, and recreation.

[17] Thomas C. Borzilleri, "The Need for a Separate Consumer Price Index for Older Persons: A Review and New Evidence," *The Gerontologist* 18, no. 3 (1978), reports a somewhat higher cumulative difference. With an older person index (OPI) and CPI both set at 100 in 1970, the OPI reaches 157.9 and the CPI 155.8 in 1977.

[18] Michael uses data from the late 1960s and the early 1970s (i.e., covering the period of the 1973–75 inflation spurt and relative price changes but before the major increase in the rate of inflation and additional relative price changes) to examine the question of how different families are affected by inflation. In his study, household-specific Laspeyres (fixed-weight) price indexes are computed for several thousand consumer units.

Michael finds that there are statistically significant differences by income level and age of the head of the household. For example, in 1973 through 1974, the poor experienced a relatively high rate of inflation. The elderly experienced a relatively high rate of inflation in the period from 1967 until early 1974. See Robert T. Michael, "Variation across Households in the Rate of Inflation," *Journal of Money, Credit and Banking* 11, no. 1 (February 1979).

[19] The weighting of the $X - 1$ index, calculated as 14 percent in 1983, is derived from a question, filled out as part of the 1972–74 Survey, in which homeowners were asked to estimate the rental value of their home.

[20] The BLS has modified the CPI rent index slightly. The most important difference is that rent changes in areas where there is a preponderance of homeownership are given a greater weight than rent changes elsewhere in the calculation of the owners' equivalent rent index.

[21] See Triplett, "The Measurement of Inflation: A Survey of Research on the Accuracy of Price Indexes."

[22] See Appendix 2.A and note 7.

[23] Jack E. Triplett suggests in "Three Studies of Indexes and Indexing: A Review Essay," that the treatment of automobile use involved significant anomalies.

[24] This includes the approximately 10 percent of wage earners who participate in union cost-of-living adjustment (COLA) contracts. See Bureau of Labor Statistics, "Escalation and the CPI: Information for Users," *The Consumer Price Index, Revision—1978,* U.S. Department of Labor, 1978.

[25] Special competitive pressures due to relative price changes may also preclude raising product prices with indexed costs in the affected sectors. Because of the differing costs of price flexibility, price movements in the manufacturing and service sector lag behind those in the commodity sector. This lag affects relative prices in both demand-pull and structural inflation. Relative price and supply-shock difficulties can be illustrated with the variable rate mortgage instrument. The borrower household may find that its income does not move with inflation while its mortgage payments and all other payments do. While the average borrower's income will move with inflation, some borrowers are employed by firms that adjust their wages infrequently. These households will suffer liquidity problems if their mortgage payments adjust more frequently. The second problem affects all borrower households. Inflation may increase, while real income and employment rates decline. If so, the households may find it very difficult to meet mortgage payments. As a result, default rates can be expected to rise with the use of these instruments.

[26] Demand shocks also may cause default problems. Short-term interest rate indexes may increase without proportional income increases, thus raising the mortgage payment burden.

[27] See Edi Karni, "On Optimal Wage Indexation," in *Journal of Political Economy* 91, no. 2 (Chicago: University of Chicago Press, 1983).

[28] For further discussion see Susan M. Wachter, "Indexing Risk: The Special Role of Pension Funds," in *Identification and Control of Risk in Thrift Institutions: Conference Proceedings,* San Francisco Federal Home Loan Bank Board, 1984.

[29] See Joel Popkin et al., "Inflation, Portfolio Balancing and Pension Indexation." in the Final Report Submitted to the United States Department of Labor, Contract No. J-9-P-1-0076, March 1983.

[30] If the rate of growth of potential output drops beneath zero, incomes and wages must decline on the average by the decline in per capita output growth. But price and wage indexation to the previous level of real income precludes such a decline. Wage claims will exceed domestic output. Under these circum-

stances, the inflation rate continues to accelerate. In addition, a foreign trade deficit will be created or exacerbated because claims to output exceed domestically produced output and will be spent on imports. As the foreign trade deficit occurs, the exchange rate will be devalued, but with indexation the devaluation will not succeed in increasing exports and decreasing imports thereby removing the deficit. Rather, the devaluation will lead to higher prices and, therefore, higher wages. Again, the wage claims will exceed domestic output leading to further devaluation and increased inflation over time.

[31] It is this effect that operates as an incentive to the government to inflate.

[32] Unanticipated growth slowdowns due to supply shocks have the same effects, since actual income falls beneath projected income.

[33] However, the payment burden to taxpayers will be less with indexed long-term than with short-term debt when supply shocks are correlated with higher real interest rates and, in general, the payment burden is made variable with short-term debt.

[34] Higher tax brackets discourage labor supply. Recent papers by Jerry A. Hausman show that payroll taxes may reduce the labor supply of husbands by about 8 percent and that of wives by about 30 percent. The labor supply decline results in an output decline. In addition, there is a welfare loss to workers because income is less than otherwise. See Jerry A. Hausman, "Income and Payroll Tax Policy and Labor Supply," in National Bureau of Economic Research, Inc., Working Paper No. 610, December 1980; and Jerry A. Hausman, "The Effect of Taxes on Labor Supply," forthcoming in H. Aaron and J. Pechman, eds., *How Taxes Affect Economic Behavior* (Washington). In addition, higher tax brackets discourage investments that generate taxable income and encourage tax sheltered investments, such as housing. Thus, higher tax brackets may have a large unintended impact on capital flows.

[35] In addition, and perhaps most politically compelling in a time of high deficits, nominal tax brackets are a convenient way to raise taxes.

[36] In the 1970s, wage earners suffered from stagflation and tax bracket creep, while the growing importance and the full indexation of social transfer payments (primarily Social Security and Medicaid/Medicare) protected the elderly from inflation. Statistics on relative per capita income show that elderly households had on average 56 percent as much disposable income as the average household in 1970 and that by 1978 this had grown to 63 percent. Per capita elderly income was 116 percent of nonelderly income in 1970 and grew to 121 percent in 1978. See Michael Hurd and John B. Shoven, "Real Income and Wealth of the Elderly," in *Financial Aspects of the United States Pension System*, ed. Zvi Bodie and John B. Shoven, (Chicago: University of Chicago Press, 1983). While the elderly were protected from stagflation, the Social Security fund was near bankruptcy due to the combination of increased expenditures and decreased payroll tax revenues. The compromise solution to this involved an increase in payroll taxes as of 1974 and a plan to automatically index Social Security benefits to the consumer price index or an index of wages, whichever is lower, if the Social Security fund reaches minimum funding levels in the future.

[37] Averages are from the data reported by the Executive Office of the President, Council of Economic Advisers, Office of Management and Budget, *Report on Indexing Federal Programs*, January 1981, Table 17, p. 37.

[38] See Alan Blinder, "The Consumer Price Index and the Measurement of Rent Inflation."

[39] Blinder, "The Consumer Price Index and the Measurement of Recent Inflation."

[40] See Laurits R. Christensen and Marilyn E. Manser, "Cost of Living Indexes and Price Indexes for U.S. Meat and Produce, 1947–1971," in National Bureau of Economic Research, Conference on Research in Income and Wealth, Vol. 40, *Household Behavior and Consumption*; and Jack E. Triplett, "The Measurement of Inflation: A Survey of Research on the Accuracy of Price Indexes."

[41] See Steven D. Braithwait, "The Substitution Bias of the Laspeyres Price Index."

[42] See the technical discussion by Jack E. Triplett, "Reconciling the CPI and the PCE Deflator," *Monthly Labor Review* 104 (September 1981), appendix.

[43] See Jack E. Triplett, "Comment on 'The Consumer Price Index and the Measurement of Inflation' by Alan S. Blinder" in *Brookings Papers on Economic Activity*, 1980:2.

[44] Such an approach is not feasible using CPI data since the weighting information is not available.

[45] See Lawrence E. DeMilner in *Indexing with the Consumer Price Index: Problems and Alternatives*, Congress of the United States, Congressional Budget Office (Washington, D.C.: U.S. Government Printing Office, document number 80-400 0-81-3, June 1981), table 3.

[46] The following material is based on the analysis of Jack E. Triplett, "Inflation Measures and Escalation Measures: What Is the Answer? What Is the Question?" *Conference Proceedings: Statistics Canada Conference on Price Measurement*, ed. W. E. Diewert and Claude Montmarquette, forthcoming.

[47] It can be constructed as a Laspeyres index or as a Paasche index, as could all the following theoretical alternative indexes. See Triplett, ibid.

[48] See Lawrence Summers, "Observations on the Indexation of Old Age Pensions," in *Financial Aspects of the United States Pension System*, ed. Zvi Bodie and John B. Shoven (Chicago: The University of Chicago Press, National Bureau of Economic Research), for a discussion of the problems involved in the construction of an intertemporal index and its overall usefulness. Summers calculates such an index for 1953 through 1979 and concludes that the CPI measured inflationary spurts of 1974, 1978, and 1979, would be dampened, since these were years of rising real interest rates. Of course, for those who already own a stream of real income, any change in the real interest rate would both decrease its price and its discounted value, thus having no net effect on their real income. For example, a rise in the real interest rate decreases the cost of an annuity fixed in real terms, at the same time that it decreases its discounted real value. A change in the real interest has no effect on real retirement income provided by an annuity purchased before the change.

Also see W. W. Brown and G. J. Santoni, "Unreal Estimates of the Real Rate of Interest," *Federal Reserve Bank of St. Louis Review,* January 1981, pp. 18–26, for a discussion of how price indexes that do not include wealth can systematically bias price and interest rate measurements. Brown and Santoni note that the prices of short-lived goods rise relative to the prices of long-lived goods when real interest rates rise. Thus, because short-lived goods predominate in the PCE and CPI, the measured inflation rate will be biased upwards when interest rates rise.

[49] See Triplett, "Inflation Measures and Escalation Measures: What Is the Answer? What Is the Question?" p. 9.

Bibliography

AZARIADIS, COSTAS, and JOSEPH E. STIGLITZ. "Implicit Contracts and Fixed Contracts." *The Quarterly Journal of Economics* 98 (1983), pp. 1–12.

BLINDER, ALAN S. "The Consumer Price Index and the Measurement of Recent Inflation." *Brookings Paper on Economic Activity* (1980:2).

BORZILLERI, THOMAS C. "The Need for a Separate Consumer Price Index for Older Persons: A Review and New Evidence." *The Gerontologist* 18, no. 3 (1978).

BOSKIN, MICHAEL J., and MICHAEL D. HURD. "Are Inflation Rates Different for the Elderly?" National Bureau of Economic Research, Working Paper No. 943, July 1982.

BRAITHWAIT, STEVEN D. "The Substitution Bias of the Laspeyres Price Index: An Analysis Using Estimated Cost-of-Living Indexes." *American Economic Review* 70, no. 1 (March 1980), pp. 64–77.

BUREAU OF LABOR STATISTICS, "Escalation and the CPI: Information for Users." *The Consumer Price Index, Revision—1978*. U.S. Department of Labor, 1978.

———. *CPI Detailed Report*, November 1980.

CAGAN, PHILLIP, and GEOFFREY H. MOORE. *The Consumer Price Index: Issues and Alternatives* Washington, D.C.: American Enterprise Institute for Public Policy Research, 1981.

CHRISTENSEN, LAURITS R., and MARILYN E. MANSER. "Cost of Living Indexes and Price Indexes for U.S. Meat and Produce, 1947–1971." *Household Behavior*, NBER, Conference on Research in Income and Wealth, Vol. 40.

DATA RESOURCES, INC. *Inflation and the Elderly*, Summary Report, Part One. Lexington, Mass., Lexington Books, January 1980.

DEMILNER, LAWRENCE E. *Indexing with the Consumer Price Index: Problems and Alternatives*. Congress of the United States, Congressional Budget Office, Washington D.C.: U.S. Government Printing Office, June 1981.

DIAMOND, DOUGLAS B., JR. "Taxes, Inflation, Speculation and the Cost of Homeownership." *AREUER Journal* 8 (1980).

DIEWERT, W. ERWIN. "Exact and Superlative Index Numbers." *Journal of Econometrics* 4 (May 1976), pp. 115–46.

EMERSON, MICHAEL. "A View of Current European Indexation Experiences." In *Inflation, Debt, and Indexation,* ed. Rudiger Dornbusch and Mario Henrique Simonsen. 1983.

EXECUTIVE OFFICE OF THE PRESIDENT, Council of Economic Advisors, Office of Management and Budget. *Report on Indexing Federal Programs,* January 1981.

FISCHER, STANLEY. "On the Nonexistence of Privately Issued Index Bonds in the U.S. Capital Market." In *Inflation, Debt, and Indexation,* ed. Rudiger Dornbusch and Mario Henrique Simonsen, 1983.

———. "Towards an Understanding of the Costs of Inflation: II." In *The Costs and Consequences of Inflation,* ed. Karl Brunner and Allen H. Meltzer, Carnegie Rochester Series on Public Policy, Autumn 1981.

———. "Welfare Aspects of Government Issue of Indexed Bonds." In *Inflation, Debt, and Indexation,* ed. Rudiger Dornbusch and Mario Henrique Simonsen, 1983.

GOLDFELD, STEPHEN M., and VAN DORN OOMS. *Research on Indexing Federal Programs,* Executive Office of Management and Budget. Washington, D.C.: U.S. Government Printing Office, January 1981.

GORDON, ROBERT J. "The Consumer Price Index: Measuring Inflation and Causing It." *The Public Interest* 63 (Spring 1981).

GRAY, JO ANNA. "On Indexation and Contract Length." *Journal of Political Economy,* February 1978, pp. 1–18.

HAUSMAN, JERRY A. "Income and Payroll Tax Policy and Labor Supply." National Bureau of Economic Research, Working Paper No. 610, December 1980.

———. "The Effect of Taxes on Labor Supply." In *How Taxes Affect Economic Behavior,* ed. H. Aaron and J. Pechman. Washington, forthcoming.

HURD, MICHAEL, and JAMES B. SHOVEN. "The Economic Status of the Elderly." In *Financial Aspects of the United States Pension System,* ed. Zvi Bodie and James B. Shoven. Chicago: University of Chicago Press, 1983.

KARNI, EDI. "On Optimal Wage Indexation." *Journal of Political Economy* 91, no. 2, Chicago: University of Chicago Press, 1983.

LAMALE, HELEN. *The Impact of Rising Prices on Younger and Older Consumers.* U.S. Department of Labor, Bureau of Labor Statistics, Report No. 238-2, December 1963.

MACKIN, JOHN P. *Protecting Purchasing Power in Retirement.* New York: Fleet Academic Editions, 1971.

MICHAEL, ROBERT T. "Variation across Households in the Rate of Inflation." *Journal of Money, Credit and Banking* 11, no. 1 (February 1979), pp. 32–46.

NORWOOD, JANET L. "The Anatomy of Price Change." *Monthly Labor Review,* March 1981.

OLSON, LAWRENCE; CHRISTOPHER CATON; and MARTIN DUFFY. *The Elderly and the Future Economy.* Lexington, Mass.: D. C. Heath, 1981.

PHELPS, EDMUND S. "Implicit Contracts and the Social Contract: Toward a Welfare Economics without Costless Mobility." In *Inflation, Debt, and Indexation,* ed. Rudiger Dornbusch and Mario Henrique Simonsen, 1983.

POLLAK, ROBERT A. "Group Cost-of-Living Indexes." *The American Economic Review* 70 (May 1980), pp. 273–78.

________. "The Theory of the Cost-of-Living Index." U.S. Department of Labor Statistics, Working Paper No. 11, June 1971.

POPKIN, JOEL, et al. "Inflation, Portfolio Balancing and Pension Indexation." Final Report submitted to U.S. Department of Labor, Contract No. J-9-P-1-0076, March 1983.

TORDA, T. S. "The Impact of Inflation on the Elderly." *The Federal Reserve Bank of Cleveland Review,* October–November 1972.

TRIPLETT, JACK E. "Comment on 'The Consumer Price Index and the Measurement of Inflation,' by Alan S. Blinder." in *Brookings Papers on Economic Activity,* (1980:2).

________. "Concepts of Quality Input and Output Price Measures: A Resolution of the User-Value-Resource Cost Debate." *The U.S. National Income and Product Accounts: Selected Topics.* NBER Conference on Research in Income and Wealth, November 1980.

________. "Inflation Measures and Escalation Measures: What Is the Answer? What Is the Question?" In *Conference Proceedings: Statistics Canada Conference on Price Measurement,* ed. W. E. Diewert and Claude Montmarquette, forthcoming.

________. "Reconciling the CPI and the PCE Deflator." *Monthly Labor Review* 104 (September 1981).

________. "The Measurement of Inflation: A Survey of Research on the Accuracy of Price Indexes." In *Analysis of Inflation,* ed. Paul H. Earl. Lexington, Mass.: Lexington Books, 1975.

________. "Three Studies of Indexes and Indexing: A Review Essay." *Journal of Money, Credit, and Banking* 15, no. 3 (August 1983), pp. 377–84.

WACHTER, SUSAN M. "Indexing Risk: The Special Role of Pension Funds." *Identification and Control of Risk in Thrift Institutions: Conference Proceedings*, San Francisco Federal Home Loan Bank, 1984.

3 Indexation of Retirement Benefits: A Survey of Existing Practices

This chapter surveys the methods that are currently used to index pension benefits to inflation.[1] In periods of rapid inflation and in the absence of attempts to update pension benefits over the worker's career, the methods can become hopelessly outdated during the accrual stage, even before retirement is reached. The first section of this chapter discusses techniques for protecting pension benefits in the accrual and disbursal stages. The next three sections survey current indexing practices in public and private U.S. plans and foreign plans, respectively, with a brief summary in the last section.

Techniques for Protecting the Purchasing Power of Prospective and Current Pension Benefits

The Accrual Stage

Employers have used several methods to protect defined pension benefits during the accrual stage. The basic objective is to provide a benefit at retirement which bears a reasonable relationship to the level of income or standard of living enjoyed by the employee immediately prior to retirement. In a period of rising wages and prices, benefits based on historical earnings or accrued at a specific dollar rate per year quickly become outdated.

This problem tends to be well recognized by employers and, in general, is more likely to be dealt with systematically than the problem associated with benefits in payment status.

The Final Average Salary Approach. By far the most common method for protecting accruing benefits in nonunionized firms is to base benefits on the highest average earnings of a number of consecutive years of service or to tie them to the average salary of the employee during a specified number of years immediately preceding retirement. This is generally three to five years, although in some cases periods as short as the last year or even the last day of employment are used.[2] This method can be found in private industry and government programs, both in the United States and in foreign countries.

Indexation of Career Earnings. To the same effect, some employers update the past earnings of the employee to reflect changes in the price or overall wage level using the adjusted amounts as a basis for determining benefits. This procedure may be found in combination with a final average salary approach, where benefits are based on the indexed earnings of the last few years of employment.

Indexation of Accruing Benefits. Alternatively, benefits accruing during a particular year of service are increased in retirement to reflect the changes in a specified wage or price index during the intervening years. This approach is typically used with plans that accrue benefits at a flat dollar amount per year or month of service, and in its pure form it provides reasonably adequate protection against inflation. Frequently, however, when this method is used, there is a limit on the amount of adjustment that can occur during one year.

Tying Benefits to Asset Values. A fourth approach is to provide a direct link between the benefit amounts and the investment performance of the assets used to fund the benefits. The participant accumulates benefits in units, the value of which is determined by the market value of the assets underlying them. The assumption, of course, is that the value of the assets will rise with prices over the long run, thus allowing benefits to increase.

If the plan is a defined benefit plan in which accruing benefits are converted into units, the employer generally takes credit initially for a certain expected investment return.[3] The net effect is that the employee benefits only from return in excess of that amount and may bear the risk of a lower return. This can be distinguished from a defined contribution plan in which the commitment refers to the funds set aside to provide benefits. In the approximately one fourth of pensions which are defined contribution plans, benefits at retirement are simply the amount that can be provided by the total accumulated contributions. Their real value at retirement depends on the underlying investment portfolio's value which may be negatively affected by inflation, as discussed in the following chapters.

Ad Hoc Adjustment in Benefit Accruals. While this is not a systematic approach for dealing with inflation, it is the one frequently found in pension plans in the unionized sector. Ad hoc increases may be made in either the level of benefits accruing or in the wage base used to determine benefits. If the adjustments are made on a regular basis with attention given to movements in a wage or price index, the results may approximate those of an adjustment mechanism which is tied directly to the index, although with a greater lag. Benefits for past service may be recalculated based on the participant's current pay or pay for a recent period. In plans with benefits not related to pay, the benefit per year of service (both past and future service) may be increased, often as the result of collective bargaining. Many employers prefer such an approach because it avoids the formal cost obligations of direct indexation, allowing consideration of the funds available for augmenting benefits.

The Disbursal Stage

The second element of the problem inflation poses to pension plans is the erosion of purchasing power during retirement years. Although benefits may be well protected during accrual by one of the methods previously discussed, it is of little satisfaction to the employee if they are subsequently allowed to fall to inadequate levels. The first two methods, indexation of benefits and ad hoc increases, are most common, the former in government and the latter in private plans.

Indexation of Benefits. The most direct way to deal with inflation is to allow the benefits to rise with movements in a specified wage or price index. This provides an automatic mechanism for protecting the purchasing power of benefits, and recent high rates of inflation have generated a surge of interest in this approach. Although infrequently found in the private sector, it is a common element of federal governmental plans. In addition, the complete indexation of Social Security benefits implies that a majority of retired individuals have some portion of their income adjusted by this method.

There are a number of ways in which indexation is applied, with many variations that attempt to limit the amount of adjustment for which the employer will be responsible. National programs in many countries provide increases without limit, while others limit indexation to a percentage of inflation, say half, or use caps. Plans at the lower levels of government and in the private sector are often capped. The majority of caps lie well below the high rates of inflation of the 1970s and are, generally, under 5 percent. In a 1975 survey of U.S. municipal retirement plans, caps were found in 77 percent of those that provided automatic indexation.[4]

The distinctive characteristic of indexation with a cap is that the employer provides complete protection against inflationary losses below the cap and none above. Alternatively, an employer may feel that the employee should bear part of the initial increases in the price level. This may be accomplished by adjusting only a portion of the benefits, either by a percentage or a specific dollar amount. Proponents of this method argue that only a portion of pension benefits are used to purchase necessities and that employers are obligated to protect only that amount against erosion of purchasing power. In another variation, indexation applies only after a specified number of years of retirement or after the individual has attained a minimum age, forcing the plan participant to bear the full costs of inflation during the first years of retirement. A third approach to limiting the amount of adjustment is to require that the increase in the index exceed a minimum level before any benefit changes will be made. An employer may adjust benefits only for movements in the index in excess of a certain amount, arguing that some inflation is expected and should be dealt with by the employee. Some plans index only the minimum benefit under this plan. With inflationary increases, then, individuals who previously had pensions below the increased minimum benefit level begin receiving the new minimum. Those with benefits above the minimum receive no adjustment for inflation.[5]

A significant element in the indexation approach is the choice of index to be used. This may be either a wage or price index or, in some cases, a combination of the two types. In the United States, price indexation seems to be the preferred method, but several countries in Western Europe tie benefits to movements in the wage level. Presumably, the latter approach allows retired persons to share in some portion of the increases in productivity and overall standard of living that they would not receive under indexation by prices.[6]

Ad Hoc Increases in Benefits. The most common method in the private sector for dealing with inflation during retirement is through ad hoc increases in benefits. Recognizing the tremendous erosion of the pension dollar in the past two decades, many firms voluntarily increased the pensions of those already retired. In some cases, the employer will provide increases that are substantially in agreement with those that would have occurred with formal indexation, although with a longer lag, while in others the increases fall far short of complete adjustment. As with ad hoc increases in accruing benefits, they allow more control over costs and free the employer to consider the resources available when increasing benefits.[7]

Automatic Increases in Benefits. A third, less used method in both private and public plans is to increase benefits by a specific percentage or dollar amount regardless of the amount of inflation. One way this can be accomplished is by giving the participant the option of a nonincreasing benefit or an actuarially equivalent increasing benefit. The increasing pension would initially be lower, eventually rising above the nonincreasing one. With this approach, the individual has the certainty of an increasing income but no guarantee that it will keep up with inflation. In fact, to provide protection against high levels of inflation, there must be substantial reduction in the initial benefit. The employer may choose to make no reduction or a smaller reduction and bear the cost of the increases himself.[8]

Recomputation. Recomputation is essentially a specific form of wage indexation. Under this procedure, benefits are related to the job classification of the individual at retirement. As the salary from that position rises, so does the pension for individuals retiring at the position. Thus, all individuals retiring at the same classification with equal service would have the same benefits, regardless of the year in which they retired. This was previously used in the U.S. military retirement system but was discontinued for cost reasons.

Asset-Linked Benefits. In addition to being tied to an asset fund during accrual as previously discussed, in a small proportion of plans benefits during retirement are increased in the same manner. This adjustment is commonly done by a variable annuity, which can be distinguished from other annuity forms by its inclusion of actual investment return in the benefit formula. Here, also, a minimum expected return is initially considered in the formula, and benefits are adjusted only by the extent to which the actual return differs. Unfortunately, the performance of these funds has not been outstanding in recent years, leaving the beneficiary open to the possibility of a benefit reduction during a period of rising prices. Some employers have resorted to ad hoc supplements in this event.[9]

Use of Excess Investment Income. This final approach could logically be included as a special case of the ad hoc or asset-linked methods, but it is distinctive enough to warrant special consideration. With this method, plan liabilities are valued at an interest rate lower than that expected to be earned, and the actuarial gains resulting from excess investment income are used to fund ad hoc increases in benefits. This approach is currently receiving much attention in Canada and in the United States. Proponents argue that part of the investment return is an inflationary component. Accordingly, any return in excess of the real interest rate plus a risk factor should be used to ease the effects of inflation on benefit recipients.[10]

Clearly, there are several mechanisms currently in use to protect pension benefits against inflation. The degree of protection varies over a wide range, as does the cost assumed by the employer, and many of the variations were developed in an attempt to limit the employer's costs, which can be substantial. The other side of the story, of course, is that inflationary losses which are not covered by the employer must be borne by the employee.

Public Sector Plans in the United States

Federal Retirement Program

Retirement programs at the federal level provide some of the most comprehensive protection against inflation found anywhere. The basic trend in federal programs is to use a form of the final average salary method for determining the initial retirement benefit and to subsequently adjust the benefit upward (but not downward) with movements in the CPI.

The Military Retirement System. Initial benefits under the military retirement system are determined with reference to the last month's pay, a form of the final average salary method. As indicated earlier, prior to 1958 benefits were adjusted automatically by the recomputation method, moving with the salary of the grade at which the individual retired. This procedure was dropped in 1958, and in 1962 benefits were tied to the consumer price index. On the basis of 1976 legislation, which also applies to the Civil Service Retirement System, adjustments were made every six months for increases in the consumer price index, rounded to the nearest tenth of a percent. This legislation was superseded by the Omnibus Budget Reconciliation Act of 1981 which allows only annual increases, based on December to December. There is no limit on the amount of increase permitted or required before adjustment takes place, nor is there a provision for a decrease in benefits in the event of a reduction in the CPI.

The Civil Service Retirement System. Benefits under the Civil Service Retirement System are based on average salary or earnings during the three highest consecutive years of service, and they are adjusted after retirement on the same basis as the military retirement system. This system is also used for the Central Intelligence Agency and the Board of Governors of the Federal Reserve System.

Some Problems. A potential problem with the military retirement system is that there is no provision for downward adjustments. For example, if the CPI fell 3 percent, there would be no adjustment in the benefit levels. If it subsequently rose 5 percent, then benefits would be increased by 5 percent, even though the actual loss of purchasing power measured over two years is much lower. To deal with this problem, indexed pension plans typically specify that if no adjustment occurs, then the previous base period will be retained.[11]

A second problem may arise if wages do not adjust fully to inflation, allowing benefits to increase faster than salaries. This shortcoming may result in an individual who continues to work receiving a lower benefit at retirement than one in the same position who retires immediately.[12] This problem is of particular importance in government plans, where there have been periods in recent years in which wage increases have not kept pace with private sector increases or cost-of-living increases.

The U.S. Social Security System

One of the most widely cited examples of purchasing power protection for retirement income is the United States Social Security System. Since the 1977 Amendments to the Social Security Act, Social Security benefits have been determined by a procedure utilizing the average indexed monthly earnings (AIME) concept. Past earnings are indexed to the second year prior to attainment of age 62 (or becoming disabled or dying, if before age 62), the increase being determined by the ratio of the average total wages in the country in that year to the average in the year being indexed. The indexed earnings (with the five lowest years dropped) are used to compute benefits at retirement.

During payout, Social Security benefits are automatically adjusted on the basis of changes in the consumer price index. Increases are made for movements in the first quarter CPI from one year to the next, with the increase, rounded to the nearest tenth of a percent, being effective for the following June. A 3 percent trigger is required and is applied cumulatively, so that if no increase occurs, the base for determining future increases is the CPI during the second quarter immediately prior to the last increase. Special provisions suspend automatic increases during periods in which there have been ad hoc adjustments by Congress, and there is no provision for a reduction of benefits in the event of a decline in the CPI. In addition, the earnings base (i.e., the maximum amount of earnings subject to the Social Security tax) is indexed to changes in the national average total wage, with a two-year lag.[13]

State and Local Plans

A study done by the Pension Task Force in 1976 provides some information on the extent to which pension benefits are protected against inflation at lower levels of government.[14] While 98 percent of all federal employees are covered by plans that adjust benefits without limit for cost-of-living increases, less than 5 percent of state and local employees enjoy such generous provisions. Almost half, however, are participants in plans that increase benefits by a constant percentage per year or provide limited automatic adjustment to a cost-of-living index, for example, by increasing only for a percentage of the change in the index or by increasing subject to a cap. There is a clear tendency for larger plans to be better protected than smaller plans. Of the plans with more than 1,000 participants, only 2.8 percent have no adjustment, ad hoc or automatic. For smaller plans, those with less than 100 participants, the figure is 63.3 percent. Surprisingly, however, smaller plans are more likely to have indexation without limit (11.3 percent) than larger plans (7.3 percent).

Plans at the state and local levels exhibit a wide range of procedures for dealing with the problems of inflation. Examples can be found of all of the basic methods discussed earlier.

The Private Sector

The most recent data on inflation adjustment is provided in a study made by Bankers Trust Company published in late 1980.[15] The study covered the activities of 325 plans from 240 companies between December 1974 and December 1979. The majority

TABLE 3–1

*Flat Rate of Annual Benefit per Year of Service**	*1960*	*1965*	*1970*	*1975*	*1980*
$60 and under	100%	100%	54%	—	—
$61–$80	—	—	39	10%	4%
$81–$100	—	—	7	28	7
$101–$120	—	—	—	45	11
$121–$140	—	—	—	2	11
$141–$160	—	—	—	13	26
$161 and over	—	—	—	2	41

*Table shows distribution of accrual rates for pattern plans that set benefits at a flat dollar amount per year of service.

of these were taken from Fortune's top 500 industrial and top 50 of other industry listing. Of these, 23 percent were pattern, or collectively bargained, plans. The remaining plans, primarily for salaried employees, were labeled conventional plans by the study.

The evidence indicates rising benefit levels during the accrual state, with benefits adjusted by periodic increases in the rates of accrual and a greater use of final average salary formulas. Post-retirement benefit increases are significantly less than inflation and are primarily ad hoc, with a slightly increasing, although still infrequent, use of capped automatic adjustments tied to the consumer price index.

Preretirement Benefit Adjustment. In most pattern plans, the benefit formula provides a uniform flat dollar amount per year of service. Not surprisingly, these rates have increased significantly during the past five years. Of the collectively bargained plans studied in 1975, 15 percent had accrual rates above $140 annually per year of service. In 1980 that figure was 67 percent, and median accrual rates have risen from $108 to $144 annually per year. Table 3–1, which has been taken from the Bankers Trust Study, shows the pronounced shift toward higher rates of accrual in pattern plans over the most recent 20-year period.

The conventional plans base benefits primarily on a career average or a final average formula. As discussed previously, a final average benefit formula provides some automatic adjustment for

TABLE 3–2
Pension Benefits of Conventional Plans (median plan benefit)

Final Year's Compensation	*Final Pay Plans*		*Career Average Plans*		*Total Plans*		*Social Security Benefit*	
	1980	*1975*	*1980*	*1975*	*1980*	*1975*	*1980*	*1975*
$ 9,000	29%	30%	35%	28%	30%	29%	55%	39%
15,000	30	33	32	31	30	32	43	25
25,000	35	36	34	35	35	35	27	15
50,000	39	38	35	37	38	38	14	8

inflation, with the more perfect the adjustment, the shorter the averaging period. It is significant, then, that the percentage of plans using an averaging period of less than five years has risen sharply, from 2 percent in 1975 to 16 percent in 1980. Of these, the majority average over a three-year period. Of the 1980 conventional plans, 85 percent use some form of final average salary formula, as compared with 78 percent in 1975.[16] In addition, of those plans which use strictly a career average formula, two thirds have updated the compensation base used in determining benefits,[17] resulting in another way to raise benefit levels.[18]

It seems clear, then, that the vast majority of conventional plans have made some attempt to offset inflation's impact during the benefit accrual years. Some insight on the degree to which they have been successful is given in Table 3–2, which is taken from the 1980 Bankers Trust Survey. The table shows for the plans covered the median percentage of final salary replaced at various incomes in 1980 and 1975 as well as Social Security replacement levels, although the table overstates average replacement rates since it is constructed for employees with 30 years of service.[19] The table indicates that private pension plans have maintained relatively constant replacement rates at each income level, with significant increases in Social Security replacement rates, especially at lower income levels.

Postretirement Benefit Increases. Postretirement benefit increases can be broadly classified as ad hoc or automatic. Approximately 70 percent of plans extended increases to retirees in the 1975 to 1980 period compared to 65 percent in the 1970 to

TABLE 3–3
Pattern Plans

Individual Retired on:	*Increases in the Form of Dollar Amount*	*Increases in the Form of Percent of Current Pension through 1980*
January 1, 1965	$681	20%
January 1, 1970	681	17
January 1, 1975	662	8

1975 period. While a majority of the plans extended benefit increases, these were largely of the ad hoc type. Automatic adjustments tied to movements in the CPI were found in only nine (4 percent) of the plans in the Bankers Trust 1980 Survey, evidence that such a provision is very much the exception. Moreover, in each case these were capped, in six plans, with a 3 percent limit. In addition, the use of a variable income feature in postretirement increases has declined and is found in only 2 percent of the plans studied.[20]

Tables 3–3 and 3–4 show average total post-1974 increases for the fixed dollar and percentage of current pension benefit adjustment forms for both pattern and conventional plans, for the hypothetical retiree with 30 years of service in those firms which extended multiple increases. One 1975 dollar lost approximately one third of its purchasing power between 1975 and 1980, one half between 1970 and 1975, and three fifths between 1965 and 1980. Increases given in the preceding 1970–74 period nearly duplicate these results. Clearly, for the average individual retiring, benefit increases have fallen far short of that required to maintain the purchasing power of his or her private pension, with earlier retirees most hurt by the continued erosion of inflation. These results are substantially confirmed by a U.S. Department of Labor study by Clark et al., which found that average benefits rose for 1973 retirees by 24 percent in 1979, a period in which the CPI rose by 63 percent.[21]

Survey of Foreign Public and Private Plans

Canada

The extent of pension indexation in Canada is similar to that in the United States, although the public retirement system re-

TABLE 3–4
Conventional Plans

Individual Retired on:	*Increases in the Form of Dollar Amount*	*Increases in the Form of Percent of Current Pension through 1980*
January 1, 1965	$525	20%
January 1, 1970	490	17
January 1, 1975	480	9

places a lower percentage of preretirement income. All federal programs are fully indexed for inflation, including the civil servants pension programs, armed forces programs, and public retirement income programs, while benefit increases in the private sector are generally made on an ad hoc basis. The provincial governments often provide indexation on the basis of changes in the consumer price index. These adjustments are usually capped, with caps ranging from 4 percent to 8 percent, but the provinces of Quebec and British Columbia have no limit.

Canada's public retirement system is comprised of two tiers, with each tier using a slightly different mechanism for adjustment. The first tier, Old Age Security, provides a basic dollar benefit per month ($182.42 in January 1980) to every male and female aged 65 and over. These amounts are tied directly to the CPI and increases, rounded to the nearest .1 percent, are made quarterly, with a three-month lag. Decreases are not allowed, and during a period in which no increase is made, the previous base quarter is retained.

At the second level, the Canada Pension Plan, individuals receive an additional benefit based on earnings (up to a ceiling) prior to retirement.[22] At retirement, the earnings report used to determine the initial benefit is adjusted to reflect the change in the earnings base, the maximum amount subject to taxation under the program. With this method, the earnings of a particular year are multiplied by the ratio of the average maximum earnings base for the three years ending with the year the pension becomes payable to the earnings base for the given year. This base is scheduled to increase by 12.5 percent each year until it reaches the average earnings of Canadian workers, after which it will rise with the average. Benefits in the course of payment are adjusted annually on the basis of changes in a specially constructed pension index, which is determined by the average of the CPI for the previous year ending in October, rounded to the nearest .1 percent. The pension index is not allowed to decrease.

A procedure similar to that found in the Canadian Pension Plan is used to adjust benefits being paid to federal civil servants and to adjust the vested benefits of those who have left the program prior to retirement. Because this procedure provides a substantial degree of protection for those employed by the federal government, an element lacking in the private sector, there is currently a movement in the legislature to limit indexation for federal employees. One recommendation is to limit increases over three-year periods to what could be financed by available resources, including accumulated past contributions made for benefit escalations and "excess" investment return (i.e., return in excess of the real interest rate).[23]

In contrast to the well-protected plans of the public sector, there are few examples of formal indexation in the private sector. Private sector plans generally base benefits on career or final average earnings, and those few that do index benefits in the course of payment are likely to have a cap on the amount of increase, typically 2 to 3 percent. These plans tend to follow the CPI or pension index and to adjust for the full increase up to the cap. Ad hoc benefit increases are used in a majority of plans but, as in the United States, do not offset inflation.

Western Europe

Most countries in Western Europe provide protection for their national programs during both the accrual and payout stages. Protection during accrual is accomplished by using a final average salary for determining benefits or indexing the past earnings record. Indexation may be done on the basis of wages (France and Germany), prices (Belgium and Sweden), or a combination of wages and prices (Norway). Those that index by prices may make occasional ad hoc changes, effectively resulting in total increases that are about equal to those that would have occurred with indexation by earnings. Benefits in payment status are also indexed to prices, wages, or some combination. West Germany and the Netherlands index on the basis of wages, and Sweden indexes by prices, using ad hoc increases to provide benefits with some share of productivity gains. As of 1975, 16 European countries had some form of automatic adjustment provision.

In Western Europe, as in North America, plans in the private sector are less likely to provide systematic protection against inflation during retirement years. Legislation in West Germany requires that private plans periodically review the adequacy of pension benefits. This review must be done every three years, and an adjustment must be made of at least 50 percent of the increase in a cost-of-living index, which refers to a four-person family. Finland has a mandatory private pension system administered by insurance companies, with benefits adjusted on the basis of a combination of the movements in the wage and price indexes.

A distinctive approach is found in Great Britain, which has a two-tiered Social Security system. Here, the employer can choose to provide a private pension plan, meeting certain minimum requirements in lieu of participating in the second tier of the government program. The principal requirement is that the earnings record be updated for changes in wages and the benefits updated for changes in prices. (Government-indexed bonds are available to use as assets for these pensions.) Private plans grant ad hoc increases in postretirement benefits, and these have been estimated to compensate for two thirds of the price level increases over time.

The trend toward protection of vested benefits is even more pronounced, with alternatives being considered in several European countries. In the Netherlands, it is being recommended that employers follow the "years of life" approach under which credit is given for service performed for past employers, but only to the extent of increases in earnings under the current employer. For an individual with no periods of unemployment, the ultimate effect is to accrue benefits at a final salary rate, with the accruals for early years being split among employers on the basis of wage increments. In Switzerland, proposals are being discussed for public financing of increases in vested benefits by imposing a charge on all employers. Finally, a procedure used in Great Britain is to transfer to the current employer the pension assets accumulated on behalf of an employee during previous employment, while giving credit for years of service. Since benefits are typically based on final average salary, with benefits accruing at a specified percentage per year of service, this method allows all accrued benefits to be expressed as a percentage of compensation.

A significant problem in Western Europe is the rising cost of the indexation provisions in the public plans. Attractive early retirement features and high unemployment levels have resulted in a continuing rise in the ratio of beneficiaries to employed participants, increasing costs substantially. Accordingly, the trend has been more toward dealing with this problem than providing additional inflationary protection. For example, West Germany has put a temporary limit on increases in benefits from indexation, and Italy has modified the formula for calculating benefits. In Italy, earnings increases resulting solely from inflation are no longer considered part of the base for computing benefits for the highly paid. Thus, the percentage of earnings that is being replaced by government programs can be expected to decline in the future, leading some to speculate that increased pressure on private employers for supplementary benefits is likely.[24] At the moment, however, the pressure on private plans may be lighter in view of the substantial benefits provided by government plans. Typically, the public sector plans provide a greater proportion of retirement income than the U.S. Social Security system at a considerable cost in average tax burden. Nonetheless, protection of private pension benefits against inflation is a widely discussed problem.[25]

Summary of Existing Retirement Benefit Indexing Practices

In the United States, Canada, and Europe, private and public pension plans use a number of procedures in the accrual period so that real benefits at retirement are not systematically lowered by inflation over the course of the employment period. In the disbursal period, in general, only national public plans are fully indexed to inflation.

In the United States, state and local plans are indexed, but with caps and limits of various forms. Private plan retirement benefits are upgraded, usually through ad hoc adjustments, which have not kept pace with inflation. A very few private plans offer some form of formal partial indexation of postretirement benefits, limited by caps.

Finally, several European countries have mechanisms in place to protect vested pensions after a job transfer, while others are evaluating alternative procedures to accomplish this.

Notes

[1] These methods of expressing benefits at retirement are called, respectively, a flat unit and a career average benefit formula. For a further explanation of this and other benefit formulas, see Dan M. McGill, *Fundamentals of Private Pensions*, 5th ed. (Homewood, Ill.: Richard D. Irwin, 1984).

[2] New York City's pension bases the initial benefit on the last day's earnings. Because overtime pay is included in the computation, some individuals have been able to manipulate the amount of their benefit by putting in long hours on their last day. Thus, it is clear that a final salary formula must also be distinguished by the types of earnings considered, including overtime, sick pay, and vacation time.

[3] A defined benefit plan is one in which the employer makes a commitment as to the amount of benefit that will be provided at retirement.

[4] "National Surveys of Employee Benefits for Full-Time Personnel of U.S. Municipalities," was conducted by Edward H. Friend & Company, Consulting Actuaries & Employee Benefit Consultants (Washington, D.C.) for the Labor-Management Relations Service of the National League of Cities, the United States Conference of Mayors, and the National Association of Counties (with the cosponsorship of the International City Management Program).

[5] Indexed plans also may be characterized by whether they allow for adjustment in both directions or consider only increases in the index. Most indexed plans of the private sector consider only increases; downward adjustment is much more likely to be found than in government programs. When found, the plan may provide for reduction in benefits only if the drop in the index exceeds a certain amount. Frequently, plans with downward adjustment specify that in no event will an adjustment be made which will reduce an individual's benefit below the initial amount.

Examples of such an approach are the National Airlines plans for pilots and communication employees. They provide for adjustment upward for inflation in excess of the first 5 percent after retirement. The pension benefit will be reduced if the CPI falls by more than 10 percent, with the reduction being limited to the amount in excess of 10 percent.

[6] In Great Britain, until 1978 a combined approach was used. The flat-benefit portion of the Social Security system (i.e., the nonearnings-related portion) was increased by the larger of the increase in the wage or price level. A similar system is currently used to adjust the minimum pension benefit under Italy's national system. For pensions above the minimum, one portion is adjusted by changes in a wage index and the remainder by the price index. Robert J. Myers, *Indexation of Pension and Other Benefits* (Homewood, Ill.: Richard D. Irwin, 1978), p. 113.

[7] While it is difficult to determine the extent to which ad hoc increases have kept pace with inflation, it is estimated that in the United Kingdom and Canada they reflect, on average, about one half to two thirds of the increases in the

price index. Ad hoc increases are estimated to provide approximately 60 percent protection in the United States. See below for further discussion and *Worldwide Benefit Review: Perspectives on International Employee Benefits*, William Mercer International, 1980.

[8] For example, to provide an annual increase of 5 percent to a male retiring at age 65, a regular monthly benefit of $400 would initially be reduced to $270.40. See McGill, *Fundamentals of Private Pensions*, p. 226.

[9] This type of plan is frequently found in educational areas. The CREF portion of the Teachers Insurance and Annuity Association—College Retirement Equities Fund (TIAA-CREF) uses a variable annuity approach in which the underlying assets are invested in common stocks. Since TIAA-CREF accounts for the retirement programs of approximately 500,000 participants of pension plans affiliated with the program, the variable annuity is a common adjustment mechanism for plans of educational institutions.

[10] Robert J. Myers, past chief actuary of the Social Security System, advocates the use of such an approach. In his book, he argues that the costs of a pension plan are "illusorily low" when any amount higher than the real interest rate is used to value plan liabilities.

[11] Myers, *Indexation of Pension and Other Benefits*, p. 76.

[12] This occurs since the retired individual's benefit is increasing faster than the salary on which the worker's benefit is based.

[13] More precisely, as noted by Robert J. Myers, "the base for a year is the previous year's one times the increase in the average wage for the second preceding year over that for the third preceding year."

[14] *Pension Task Force Report on Public Employee Retirement Systems*, Committee on Education and Labor, U.S. House of Representatives, March 15, 1978.

[15] In a 1975 study made by Bankers Trust, only 8 out of 271 plans (3 percent) studied automatically adjusted benefits, 7 by the consumer price index with a 3 percent limit and 1 by 65 percent of the increase in the CPI. See *1975 Study of Corporate Pension Plans* (New York: Bankers Trust, 1975). Several plans provided the variable annuity as an option at retirement. By 1977, a survey done by Hay-Huggins found that 6 percent of the pension plans responding made automatic adjustments by the CPI, with caps ranging upward to 5 percent. A number of plans with indexing provisions allowed benefit reduction, but never below the initial amount, and several required a minimum increase in the CPI before adjustment would occur. Finally, a fraction of the plans increased benefits by a constant percent (1 percent or 3 percent) regardless of changes in the CPI. See Myers, *Indexation of Pensions and Other Benefits*, p. 122.

In general, earlier evidence indicates that automatic indexation provisions were infrequent in private pension plans, and ad hoc adjustments only partially adjusted for inflation. Earlier evidence indicates, however, that many plans based benefits on final average salary, in which case accruing benefits are fully protected. A 1978 study of 131 pension plans by the Department of Labor found 23 using a final average salary for determining initial benefits. Of the remaining 108, 94 liberalized their benefit formula between 1974 and 1978, either by adopting a new method or by making ad hoc adjustments in the current formula. This trend is supported by the 1975 Bankers Trust Study, which found a significant percentage of pension plans using final salary, the majority of these (93 percent) with a five-year average. In addition, those plans which based benefits on a flat dollar amount per year of service made substantial increases in the rate of accrual between 1970 and 1975. See Robert Frumkin and Donald Schmitt, "Pension Improvements since 1974 Reflect Inflation, New U.S. Law," *Monthly Labor Review* 102, no. 4 (April 1979), pp. 32–37.

An unusual approach to adjusting benefits which differs from those described above has been taken by the Rockefeller Foundation of New York. Under this plan, benefits are increased for movements in the CPI, but with qualification for increases greater than 4 percent. In such cases, the increase in the index is compared to the amount by which the average prime interest rate over a 12-month period (ending in September) exceeds 3 percent, with the lesser figure being used to adjust benefits. Essentially, this discrepancy involves two estimates of the level of inflation: the rise in the CPI and the excess of the nominal interest rate over (3 percent estimate of) the real rate, with the lower estimate being applied. Since the smaller of the two is always used to adjust for increases of over 4 percent, this adjustment should result in a long-run increase in benefits somewhat lower than the increase in the CPI. See Myers, *Indexation of Pension and Other Benefits*, p. 127. Myers indicates that this method would have resulted in benefit increases over the period 1955–74 of about 90 percent of the increase in the CPI.

[16] Of the conventional plans, 76 percent are exclusively final pay, as compared to 54 percent in 1975. The 85 percent figure includes plans which have a minimum pension benefit determined by a final average formula in addition to standard career average benefit formula.

[17] The following is a breakdown of conventional plan changes by broad categories:

1. Forty-four plans increased their benefit rates. These included 22 plans which increased the rate in a final average formula, 8 which increased future and prior service rates in a career average formula, and 14 which increased rates above or below the "break point" in a step-rate integration program. (Integration refers to a procedure which explicitly recognizes Social Security benefits in designing a pension plan. With the step-rate method of integration, benefits accrue at a higher rate above the "break point" than below, with IRS rules placing a maximum on the differential. Frequently the break point is set at the SS taxable wage base in career average plans or at SS covered compensation in final average plans.)
2. Fifty-two plans revised their compensation bases, with 15 changing to a final average salary formula and 8 adjusting prior service benefits to reflect current compensation levels. Twenty-nine plans had a final average salary formula and shortened the averaging period or otherwise liberalized it.
3. Six plans with a flat dollar benefit increased the benefit.
4. One plan with a flat dollar benefit changed to a final average formula.

[18] In addition, approximately 60 percent of the conventional plans offer a minimum pension benefit. This amount averaged $3,817 annually after 30 years of service in 1980 as compared with $550 in 1960. Of those plans without minimum benefits, 96 percent based the regular normal retirement benefit to some extent on final average pay. Another interesting trend is the movement away from the variable income option for dealing with inflation. Of the plans studied, nine were amended to eliminate such a feature.

[19] The figures in Table 3–2 are excerpted from the Bankers Trust Study and assume an individual retiring on January 1, 1980 or on January 1, 1975 with 30 years of credited service and a 5 percent annual increase in compensation. Because plans covered by the Bankers Trust Survey are disproportionately large and well funded and because 30 years of continuous service is unusually high, the table may give a misleading picture of the amount of income replaced by organized savings plans, although the table still can give insight on the lack of impact of inflation on real benefits in the accrual period. It should also be noted that after-tax real wages in the 1975 through 1980 period declined, as reflected in the assumed 5 percent minimal wage increase.

[20] In collectively bargained plans, 69 percent had increased benefits during the five-year period ending December 1979. Of these, three fifths had more than one increase during that time. The predominant form of increase was a flat dollar amount (typically $180) or a dollar amount per year of service (e.g., $15), although some increases were expressed as a percentage of current pension benefit. The latter group includes four plans providing a fixed percentage of current pension, in one case varying by length of retirement period, and eight plans providing a fixed percent per year of retirement. Six of these placed a maximum on the number of years of retirement recognized, and one applied increases only to years of retirement after age 65.

Among conventional plans, 72 percent extended benefit increases between 1975 and 1980, compared to 65 percent between 1970 and 1975. Of these, two fifths provided multiple increases during that period. In contrast to the collectively bargained plans, conventional plans tended to structure increases as a percent of current pension benefit (73 percent of those with benefit increases).

Twelve plans offered a flat percent of current compensation (ranging from 3 percent to 15 percent), with 4 of these placing a dollar ceiling on the increase. Ninety-three plans gave percentage increases that varied with the length of time the individual had been retired. These plans included 65 which increased pensions by a fixed percent per year of retirement (commonly 2–3), 45 percent of which limited the number of years recognized. Thirteen plans provided a flat percentage of current pension benefit plus an additional percentage per year of retirement, and 11 of these placed a maximum on the total additional percentage.

Eighteen plans used dollar formulas, either a fixed-dollar amount or a stated-dollar increase per year of service. Three of these used a fixed-dollar amount which varied by year of retirement.

Finally, 13 plans provided cost-of-living adjustments based on changes in the CPI. Four of these, however, were not automatic increases but were "one-shot" adjustments. No information was provided on two of the plans. Of the nine plans that did have automatic adjustments based on the CPI, all had maximum limits on the increase, as follows:

1. Six adjusted benefits by the full amount of the change in the CPI, subject to a maximum change of 3 percent in either direction. In no event was the benefit allowed to fall below its initial amount.
2. One increased current benefits by a percentage of the original benefit, the amount being determined by the change in the CPI and subject to a 3 percent maximum.
3. One increased current benefits by 50 percent of the change in the CPI, limited to a maximum increase of 2.5 percent.

4. One adjusted benefits by the full amount of the change in the CPI, with a limit of 4 percent. These adjustments were not allowed to reduce the pension below its original level.

[21] See Robert Clark, Steven Allen, and Daniel Sumner, "Inflation and Pension Benefits," U.S. Department of Labor, 1983.

[22] The province of Quebec opted out of the Canada Pension Plan and maintains a separate Quebec Pension Plan nearly identical to the national plan.

[23] Under the federal pension plan, the employee and government both contribute to a special fund to provide benefit increases.

[24] *Worldwide Benefit Review: Perspectives on International Employee Benefits,* William Mercer International, 1980.

[25] A distinctive approach to providing retirement income is the French repartition system, which developed following World War II in response to the high levels of inflation experienced by the French economy. It is operated essentially on a pay-as-you-go basis, with current contributions used to fund benefits for retired persons. The system was imposed by the government on about two thirds of the employees of industry and commerce, with separate subsystems applying to management and supervisory personnel and to manual workers. Employers and employees are required to contribute at a specified percentage of the defined earnings base, with the contributions being made to one of a number of privately administered "caisses." The rate at which contributions are made can vary within a range between employers, and the defined earnings base varies between subsystems. See McGill, *Fundamentals of Private Pensions,* p. 230.

Bibliography

FRUMKIN, ROBERT, and DONALD SCHMITT. "Pension Improvements since 1974 Reflect Inflation, New U.S. Law." *Monthly Labor Review* 102, no. 4 (April 1979), pp. 32–37.

MCGILL, DAN. *Fundamentals of Private Pensions.* 5th ed. Homewood, Ill.: Richard D. Irwin, 1984.

MYERS, ROBERT J. *Indexation of Pension and Other Benefits.* Homewood, Ill.: Richard D. Irwin, 1978.

"National Surveys of Employee Benefits for Full-Time Personnel of U.S. Municipalities." Edward H. Friend & Co.

1975 Study of Corporate Pension Plans. New York: Bankers Trust, 1975.

Pension Task Force Report on Public Employee Retirement Systems, Committee on Education and Labor, U.S. House of Representatives, March 15, 1978.

Worldwide Benefit Review: Perspectives on International Employee Benefits. William Mercer International, 1980.

PART TWO

The Impact of Inflation on Capital Markets

It has sometimes been presumed that it would be a relatively simple matter to index defined benefit pension plans fully to an inflation index. The accuracy of this assertion depends on the assumptions that, in real terms, capital markets are unaffected by inflation and, specifically, that inflation is not correlated with increased risk or decreased real rates of return. These assumptions are not accurate because unanticipated inflation is likely to be correlated with both. Thus, guaranteeing a real rate of return in an inflationary economy is riskier and/or more costly than guaranteeing the same nominal rate of return in a noninflationary economy.

Inflation-hedging variable pensions could be constructed without risk to the sponsoring firm by investing in inflation-hedging assets with lower rates of return. However, the cost would be passed on to plan participants in the form of lower overall lifetime remuneration. The necessary decreases in either wages or retirement benefits means that benefit plans that more closely track inflation may not be desired by plan participants themselves. Agreements that result in shared risk through partial indexation also may not be preferable to existing arrangements. Whether or not such agreements are preferable to current practice depends on the pension recipient's desired stream of income and expected (indexed) Social Security benefits, among other factors. The optimal structure of pensions also depends on the nature of inflation's impact on capital markets.

Part Two examines the impact of inflation on the variance and levels of real rates of return. Chapter 4 reviews the theory and Chapter 5, the empirical evidence of capital market effects of inflation. Chapter 5 ends with a discussion of the implications of the analysis for pensions.

Theory of the Impact of Inflation on Capital Markets

4

This chapter analyzes the theory of inflation's effects on capital markets with and without taxes.

Inflation's Effects with No Taxes

Under certain assumptions, inflation has no capital market impact and is neutral in both the short and long run. The first section begins by discussing the short- and long-run neutrality hypothesis, not because it is realistic but rather to show the stringent assumptions necessary to sustain it. The short-run capital market effects of money and real shocks are discussed in the second and third sections, respectively. The fourth section analyzes the short- and long-run effects of changes in the anticipated inflation rate and money illusion. In the fifth section the long-run effects of increased uncertainty are considered. The last section summarizes inflation's effects with no taxes. The theory is briefly presented in each section with a more detailed explication provided in the chapter's appendixes.

Assuming rational investors, without money illusion, and no increase in inflation uncertainty, inflation should be neutral in the long run, although not in the short run. Chapter 1 identified two kinds of inflation: long-run inflation which results only from sustained excessive money supply growth and short-run inflation which results from short-run monetary and nonmonetary shocks. Eventually long-run inflation becomes anticipated, assuming no persistent money illusion. In itself, anticipated inflation is neutral. Capital market participants—lenders and borrowers, savers and investors, alike—expect inflation and raise the nominal rate of return that they require and are willing to pay by the amount of the expected inflation. However, as Chapter 1 also indicates, higher levels of sustained inflation are generally accompanied by greater uncertainty over future rates of inflation. Greater uncertainty raises the required real rate of return. Uncertainty over future inflation rates makes inflation-hedged pensions desirable, if preservation of a given real pension is desired. However, the nonneutrality of short-run unanticipated inflationary spurts makes such indexation risky or costly. Returns on traditional assets (stocks and bonds) are negatively correlated with inflationary spurts. Hedging assets generally have lower rates of return. Thus nonneutrality of inflation makes it costly to redesign pensions to compensate for inflation. We begin with a discussion of necessary assumptions for inflation neutrality to clarify why inflation is not neutral.

Neutral Inflation in the Short and Long Run: Necessary Assumptions

Long- and short-run neutrality requires a number of assumptions. We must assume that inflation occurs through a neutrally distributed money supply increase in which everyone's money holdings are increased by the same percentage. A neutral distribution of money precludes a wealth redistribution or wealth-shift effect. The former could raise or lower real interest rates. Lower real rates would result, for example, if money supply increases were distributed disproportionately to individuals with a relatively high propensity to save. Although the distribution of the increased money supply does matter, there is no political or economic reason for savers or borrowers to gain disproportionately from a money supply increase; therefore, we can hypothesize a money supply distribution that is neutral in this respect.

However, money supply increases still may cause a wealth-shift effect that would reduce equilibrium real interest rates. Higher inflation rates erode the value of cash more rapidly. Thus, an increase in the anticipated inflation rate decreases the desired holdings of cash (i.e., real money balances). If individuals wish to preserve their overall wealth, they may then choose to save more in interest-earning forms of wealth. If so, equilibrium real interest rates will be lower.[1] If desired savings in other forms do not increase, real interest rates would not be affected through this route. We must assume a zero or negligible increase in nonmonetary savings to conclude that real rates are invariant to inflation. Alternatively, we must assume a neutral money supply distribution in which money supply increases are (and are expected to be) distributed proportionately to currency holders according to the size of their money holdings, in order to compensate for the decline in the purchasing power of money. The empirical evidence, considered below, implies that for the United States the largest possible magnitude of a wealth-shift effect is negligible. Thus, the neutrality result may hold, approximately, even if a wealth-shift effect does occur.

The additional assumptions that we must make are more troublesome, and the short- and long-run capital market effects of their violation are separately discussed in the sections that follow. Inflation must be the result of an anticipated increase in the money supply. An unanticipated increase in the money supply or a short-run spurt in the inflation rate due to nonmonetary factors will be accompanied by capital market effects. More precisely, we must assume a money supply increase that is anticipated *before* all current nominal contracts are negotiated and that does not affect the expected dispersion of future anticipated inflation rates (i.e., inflation uncertainty). Otherwise nominal contracts, to be negotiated in the future, would have to include increased expected inflation and money risk premiums, and already negotiated contracts would decline in value.

As Chapter 1 showed, long-run inflation always is the result of long-run excessive growth in the money supply. Inflation that is the result of long-run excessive money supply growth is predictable and should be anticipated by rational investors. Thus, if investors are rational, and assuming no increases in real or inflation uncertainty and a negligible wealth-shift effect, inflation may be neutral in the long run.

Unlike long-run inflation, short-run spurts of inflation tend not to be anticipated, since they are the result of money and real shocks. Unanticipated inflation, whatever its source, has real effects. Since nominal contracts are based on an anticipated inflation rate, unanticipated inflation reduces the realized rate of return, causing it to fall beneath the expected rate of return. Moreover, real and money shocks may cause short-run changes in the expected rate of return as well, since real output and relative prices are affected. Thus, to be neutral in the short run as well as in the long run, inflation must be the result only of a neutrally distributed fully anticipated money supply increase.

Indexing cannot undo the effects of nonneutrality. We will show below that the short-run capital market effects of shocks on stocks and bonds are negative; that is, the inflation they produce is correlated with decreased holding period rates of return. It is this inverse correlation which precludes the guaranteed indexing of an average real rate of return from an investment portfolio, to provide real annuities, as a costless alternative to nominal annuities. While short-term bonds and other hedges are likely to track inflation, over the long term such assets provide lower yields. Thus, it is costly to index the average real return of an investment portfolio to provide a guaranteed real income stream. Indexing is possible at no extra costs only if the assumptions of short- and long-run neutrality hold.

In summary, assuming short- and long-run neutral inflation, borrowers pay and lenders and equity holders receive the same real payments that they would in the absence of inflation. Real activity, prices, real rates of return are invariant to neutral inflation; a positive neutral inflation rate does not differ from a zero inflation rate in its effects, in the short or long run. Appendix 4.A details long- and short-run neutrality's lack of impact on expected and actual real yields of specific assets. To arrive at this neutrality conclusion, we must assume (1) that inflation is only caused by a neutrally distributed fully anticipated expansion in money supply growth and (2) that there are no tax effects.[2] The following sections withdraw these assumptions and describe the theoretical reasons that inflation may have an impact on real rates of return and the direction of this impact.

Money Shock Effects

Obviously, we do not live in a world of certainty. We can be surprised by inflation. Appendix 4.B discusses in detail the short-run effects of inflation caused by unanticipated (neutrally distributed) money supply growth.[3] Money shocks reduce expected (i.e., equilibrium or ex ante) real rates of return on short-term debt due to excess liquidity. They also reduce holding period returns on longer-term debt, since unanticipated inflation exceeds the anticipated inflation rate, previously built into nominally fixed-interest rates.

Equity holders also are affected by money shocks with the resulting unanticipated inflation inversely related to yields. Earnings increase, initially, in response to a money shock as aggregate demand, output, and sales increase with fixed labor input costs.

Employees purchase more goods with increased aggregate demand, and at the same time their productivity increases as they produce more goods for the same money wage. However, as commodity prices rise and produced good prices also begin to rise, employees demand higher nominal wages to catch up. The resulting increased labor and raw material costs lead to increased prices across the board and reduced purchasing power so that aggregate demand, output, sales, and earning growth decline to their previous levels. The result is an inverse correlation of unanticipated inflation with the growth of earnings. On the other hand, investors in commodities find their yields are directly related to unanticipated inflation, since raw material prices adjust more quickly to money shocks than other prices.

If money shocks are random, some positive and some negative (with their frequency and average size unchanged) over time, no increase in the long-run inflation rate is observed. Real rates of return over the business cycle, induced by money shocks, also do not change. However, the negative short-run correlation of real returns and unanticipated inflation on stocks and bonds remains.[4]

Overall, firms tend to be net debtors. Their gain, as borrowers, offsets to some extent the negative correlation of inflation with earnings. Investors in equity thus lose less, with unanticipated money shock inflation, at the expense of nominal debt holders.

Real Shock Effects

Unanticipated inflation results from supply and demand shocks. In both cases, the impact on actual inflation and equity yields is an inverse one. At base, the inverse outcome derives from the inverse relationship, between real output growth and inflation, in the quantity theory equation.

The earnings/inflation negative correlation is most obvious in response to a supply shock. With a constant rate of money supply growth, if real output and earnings slow, inflation accelerates.

A negative earnings/inflation correlation also results from a demand shock, just as from a money shock. With a constant rate of money supply growth and increased aggregate demand, earnings first increase and then decrease, since output responds, initially; and then prices adjust fully upward, concomitant with a decline in output growth. Hence, the delayed impact on prices is correlated with a slowdown in earnings growth.[5]

To the extent firms are leveraged with nominal—not indexed—debt, they gain from unanticipated inflation's negative impact on ex post real interest costs. With real shocks, firms' nominal interest payments are reduced in real terms by higher unanticipated inflation rates. This gain may mitigate the earnings declines that are correlated with unanticipated inflation, arising out of supply and demand shocks. Thus, firms may be able to leverage themselves to minimize profit rate declines that accompany unanticipated inflation. Because profit declines are not likely to be entirely prevented by this hedging, the real returns from equity, as well as from debt, will be inversely related to unanticipated inflation.

Raw materials' yield is directly related to real shock inflation. First, as with money shock inflation, these prices adjust quickly to shocks that derive from nonmonetary increases in aggregate demand; their yield then declines as other prices catch up. Second, supply shock inflation is likely to derive from specific sectors, and prices of raw materials in these sectors will rise more than overall prices with unanticipated inflation. In particular, internationally traded goods are, for the United States, heavy in the raw material sectors, and their prices rise relative to other prices with a supply shock that is caused by exchange rate decline.

Unanticipated Changes in the Inflation Rate

Capital markets should adjust perfectly to anticipated changes in the inflation rate through a proportionate increase in expected nominal rates of return. Rational investors should require and debtors should be willing to pay the same real rate of return regardless of the anticipated inflation rate. Thus, the value of existing nominally denominated debt instruments must fall, when a new, higher unanticipated inflation rate becomes anticipated. This creates negative distribution effects for nominally fixed-debt holders. Lenders who hold the longest term nominally fixed debt are most harmed, since the earning power of their fixed-dollar return is eroded by the unanticipated higher inflation over the longest period. Holders of short-term debt suffer a loss for only a short period. Commodity and stock investors are unaffected by this, since their return is not nominally fixed.

If the newly accelerated inflation persists and is not recognized, low real returns are earned on newly issued as well as on existing debt. If they do not recognize inflation's negative impact on real returns, equity holders also suffer lower real rates of return. Thus, money illusion may cause persistently lower real rates of return, in the presence of sustained inflation on all assets. The existence, degree, and persistence of money illusion are empirical issues, addressed in the following chapter.[6]

Increased Real and Inflation Uncertainty

Up to this point we have assumed that the risks of holding various capital market assets are unchanged in the presence of inflation. However, long-term inflation is likely to be accompanied by greater real and inflation uncertainty which raise the required rate of return. Inflation uncertainty may become sufficiently severe as to eliminate long-term nominally fixed debt completely.

Increased Real Uncertainty. If money authorities increase the long-term rate of monetary expansion in periods of increased real shocks or simply increase the money supply erratically, higher sustained inflation will accompany increased real earnings variability.[7] Political incentives may lead to these results.

Government spending may create a political cycle, and monetary authorities may respond to increased inflation with a higher rate of monetary expansion. Alternatively, monetary authorities themselves may create a political cycle. In either case, the result is a spiral with a higher variance in earnings associated with higher rates of inflation over time. There is evidence that the sustained inflation of the 1960s and 1970s in the United States did originate, in part, out of fiscal and monetary policies such as these.

Supply shocks also resulted in an increased output and earnings variance in the 1970s. The factors that cause supply-shock inflation increase the variability of output, primarily by decreasing the previously anticipated level or rate of growth of real output, thus deflecting output growth rates from their previous path.[8]

Monetary authorities are more likely to increase monetary growth in response to positive supply shocks (in an attempt to mitigate output declines) than to decrease monetary growth in response to negative supply shocks. As a result, higher levels of inflation accompany the increased earnings variance that the shocks create. Thus, innovations in the long-run money supply growth process may be determined, in part, by real shocks and correlated with the real shock's capital market effects. There is also evidence of an autoregressive monetary process, so that the previous rate of monetary growth is an important determinant of the current rate of monetary growth. If monetary expansion increases in response to shocks and a portion of that expansion is sustained over time, sustained inflation is likely to occur in periods of increased real uncertainty.[9] In sum, long-term inflation may be accompanied by increased real risk due to an increased variation in real output and profits, accompanied by long-term increases in the rate of money supply growth.

Increased Inflation Uncertainty (Money Risk). Besides a possible increase in the variance of real earnings, ongoing effects on capital markets may occur through increases in the variance of the expected inflation rate. Monetary authorities' surprising increases in the rate of monetary expansion and their tendency to ratify supply-shock inflation will increase uncertainty about future inflation rates along with actual inflation.

An increase in long-run inflation uncertainty will have its greatest impact on long-run debt instruments denominated in nominally fixed terms. This holds true because the compensating premium that must be paid varies directly with the increased money risk which itself varies (with any given increase in inflation) with the duration of nominally denominated assets. To illustrate with two extremes, a consul of $100 with a $2 ongoing annual fixed payment with zero expected inflation and 2 percent interest rate is valued at $100, as is a one-day note. If interest rates increase to 4 percent because of an increase in expected inflation to 2 percent, the consul's value declines to $50. The overnight debt is still valued at $100.

The risk is symmetrical to lenders and borrowers. As inflation rises above its anticipated rate, lenders are hurt; and as inflation falls below its anticipated rate, borrowers are hurt. Thus, both lenders and borrowers should be less willing to enter into long-term nominally fixed contracts. However, in practice, long-term debt markets adjust to increased inflation uncertainty by the increased use of call provisions. These provisions allow borrowers to repay debt before maturity, so that if inflation rates decline significantly, the borrower is not saddled with a large increase in real debt payments.[10] They also allow borrowers to continue to borrow long at higher inflation rates since without such protection both borrowers and lenders would require risk premiums. With call protection, all the money risk is on the lender's side, and the lender can be appropriately compensated with a higher risk premium.

This raises the cost of long-term funds to finance long-term investment. The required yield on acceptable long-term projects is now higher. This means that fewer long-term projects are accepted.

This decline is lessened by the existence of funding alternatives. Because substitutes are imperfect, they mitigate the decline rather than eliminate it.[11] Substitutes are equity or short-term or variable debt. Issuing short-term or variable debt is risky. Because there is uncertainty over what the real short-term interest rate will be in the future, long-term projects cannot be hedged with short-term debt or variable debt that is linked to short-term interest movement. Extra interest rate risk is taken on. Equity funding can be used without added risk, but if doing so was not optimal before, there will now be extra costs involved—all the more so because, as we saw in the previous section, the required yield on equity funds increases with higher real uncertainty.

Thus, long-term investment becomes more expensive and/or riskier. The result is that less of it is undertaken. In response to the increased risk premium on long-term debt, borrowers demand fewer long-term investment projects and more short-term investment projects. In addition, they pay increased risk premiums on both long-term and short-term debt as the latter replaces the former. Risk premiums rise on short-term debt because of increased default risk due to greater dependence on short-term debt.

While the return on long-term instruments is higher to reflect the increased risk of capital losses to lenders due to increased money and default risk, risk-averse lenders who wish a future real income stream are likely to be made worse off by the increased risk. If the long-term fixed-income instrument was used to hedge a future long-term liability of a nominally fixed payment stream, the increased inflation uncertainty has a limited negative effect that is compensated by a higher return. The long-term asset will still pay off in fixed dollars. There is increased risk because such assets will now have call protection and an increased likelihood that the asset will be called. Although other assets can then be invested in with the receipts, the asset that guarantees a 30-year fixed-payment stream may no longer exist.

Increased money risk is more troublesome if the asset was to be used to hedge liabilities fixed in real terms. If an individual desires to retire with a fixed-real-income stream, the future liability is fixed in real terms. A long-term nominally fixed debt instrument can be used as an asset to hedge that liability, if the risk of unanticipated inflation is small. In the face of inflation uncertainty, long-term nominally fixed assets provide a high real rate of return, but they can no longer be used to hedge a liability that is fixed in real terms.

Stock market shares are too volatile to do so, even absent a negative effect of inflation. Short-term interest rates and commodity returns will be likely to move in tandem with inflation rates and so can provide an income stream to hedge inflation, but they do so only at a cost to the saver who must accept a significantly lower rate of return. The cost reflects the lesser usefulness of short-term debt to the borrower who wishes to hedge a long-term investment. Thus, both the borrower and lender who wish to hedge a real income stream are made worse off by uncertain inflation.

Capital Market Effects of Inflation without Taxes: Summary

Neutral inflation, by definition, has no impact on holding period or equilibrium real rates of return. A necessary assumption, for both long- and short-run neutrality to hold, requires inflation to be anticipated before all current contracts have been negotiated.

Short-run inflation neutrality can be ruled out. Short-run inflationary spurts result from shocks and thus are unanticipated. Unanticipated inflation causes a decline in the real yield of nominally fixed assets. Shocks also result in a negative correlation of earnings growth and equity values.

Shocks that are ratified by ongoing increases in the money supply cause an unanticipated increase in the anticipated inflation rate. This lowers the value of nominal debt. Since the previously negotiated nominal interest rate is too low, asset values of existing debt decline. The loss to debt holders varies directly with the duration of the debt. Money illusion may cause continuing losses on debt and equity if the increased inflation rate is not recognized.

In the long run, rational investors should anticipate sustained inflation since it must be the result of long-run predictable excessive monetary growth. Once anticipated, inflation may have no further effects. This requires, however, no increases in inflation or real uncertainty.

Inflation risk is likely to increase with higher levels of inflation, since rational investors view past accelerations of monetary growth as revealing an increased likelihood of future accelerations, even more so if a return to zero inflation remains a possibility. Real risk is likely to increase with higher sustained inflation rates since these originate when monetary authorities respond to or initiate shocks with accelerated money supply growth. This then adds to inflation risk since such shocks and the long-run inflation that they give rise to are not predictable.

It is the violation of the no increase in uncertainty assumption that is most likely to cause the nonneutrality of inflation and abiding capital market effects. Higher long-term inflation rates can only be reached with increased long-term money supply growth rates. There would be no gain to monetary authorities or purpose for these increases unless these growth rates were not anticipated. Thus, higher levels of inflation are likely to be the result of previous unanticipated increases in money supply growth rates, which result in increased expectations of such future changes. Monetary authorities may be disposed to unanticipated money supply accelerations either because they respond passively to real shocks with money supply increases in order to dampen the negative output effects of these shocks or because they actively accelerate money growth to create positive output effects, perhaps, to create a political cycle. These short-run accelerations are then likely to be followed by continued growth of the money supply at the new rate (or at a rate that somewhat exceeds the old rate) to avoid the negative output dislocations of decreasing money supply growth once a new money growth rate and a new long-run inflation rate become anticipated. Markets anticipate this monetary policy and recognize that long-run inflation prediction is now more difficult. The result is increased inflation uncertainty.

With increased uncertainty over future rates, hedging inflation becomes more important for those who wish to save for future real income needs. Nominal pensions are the exact opposite of an inflation hedge. If inflation were to rise, these nominal dollars would buy less. Indexed pensions are not feasible since there are no perfect hedges to fund such pensions.

Even though no asset is a perfect hedge, returns on short-term debt and commodities move closely with inflation and so can provide an income stream to hedge inflation. They do so, however, at a cost to the saver who must accept a significantly lower rate of return on earnings and, thus, must save commensurately more to achieve a given retirement income.

Inflation's Effects with Taxes

The previous discussion concerns the effects of inflation on asset yields in a world without taxes. To analyze tax effects we assume that inflation results from neutral fully anticipated money supply expansion and that any wealth-shift effect is insignificant. Thus, we assume that inflation has no impact on capital markets in the absence of taxes. A discussion of tax effects due to interest deductibility, capital gains taxation, and the use of historical cost accounting is presented in the next three sections, respectively. The effects deriving from the federal income taxation of nominal interest rates are discussed in the last section.

The Interest Deductibility Effect

To discuss the impact of inflation on real rates of return through what is termed the *interest deductibility effect,* first assume that the firm is financed entirely by debt and then extend the analysis to the equity financed firm. To illustrate the impact of this effect, use a simple numerical example. The example is first developed under the benchmark case of no taxes and then is developed to indicate the effect of taxes.

The Debt-Financed Firm in a World without Taxes. Consider a world without taxes where the inflation rate is 10 percent per period, and the real rate of interest is 1 percent, implying that the nominal rate of interest is approximately 11 percent.[12] We focus on an investment where a firm purchases a nondepreciating machine at date zero for $1,000. We also assume that at any date, the real cash flows are equal to the real interest rate times the initial investment. For example, the machine yields a cash flow of $1,000 × 1% × 1.10 = $11 on the first date. Had there been no inflation over the first period, the cash flow would have only been $1,000 × 1% = $10. The cash flow on the second date would be $1,000 × 1% × $(1.10)^2$ = $12.10. As we will see below, the example has been constructed so that this investment is marginal. The cash flows generated by the machine are examined in more detail below and are summarized in Table 4–1. We assume initially that the $1,000 investment is financed solely by debt. Here, interest costs at date 1 are $111, a number far exceeding the cash flow of only $11. The $100 deficit can be financed by additional borrowing. It appears as though the project is losing money. This first impression is reinforced by the operation on the second date. Here, since total debt is $1,100, interest costs are $1,100 × 11.1% = $122.10. As pointed out earlier, cash flow at date 2 is only $12.10, yielding a deficit of $122.10 − 12.10 = $110, to be financed by further borrowing.

TABLE 4–1
Example under Debt Financing

Date	*1*	*2*	*3*	*t*
Cash Flows in a World without Taxes				
Cash flow from machine	$1,000 × 1% × 1.10 = $11	$1,000 × 1% × $(1.10)^2$ = $12.10	$1,000 × 1% × $(1.10)^3$ = $13.31	$1,000 × 1% × $(1.10)^t$
Interest payable	$1,000 × 11.1% = $111	$1,100 × 11.1% = $122.10	$1,210 × 11.1% = $134.31	$1,000$(1.10)^{t-1}$ × 11.1%
New borrowing (interest payable minus cash flow)	$111 − 11 = $100	$122.10 − 12.10 = $110	$134.31 − 13.31 = $121	100(1.10)^{t-1}$
Cash Flow in a World with Taxes				
Taxable income (or loss)	($100)	($110)	($121)	$100 × $(1.10)^{t-1}$
Tax subsidy assuming 50 percent tax bracket	$50	$55	$60.50	$50 × $(1.10)^{t-1}$

However, once capital appreciation is taken into account, one can see that the machine's value rises to \$1,100 by date 1 and to \$1,230 by date 2, implying that the equity position stays at zero. This analysis can be extended to date 6, where the firm's debt is (\$1,000)(1.10)^t, a value just equal to the value of the machine at that date.

Since the equity position is always equal to zero, we have shown that, in a world without taxes but with inflation, an investment whose real rate is equal to the real rate of interest is of no value to the firm (i.e., the cutoff rate is the real interest rate). This result will now be contrasted with the findings under taxes.

The Debt-Financed Firm in a World with Taxes. The corporation's taxable income is cash flow minus interest payments. Therefore, the taxable income for the project is \$11 − 111 = −\$100 at date 1 and is \$12.10 − 122.10 = −\$110 at date 2. Note that a loss is reported each period on the machine. Given that earnings are positive for the rest of the firm, the firm's total taxes will be reduced should the machine be employed. While the project would be of no value to the firm without taxes, it now is valuable since it reduces the company's total taxes. In other words, the introduction of taxes spurs debt-financed investment in an inflationary environment.

In essence, the firm gets a tax subsidy on interest deductions during inflationary periods because it can deduct the entire nominal rate of interest of 11.1 percent. However, it is not forced to declare the capital gain of 10 percent on the machine. Due to the lack of symmetry, the cutoff rate (as expressed as a function of the real interest rate) falls as the rate of inflation increases. The net result is to shift the after-tax demand for capital curve to the right as shown in Figure 4–1. Given the rightward shift in the investment schedule, nominal and real rates of return rise.

We can also relate cash flows to earnings in an inflationary environment, a task which our example simplifies. We see in Table 4–1 that earnings after interest must fall when the rate of inflation rises. However, we showed earlier that for a constant real rate of interest, the present value of the cash flow must increase with inflation. Thus, our debt-financed firm with no depreciable assets is improved by inflation although stockholders may believe that the firm has been hurt.

FIGURE 4–1
Shift in the After-Tax Demand for Capital with Increased Inflation Due to the Interest Deductibility Effect

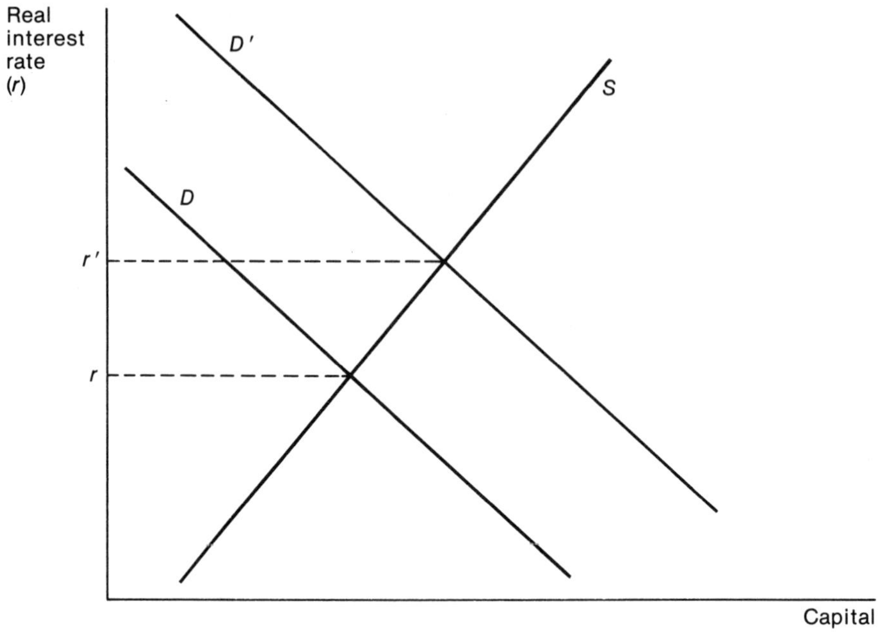

The same effect is responsible for the appreciation of real estate in an inflationary economy. While interest is fully deductible, the appreciation on the house generally goes untaxed. Like any other asset, capital gains are not recognized by the IRS prior to a sale. Also, due to various rollover provisions, an individual pays no tax if another house is bought within 18 months following the sale of the original dwelling.

In summary, inflation increases the investment demand of debt-financed firms, thus driving up the real rate of interest. As the following section indicates, this benefit does not accrue to an all-equity firm, so that the real rate of interest will not rise with inflation if all firms are equity financed without depreciable assets.

The Equity-Financed Firm in a World without Inflation. To illustrate the dependence of the above effect on debt financing we consider the case where a $1,000 investment is financed by equity. In a world without inflation, let us now consider a machine yielding pre-tax cash flow at each date of $20. If the corporation tax rate is 50 percent, the after-tax cash flow is $10. These cash flows are presented in Table 4–2.

If the interest rate is 1 percent and there are no personal taxes, the firm is indifferent between accepting and rejecting the project. That is, a new equity investor raising $1,000 must be promised an after-tax return of $10 per date, leaving no cash runoff from the machine for the firm's original stockholders. Note that, with equity capital, the project is marginal when pre-tax cash flows are $20 per date, while only $10 of pre-tax flow is needed for the debt-financed example of the previous section. This occurs, of course, because the interest payments to debt holders reduce corporate taxable income, while any payments to stockholders are not deductible. Thus, in keeping with the work of Modigliani-Miller and others, our examples show that the cost of equity capital is higher than the cost of debt capital in a world with taxes.[13]

The numbers in the example would be changed slightly if we included a personal tax of, say, 50 percent. Here, an individual with $1,000 would be indifferent between (1) putting the money in the bank, yielding a pre-tax income of $10 and an after-tax income of $5, or (2) forming a corporation in order to purchase a machine where the pre-tax and after-tax cash flows are $10 and $5, respectively. Note that with a personal tax rate of 50 percent the machine becomes marginal with precorporate tax income of $10, while it is marginal with precorporate tax income of $20 in a world with no personal tax.

The Capital Gains Tax Effect

To consider the effect of a capital gains tax in a world with inflation, we assume that the corporate tax rate is 50 percent but that the personal tax rate is zero, in an equity financed firm in a world with inflation. If the inflation rate is now 10 percent, pre-tax cash flows at dates 1, 2, and t will be $22, $24.20 and ($20)$(1.10)^t$, respectively. The after-tax cash flows are $11, $12.10 and ($10)$(1.10)^t$. While the after-tax cash flows have risen with inflation, the real cash flows have not been affected by changes in the price level. The figures are presented in

TABLE 4–2
Example under Equity Financing

Date	1	2	3	t
		Cash Flows in a World without Inflation		
Pre-tax cash flow from machine	$1,000 × 2% = $20	$20	$20	$20
Post-tax cash flow from machine	$20/2 = $10	$10	$10	$10
		Cash Flows with 10 Percent Inflation		
Pre-tax cash flow from machine	$1,000 × 2% × (1.10) = $22	$1,000 × 2% × $(1.10)^2$ = $24.20	$1,000 × 2% × $(1.10)^3$ = $26.62	$20 × $(1.10)^t$
Post-tax cash flow from machine	$22/2 = $11	$24.20/2 = $12.10	$26.62/2 = $13.31	$10 × $(1.10)^t$
Real value of cash flow from machine	$11/1.10 = $10	$12.10/$(1.1)^2$ = $10	$13.31/$(1.1)^3$ = $10	$10 × $(1.10)^t/(1.10)^t$ = $10

FIGURE 4–2
Shift in the After-Tax Demand for Capital with Increased Inflation Due to the Historical Cost Accounting Effect or to the Taxation of Capital Gains

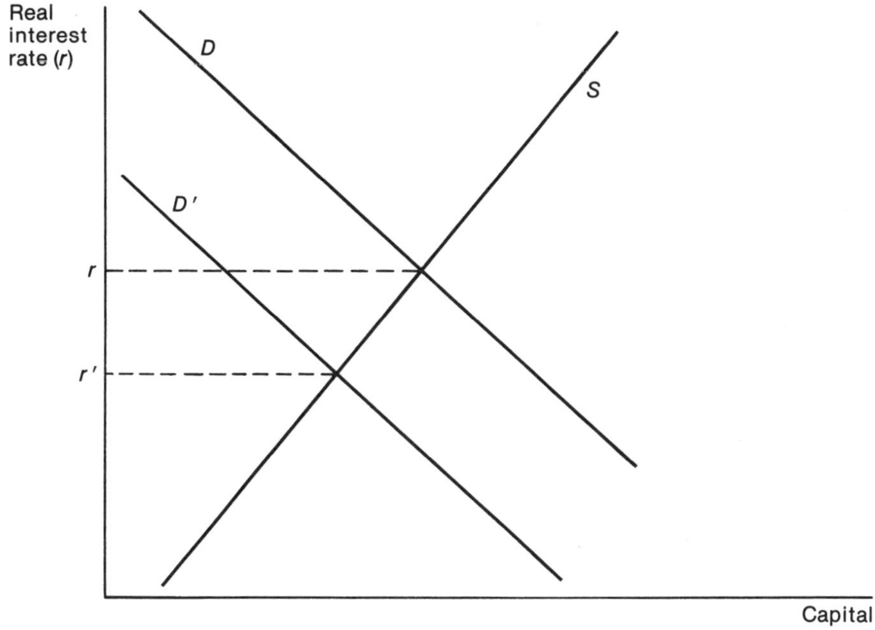

2. Thus the project, which was marginal in a world without inflation, stays marginal in a world with inflation. This implies that the level of real investment is not a function of the inflation rate and, hence, the pre-tax real rate of interest can be expected to be invariant to anticipated changes in the price level.

Inflation would influence the level of real investment only if a tax were applied to capital gains. Since the value of the machine would stay at $1,000 in a no-inflation world, no capital gains would be recognized when the asset was sold. However, in an inflationary environment, the value of the asset would be ($1,000)$(1.10)^t$ for any date t. Capital gains of ($1,000)$[(1.10)^t - 1)]$ would be recognized upon sale of the asset at date t. Therefore, in a capital gains tax world, a machine that is marginal if held to eternity becomes less than marginal if sold prematurely. The result is that, with capital gains taxation, the after-tax demand curve for capital shifts to the left, and the after-tax rate of return on investment declines, as shown in Figure 4–2.

The Historical Cost Accounting Effect

In this section we consider the impact of the use of historical cost accounting, first for depreciable assets and then for inventories on real rates of return in a world with anticipated inflation.

Depreciable Assets. To demonstrate the impact of the use of historical cost accounting on depreciable assets, we use the following example. Imagine a firm in a no-inflation world purchasing for $300 an asset which yields a pre-tax cash flow of $105 per year. The asset fully depreciates via straight line in three years. Each year, pre-tax earnings are equal to Cash Flow − Depreciation = $105 − 100 = $5, implying after-tax earnings of $2.50, and an after-tax cash flow of $2.50 + 100 = $102.50. These numbers are presented in Table 4–3. With an interest rate of 1 percent, the present value of the investment is zero.

Table 4–3 also presents the figures in a world with a 10 percent inflation. Here, pre-tax cash flows at date t are ($105)(1.10)^t, yielding after-tax cash flows of $107.75, $113.525, and $119.88 for the three dates. If the company employs a discount rate of 1 percent in a no-inflation world, it should use one of 11.1% = [(1.01)(1.10) − 1] in an inflationary world, given that the real rate is invariant to inflation. The bottom of Table 4–3 shows that the present value of the project is negative, indicating that a project which is marginal under constant prices is of negative value when prices rise.

The explanation is quite simple. Pre-tax flows are assumed to rise with increases in the price level. Thus, the present value of these pre-tax flows is invariant to the rate of inflation. However, the depreciation of $100 per year is not changed by inflation, implying that the present value of the depreciation deductions is negatively related to the inflation rate. Since after-tax cash flows are a function of (1) pre-tax cash flows that rise with inflation and (2) depreciation deductions that do not increase with inflation, these after-tax cash flows do not quite keep pace with the rate of inflation.

The above discussion does not imply that inflation alone reduces corporate investment, since we see above that the present value of pre-tax cash flow is invariant to price level changes.

TABLE 4–3
Cash Flows from Depreciable Asset

No Inflation

Date			
Pre-tax cash flows	$105.	$105.	$105.
− Depreciation	−100.	−100.	−100.
Pre-tax earnings	5.	5.	5.
− Taxes	−2.50	−2.50	−2.50
After-tax earnings	2.50	2.50	2.50
+ Depreciation	+100.	+100.	+100.
After-tax cash flow	$102.50	$102.50	$102.50

$$PV = -\$300 + \frac{\$102.50}{1.01}$$

Inflation of 10 Percent

Date			
Pre-tax cash flows	$115.50	$127.05	$139.76
− Depreciation	−100.	−100.	−100.
Pre-tax earnings	15.50	27.05	39.76
− Taxes	−7.75	−13.525	−19.88
After-tax earnings	7.75	13.525	19.88
+ Depreciation	+100.	+100.	+100.
After-tax cash flow	$107.75	$113.525	$119.88

$$IV = -\$300 = \frac{\$107.75}{1.111} + \frac{\$113.525}{(1.111)^2} + \frac{\$119.88}{(1.111)^3} - \$20.72$$

Rather, the investment reduction is caused by the relationship between inflation and taxes. Note that taxes at date 1 rise from the no-inflation case of $2.50 to the inflation case of $7.75—an increase of 210 percent. As a result, the after-tax demand curve for capital shifts to the left, and the after-tax rate of return on investment declines, as illustrated in Figure 4–2.

The above results do not hold with the use of replacement cost accounting for depreciation. Here, depreciation would be related to the current value of the asset, rather than its historical cost. For example, with an inflationary regime of 10 percent, the replacement cost of an undepreciated asset would be $300 at the end of the first year. This yields a first-year depreciation of $110, which is greater than the historical cost depreciation of $100. It can easily be shown that the present value of the asset would rise from −$20.72 to zero if replacement cost accounting were allowed for tax purposes.

However, for corporations, replacement cost depreciation is not allowed for tax purposes, although the tax code has been liberalized in ways that substitute for replacement cost depreciation. Accelerated depreciation methods were introduced in 1954. Investment tax credits were first permitted in 1962 and have been liberalized in recent years. Depreciation schedules for certain assets permit premature full write-offs. For example, buildings generally have a 40- to 50-year life while these structures may still be functioning, say, 200 years from now. But the Tax Recovery Act of 1982 allows companies to depreciate buildings in 15 years, equipment in 5 years, and cars in 3 years. Though depreciation schedules are now more generous than ever before, most economists argue that this liberalization falls short of replacement cost depreciation. Nonetheless, the negative impact of historical cost accounting and inflation on profits has been to a considerable extent undone, and in some cases reversed.

The above discussion has argued that the use of historical cost depreciation by an all-equity-financed firm reduces investment for a constant real rate. Thus, the real interest rate tends to fall in an inflationary environment to coax out investment. This result must be contrasted with debt-financed firms without depreciable assets. These firms will increase investment during inflationary periods if the real rate remains constant. Thus, the real rate will rise with the rate of inflation for an economy composed of only this type of firm. Of course, we know that the real world is composed of various combinations of the two types of firms. Some employ all-equity, some use all-debt, and some have a mixed capital structure. Similarly, the assets of some firms are primarily nondepreciable (e.g., land). Because of this, the real rate has tendencies to both rise and fall with the inflation rate.

Inventories. The previous example concerns the negative effect of inflation on the worth of depreciable assets. Below is a discussion of the effect of inflation on the worth of inventories.

Imagine a world without inflation where a firm raises $100 of

TABLE 4–4
Example of Cash Flow and Profit with and without Inflation

	No Inflation	*Inflation of 10 Percent*
Sale price on December 31	$112	$123.20
Purchase price on January 1	−100	−100.00
Pre-tax profit	12	23.20
Taxes	− 6	− 11.60
After-tax profit	$ 6	$ 11.60

Free Cash Flow under Inflation

$123.20	Sale price on December 31
− 11.60	Taxes
−110.00	Replacement cost of inventory on next January 1
$ 1.60	Free cash flow

equity capital. These funds are used to purchase inventory on January 1. This inventory is sold for $112 on December 31, implying an inventory holding period of 365 days. If we ignore all other expenses of the firm, pre-tax profit is $112 − $100 = $12. With a corporate tax rate of 50 percent, profit after taxes is $6. These figures are presented in Table 4–4. This profit of $6 is repeated year after year in a steady state economy and can be paid out to investors as dividends. That is, of the $112 received at the end of the year, $6 goes to taxes, $100 is used to repurchase new inventory, and the remaining $6 is free cash flow.

Now, imagine that a yearly inflation rate of 10 percent begins on January 1 of a particular year. If all prices in the economy rise at this rate, the inventories can be sold at $112 × 1.10 = $123.20 on December 31. Since the cost of the inventory purchased on January 1 is still $100, the reported pre-tax profit is $123.10 − $100 = $23.20, leaving a profit after taxes of $11.60.

Though this net profit of $11.60 is reported in the financial statements, it is *not* meaningfully related to the firm's cash flow. The firm must buy new inventory for $110 on the following January 1, implying that free cash flow, *after* the purchase of new inventory, is only $1.60. This number is calculated in the bottom half of Table 4–4. In other words, the maximum dividend should be $1.60 in an inflationary world, while the maximum dividend should be $6.00 in a noninflationary world.

The key to this example is taxes. Revenues and cost of goods sold rise at the annual inflation rate of 10 percent. Selling, general, and administrative costs would also rise at the inflation rate had we included them in our example. However, the firm is worse off under inflation because taxes increase by 93⅓ percent from $6 to $11.60. Note that under inflation the firm is taxed on the total appreciation of inventory from $100 to $123.20. However, only the increase from $100 to $112 can be viewed as real economic gain above and beyond inflation. The further increase from $112 to $123.20 is merely appreciation due to inflation. Thus, firms experience tax on the gain due to inflation, a term accountants call an *illusory holding period gain*.

The above case was constructed to present the impact of inflation on inventories in the strongest possible light. For example, inflation affects a company with an inventory holding period of 365 days more than it affects a company with a more normal holding period of, say, one or two months. Similarly, the last-in, first-out (LIFO) inventory valuation method, which was not used in our example, can reduce inflation's painful effects somewhat.

However, as with the depreciable assets case, the adverse implications of inflation can be eliminated only if replacement cost accounting is allowed for tax purposes. Here, income and free cash flow under inflation are calculated as:

Sales	$123.20
Less replacement cost of inventory	−110.00
Pre-tax profit	13.20
Less taxes	− 6.60
After-tax profit and free cash flow	6.60

Note that the free cash flow of $6.60 is 10 percent greater than it is in the no-inflation case, implying that the real free cash flow is the same in both cases. Of course, as mentioned earlier, replacement cost accounting is not allowed for tax purposes at the present time.

The above results show that the after-tax earnings of an all-equity firm with inventories are hurt by inflation. With historical tax accounting, the after-tax demand curve for capital shifts to the left, and the after-tax rate of return on investment declines, as shown in Figure 4–2. Capital gains taxation adds to this effect. However, these effects are mitigated for the firm with debt. The negative effects of inflation may be offset by the tax advantages to debt financing under inflation. The combined effects of historical tax accounting, capital gains taxation, and debt financing on the real interest rate depend on the magnitudes of the rightward and leftward demand curve shifts, shown in Figures 4–1 and 4–2, respectively. Thus, the net impact of the interaction of inflation and the corporate tax structure on the real interest rate is indeterminate, without empirical evidence.

Federal Income Taxation of Nominal Interest Rates

While the firm gains from higher inflation due to the full deductibility of higher nominal interest payments, investors are hurt by the full federal income taxation of nominal interest rates. The effect of the interaction between inflation and the federal income taxation of nominal interest rates is shown in Table 4–5. Assuming no inflation, a 50 percent federal income tax bracket, and a nominal and real interest rate of 1 percent at the end of the first period, the pre-tax wealth is \$101, and the after-tax wealth is \$100.50. With an inflation rate of 10 percent, the nominal interest rate rises to 11 percent. The end-of-period pre-tax wealth is now \$111. The investor is fully compensated for the 10 percent decline in the value of the dollar with a 10 percent increase in nominal wealth. Thus, the end-of-period real wealth is unchanged by inflation. However, the 50 percent tax rate reduces the post-tax nominal wealth to \$105.50, which in real terms is approximately equal to \$95.50, given the 10 percent inflation. In order to preserve the same real post-tax end-of-period wealth with a 10 percent inflation rate as without, the 50 percent tax bracket investor would have to require a nominal return of 21 percent, as shown in the third row of Table 4–5.

To generalize the above for an average tax bracket of β, interest rates will have to rise by $1(1 - \beta)$ for each one-point increase in the inflation rate to compensate savers for the federal income taxation of nominal interest rates. To accomplish this, the savings function shifts backwards, as shown in Figures 4–3a and 4–3b. The effect of the backwards shift depends on the interest elas-

TABLE 4–5
Interaction between Inflation and Taxes

Inflation Rate	*Nominal Interest Rate*	*End-of-Period Pre-Tax Wealth*	*End-of-Period Post-Tax Wealth*	*Real End-of-Period Post-Tax Wealth*
0%	1%	$101	$100.50	$100.50
10	11	111	105.50	~ 95.50
10	21	121	110.50	~ 100.50

ticity of the savings function, as shown by the slopes of the curve in Figures 4–3. With an infinitely elastic curve, as in Figure 4–3a, the interest rate rises by the full amount of the upward shift. With a less than fully elastic savings function, this effect is reduced but not undone, as in Figure 4–3b.

Capital Market Effects of Inflation through Taxes: Summary

The sum of the historical cost accounting, capital gains taxation, and interest deductibility effects on the after-tax rate of return on capital is unknown since the last counters the first two effects. The net impact is an empirical issue, which is addressed in detail in the following chapter. To anticipate the conclusion of that discussion, these effects probably do counterbalance each other with little net impact of inflation on after-tax corporate yields, especially with the liberalization in depreciation rules implemented by the Economic Recovery Tax Act of 1981.

Federal income tax effects have an obvious negative impact on after-tax yields of taxable investment returns. Here too, however, the net impact on overall rates of return is unclear. Higher anticipated inflation rates raise nominal yields. Higher nominal yields represent early repayment of principal. Thus, higher anticipated inflation leads to federal income taxation of early repayment of principal, which raises the effective tax rate on the real yield and lowers the after-tax rate of return. However, investors can avoid this result by channeling more savings into tax-exempt investments, such as pensions or housing and equities (which are only subject to capital gains taxation upon sale). Thus, these shifts are an expected outcome of the interaction of inflation with the federal income tax.

FIGURE 4–3
Shift in the Supply of Savings with Increased Inflation Due to the Federal Income Taxation of Nominal Interest Rates

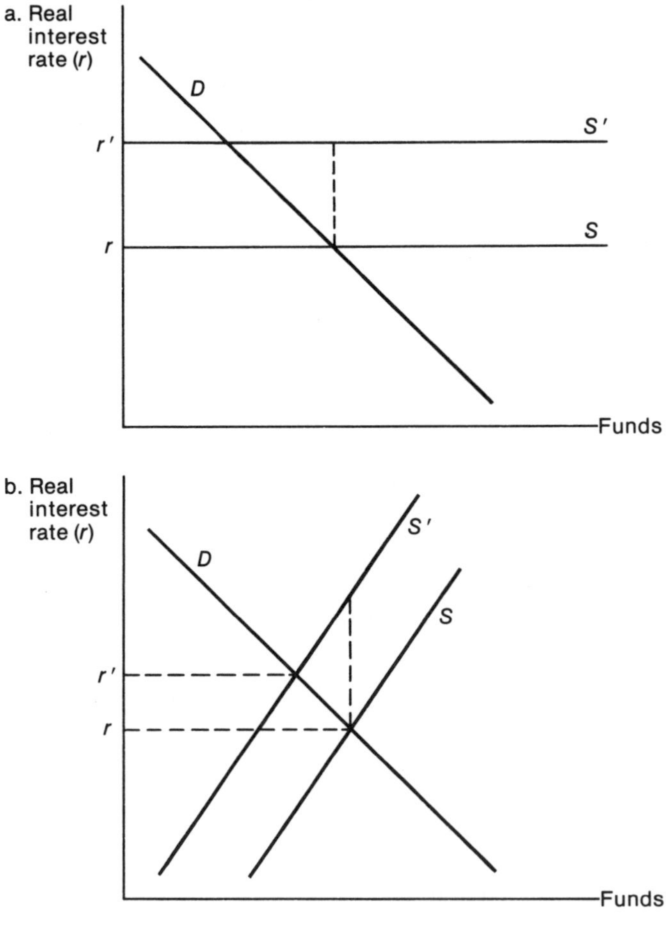

To the extent that capital can be shifted into tax-exempt forms of savings, the after-tax rate of return will not fall as much, since those investors who continue to save in nontax-exempt instruments will tend to have lower tax brackets. However, limits of various sorts are placed on these shifts. Some decline in after-tax rates of return may then persist unless savings are interest-elastic, in which case before-tax interest rates rise as savings decline. If not, the only effects of inflation's interaction with taxes are shifts to tax-exempt instruments and lower rates of return than otherwise on taxable investments.

APPENDIX 4.A
Neutral Inflation's Lack of Real Impact

With long-run neutrality, all yields are adjusted upwards by the expected inflation rate, so that real yields are unchanged by the level of the expected inflation rate. We show this separately for bonds, commodities, stocks, and the underlying value of the firm's plant and equipment.

To illustrate the lack of real impact on bonds, suppose short-term government securities (i.e., Treasury bills) are expected to pay interest at a real rate of $E(r_f)$ equal to the nominal rate of $E(R_f)$, in the absence of inflation. The real rate of interest is a function of production possibilities for the economy and individuals' rates of time preference. In equilibrium, it equals the marginal productivity of capital. Thus, real factors determine $E(r_f)$. Now let us examine what happens when inflation is equal to the expected rate $\dot{P}_e$. In this case, borrowers and lenders expect inflation next period to be $\dot{P}_e$. Assuming that there are no other changes in the economy, lenders will require and borrowers will be willing to pay (approximately) an expected nominal interest rate $E(R_f)$ equal to $E(r_f)$ plus $\dot{P}_e$. Therefore (in constant purchasing power), they will still expect to earn and to pay $E(r_f)$ net of inflation.

More precisely, if a nominally denominated instrument is expected to be worth $(1 + r_f)$ multiplied by the amount of the principal in a year, with an anticipated change in the price level of $(1 + \dot{P}_e)$, a rational lender would require and a rational borrower would be willing to pay the principal multiplied by

$$1 + E(R_f) = [1 + E(r_f)](1 + \dot{P}_e) = 1 + E(r_f) + \dot{P}_e + E(r_f)\dot{P}_e$$

which, for small $E(r_f)$ and $\dot{P}_e$, is approximated by

$$1 + E(R_f) = 1 + E(r_f) + \dot{P}_e$$

as above.

TABLE 4–6
An Inflation-Neutral 10-Year Bond (2 percent real return)

0 Percent Inflation Pay for Bond $100 in Period:			*100 Percent Inflation Pay for Bond $100 in Period:*		
Period	*Value of Bond*	*Coupon*	*Period*	*Value of Bond*	*Coupon*
0	$100	0	0	$ 100	0
1	100	2	1	200	4
2	100	2	2	400	8
3	100	2	3	800	16
4	100	2	4	1,600	32
5	100	2	5	3,200	64
6	100	2	6	6,400	128
7	100	2	7	12,800	256
8	100	2	8	25,600	512
9	100	2	9	51,200	1,024
10	Principal + coupon	102	10	Principal + coupon	104,448

The adjustment of the nominal return on Treasury bills to neutral inflation is repeated for all debt instruments. In the absence of inflation, the expected holding period return on a long-term government bond, $E(R_g)$, is likely to be greater than the return on bills, because the probability of capital gains or losses (due to a change in interest rates) increases with the maturity and duration of a bond.[14] Furthermore, the expected holding period return on corporate bonds, $E(R_c)$, should exceed the holding period return on government bonds to compensate for the extra default risk.[15] With an expected inflation rate of $\dot{P}_e$, the expected nominal holding period returns on long-term government and corporate bonds also adjust upwards by $\dot{P}_e$. As a result, the expected real and relative rates of return on these assets are unchanged.

It should be noted that if inflation is neutral, both principal and interest payments of a bond rise by the expected inflation rate, $\dot{P}_e$, so that the bond's maturity and duration are unaffected by inflation. Table 4–6 illustrates an inflation-neutral 10-year bond, with a 2 percent real rate of return, without inflation and with a 100 percent inflation rate. In contrast to this, an instrument whose interest payments alone (coupon) are adjusted upwards to yield the expected inflation rate plus the real rate would pay in nominal terms, 104 percent, at the end of the first year; and the debt would be repaid in 1 year rather than 10. Although the results are far less extreme with single-digit inflation, the duration of any bond whose coupon alone is adjusted upwards to reflect the deterioration in the principal (so that the outstanding principal declines in real terms) is shortened with inflation. Thus, with neutral inflation both the principal and the interest rate are increased by $\dot{P}_e$ in each period.

The expected return from holding real assets is similarly invariant to neutral long-run inflation. Assume that a commodity, such as gold, is a means of storing wealth that is expected to yield a zero real rate of return. The price of gold will rise with the general price level. Thus, it will be expected to yield a nominal return of $\dot{P}_e$, but in real terms the expected return will still be zero. The prices of gold and other commodities, including real estate, adjust upwards with neutral inflation. Relative prices change with shifts in the underlying factors that determine supply and demand, but no more or less than they would in the absence of neutral inflation.

Expected stock yields are also unaffected. In symbols assume, for the purpose of simplicity, a pure equity firm that distributes all its earnings as dividends. Without inflation, the present market price of the stock, P_0, is determined by its expected constant stream of (real and nominal) dividends, D, and the expected (real and nominal) interest rate, $E(r)$, so that:

$$P_0 = \frac{D}{E(r)}$$

With an anticipated inflation rate of $\dot{P}_e$, dividends will increase by $\dot{P}_e$ each year, so that the price of the stock will also increase by $\dot{P}_e$, each year,

$$P_0\,(1 + \dot{P}_e) = \frac{D(1 + \dot{P}_e)}{E(r)}$$

and the expected real rate of return, $E(r)$, will remain unchanged, since

$$E(r) = \frac{D(1 + \dot{P}_e)}{P_0\,(1 + \dot{P}_e)}$$

We have assumed long-run neutrality so that inflation is anticipated. As a result, expected real rates of return are unchanged. As we will see in the next section, in the short-run random shocks will cause actual real rates of return to deviate from expected real rates of return. If the variance (the probability distribution) of these random shocks is unchanged, then expected rates of return remain invariant to inflation. As a result, inflation is neutral in the long run but not in the short run. For short-run neutrality there can be no shocks. If such (a most unrealistic) condition holds, the real return on all assets always equals the expected return. Thus, for short- and long-run neutrality all inflation is anticipated, and the real return on nominal instruments is not affected by inflation, in the short or long run. Short-run inflationary episodes can occur due to shocks without violating long-run inflation neutrality as long as shocks are no greater with or without expected inflation. Long- and short-run neutrality are illustrated in Figure 4–4 (see p. 150).

APPENDIX 4.B
Money Shock Effects: Liquidity, Distribution, and Correlated Real Earnings Effects

Economic theory indicates that unexpected changes in the money supply will have a series of short-term real effects on markets. In Chapter 1, an unanticipated increase (decrease) in the money supply was shown to increase (decrease) aggregate real output and employment and to affect relative prices across sectors temporarily. Capital markets are affected by money shocks through liquidity and distribution effects.[16]

Figure 4–5 illustrates the excess liquidity effect of a positive money shock. Assuming zero inflation and zero inflationary expectations, D_1 and S_1 indicate the demand for and supply of money at the original price level, P_1.

The supply of money increases from S_1 to S_2, but because the increase is unanticipated and prices do not immediately adjust, the demand for money does not immediately increase. Thus, the increase in the supply of money depresses the equilibrium (ex ante) real interest rate, r, from the equilibrium real rate, r_e, to r_0.

FIGURE 4–4
Neutral Inflation's Impact on the Bond Market

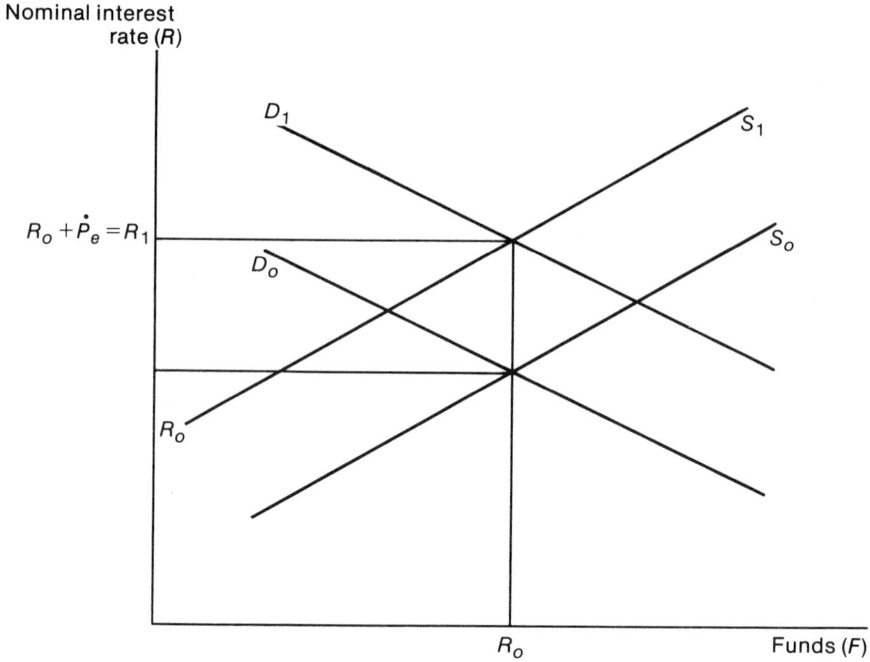

Lower than equilibrium interest rates may persist for some time. Pervasive explicit and implicit price contracts prevent monetary increases from having a full immediate impact on the price level.[17] Eventually, however, the excessive money supply bids up the price level. At the new price level, P_2, the demand for money increases by the percentage increase in the money supply. Money supply no longer exceeds demand. As shown in Figure 4–5, D_1 shifts to D_2, and the result is that the real (and nominal) interest rate returns to its original level, r_e. The result of a negative money shock is the reverse of the above. The real interest rate climbs, due to a liquidity shortage, until the price level declines to reestablish the original equilibrium.

Money shocks may also have a short-run liquidity (lagged price) effect on the return from holding commodities, such as gold. Because commodity prices are likely to adjust more rapidly

FIGURE 4–5
Inflation Due to Unanticipated Money Supply Growth: The Excess Liquidity Effect

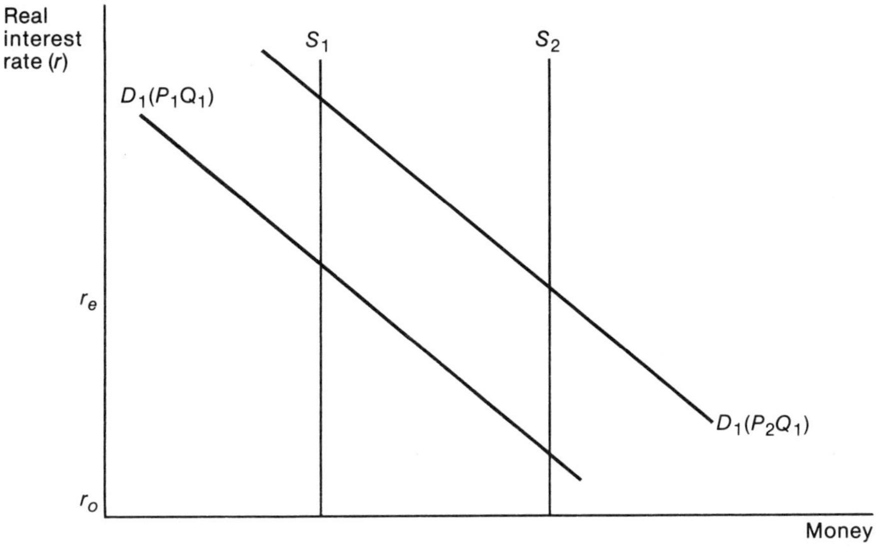

than other prices, in the short run the price of a commodity such as gold will rise faster and then slower than the general price level after a positive money shock. Thus, assuming gold yields zero real return in the absence of unanticipated inflation, it may yield a positive return for a period before the general price level adjusts upwards, at which point the holding period return is no longer affected.

The short-run impact of unanticipated money supply growth on output and profits is also positive since sales and capacity utilization will increase, although the results will vary with the industry. Again, those sectors whose prices adjust relatively rapidly (if their costs do not) will gain while others will lose in the short run. Overall, however, a short-run positive impact on earnings, and consequently on stock values, may be expected due to a lag in wages and increased labor productivity. In addition, the interest rate decline may raise stock values. As prices begin to increase, however, the positive impact on stock values reverses itself. The inflation signals that previous profit increases are not sustainable (i.e., that they were merely an artifact due to lags in price and wage adjustments). In addition, interest rates rise again to their original levels. Thus, unanticipated money supply growth may be correlated with stock market value increases and the resulting unanticipated inflation with stock market value declines.[18] Essentially, the inverse correlation of earnings with inflation results from the quantity theory relationship combined with price and wage lags. A money shock has an immediate positive impact on output (not prices). When prices accelerate in response to excess aggregate conditions, output growth decelerates. Thus, the earnings and inflation outcomes of a money shock are inversely related. As a result of the liquidity effect, nominal debt and equity holders find their short-run real rate of return inversely related to inflation.

The second short-run impact of money shocks is on the real value of assets that are denominated in nominal terms. We term this the unanticipated inflation distribution effect since it redistributes wealth away from holders of cash and from lenders to borrowers.

To illustrate, consider the impact of a price level increase of $\dot{P}_0$ on bonds. With the maintained assumptions that neither $\dot{P}_e$ nor $\sigma_{\dot{P}_e}$ change, the nominal return remains R. However, because it is a nominal "fixed-income" instrument, the bond's purchasing power (or constant dollar value) declines by $\dot{P}_0$. Thus, its real return is $(R - \dot{P}_0)$. Lenders lose and borrowers gain as a result of unanticipated inflation since payments fixed in nominal terms decrease in real terms with a price level rise.

Holders of cash suffer similar distribution effects from an unanticipated increase in the price level or in inflation, unless they are compensated by the way in which the increased money supply is distributed.

Stock prices are also affected by unanticipated inflation through both these distribution effects. Net debtor firms can repay borrowings with depreciated dollars and, thus, gain from unanticipated inflation, while firms that are net lenders lose. In addition, firms, as individuals, suffer losses through the decline in their value of cash balances.

APPENDIX 4.C
Real Shock Effects: Correlated Short-Run Effects

Real shocks are divided, in the following, into aggregate demand and supply shocks. The unanticipated inflation that these shocks (of either origin) cause is likely to be associated with declines in profit growth rates. In addition, the unanticipated inflation causes distribution effects that harm holders of nominal assets. Liquidity effects vary. Demand shocks will be associated with higher interest rates, while supply shocks may be associated with higher or lower interest rates, depending on their source.

Aggregate Demand Shocks

The liquidity effects of an aggregate demand shock are the reverse of those of a money shock. An aggregate demand shock increases output initially and then prices. This raises the demand for money. (See Chapter 1 for a fuller discussion.) As illustrated in Figure 4–6, the real interest rate climbs from r to r_0. Increased real interest rates and asset yields allow a onetime price level increase to persist.[19] But they also result in a decline in the asset value of outstanding debt; similarly, equity values decrease in response to higher interest rates. Furthermore, for all firms, whether net debtors or lenders, due to lagging prices and the quantity theory relationship the demand shock is likely to result first in increased earnings growth, then in a decline in earnings growth as prices adjust to the increased aggregate demand. Thus, as with money shock inflation, equity holders find their returns inversely related to demand shock inflation. Earnings may also be negatively affected by the demand shock. Higher interest rates raise borrowing costs for net debtor firms with short-term debt, while those with long-term debt gain by the higher inflation, which reduces real interest cost.

FIGURE 4–6
Exogenous Spending Increase's Effect on the Real Interest Rate

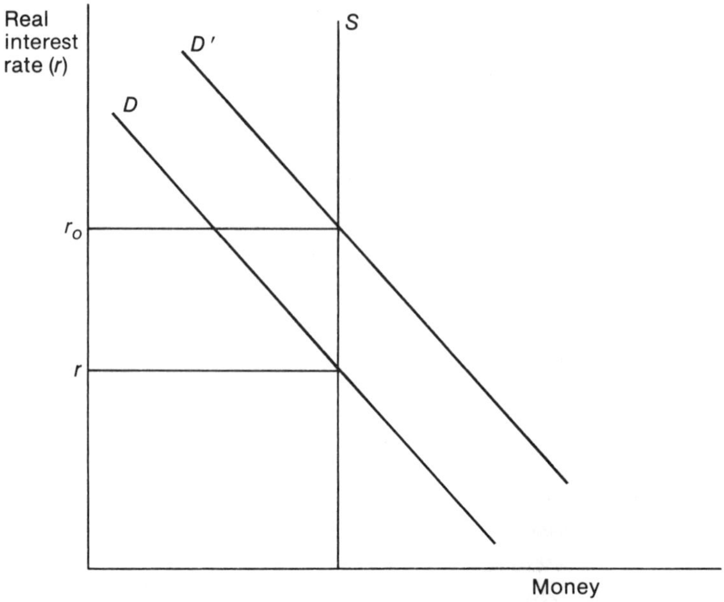

Supply Shocks

Supply-shock inflation is caused by an exogenous increase in prices or by an exogenous decrease in rate of growth in output. Liquidity effects vary depending on whether an exogenous price rise or an output slowdown predominates as an initiating factor. In either case, output growth and underlying capital values decrease.

Output Slowdowns

One source of supply-shock inflation is an unexpected output slowdown.[20] As in the case of a positive money shock, money supply is excessive, which results temporarily in excess liquidity and lower real interest rates. This then causes increased spending, higher prices, an increased demand for money, and a return to higher original interest rates. As illustrated in Figure

4–5, such excess liquidity effects last only until prices and the demand curve shift upwards. In the same way, as a result of the unanticipated inflation, distribution effects ensue. Debtors gain and lenders lose. In these outcomes, supply-shock inflation mimics money-shock inflation. The difference lies in the real output and consequent capital market effects.

When potential (full-employment) output growth, for whatever reason, is less than anticipated, lower sales, profits, and stock market share values follow.[21] As long as output growth rates are lower, earnings will be lower. This will depress the yields on existing and new capital. Thus, ex ante yields on all assets will be depressed.[22]

In sum, with this scenario unanticipated output slowdowns are reflected in unanticipated declines in stock market values and asset yields, which persist until growth rates recover. Additionally, the unanticipated output slowdown creates unanticipated inflation and temporary excess liquidity. The unanticipated inflation also has distribution effects on bond markets identical to those described above.

Exogenous Price Rises

Supply-shock inflation can have a temporary positive effect on interest rates if prices rise along with output slowdowns. However, negative effects on output growth, profits, and stock market share values remain.

Several possible causes of supply-shock inflation in which price rises initiate or accompany, rather than follow, output slowdowns were discussed in Chapter 1.[23] In these cases, the initial price rise in the offending sector leads to an overall price rise even though the money supply is not excessive, because other prices do not immediately fall. Interest rates rise because the price rise shifts the demand curve for money upwards. But prices will then decline due to the higher interest rates, and the demand curve will shift back with a return to the original interest rate equilibrium. As in the scenario of Figure 4–5, the liquidity effect is temporary.[24]

In this case there will also be relative price effects. These can lower or raise the yield on specific assets, depending on whether the asset is a substitute or a complement to factors in newly scarce supply.[25]

APPENDIX 4.D
Changes in the Anticipated Inflation Rate and Money Illusion

We assumed in previous sections that anticipated inflation was not affected by price level changes, because they were not serially correlated (i.e., price level increases are not followed by similar price level increases). If price level changes are serially correlated, rational investors will anticipate inflation. The evidence presented in Chapter 1 indicates that price level increases in the United States have been serially correlated. Unanticipated inflation in the current period results in somewhat higher future inflation rates in future periods as well. Evidence on expectation formation indicates that, eventually, the anticipated inflation rate increases in response to changes in the actual inflation rate. This section considers the capital market effects of changes in the inflation rate that are fully anticipated and those that are not fully anticipated because of money illusion.

While money and real shocks can cause temporary changes in the inflation rate, ongoing higher (lower) inflation requires a higher (lower) rate of monetary growth. Thus, the only effects of long-run inflation are those that accompany long-run monetary growth.

If investors are rational, their predictions of future inflation will be unbiased. The alternative is that investors are "fooled" by inflation and do not understand that they are being repaid with depreciated dollars. Nonetheless, the costs of gathering information may cause delays in perception of changes in inflation and in the inflation-generating (monetary expansion) process. If so, and if monetary expansion accelerates over time, anticipated inflation will lag actual inflation. Thus, for a time, lenders, who suffer from money illusion, will be fooled by inflation and may agree to too low nominal interest rates. Once higher (lower) inflation is anticipated, nominal interest rates will increase (decrease). Even assuming strictly rational expectations, so that predictions of inflation are unbiased estimates, unanticipated changes in the anticipated inflation rate will have an impact on the real value of already negotiated long-term contracts. Distribution effects result. Additionally, anticipated changes in the inflation rate may lower real equilibrium yields through the Mundell effect. Distribution effects occur because the change in the anticipated inflation rate was not previously anticipated. The Mundell (wealth-shift) effect occurs if and when the change becomes anticipated. Money illusion effects occur if the change is neither anticipated nor recognized. Each of these effects of changes in the inflation rate is discussed in the following.

Distribution Effects

To illustrate the impact of unanticipated changes in the anticipated inflation rate, the theoretical relationship between the holding period return on a bond and unanticipated inflation is derived as follows:

$$V_B = \frac{C}{1+R} + \frac{C}{(1+R)^2} + \frac{C}{(1+R)^3} + \cdots + \frac{C}{(1+R)^{n-1}} + \frac{P+C}{(1+R)^n}$$

where R = The nominal return on an n period bond
C = The coupon
P = The principal to be repaid in the Nth year
V_B = The present value of the bond.

If the inflation rate has a once-and-for-all sudden and unanticipated increase at time t, but the inflation rate is expected to return to its original rate, after the jump we saw that the value of the bond remained unchanged. This occurred because the nominal rate of return, R, which is a function of the anticipated inflation rate, remained the same. However, if the anticipated inflation for future periods rises (falls), the value of the bond must fall (rise), because R must adjust with the anticipated inflation rate so that the real return remains unchanged.[26]

Holders of very short-term debt suffer relatively little of the capital loss inflicted by an unanticipated increase in inflation.

FIGURE 4–7
Anticipated Inflation's Wealth-Shift (Mundell) Effect

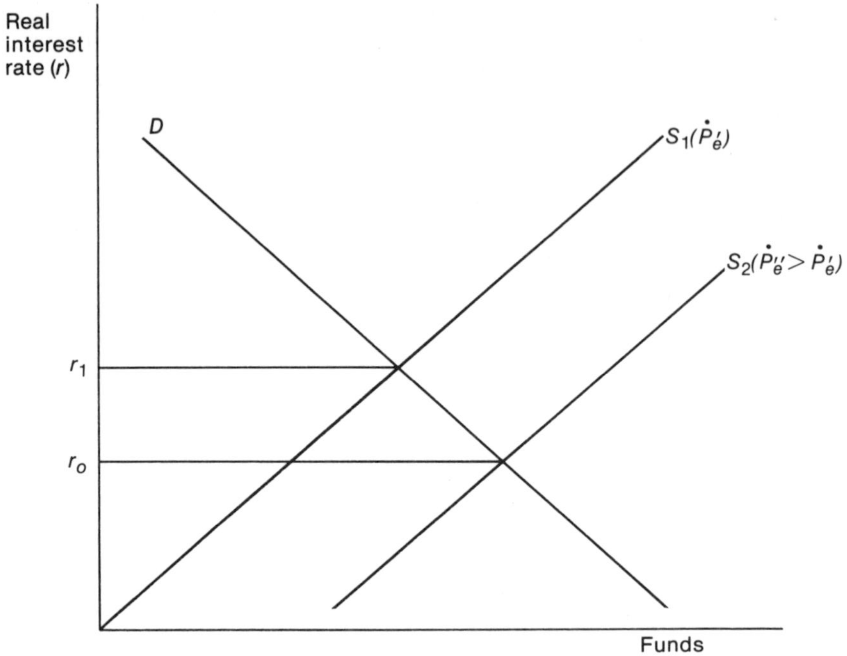

This is because they are not locked into a too low nominal rate of return, but can purchase the new higher yielding instruments relatively soon as their debt comes due. The extent of the capital loss varies directly with the duration of the nominally denominated debt.

The Wealth Shift (Mundell) Effect

While the nominal rate of return on nominal debt instruments can and does adjust, the zero nominal return on cash holdings cannot adjust. The result of an increase in the anticipated inflation rate is an increase in the cost of holding cash balances. As Mundell originally observed, an ongoing wealth-shift effect (which lowers real rates of return) may result.[27] That effect is shown for the bond market in Figure 4–7. As P_e increases from

$\dot{P}'_e$ to $\dot{P}''_e$, savers desire to hold less cash balances and more interest-bearing savings. Thus, an increase in the anticipated inflation rate causes the supply of loans to shift back at a given nominal interest rate, but not sufficiently to result in a full adjustment of nominal interest rates to the increases in anticipated inflation. As a result, the new real interest rate, r_0, is less than the original r_1.[28]

Money Illusion

Capital losses (on nominal loans as nominal rates adjust upwards) and a decrease in real cash holdings reflect rational investor responses to serially correlated increases in the price level. Yet it is possible that investors are irrational and do not respond to serially correlated price level increases by requiring higher nominal rates of return. The converse may also be true. Required nominal rates of return may not drop with a serially correlated decline in price level changes. Lenders and borrowers, as well as equity holders, may confuse nominal returns with real returns. If they do, they are said to suffer from money illusion. The consequence of money illusion is that real rates decline with increases in inflation and rise with decreases in inflation.

To demonstrate these effects, we first review the rational response. In symbols, rational lenders and borrowers neutralize the effect of expected inflation when $\dot{P}_e$ is not zero by adjusting R upwards. If the real return expected is $1 + r$, this must be multiplied by $1 + \dot{P}_e$ to keep the purchasing power of $1 + r$ constant. Thus, the nominal return $1 + R$ fully adjusts, as follows:

$$1 + R = (1 + r)(1 + \dot{P}_e)$$

Equivalently, this equation indicates how the real rate of return, r, changes if this adjustment does not take place. That is because

$$1 + r = \frac{1 + R}{1 + \dot{P}_e}$$

If $1 + R$ does not adjust upwards by $1 + \dot{P}_e$, $1 + r$ is thereby lowered.

To illustrate, if $\dot{P}$ and $\dot{P}_e$ are 0,

$$1 + r_0 = \frac{1 + R_0}{1}$$

If $\dot{P}$ and $\dot{P}_e$ increases to .03 and if the $1 + R_0$ is multiplied by 1.03,

$$1 + r_0 = \frac{(1 + R_0)(1.03)}{1(1.03)}$$

$1 + r_0$ is unchanged and the new nominal return

$$1 + R = (1 + R_0)(1.03) = 1 + R_0 + .03 + .03R_0$$

rises by approximately 3 percent, which is $\dot{P}_e$. If the increase in R is less than 3 percent, $1 + r$, the new return, is less than $1 + r_0$, the initial and expected real return.

Capital markets may be "infected" with money illusion. If so, nominal returns will not adjust upwards (downwards) with predictable inflation (disinflation), and real rates of return will be inversely correlated with inflation.

The confusion of bond market participants may also affect stock market investors.[29] For example, if a rise in inflation increases nominal interest rates somewhat (although perhaps not as much as it should because of bond market money illusion), stock market investors may perceive this as an increase in the *real* rate of return, which will depress stock market prices. Stock prices may fall because investors consider higher nominal interest payments an increased expense (rather than early repayment of capital) and because investors capitalize profits at nominal rather than real rates of return. In addition, equity holders may experience a loss inflicted by the lagged adjustment of the bond market to higher inflation rates, once inflation becomes anticipated. As nominal rates incorporate anticipated inflation, real rates of return in bond markets rise. The rise in real rates of return in the bond market means that investors in the stock market may also demand a higher yield. All other things constant, this requires that stock market values decline. Again, this results from money illusion, primarily in the bond market (as evidenced in the original failure of bond market participants to recognize the needed upward adjustment in R), but also among equity investors, if they allow the money illusion-caused gyrations of the bond market to influence real yields in the equity market.

The lack of sufficient adjustment of nominal yields in all markets to serially correlated price level changes may be an ongoing effect of monetary expansion. Rational investors should catch on to the "veil" of money if inflationary monetary increases are otherwise neutral. Whether they do so or not is an empirical question.

APPENDIX 4.E
Increased Uncertainty's Impact on Relative and the Risk-Free (Shadow) Yields

Increased inflation uncertainty also has an impact on the yield spread between assets and on the real (shadow) riskless rate of return. In an analysis of the impact of increased inflation uncertainty, Gordon and Halpern assume that equity investments are at least a partial hedge against inflation and show, first, that the share of bonds relative to real assets, such as equities, will decline.[30] This is in direct reaction to the increased riskiness of bonds. Second, insofar as relative quantities of assets fail to adjust fully to investor preference, the rate of return on bonds relative to real assets will increase. Thus, borrowers will either have to cease funding with bonds or provide an increased risk premium to lenders. The result will be a narrowing in the historical positive spread between the yields on equity and bonds and, possibly, a reversal of this spread.

Once assumptions are made about relative increases in long-term and short-term inflation uncertainty, the analysis can be extended to derive implications for long-term versus short-term debt premiums. Assuming, as noted by Klein,[31] that the ratio of long-term to short-term inflation uncertainty rises with the level of inflation, the risk premiums and the nominal rates of return on long-term versus short-term debt instruments would rise.[32]

Increased inflation uncertainty may also have an impact on the real (shadow) riskless rate of return depending, first, on whether alternative funding instruments are perfect substitutes for increasingly risky nominal debt instruments and, second, on the reaction of savers. Assuming that the alternative instruments are not perfect substitutes for the reasons noted above, the demand for capital shifts backwards. The negative impact of this shift on the real riskless rate of return may be counterbalanced by the reaction of savers if the interest elasticity of demand for savings is infinite, or if savings decrease in reaction to increased inflation uncertainty. (With an infinite interest elasticity, savings decrease until the original interest rate is restored. If the savings rate decreases in reaction to increased inflation uncertainty, the real shadow riskless rate can increase.)

Notes

[1] See Robert Mundell, "Inflation and Real Interest," *Journal of Political Economy* 71, no. 3 (June 1963), pp. 280–83, and discussion below, pp. 321–22.

[2] Irving Fisher originally proposed and tested the theory that anticipated inflation has no real impact on interest rates. The theory has since become known as the Fisher hypothesis, although Fisher did not subscribe to it. See Irving Fisher, *The Theory of Interest* (New York: Macmillan, 1930).

[3] We assume that money shocks are random and that their variance is unchanged over time, so that individuals' expectations of future inflation rates and their dispersion do not change. As a result, expected rates of return remain constant in the long run.

[4] We have assumed no anticipated inflation prior to the unanticipated money supply increase. The results would not be materially changed if we had started with a positive anticipated inflation rate. Lagged price adjustment effects identical to those described above will occur. An unanticipated increase (decrease) in the rate of the money supply will decrease (increase) real interest rates in the short run. Inflation acceleration will be correlated with earnings deceleration.

In addition, lenders, borrowers, and holders of cash experience similar distribution effects. Rational lenders' predictions of future inflation will be unbiased estimates of inflation, and the rate that lenders demand and borrowers offer will be the real rate plus the anticipated inflation rate. Lenders will then experience losses (gains), and borrowers will experience gains (losses) if the actual inflation is greater than (less than) anticipated inflation, as before.

For the temporary increase in the price level or inflation rate not to result in an increase in anticipated inflation, assume that the stochastic changes in the price level or inflation rate are serially uncorrelated (i.e., random). As a result, all holding period rates of return on assets that are denominated in nominal terms, regardless of maturity, suffer the same losses. Random money shocks result in onetime losses and gains that do not have ongoing capital market effects. Assuming rational investors (nonrandom), serially correlated price changes will become anticipated and, once anticipated, holding period rates of return of nominal assets of varying maturities are affected differentially, as is discussed below.

[5] Again, it should be emphasized that we assume random shocks so that while the price level (or inflation rate) may rise or fall in the short run, on the average it remains unchanged over time, as does the average and expected profit rate. As discussed below, if inflation increases over time and is accompanied by increases in perceived risks of future monetary contractions, the negative earnings/inflation correlation may be exacerbated.

[6] Even without money illusion, a wealth-shift effect may lower real rates of return when there is an increase in the anticipated inflation rate. However, to anticipate the discussion of the following chapter, it is clear that, at its possible maximum in the United States, this effect is negligible.

[7] Real shocks of either demand-pull or supply-shock origin may increase the variance of output growth and, consequently, earnings. Because the wage bill and other production costs cannot be reduced (expanded) proportionately with sales declines (increases), increased output and sales variance result in an increased variance in the firm's earnings.

Demand-pull inflation that commences with an unanticipated surge in money supply growth or aggregate demand will cause output to temporarily rise above the full-employment level before it returns to normal. This temporarily increases profits. As prices rise, lowered output growth and higher wages reduce earnings growth. The result is increased variance in earnings.

An additional source of variation of profits occurs because prices do not all adjust to an increase in aggregate demand with the same speed. However, this risk is diversifiable with a sufficiently large portfolio.

[8] If the economy becomes more vulnerable to supply shocks, for whatever reason, output will be more variable. As economies become more interdependent they may become more vulnerable to internationally transmitted sectoral shocks as well as to shocks induced by a decline in competitiveness and exchange rate devaluations.

[9] Whatever the cause of the increased variation in output, the result will be an increase in the variation of profits as well. A greater variance in underlying profits will lead to a greater variance in dividends and equity values. The increased variance in the value of these assets will diminish their value to individual investors who are risk-averse. The value of these now riskier assets declines, which means that their holding period rate of return declines when the increased risk is recognized. The price of these assets drops until their expected yield increases sufficiently to compensate for the increased risk involved in holding them.

[10] A payment of a penalty fee is generally required with repayment prior to maturity, but the amount of the penalty is fixed. Since money income growth is likely to decline with inflation, without such provisions the possibility of bankruptcies would be increased, and borrowers would have to pay lenders for this risk as well. Thus, rates would be higher with or without the call provision, but the diminished risk of bankruptcy makes the higher rates that accompany call protection more desirable. Call provisions are widely used with corporate and municipal long-term debt. The Federal Treasury has proposed using a five-year call provision on its long-term debt.

[11] See Benjamin M. Friedman, "Substitution and Expectation Effects on

Long-Term Borrowing Behavior and Long-Term Interest Rates," *Journal of Money, Credit, and Banking* 11, no. 2 (May 1979).

[12] To be more precise, the nominal rate of interest is (1.10)(1.01) − 1 = 11.1%. See above.

[13] See Franco Modigliani and Merton H. Miller, "The Cost of Capital, Corporation Finance, and the Theory of Investment," *American Economic Review* 48 (June 1958); see also Franco Modigliani and Merton H. Miller, "Corporation Income Taxes and the Cost of Capital, a Correction," *American Economic Review* 53 (June 1963).

[14] Duration reflects the average amount of time required for the money invested in the bond to be repaid.

[15] The estimation of the size of the liquidity, maturity, and default premiums over the past three decades by Roger G. Ibbotson and Rex A. Singuefield in *Stocks, Bonds, Bills, and Inflation: 1926–1978* (Charlottesville, Va.: Financial Analysts Research Foundation, 1979), is discussed below.

[16] To illustrate these, we assume initially a zero anticipated inflation rate and then assume $\dot{P}_e > 0$, maintaining the assumptions that whatever the initial levels of $\dot{P}_e$ and of the variance of inflation, $\sigma\dot{P}_e$, they are not changed by the unanticipated inflation. It is also assumed that the economy initially is at full employment, that is, at the nonaccelerating inflation unemployment rate defined in Chapter 1.

[17] As is discussed below, empirical evidence supports the existence of a two- to three-quarter price adjustment lag in the post–World War II U.S. economy.

[18] Also, unanticipated inflation may provoke fears among investors of a future monetary correction with consequent temporary output and profit declines and interest rate increases. If so, this negative correlation is heightened.

Similarly, any perception that contractionary policy is no longer as likely to be embraced in the future, already having had its desired effects, will strengthen the negative short-run correlation of inflation and equity values.

Negative money shocks temporarily depress output and earnings growth, which together with the boost in interest rates reduce equity values. But as inflation decreases, output and earnings growth accelerate while interest rates decline with a positive impact on equity values. Thus, equity values vary inversely with inflation caused by money shocks.

[19] Higher real interest rates and asset yields continue as long as the aggregate demand shock does. Inflation, however, cannot unless the money supply is expanded at a faster rate. As long as the positive (negative) aggregate demand shock persists, interest rates and the price level are lower than otherwise, but inflation, after slowing down (increasing), in the short run resumes at the rate determined by monetary growth relative to real growth. Thus, aggregate demand shocks cause and are correlated with inflation only in the short run.

There will be a one-period correlation of higher interest rates and inflation, if monetary expansion does not increase. If it does, the correlation persists. One possible scenario in which a rise in real interest rates and inflation are correlated occurs through a surge in inflation caused by an increase in government spending, initially financed by debt. The increased debt may then be monetized through expansion of the money supply to purchase the debt. Although nominal interest rates may be depressed temporarily, depending on the rate at which the money supply is expanded, in the long run the effort will be self-defeating. The result will be ever-higher nominal interest rates, with real rates remaining high as long as the underlying aggregate demand for goods and services from firms, consumers, and government (relative to the savings of these sectors) remains high. See Chapter 1 for further discussion.

[20] According to the Harberger and quantity theory equations, inflation, $\dot{P}$, is the result of an excessive growth of the money supply, where excessive is defined relative to potential growth in output for given interest rates. Thus, unanticipated inflation can occur as the result of an unanticipated surge in the money supply or, as the result of an unanticipated decline in the rate of output growth. See Chapter 1.

[21] The underperformance of sales and earnings is temporarily abated by the negative impact of lower output on interest rates. The temporary excess liquidity effect on interest rates stimulates purchases of interest-sensitive consumer durables and investment goods. Thus, the original sales and output decline is mitigated by the temporary decline in interest rates. But the excess supply of money, for a given full-employment output level, will eventually bid up prices or the inflation rate and reduce excess liquidity to zero. At that point, interest rates return to their previous level. Output, sales, and earnings are no longer artificially supported by the temporary interest rate decline. Thus, because stock market share values will depend positively on all earnings and inversely on interest rates, they may not be immediately fully affected by the potential output slowdown. As inflation becomes apparent, excess liquidity is absorbed and interest rates recover. At this point, interest-sensitive purchases decline once again, and the earnings decline will be fully apparent and fully reflected in declines in stock market share values.

[22] Depressed asset yields will not be correlated with continued inflation if monetary authorities decrease the rate of expansion of the money supply. Inflation decelerates to its original rate if either money supply growth declines to the lower output growth rate or the output growth rate recovers. To maintain the assumption that anticipated inflation, $\dot{P}_e$, is unchanged, one of these must occur.

[23] To recapitulate briefly here, first, a group of firms (or unions) may exert monopoly power to raise prices (wages) and artificially restrict output (services) (e.g., the OPEC price rises of 1974 and 1979). Second, natural scarcities of important raw materials or agricultural goods will result in immediate price rises with noticeable impact on the price level, if the scarcities are sufficiently broad-based. Third, as economies become more open, with a greater proportion of traded goods, international as well as domestic scarcities will affect domestic price levels. In addition, in open economies any factor that results in a significant exchange rate devaluation will put temporary upward pressure on the overall price level due to the increased demand for exports and import substitutes.

[24] Thus, supply-shock liquidity effects initially cause an excess demand or supply of money depending on whether output declines or exogenous price increases predominate. In either case, overall prices rise. However, in the first instance the price rise is due to too much liquidity, given the output decline, so that interest rates fall. In the second instance, the price rise is due to the exogenous upward price pressure in selected sectors, with price rigidity elsewhere, so that without a balancing potential output decline, interest rates rise. In this case, a secondary output decline will result because the percentage rise

in the price level or inflation rate is greater than the percentage output decline; hence, total expenditures (*PQ*) increase. As indicated by the Harberger or quantity theory equations, greater total expenditures for the given money supply entail increased real interest rates. The real interest rate increases place downward pressure on interest sensitive investment and consumer durables outlays, lowering aggregate demand and output growth.

[25] The focus of this section has been on the capital market effects of unanticipated inflation resulting from unanticipated output growth rate declines. Unanticipated *increases* in output growth rates have symmetrically opposite effects. The principal impact is an increase in equity values, due to the unanticipated increase in sales and profits. There is also an unanticipated decrease in the price level or rate of inflation which has distribution effects that benefit lenders and harm borrowers. The liquidity impact on real interest rates is again ambiguous with the real rate decreasing or increasing depending on whether the increase in output is proportionately less than or greater than the decrease in the inflation rate. Finally, accompanying relative price effects may increase or decrease asset yields.

[26] Newly issued bonds will incorporate the new anticipated inflation rate. Nominal yields offered by such bonds will be higher (lower) if there is an unanticipated increase (decrease) in the anticipated inflation rate. Thus, sellers of existing bonds will match the real return offered by newly issued bonds, and to do so will experience a capital loss (gain). Of course, even those who wish to hold their bonds until maturity do not escape the capital loss inflicted by an unanticipated increase in anticipated inflation. Those who invest in newly issued bonds get a higher yield on the same dollar investment. The loss of those who invested before the rise in the anticipated inflation is real whether it is viewed as occurring in every period in which "old" investors receive a lower rate of return or as a one-shot capital loss which then equalizes future rates of return. Similarly, capital gains are experienced by holders of long-term bonds if anticipated inflation decreases, since their real yield is higher than otherwise.

[27] See Mundell, "Inflation and Real Interest."

[28] The increase in the cost of holding cash and the decrease in the desired real cash holdings also have consequences for the conduct of monetary policy itself. An increase in the rate of monetary expansion on the part of monetary authorities will induce cash holders to reduce their cash holdings. The result is that inflation temporarily increases at a rate above the money supply growth rate. On the other hand, if interest rates are declining because of money supply contraction, and actual and expected inflation are slowing, people will wish to hold more money balances than otherwise, and inflation will be less than if interest rates had not declined. The effect is that $\dot{P}$ initially will undershoot (overshoot) a decline (rise) in $\dot{M}$.

[29] See Franco Modigliani and Richard Cohn, "Inflation, Rational Valuation and the Market," *Financial Analysts Journal* 35 (March–April 1979).

[30] See Myron J. Gordon and Paul J. Halpern, "Bond Share Yield Spreads under Uncertain Inflation," *American Economic Review* 66, no. 4 (September 1976), pp. 559–65.

[31] See Benjamin Klein, "The Measurement of Long- and Short-Term Price Uncertainty: A Moving Regression Time Series Analysis," *Economic Inquiry*,

July 1978; and Benjamin Klein, "The Social Costs of the Recent Inflation: The Mirage of Steady 'Anticipated' Inflation," *Carnegie-Rochester Conference Series on Public Policy: Institutional Arrangements and the Inflation Problem*, Vol. 3, ed. Brunner and Meltzer, 1976.

[32] Money risk is reflected in the term structure of interest rates. However, the prevailing term structure of interest rates is determined by a number of factors. Theory indicates that expectations of future interest rates are an important determinant of the term structure. While normally upward sloping, with zero inflation uncertainty, the term structure of interest rates is downward sloping when interest rates are high and future rates are expected to fall. This is because lenders will want to lend long-term funds, when nominal and real rates are expected to fall, putting downward pressure on long rates, and borrowers will want to borrow short-term funds putting upward pressure on short rates. In addition to expectations, the increased threat of business decline and default in outgoing years for which there is less information is likely to make long-term loans riskier. This contributes to a more positive slope.

A fourth set of factors which influences the shape of the term structure has been termed the *preferred habitat* of lenders and borrowers. Because, in general, lenders and borrowers are risk averse, they will wish to hedge risks when they can. By borrowing long-term funds, investors can hedge the interest rate risk involved in long-term investment.

In an environment without inflation uncertainty, hedging demands of lenders for long-run real income streams are met by long-term nominally fixed debt. In addition, such hedging demands of lenders are matched by similar hedging demands of borrowers. But the quantity of funds that need to be hedged on the two sides may differ. If the demand by hedging borrowers for long-term funds exceeds the hedging lenders' supply of long-term funds, borrowers will have to pay a premium to attract lenders who wish to hedge their liabilities by lending to the short-term market. Thus, long-term borrowers may have to pay higher rates on long-term loans, even in the absence of expectations of increased interest rates, extra business risk, or money risk.

The preferred habitat theory could also explain a negatively sloping yield curve if long-term lenders' hedging demands for funds exceeded long-term borrowers' demand. In either case, the slope of the term structure of interest rates increases with an increase in money risk.

Bibliography

FISHER, IRVING. *The Theory of Interest*. New York: Macmillan, 1930.

FRIEDMAN, BENJAMIN M. "Substitution and Expectation Effects on Long-Term Borrowing Behavior and Long-Term Interest Rates." *Journal of Money, Credit, and Banking* 2, no. 2 (May 1979).

GORDON, MYRON J., and PAUL J. HALPERN. "Bond Share Yield Spreads under Uncertain Inflation." *American Economic Review* 66, no. 4 (September 1976).

IBBOTSON, ROGER G., and SINGUEFIELD, REX A. *Stocks, Bonds, Bills, and Inflation: 1926–1978*. Charlottesville, Va.: Financial Analysts Research Foundation, 1979.

KLEIN, BENJAMIN. "The Measurement of Long- and Short-Term Price Uncertainty: A Moving Regression Time-Series Analysis." *Economic Inquiry*, July 1978.

———. "The Social Costs of the Recent Inflation: The Mirage of Steady 'Anticipated' Inflation." *Carnegie-Rochester Conference Series on Public Policy: Institutional Arrangements and the Inflation Problem*, vol. 3, ed. Brunner and Meltzer (1976).

MODIGLIANI, FRANCO, and RICHARD COHN. "Inflation, Rational Valuation and the Market." *Financial Analysts Journal* 35 (March–April 1979).

MODIGLIANI, FRANCO, and MERTON H. MILLER. "The Cost of Capital, Corporate Finance, and the Theory of Investment." *American Economic Review*, June 1958.

———. "Corporation Income Taxes and the Cost of Capital, A Correction." *American Economic Review*, June 1963.

MUNDELL, ROBERT. "Inflation and Real Interest." *Journal of Political Economy* 71, no. 3 (June 1963).

5 Capital Market Empirical Evidence and Implications for Pensions

This chapter reviews the empirical evidence on the capital market effects of inflation. In the long run, rational investors should anticipate inflation. They should come to expect the inflationary effects of excessive money supply growth and adjust their required nominal rates of return upward by the expected inflation rate. Required nominal and real rates of return also should rise to include any increased risk premiums due to increased real and inflation uncertainty. This assumes no capital market effects through taxes. Given the effects of the federal income tax structure, in particular, investors may require higher before-tax nominal and real rates to compensate for decreased after-tax real rates. Thus, theory suggests that real rates should at least remain constant or increase with inflation in the long run, although in the short run unanticipated inflation lowers real rates of return on traditional assets.

Historical data demonstrate that lower real rates have accompanied higher inflation. The observed fact is that real rates tend to be lower in periods of higher inflation over long periods of time.

The following two sections review the conclusions of empirical work to assess inflation's short-run and long-run impact on bond and equity markets. The concentration is on interpreting empirical work based on post–World War II U.S. data; studies that review earlier U.S. data and foreign data are briefly examined. The third section provides an overview of the impact of inflation on capital markets, and the last section discusses implications for pensions.

Inflation's Impact on Bonds

Inflation in the United States in the post–World War II period has been accompanied by reduced short-term and long-term real bond yields. First, the negative correlation of inflation and real yields can be explained by the nature of short-run shocks. Supply shocks reduce the underlying productivity of capital; money shocks create excess liquidity effects, which reduce real yields; demand shocks raise real interest rates, but in general in this period these were neutralized by excessive monetary expansion and reduced real productivity. (Appendix 5.A discusses the evidence for the impact of short-run shocks on bond yields.) Second, holding period returns were reduced because increases in inflation were unanticipated. Third, inflation may have been accompanied by money illusion which further contributed to reduced real yields. Below is a review of the evidence on unanticipated inflation's impact on holding period returns and the long-run effects of inflation.

Bond Yields and Unanticipated Inflation

Increases in unanticipated inflation decrease bond holding period returns. Moreover, if such increases raise the anticipated inflation rate, the entire term structure of interest rates will rise. This will decrease the value of previously issued longer-term bonds more than the value of short-term bonds.

Jaffe and Mandelker and Fama and Schwert tested for the impact of unanticipated inflation with the following regressions:

(5.1) $$Rbxt = a + b\,(\Delta t - Rt)$$

where *Rbxt* is the holding period return over a one-month period *t* on bonds with maturities (x), which vary from two months to 20 years. R_t is the return on the one-month maturity T-bill, and Δt is the inflation rate over period *t*.

Since *Rt* (as indicated below) appears to be proxy for anticipated inflation, $\Delta t - Rt$ is used as a measure of inflation that was unanticipated at the beginning of the period. The coefficients for *b* reported in both papers are uniformly negative, whether the holding period return is measured for a short-term Treasury bill, intermediate-term Treasury note, or long-term Treasury bond.

Also, the coefficient of *b* is generally more strongly negative for the longer-term instruments than for the shorter-term ones. This implies that an increase in unanticipated inflation leads to increases in anticipated inflation in the future, so that holding period returns on bonds of longer duration are bid down more than those on shorter duration bonds.

Sustained Inflation: Wealth-Shift, Money Illusion, Tax, and Uncertainty Effects in the Bond Market

In the long run, inflation must be accompanied by predictable excessive monetary growth; thus, it should be anticipated. While unanticipated increases in the inflation rate reduce holding period returns, rational investors should anticipate predictable money supply increases and require higher nominal interest rates to compensate for increased inflation. Thus, in the absence of wealth-shift, tax, and uncertainty effects, the theoretical relationship between anticipated inflation and the real interest rate is clear. Interest rates should rise one-for-one with an increase in the anticipated inflation rate. While the wealth-shift effect, in theory, decreases real interest rates, the largest potential size of this effect in the United States is negligible.[2]

Tax and uncertainty effects should raise real interest rates. Hence, the evidence of persistently lower real yields over the inflationary 1960 and 1970 decades in the United States indicates either that the underlying yields on capital (productivity) were lower or that there has been persistent money illusion.

The most important early study, done by Fama, concludes that for the testing period 1953 to 1971, there was no money illusion.[3] This and other earlier studies are reviewed in depth in Appendix 5.B.

Three recent studies question the Fama results. Steven Leuthold has compiled 200 years of U.S. data, sorted by inflation rate.[4] The data indicate that years of higher than average inflation were not years of higher than average nominal interest rates. In general, deflation was accompanied by high real interest rates, and inflation was accompanied by low real interest rates, except for one period, the period of Fama's analysis.

A second study, by Lawrence Summers, uses econometric analysis to analyze U.S. inflation from 1860 through 1980.[5] In part of the analysis, Summers subjects the data to the same procedural test used by Fama. Summers reproduces Fama's results for 1953 to 1971, the period of Fama's study, but finds that, both before and after, inflation is associated with a decline in real rates of return.

A third study by Robert J. Shiller and Jeremy J. Siegel finds similar results for the United Kingdom.[6] In the pre–World War II period there is no response, short or long run, to inflation; there is little response through the mid-1960s. Analysis of post-1965 results does reveal a positive, although not a full response of nominal interest rates to inflation.

In explanation of these results, these studies conclude that lenders and borrowers suffer from money illusion. However, if results for the 1953 through 1971 period show no money illusion, how is this consistent with the finding of money illusion both before and after?

Summers argues that significant money illusion existed even in the 1953 to 1971 period because, given tax effects, nominal rates of return should have increased by more than 1 percent for a 1 percent increase in expected inflation.

To determine overall tax effects, Summers puts bounds on the combined size of the four corporate tax effects of inflation, discussed in the preceding chapter.[7] Summers calculates that the combined negative capital gains tax and historical depreciation effects on profits are almost balanced by a positive interest rate deduction effect.[8] He finds an overall negative effect on the after-tax real rate of return on equity of approximately .14 percent for a 1 percent increase in inflation.

Assuming only corporate taxes and a zero interest rate elasticity, this would be the only effect. Thus, the impact of inflation, $\dot{P}$, on the after-tax real interest rate, r, would be equal to:

$$\frac{dr}{d\dot{P}} = 1 - .14 = .86 \tag{5.2}$$

The after-tax real rate of return on equity would only rise by .86 of a percent for a 1 percent increase in inflation. However, this ignores any personal income tax effect. The personal income tax lowers the after-tax real rate of return received by investors on taxable interest income. This lowers the yield that firms must offer on equities which, if held for the long term and if they pay no dividends, are essentially nontaxable. The impact of this depends on the interest elasticity of savings. Assuming a zero elasticity so that savings and capital investment is unchanged, the after-tax real rate of return on equity that investors would have to offer savers would decline by $1(1 - B)$, where B is the marginal tax rate. Higher personal income taxes due to inflation may lower the after-tax required real yield on capital investment.[9] On the basis of Gordon and Malkiel's study, Summers accepts as realistic a marginal tax rate of one third.[10] Using this and maintaining the assumption of zero interest elasticity of savings, he finds the combined effect on inflation would be equal to

$$\frac{dr}{d\dot{P}} = \frac{1 - .14}{1 - .33} \approx 1.3 \tag{5.3}$$

Removing the assumption that interest rate elasticity of savings is zero implies a backward shift of the savings function, in the extreme by the full amount of the tax increase, if savings are infinitely interest rate elastic. An infinitely interest rate elastic function means that savings will continue to decrease unless the after-tax real rate of return is unchanged. If after-tax interest rates are to remain unchanged with inflation, pre-tax, nominal interest rates must increase. Assuming a marginal tax rate of B, the before tax rate of return, r, must increase by $1(1 - B)$ for every 1 percent increase in inflation.[11] Assuming again a marginal tax rate of one third, the upward bound on interest rates movements would be 1.5. On the basis of Summers' estimates, the before-tax interest rate should increase between *1.3* and *1.5* percentage points for every 1 percentage point increase in inflation.

As the above theoretical discussion indicates, uncertainty also should lead to a greater than unitary response in nominal rates to inflation.[12] Thus for Summers, the finding of a less than unitary response in all periods conclusively demonstrates persistent money illusion.

The lower bound of Summers' estimated tax effect, however, may be considerably overstated. If capital markets are segmented (so that tax-exempt and low-income investors hold bonds while high-bracket investors hold low-dividend stocks), a decrease in the after-tax rate of return in the bond market may not lower investors' interest costs significantly.[13] The relevant marginal tax bracket is somewhere between zero and one third, assuming a .15 tax bracket results in a lower bound of one. Evidence, cited below, provides confirming evidence of this.[14]

In addition, there is evidence of a continuous rise in the response of nominal interest rates to anticipated inflation in the post–World War II period. Using Summers' results, there is a change from no response before World War II to a nearly unitary response after the 1950s through the 1970s. There would seem to be evidence, in any case, of a lessening of money illusion.

If the studies of inflation expectation formation, discussed above, are correct, it may indeed have taken time for investors to recognize the change in the money supply determination process away from a de facto gold standard to an autoregressive process in which money and real shocks were ratified by an increase in money supply growth rates which then persisted. Individuals may have continued to expect a return to "normal" near zero inflation rates for some time after an autoregressive monetary policy had in fact been implemented.

The regulatory environment of the 1970s itself lagged behind the new monetary process. Regulation Q fixed interest rates on savings deposits at negative real rates. Unregulated money market funds, which by their growth forced deregulation of financial institutions, were only in the early stages of development in the 1970s. Thus, there was an institutionally based rationale for the persistence of lower real rates through the 1970s.

In addition, the apparent decreased responsiveness of nominal rates to inflationary expectations in the 1970s decade may be specious and attributable rather to a decrease in the marginal productivity of capital, which lowered the real interest rate. To test for this, James A. Wilcox incorporates variables to measure the marginal productivity of capital in his study of post–World

War II U.S. interest rate determination.[15] [16] He avoids Fama's assumption of rational expectations by using survey data on inflation expectations.[17] He includes, as exogenous variables that might have influenced the real interest rate, the acceleration in money growth, real defense spending, export demand as a fraction of real output, and supply shock proxies. As expected, the acceleration in money growth has a significant negative coefficient, demonstrating the liquidity effect found in Hafer and Hein as well.[18] Wilcox then also finds that real shocks can explain the increases in the real interest rate found in the 1950s and the declines of the 1970s. With inclusion of these real variables, nominal interest rates are found to adjust *almost* completely to the expected inflation rates predicted in the survey data.[19] In addition, estimates of the size of the coefficient on expected interest rates rise over time. These findings are consistent with a growing income tax effect (assuming nonzero interest elasticity), diminished money illusion, and diminished impact of expectations of a return to a "normal" zero or low inflation rate, over time.

International data confirm these results. Gultekin tests the Fisher hypothesis for 14 countries in the period 1965 to 1979, using the short-term interest rate as a predictor of inflation. In general, regression coefficients are positive and significant, with many indistinguishable from unity.[20]

The high interest rates, apparent in the deregulated U.S. environment of the 1980s, may provide further evidence that money illusion no longer has a significant role in interest rate determination, if it had in the past. If so, short-term interest rates may show a unitary response to long-run inflation in the future. Before-tax rates may show a greater than unitary response, if savings decrease as a result of lower after-tax rates.

Finally, we have held aside the issue of how increased money risk may have affected expected real rates of return on longer-term bonds. Autocorrelated unanticipated price changes in the 1970s caused a sharp increase in the riskiness of longer-term bonds. A study by Zvi Bodie, Alex Kane, and Robert McDonald indicates that the 1973 to 1980 standard deviation on longest-term (eight-year duration) bonds increased fourfold and exceeded the standard deviation on the rate of return on equity.[21] This standard deviation was about 50 times as large as that on one-month Treasury bills, which changed little. The increased variance of the rate of return should have increased the risk premium on long-term bonds since the correlation of long-term bond returns with equity returns also increased. Depending on the estimated level of aggregate risk aversion, the induced risk premium increase was between 110 and 700 basis points. This could explain the especially large increase in *long-term* real expected returns in the early 1980s.

Inflation's Impact on Stocks

Early studies of the impact of inflation on stock returns focused on whether equity investments hedged inflation.[22] They show that stocks do not provide a consistent or complete hedge against inflation.[23]

More recent studies have separated inflation into its anticipated and unanticipated components and analyzed each component's impact on stock market yields.

Stock Market Yields and Unanticipated Inflation

The empirical relationship between unanticipated inflation and the return on common stocks in the United States, over the 1958–71 period, has been analyzed by Jaffe and Mandelker and by Nelson.[24] Jaffe and Mandelker perform the following regression:

$$Rmt = a \pm b(\Delta t - Rt) \tag{5.4}$$

where Δt is the inflation rate in period t, Rt is the interest rate on a one month to maturity Treasury bill (which is assumed to be a good proxy for the expected inflation rate, over these years), and Rmt is the nominal return on the stock market in period t. They define real stock returns as the sum of dividend yields and capital gains on the Standard & Poor's Composite Index of Common Stocks, with both value-weighted and equally weighted indexes used. The coefficient of unanticipated inflation, b, is significantly negative. Nelson runs the following regression as part of a series of regressions described below:

$$Rmt = a \pm bPt \tag{5.5}$$

where Pt is current inflation. Nelson also finds a significantly negative value of b.[25]

Stock Market Yields and Anticipated Inflation

One of the most surprising findings in finance is the relationship between the expected return on stocks and anticipated inflation. Most researchers have found a negative relationship between anticipated inflation and the expected *nominal* return on stocks, while virtually all researchers have found a negative relationship between anticipated inflation and the expected *real* return on stocks.

It is beyond the scope of this chapter to cover all the results in this area in depth. Instead, the early results of Jaffe and Mandelker, who perform the following pair of regressions over the period from 1953–71, are primarily discussed.

(5.6) $$Rmt = a + bRt$$

and

(5.7) $$rmt = a + bRt$$

where Rmt and rmt are the nominal and real returns, respectively, on the stock market over period t. [26] Both value-weighted and equally weighted indexes were used. If the joint hypotheses that (1) the expected rate of inflation is independent of the expected rate of return and (2) the market is efficient hold, then b should be 1 in Equation 5.6 and should be zero in Equation 5.7.

Surprisingly, Jaffe and Mandelker find the coefficient b to be -5.43 and -6.40 in Equations 5.6 and 5.7, respectively. These numbers imply that when expected inflation rate rises by 1 percent, the expected nominal return on the stock market falls by approximately 5.5 percent. The expected real return on the market falls by about 6.5 percent.[27]

Empirical Evidence on Explanations for the Negative Correlation between Yields and Inflation

In the past, it was commonly believed that equity investments would hedge inflation. Thus, the empirical evidence that nominal returns on equities moved inversely with both unanticipated and anticipated inflation has been met with surprise. These results have been cited as evidence that stock market investors are irrational and, in particular, that they suffer from money illusion.[28] Nonetheless, the negative correlations of real equity returns with unanticipated and anticipated inflation could also be consistent with the models of rational investor behavior.

The theoretical discussion of the preceding chapter suggested several explanations for a negative correlation between unanticipated inflation and stock market yields. Tax and distribution effects associated with inflation were shown to have an indeterminate (possibly negative or positive) impact on equity holding period returns. The broad weight of empirical evidence, reviewed in Appendix 5.C, suggests that tax and distribution effects have in fact neither a strong negative nor a positive impact on earnings. Thus, neither explains the negative correlation of unanticipated inflation and stock market yields. Unlike the theoretically indeterminate impact of these factors, theory implies that shocks should produce a negative correlation between earnings and unanticipated inflation.[29] In addition, theory implies that the increased real risk that may accompany increased inflation should result in lower equity values and a decline in holding period returns. The empirical evidence that supports both of these hypothetical explanations of a negative correlation between stock yields and unanticipated inflation is discussed in the following.

Neither of these theories, however, can explain a negative relationship between *anticipated* inflation and negative holding period returns.[30] Rational investors should forecast any negative impact of ongoing inflation at the same time that inflation is expected.[31] While money illusion can explain a negative anticipated inflation/yield relationship, the evidence of direct tests (discussed in Appendix 5.C), however, is not supportive of this hypothesis as the sole explanation of this relationship for the post–World War II period. Moreover, the negative correlation of anticipated inflation and negative yields may be a statistical artifact, since it may disappear when the impact of shocks on the yield of the underlying capital is included, in the same way that the negative relationship between anticipated inflation and negative real bond rates of return *almost* disappears when shocks are included as explanatory factors.

The evidence presented below suggests that this is indeed the case, at least for the post–World War II period. When other factors that affect real holding period yields are included, the coefficient of anticipated inflation becomes statistically insignificant, as would be expected if money illusion were not an important factor in determining equity yields. Nonetheless, the statistical results are open to several interpretations. Some amount of persistent money illusion cannot be ruled out in the post–World War II period, as one explanation for the negative relationship of inflation to equity yields, along with other explanations based on the negative earnings impact of shocks and increased real uncertainty.

Effects of Productivity Declines. Theory and empirical evidence can explain much of the apparent negative correlation between expected inflation and expected yields, without an appeal to investor irrationality. In theory, an inverse relationship between expected inflation and expected real yields results, if long-term monetary expansion is not adjusted downward for downward shifts in long-term output growth rates. Excess monetary growth is correlated with depressed output growth, if monetary authorities are slow to perceive and to act on declines in potential output growth. Evidence that excess monetary and fiscal stimulus of the 1970s in the United States is attributable to a failure to recognize or to act on reduced growth potential (due to supply shocks as well as to secular factors) was presented in Chapter 1.[32]

Effects of Shocks. A second theoretical explanation offered is that, with monetary policy constant, real activity varies inversely with inflation due to supply shocks. Real stock market returns then vary positively with real activity. Thus, the negative simple correlation of real stock returns and inflation may be due to the negative simple correlation of inflation and real activity.

To test this, Fama regresses real stock returns on unanticipated inflation, anticipated inflation, real activity, and monetary base growth rates.[33] In the multiple regressions of stock returns which include each of these independent variables, the coefficient of the real activity variable is significant, and the coefficient of the expected inflation variable is not significant. Fama's results demonstrate that output measures positively affect the average real rate of return on capital, and that with the inclusion of real and money supply growth variables, the negative effect of expected inflation on real stock returns disappears.[34] The continued significance of money supply, which in this period acts like a trend variable, indicates the presence of a long-run productivity decline effect, money illusion, or of some other excluded trendlike variable.

In their study of U.S. inflation for the period 1926 through 1978, Friend and Hasbrouck regress real stock returns against unanticipated and anticipated inflation rates.[35] As do the other studies cited above, they proceed by defining real stock returns as the sum of dividend yields and capital gains on the Standard & Poor's Composite Index of Common Stocks minus the contemporaneous inflation rate. They model the expected inflation rate, using either an autoregressive forecasting model or the Treasury bill interest rate. In either case, they find that the coefficients of both the unanticipated and anticipated inflation rate are significantly negative. Again, the finding of a negative coefficient for unanticipated inflation does not contradict economic theory. However, rational investors should forecast any negative impact of ongoing inflation at the same time that inflation is expected.

Changes in the expected inflation rate, however, may have a negative impact on the real stock returns, without contradicting rationality. If a sustained increase in inflation has a negative impact on earnings, information of an increase in expected inflation should depress holding period returns, assuming investor rationality. Since Friend and Hasbrouck's earlier results demonstrate this effect, they redo their regressions, including as a measure of the change in the expected inflation the first difference in the Standard & Poor's municipal bond yield. The coefficient of this variable is always significantly negative. In addition, they include the rate of change in the Federal Reserve Board Total Index of Industrial Production as a real output measure.

A trend to represent a decrease in the marginal productivity of capital and required rates of return over time is also included.[36] Using these independent variables does not change the finding of a significant and negative coefficient of the expected inflation variable for the whole of the period. However, when these variables are included in the post–World War II regression, the coefficient of the expected inflation rate variable is no longer significant. In the annual data in the post–World War II period, including the real output variable alone depresses the impact of expected inflation to the point of marginal statistical insignificance. These results indicate that the significance of the expected inflation variable in other studies in the post–World War II period may be due to its close correlation with changes in expected inflation.

Increased Real Uncertainty. The change in expected inflation rate variable may also proxy an increase in real uncertainty. While increased money and real shocks should only affect stock yields temporarily, an increased likelihood of shocks, and consequent earnings variations, should raise the required rate of return to compensate for the increased risk.

Robert S. Pindyck provides evidence of a substantial increase in the riskiness of capital investments since 1965. His results "show that the variance of the firm's real marginal return on capital has increased significantly over the past two decades, that this has increased the relative riskiness of investors' net real returns from holding stocks, and that this in turn can explain a large part of the market decline."[37] Pindyck also shows that the variance of stock returns is closely related to expected changes in inflation. In fact, including it along with the change in expected inflation variable in a regression to explain changes in stock return results in the change in expected inflation variable's insignificance. Thus, the significance of the expected inflation and the change in the expected inflation rate variables, in studies which exclude the variance of stock returns variable, may be in part due to their proxying of an increase in the variance of stock returns.[38]

In sum, the decline in real stock market returns through the 1970s can be explained by unanticipated increases in the expected inflation rate (associated with increased real risk), together with a trend variable (associated with a secular decline in the productivity of capital) and declines in real output growth (associated with supply shocks). With inclusion of these variables, the level of the expected rate of inflation is not found to influence the ex ante real rate of return. However, since other included variables are highly correlated with expected inflation, its possible influence, indicating persistent money illusion, cannot be ruled out.

Overview of Inflation's Impact on Capital Markets

Summary statistics of inflation's impact on stock and bond markets are presented in Tables 5–1 through 5–5.[39] Rates of return and correlations of returns with inflation in U.S. capital markets for 1947 through 1982 are shown in Tables 5–1, 5–2, and 5–3. Nominal returns of all listed assets, except U.S. Treasury bills, are negatively correlated with inflation, and real yields of all assets are negatively correlated with inflation.

Table 5–4 gives year-by-year returns in the 1947 to 1982 period. These data are derived from studies by Ibbotson and Sinquefield.[40] Table 5–5 presents data aggregated by Benjamin Friedman, comparing before- and after-tax real rates of return for the 1960 to 1980 period of accelerated inflation.[41] In this period before- and after-tax real yields on all assets but equities were negative.

The low real rates of return of the 1960s and 1970s on stocks and bonds and the inverse correlation of inflation and real returns from 1947 to 1982 can be explained by the major capital market effects of unanticipated inflation.

Theoretical and empirical analyses identify these as (1) money illusion effects; (2) negative distribution effects of unanticipated inflation, unanticipated increases in anticipated inflation, and increased inflation risk on bond holding period real yields; (3) negative effects of supply, demand, and money shocks, and real risk increases on equity real yields; and (4) tax effects. The past impact and the likely future impact of these on capital market yields is reviewed here, in brief.

Money illusion effects on stocks and bonds. The predominance of empirical evidence indicates that real yields have been systematically lowered when inflation has increased, and that real yields have been systematically raised when inflation has decreased.[42] This may have been due in part to money illusion. Even in the absence of persistent money illusion, investors' predictions are likely to be based to some degree on past observations of inflation. If inflation is changing, expectations are likely to continue to take time to catch up to reality, so that real yields move inversely with inflation.

TABLE 5–1
U.S. Capital Market Total Annual Returns (percent per annum compounded annually)

	1926–1947	*1947–1982*
	a. Nominal Returns*	
Common stocks†	6.3	10.9
Long-term bonds‡	4.7	3.2
U.S. Treasury bills	1.0	4.4
Money (inflation rate)§	1.2	4.0
	b. Real Returns*	
Common stocks†	5.1	6.9
Long-term bonds‡	3.5	−1.2
U.S. Treasury bills	−.02	.04
Money§	−1.2	−4.0

*Values in percent per annum compounded annually.

†Standard & Poor's 500 Stock Index.

‡Corporate and government bonds.

§Including currency and demand deposits.

SOURCE: R. G. Ibbotson and R. A. Singuefield, *Stocks, Bonds, Bills, and Inflation: The Past and the Future*, Financial Analysts Research Foundation, 1982. Updates published as *Stocks, Bonds, Bills and Inflation Yearbook* (Chicago: R. G. Ibbotson Associates, 1984. Annual).

TABLE 5–2
U.S. Capital Market Cross- and Serial Correlations of Asset Total Returns, 1947–1982

	S&P 500 Stocks	*Long-Term Corporate Bonds*	*Long-Term Government Bonds*	*U.S. Treasury Bills*	*Inflation Rates*
S&P common stocks	1.00				
Long-term corporate bonds	0.14	1.00			
Long-term government bonds	0.01	0.95	1.00		
U.S. Treasury bills	−0.25	0.15	0.21	1.00	
Inflation rates	−0.27	−0.19	−0.15	0.70	1.00
Serial correlation	−0.10	−0.00	0.06	0.90	0.68

SOURCE: R. G. Ibbotson and R. A. Singuefield, *Stocks, Bonds, Bills, and Inflation: The Past and the Future*, Financial Analysts Research Foundation, 1982.

TABLE 5–3
U.S. Capital Market Inflation-Adjusted Cross- and Serial Correlations of Asset Total Returns, 1947–1982

	S&P 500 Stocks	*Long-Term Corporate Bonds*	*Long-Term Government Bonds*	*U.S. Treasury Bills*	*Inflation Rates*
S&P common stocks	1.00				
Long-term corporate bonds	0.30	1.00			
Long-term government bonds	0.20	0.96	1.00		
U.S. Treasury bills	0.17	0.57	0.59	1.00	
Inflation rates	−0.46	−0.50	−0.50	−0.52	1.00
Serial correlation	−0.00	0.12	0.17	0.65	0.68

SOURCE: R. G. Ibbotson and R. A. Singuefield, *Stocks, Bonds, Bills, and Inflation: The Past and the Future*, Financial Analysts Research Foundation, 1982.

Negative distribution effects on bonds. Unanticipated increases in anticipated inflation decrease the value of long-term bonds because they bear interest rates negotiated at the previous lower nominal rates. As a result, holding period returns decline. The theory of why this happens and the empirical evidence that it does happen are not in dispute. This has been one of the clearest-cut effects of unanticipated increases in inflation in the post–World War II period and the major cause of the negative real yield on long-term bonds, shown in Table 5–1. Even if in the future money illusion is overcome, the value of long-term bonds will decline with an unanticipated increase in the anticipated inflation rate, with the only difference being that the decline will occur more rapidly. The experience of loss in value has made bond investors more aware of inflation risk. As a result, the risk premium in interest rates on longer-term bonds has increased.

Negative effects of shocks and risk on stocks. Equity investors also require higher risk premiums to compensate for the greater earnings variance that has accompanied heightened inflation. With the recognition of increased risk, investors bid down equity values, lowering holding period and raising expected future real rates of return.

TABLE 5–4
Year-by-Year Returns on Selected Asset Classes (1947–1982*)

	Total Returns				
Year	*S&P 500 Stocks*	*Long-Term Corporate Bonds*	*Long-Term Government Bonds*	*U.S. Treasury Bills*	*Inflation Rates*
1946					
1947	5.71	−2.34	−2.63	0.50	9.01
1948	5.50	4.14	3.40	0.81	2.71
1949	18.79	3.31	6.45	1.10	−1.80
1950	31.71	2.12	0.06	1.20	5.79
1951	24.02	−2.69	−3.94	1.49	5.87
1952	18.37	3.52	1.16	1.66	0.88
1953	−0.99	3.41	3.63	1.82	0.62
1954	52.62	5.39	7.19	0.86	−0.50
1955	31.56	0.48	−1.30	1.57	0.37
1956	6.56	−6.81	−5.59	2.46	2.86
1957	−10.78	8.71	7.45	3.14	3.02
1958	43.36	−2.22	−6.10	1.54	1.76
1959	11.95	−0.97	−2.26	2.95	1.50
1960	0.47	9.07	13.78	2.66	1.48
1961	26.89	4.82	0.97	2.13	0.67
1962	−8.73	7.95	6.89	2.73	1.22
1963	22.80	2.19	1.21	3.12	1.65
1964	16.48	4.77	3.51	3.54	1.19
1965	12.45	−0.46	0.71	3.93	1.92
1966	−10.06	0.20	3.65	4.76	3.35
1967	23.98	−4.95	−9.19	4.21	3.04
1968	11.06	2.57	−0.26	5.21	4.72
1969	−8.50	−8.09	−5.08	6.58	6.11
1970	4.01	18.37	12.10	6.53	5.49
1971	14.31	11.01	13.23	4.39	3.36
1972	18.98	7.26	5.68	3.84	3.41
1973	−14.66	1.14	−1.11	6.93	8.80
1974	−26.47	−3.06	4.35	8.00	12.20
1975	37.20	14.64	9.19	5.80	7.01
1976	23.84	18.65	16.75	5.08	4.81
1977	−7.18	1.71	−0.67	5.12	6.77
1978	6.56	−0.07	−1.16	7.18	9.03
1979	18.44	−4.18	−1.22	10.38	13.31
1980	32.42	−2.62	−3.95	11.24	12.40
1981	−4.91	−0.96	1.85	14.71	8.94
1982	21.41	43.79	40.35	10.54	3.87

*Total returns in percent.

SOURCE: R. G. Ibbotson and R. A. Singuefield, *Stocks, Bonds, Bills, and Inflation: The Past and the Future*, Financial Analysts Research Foundation, 1982.

TABLE 5–5
U.S. Capital Market Total Annual Real Returns (1960–1980*)

	Before-Tax	*After-Tax*
Common stocks†	5.24	3.13
Long-term bonds‡	−1.60	−3.83
U.S. Treasury bills§	.78	−1.16
Money ‖	−5.43	−5.43

*Values in percent per annum.

†Standard & Poor's 500 Stock Index.

‡Corporate and government bonds

§Plus other debt maturing in less than one year.

‖ Including currency and demand deposits.

SOURCE: Benjamin M. Friedman, "The Substitutability of Debt and Equity Securities," NBER Working Paper No. 1130, May 1983.

The origin of the increased earnings variance of the 1960s and 1970s was the shocks which also caused the unanticipated inflation of this period. These shocks lowered real rates of return as well.[43]

Tax effects. The capital market impact of inflation's interaction with taxes over the past two decades is less clear than inflation's other effects. The impact of the interaction of corporate and federal income taxes with inflation cannot be known with certainty. The evidence, however, suggests that corporate tax effects largely offset each other, with the positive impact on after-tax profits due to nominal interest deductibility, counterbalancing the negative impact due to historical cost accounting and capital gains taxation, especially with liberalized depreciation rules.

On the other hand, the federal income taxation of nominal returns does lower after-tax rates of return on taxable investment income, as is evident from Table 5–5, but it is not known whether the reaction of savers eventually causes a compensating rise in before-tax rates of return. Lowered after-tax yields induce a shift to capital-gains-only taxed equities and housing and to tax-exempt savings vehicles, such as pensions, IRAs, and Keogh plans. Whether they have any additional impact depends on the response (elasticity) of savings to interest rates. Before-tax rates may be bid up if savers restrict their savings in response to lower after-tax interest rates, but there is no evidence that they do.

As expected in a period of increased inflation uncertainty, assets that hedge inflation such as commodities and real estate do well. In particular, tax effects, while potentially neutral for traditional assets, clearly aided real estate in the 1970s. Highly leveraged real estate investors gained from inflation through the deductibility of nominal interest payments as well as through the decline in before-tax real interest rates.

In sum, we know that the low real rates of return on traditional assets in the 1960s and 1970s were due to shocks (especially but not solely supply shocks), to sustained excessive monetary expansion that followed the shocks, and to accompanying money illusion and distribution effects.

The propensity of the Federal Reserve to respond to and initiate shocks with increased monetary expansion over time was responsible for unanticipated increases in inflation and increased money risk.[44]

In October 1979, the Federal Reserve decided no longer to attempt the impossible task of making interest rates permanently lower with increased monetary expansion. The restriction of monetary growth reduced inflation and raised real interest rates and real yields except on real estate and commodities. The decline in inflation and the rise in real yields on traditional assets, shown in Table 5–4, are not coincidental but rather a continuation of the previous pattern of negatively correlated inflation and real yields. Just as increased money supply growth contributed to low yields in the 1970s, restricted money supply growth contributed to high yields in the early 1980s, before lower inflation and inflationary expectations could be reflected in lower nominal required yields. The nontraditional hedging assets of commodities and real estate have also reversed direction and dramatically declined in value.

The continued inverse pattern of yields and inflation is also due to the simultaneous negative impact on unanticipated inflation and positive impact on yields of positive supply shocks. The underlying productivity of capital has increased, and there has been unanticipated disinflation as a result of the partial undoing of the OPEC supply shocks of the 1970s.

High real interest rates of the early 1980s are also due to increased inflation risk. Contractionary monetary policies, paradoxically, resulted in more variance in monetary growth and increased money risk (since zero future inflation rates were now a more likely possibility). In the interim, before it is clear that inflation can be permanently subdued, long-term nominal (callable) bonds are riskier to the investor: Possible higher future inflation rates will lower the real yield, and possible lower future inflation rates will cause the bonds to be recalled (so that bond holders might no longer be able to achieve high nominal portfolio returns). Thus, the higher interest rates of the early- to mid-1980s were due to a combination of higher deficits, increased money risk, increased productivity of capital, and (in the early 1980s), a liquidity shortage.

The experience of the past two decades can instruct us on the likely impact of future unanticipated increases in the inflation rate. Once again unanticipated increases in inflation and in anticipated inflation would lower holding period returns on nominal bonds, with bonds of longest duration most affected. Equity values also would fall if future monetary contractions were perceived as more likely. While the supply shocks of the 1970s were unusually strong, the increased involvement of the United States in worldwide trade and capital flows makes the economy more vulnerable to continued shocks from abroad. For example, a decrease in U.S. yields could stimulate an exodus of foreign capital, which would raise exchange rates and the inflation rate (due to an increased cost of domestic goods) and decrease real output growth.

Of the possible future inflation scenarios, a return to price level stability is consistent with the ability of nominal pensions to provide a safe retirement income. Low to moderate inflation may also be consistent with the current institution of nominal pensions, given that a large percentage of preretirement income is indexed after retirement through Social Security and Medicare benefits. As inflation increases, a nominal pension's value erodes faster. Clearly, if inflation reaches and becomes chronic at the double-digit highs of the 1970s, private nominal pensions will no longer provide a secure retirement income. Yet, given the capital market effects of inflation, there is no easy adjustment that pensions can make to adapt to an inflationary economy.

Implications for Indexed Pensions

As discussed in Chapter 3, the great preponderance of pensions provide nominally fixed retirement benefits. In a time of limited or zero inflation, nominally fixed pensions offer a secure retirement income. In a time of chronic ongoing inflation, nominal benefits can be rapidly eroded.

Ongoing inflation, supported by money supply growth, may threaten recipients of nominal pensions who depend on their pension income for retirement expenditures. The extent of harm of ongoing inflation to nominal benefit recipients depends positively on the rate of inflation and on the number of years spent in retirement, as shown in Table 5–6. Assuming a 5 percent inflation rate, real income is halved after 20 years of retirement. Thus, even with moderate ongoing inflation, a nominally fixed income stream no longer provides a secure retirement income.

Is it possible to restructure pensions to index benefits to inflation, at the same risk and cost of nominal pensions in a period of price stability? This could be done if investment portfolios could be constructed to yield the same real rate of return, with or without inflation.

In reality, indexing a real rate of return to inflation is not economically feasible. An indexed stream of income is only possible if an increase in inflation does not lower real rates of return. As theory and empirical evidence show, however, real rates of return on equities and bonds are likely to be lowered coterminously with an unanticipated increase in the inflation rate. Money illusion, shocks, distribution effects, and increased risks are all likely to result in lowered holding period returns. Therefore, a portfolio invested in stocks and bonds cannot be used to index the same average real rate of return that the portfolio earns in noninflationary periods.[45]

Even if inflation does not increase over time, and if real rates of return on the average remain unchanged over time, reduced earnings and reduced holding period returns are likely to be associated with unanticipated inflation. This inverse correlation of real returns and unanticipated inflation makes guaranteeing an

TABLE 5–6
Purchasing Power of $100 of Fixed-Pension Benefits under Various Rates of Inflation

Number of Years after Retirement	*Rate of Inflation*			
	5 Percent	*10 Percent*	*12 Percent*	*15 Percent*
5	$78	$62	$57	$50
10	61	39	32	25
15	48	24	18	12
20	38	15	10	6

indexed stream of income riskier when the inflation rate is positive than guaranteeing a nominal income stream when the average inflation rate is zero.

Nominally denominated debt, including pension debt, reduces the risk of random shocks to the firm. Shocks reduce real output growth and the productivity of all inputs. Shocks also reduce real payments because with constant money supply growth unanticipated inflation tends to rise proportionately to the fall in real output and productivity growth (as indicated by the quantity theory). In general, it is efficient for inputs to be paid according to their productivity. Moreover, risk of the enterprise's failure due to external shocks is minimized if positive and negative shocks can be absorbed by the enterprise's contractual suppliers of inputs, most importantly, employees. Hence, nominal contracting can be an efficient form of risk bearing for the firm's employees as well as owners. This assumes long-term (although not short-term) price stability, so that the real expected value of long-term nominal contracts is not eroded by inflation.

Indexation of contracts prevents such erosion. However, with indexation, unanticipated declines in a firm's productivity, caused by unanticipated declines in economywide real output growth, can no longer be shared with the firm's inputs. These commitments are then fixed in real terms, no matter what the unanticipated decline in output and earnings growth due to a shock. As a result, the firm is more vulnerable to shocks.

Table 5–7 illustrates the major dilemma posed by inflation for those who desire an income stream that is not expected to decline over time. The "solution" to inflation caused by money

TABLE 5–7

The Cost to Firms of Alternative Debt Instruments and the Source of Inflation and Disinflation Episodes

	Inflation	*Money Supply*	*Real Cost with Nominal Long-Term Debt*	*Real Cost with Indexed Debt*	*Profits*
Sources of unanticipated inflation					
Demand-pull					
1. Money supply					
a. Increases	↑	↑	↓	–	↑
b. Decreases	↓	↓	↑	–	↓
2. Expenditure					
a. Increases	↑	↑	↓	–	↑
b. Decreases	↓	↓	↑	–	↓
Supply-shock					
1. Increases	↑	–	↓	–	↓
2. Decreases	↓	–	↑	–	↑

shocks is indexation of all contractually determined prices, including pension debt. But this is precisely the wrong solution for inflation caused by supply shocks. Supply shocks entail an economywide slowdown in sales and profit growth and, for firms in sectors heavily dependent on affected raw materials, an extra increase in costs. Firms are not in the position of passing on the increase in costs to the consumer. If they attempt to do so, further declines in sales, output, and profit growth rates will result. In general, relative prices and wages must change as a result of supply-shock episodes. Indexing prices, wages, debt payments, and pensions prevents the adjustment and exacerbates the real dislocations associated with the causes of the supply-shock episodes.

Thus, firms should not be and are not indifferent between (1) a long-run noninflationary monetary policy and nominal debt and (2) a long-run inflationary monetary policy and indexed debt. The first alternative involves less risk. Moreover, the second alternative increases risk exposure by an unknowable amount since the size of future supply shocks are not predictable.

Although the currently prevalent defined benefit pension cannot be transformed into an indexed pension, there are alternatives that can serve as near substitutes. One possibility is the transformation of a defined benefit pension upon retirement into a defined contribution pension, which is funded with assets whose returns closely track inflation, such as short-term debt. The income that this portfolio would provide could then be indexed not to inflation but rather to the changes in the short-term interest rate. Since, as shown by Bodie, these short-term interest rate movements have been very closely correlated with inflation, there would be little money risk to beneficiaries in choosing this route.[46] Such performance-type indexing, which includes excess investment return arrangements, is described in Chapter 7.

Although it is possible to construct such alternatives to the conventional nominal defined benefit plans, there are significant costs in doing so.[47] These costs occur because of the lower real rate produced by the assets of an inflation-tracking portfolio. If pensions that preserve real income are desired, in a time of increased inflation uncertainty it is necessary to fund with a mix of short-term securities, commodities, and real estate, rather than with a mix of debt of various maturities and equity. Such assets cannot yield the high real return produced by equity or long-term nominal debt. Investors are willing to pay a higher expected return on these because they reduce the risk of long-term investment.

The magnitude of the cost of this shift is unknown. However, the approximate cost may be estimated very roughly on the basis of the Bodie results and the Ibbotson-Singuefield[48] historical data, together with the assumption frequently made in the pension cost literature that a 1 percent decline in real interest rates raises pension costs, as a percentage of the wage bill, by 25 percent.[49] Ibbotson-Singuefield's historical data are used as the basis for the assumption that the rates of return of equities and long-term bonds exceed the rate of return of an inflation-hedging (short-term bond, real estate, and commodity) portfolio by approximately 6 percent and 2 percent, respectively, for an average rate of return markup on these assets over inflation-hedging assets of 4 percent. As shown by Bodie, historically the return on a risk-free minimal variance portfolio (that is, a portfolio made up predominantly of Treasury bills hedged against unanticipated inflation by a small position in a diversified portfolio of commodity futures) has been approximately zero. Using these assumptions, pension costs, as a percentage of wages, would rise by 100 percent if the firm had to shift all its funds into an inflation-hedging portfolio in order to preserve real pensions.

This, however, is unlikely to be the case. In the early portion of the working career, defined benefit pension credits need not be funded by inflation-hedging assets. Real wages can decline and the firm is only obligated to provide a pension that is in proportion to the real wage. Equity funding is appropriate for the first half of a worker's career, even with sustained and uncertain inflation, because real wages and equity values are both likely to move with the overall growth rate of the economy and because, if equity values do not keep up with the real wage, the divergence can be funded by small increases in contribution rates over the long-term worklife of the employee.

These conditions do not hold for the latter portion of the worker's career. In the years prior to retirement, the firm may feel that it must maintain a worker's real income for morale purposes, even if not obligated to do so. If so, after-retirement income and the immediately preceding retirement income need to be maintained in real terms.

Thus, assuming that inflation-hedging returns are necessary only in the latter part of the career and during retirement and that these two periods taken together are roughly one half of the pension-holding period, this implies an overall increased cost of 50 percent.

Other assumptions are possible. For example, nominal pension liabilities can be funded without risk to firms with long-term bonds. Assume firms switch to providing inflation-hedging, defined contribution pensions, which also impose no risk to firms while protecting workers against inflation. Using historical data that suggest a 2 percent differential between long-term and (inflation hedging) short-term bond portfolio yields, this also would raise the cost of pensions by 50 percent.

This cost differential, due to uncertain and sustained inflation, is relevant for a firm starting up a new inflation-hedging pension for a given expected real benefit. The expected real benefit of an already existing nominal pension plan is, of course, lowered over time by expected inflation.

Table 5–6 shows how the real purchasing power of nominally fixed-pensions is eroded for various rates of expected inflation. The table can also be used to show how the funding costs of a given nominally fixed pension decline with expected inflation. The loss to retirees in real purchasing power is identical to the gain to firms in lowered real pension costs, assuming neutral inflation.

With a 5 percent inflation rate, funding requirements of a nominal pension are lowered by 50 percent, given a 15-year average retirement period (since the real value of a nominal pension declines by 50 percent with a 5 percent inflation rate in 15 years). Thus, if the initial real value of a pension is to be preserved, with an inflation-hedging portfolio, pension costs may increase by approximately 100 percent.

Double-digit expected inflation rates nearly wipe out the value (and the cost) of pensions within the normal 15-year retirement period. Even a moderate 5 percent inflation rate reduces real purchasing power by more than half for those who live longer than average. If the decline in the expected future value of pensions is not perceived by workers—and they may not be, at least for some period of time—firms need not compensate workers with higher current wages. If so, the tax advantages to pensions granted by the government would result in higher profits and lower lifetime remuneration without assuring old age income security.

Workers may be aware of expected inflation's erosion of their expected benefits and receive commensurate increases in current wages. Nonetheless, the role of pensions in providing old age income security is diminished by sustained inflation. Tax advantages may be granted by the government to pensions in large measure because they encourage private provision of old age income security. If so, their continued public policy justification may require inflation-hedging performance indexed pensions, in spite of their greater cost. The public policy issues involved are discussed further in Part Four.

APPENDIX 5.A
Demand, Supply, and Money Shocks

Empirical evidence generally confirms the theoretical discussion of the short-run correlation of inflation and capital market effects. The three sources of short-run inflation are identified above as demand, supply, and money shocks. In theory, demand shocks were shown to have a positive impact on real interest rates together with a once-and-for-all positive impact on inflation. A study of the period 1955 through 1980 in the United States by Hafer and Hein confirms that increased deficits resulted in higher real interest rates and in higher inflation.[50] These effects, however, were minor.[51]

A direct test for the impact of supply shocks on real yields in the United States in the period 1952 through 1978 has been undertaken by James A. Wilcox as part of a comprehensive study of interest rates and inflation (discussed below).[52] Wilcox finds that positive shocks, deriving from declining oil prices, contributed to higher real and nominal interest rates and lower inflation rates than otherwise from the beginning of the period studied through the early 1970s. In the mid-1970s through 1978, negative supply shocks due to sharply increased oil prices resulted in a decline in the productivity of capital and lower yields. Nonetheless, although these effects are detectable and economically significant, they do not play a major role in explaining interest rate variation in the postwar U.S. economy, except for the mid-1970s.[53]

In theory, the impact of a money shock on interest rates must be negative due to the liquidity effect. Evidence of this effect is found in a study by Hafer and Hein, which examines the impact of monetary policy on short-term real interest rate movements in the United States in the post–World War II period.[54] To test for a liquidity effect, Hafer and Hein construct a measure of real balances, defined as the ratio of money supply to prices. Positive money shocks augment real balances and create excess liquidity if prices do not adjust upward immediately and fully. As predicted, the study finds that real interest rates decrease within the quarter of a real balance increase. In the following quarter, as prices rise real balances and the interest rate return to their equilibrium levels. Thus, real interest rates decline in the quarter after a money shock, with the decline reversed in the following quarter. This implies that prices adjust to money shocks on the average in six months in the U.S. economy in the post–World War II period. Hafer and Hein also find that the variation in real balances explains only a small proportion of real interest rate fluctuations. This study as well as the others cited here confirm that real interest rates have not been constant in the post–World War II period and that a large proportion of their variation needs to be explained by variables other than the direct effects of money or real shocks on ex ante returns.

In sum, measurable demand, supply, and money shocks explain some portion of yield variation in the post–World War II U.S. economy, due to their impact on ex ante yields. Partial equilibrium empirical studies that focus on these leave a good deal of yield variation unexplained. Nor is the net impact of these shocks on interest rates indicated by these partial equilibrium studies. The direction of this impact, however, can be inferred from the course of inflation and monetary policy over this period. Evidence presented in Chapter 1 indicates that increases in inflation in the post–World War II period were caused by money, demand, and supply shocks and that monetary expansion increased with these shocks. Since monetary authorities responded to demand and supply shocks with monetary expansion, and also excessively expanded the money supply through money shocks, short-term equilibrium (ex ante) interest rates on the average were reduced below their previous levels.

APPENDIX 5.B
Money Illusion: The Empirical Debate

Given a negligible wealth-shift effect and maintaining the assumption of no tax or uncertainty effects, the reasons for the neutrality of anticipated inflation in the long run are (1) that ongoing anticipated inflation must be a monetary phenomenon and (2) that rational investors require full compensation for expected deterioration in purchasing power. As a result, the expected real return is independent of the expected inflation rate in the long run. Under these circumstances, as stated in the Fisher hypothesis, the nominal interest rate is the sum of an expected real rate of return and the expected inflation rate; sustained inflation does not affect capital markets.

To test the Fisher hypothesis, the relation between the expected nominal return on any asset and the expected inflation rate (in an efficient market with rational investors) can be algebraically stated as:

$$E(\tilde{R}_t/\phi_{t-1}) = E(\tilde{r}_t/\phi_{t-1}) + E(\tilde{\pi}_t/\phi_{t-1})$$

where R_t is the nominal return on any asset; r_t is the equilibrium real rate; π_t is the inflation rate; E is the expectations operator; and ϕ_{t-1} is the information set that investors use in forming their expectations on inflation and real rates for the period t. Thus, $E(\tilde{r}_t/\phi_{t-1})$ and $E(\pi_t/\phi_{t-1})$ are the expected real rate and expected inflation rate.

The difficulty in testing this hypothesis is that neither the expected real rate nor the expected inflation rate is observable. In the absence of a general equilibrium model for the determination of real interest rates, a major assumption made is that the equilibrium expected real rate and the expected inflation rate are uncorrelated. With this assumption a value of unity for β is implied in the following regression model:

$$\tilde{R}_t = \alpha + \beta E(\tilde{\pi}_t/\phi_{t-1}) + \tilde{\varepsilon}_t$$

A test of the above equation is a test of the joint hypothesis that the market is efficient and the expected real return and expected inflation rate vary independently. (Thus, rejection of the equation would be an indication of either of the two conditions not holding.)

Three techniques have been used to model the anticipated inflation rate: (1) the assumption that the anticipated inflation rate is a function of past inflation rates (i.e., adaptive expectations), (2) the use of survey data to estimate inflation expectations, and (3) the assumption of rational expectations.

Early research relied for the most part on the assumption of adaptive expectations. Thus, Meiselman regressed various interest rates against a distributed lag function of past percentage price level changes.[55] His results support a less than one-to-one relationship between interest rates and inflation rates. William Gibson used a similar procedure and obtained similar results.[56] His study for the period 1869 through 1963 finds an extremely long lag in the response of interest rates to inflation; by the 10th year, interest rates increase only one third of 1 percent for a 1 percent increase in inflation.

Other authors used more sophisticated methods of assessing expected inflation. Using adaptive expectations, Yohe and Karnosky,[57] Feldstein and Eckstein,[58] and Elliot expressed anticipated inflation as an Almon polynomial of past inflation rates.[59] In general, these authors find that "expected real rates are systematically lowered when the most current realized rate of inflation is increasing."[60]

A problem in these studies derives from their use of adaptive expectations to model the expected inflation rate. If shocks, such as those discussed above, cause actual inflation to differ from its expected level, expected inflation may remain unchanged, but measured expected inflation will increase. Unavoidable bias in the measurement of the expected inflation rate results. This then biases the measure of the expected real interest rate, since it is constructed by subtracting the measured expected inflation rate from the nominal interest rate. When expected inflation is wrongly measured as high, expected real interest rates will be wrongly measured as low. The conclusion of money illusion may be an artifact of this bias rather than a true description of the lack of responsiveness of expected nominal rates of return to expected inflation.[61]

Perhaps the most significant and also the most controversial piece of research in recent years on this topic is that of Fama.[62] The major innovation of this study is the use of rational expectations to avoid the adaptive expectation measurement bias. His work is built around the following regression:

$$\overset{n}{\Delta}_t = \alpha_0 + \alpha_1 R_t + E_t$$

where Δ_t is the inflation rate over period t. Note that the interest rate is quoted at the beginning of the period, and the inflation rate is published in government statistics at the end of the period. Thus, the interest rate, which is viewed as a predictor of inflation and an estimate of anticipated inflation, should be the independent variable. An errors-in-the-variables problem would arise if Δ_t were the independent variable, since inflation is measured with error.

Fama argues that if the estimated value of α_1 is significantly different from 1, we can reject the joint hypothesis that (1) the expected real rate of interest is constant and (2) the market efficiently incorporates all relevant information in setting interest rates.[63]

The notion that the regression tests a joint hypothesis is quite important. A value of α_1 different from one does not imply inefficiency since the market may rationally set an expected real rate that varies with inflation because the expected real rate is a function of the expected inflation rate for the theoretical reasons presented in the previous chapter. Also, a value different from one does not imply that the expected real rate is a function of the expected inflation rate, since the market may so inefficiently process information that expected rates differ widely from the realized ones. Money illusion may cause α_1 to be less than one.

To measure inflation, Fama primarily uses the consumer price index (CPI). (A confirming regression also employs the WPI.) The interest rate is measured by Treasury bills of different maturities. Fama performs regressions between 1953 and 1971. He uses data after 1953 because earlier price data are measured with a lag which would result in downward biased estimates of the value of α_1. The estimated values of α_1 are not significantly different from one for the whole of the period and for subperiods, leading Fama to conclude that the above joint hypothesis cannot be rejected. This latter result is rather strong since it holds for all T-bill maturities between one month and six months.

Fama's results have been subject to criticism and reexamination. The basis of the criticism has been the assumption of the constancy of the real interest rate in the early work, and the assumption in the later study that the expected real rate of interest is invariant to the inflation rate.[64] Thus, the Fama procedure, as that of earlier studies, suffers from the lack of a general equilibrium model for the determination of real interest rates. In the absence of such a model, the positive or negative short-run correlation of changes in the expected real interest rate and the expected inflation rate may bias the results of regressions, which assume no correlation or a constant interest rate.

Fama himself points out that the nominal interest rate may merely be a proxy for more fundamental variables.[65] For example, the coefficient of R_t may be biased upwards, if R_t is a proxy for a variable such as employment or output which may be positively related to both inflation and real interest rates in the time period of his study. If such variables were included in the regression equation, the coefficient of R_t might be significantly less than 1. Since there is an infinite number of variables that could conceivably be added to the regression equation, one can never completely reject the hypothesis that a proxying effect exists. However, Fama limits his analysis to the following regression:

$$\Delta_t = \alpha_0 + \alpha_1 R_t + \alpha_2 \Delta_{t-1}$$

arguing that Δ_{t-1} should pick up much of the information predicting Δ_t that R_t might miss. The joint hypothesis would be rejected if α_1 is significantly different from one. The values of α_1 in this set of regressions are not significantly different from 1, lending further support to the joint hypothesis.

The Fama paper has received a great deal of attention, discussion, and criticism. We present a sampling of this controversy below. As a group, the criticism primarily attacks Fama's limited search for proxies.

Joines performes the following set of regressions over the same 1953–71 period:

$$\Delta_t = \alpha_0 + \alpha_1 R_t + \alpha_2 W_{t-1} + \alpha_3 W_{t-2} + \alpha_4 W_{t-3}$$

where W_t is the inflation rate over period t, as measured by the WPI. His results indicate that α_1 is significantly less than 1 and that α_2, α_3, and α_4 are significantly greater than 0. Because W_{t-2} and W_{t-3} are certainly observable at the beginning of period t and W_{t-1} may be observable at this time, Joines argues that variations in the real rate are predictable.

Both Nelson and Schwert[67] and Hess and Bicksler argue that W_{t-1} does not capture all the predictive power concerning α_t that all the past rates of inflation provide.[68] Both studies first estimate an autoregressive moving average (ARIMA) model where the expected inflation rate is a function of past inflation rates. Thus, Nelson and Schwert argue that at each date t, $\hat{p}_t$, the expected inflation rate calculated from the ARIMA model can be placed in the following regression:

$$\Delta_t = \alpha_0 + \alpha_1 R_t + \alpha_2 \hat{p}_t$$

The authors find this yields a value of α_1 significantly below 1, and positive values of α_2 suggesting that the real rate of interest is a function of $\hat{p}_t$.

Noting that both R_t and $\hat{p}_t$ are predictors of inflation, Hess and Bicksler measure the forecast errors of these parameters over the period 1953–71. The authors conclude that R_t does not capture all the information available to the marketplace concerning Δ_t.

Carlson performs the following regression:

$$\Delta_t = \alpha_0 + \alpha_1 R_t + \alpha_2 (\mathrm{E/P})_{t-6}$$

where E/P is the ratio of seasonally adjusted employment to population.[69] He finds that α_1 is significantly less than 1, implying that the real rate of interest is a function of a lagged value of E/P.

Fama's rejoinder stresses two points.[70] First, the Bureau of Labor Statistics samples the prices of many items less than once a month, inducing a spurious serial correlation in the inflation rates from the CPI and WPI. This could easily cause the coefficients on the lagged values of W_{t-1} and P_t to be positive. Second, the R^2's of the other studies' regressions are only slightly higher than the R^2 from Fama's. Thus, Fama concludes, "Taking the data at face value, the interest rate remains the best single predictor of the inflation rate; and nobody has uncovered variables that make substantial contributions to the prediction of inflation beyond that provided by the interest rate alone."[71]

APPENDIX 5.C
Tax, Distribution, and Money Illusion Effects on Equities: The Empirical Evidence

This appendix discusses the empirical evidence for the hypothetical impact of taxes, distribution effects, and money illusion as explanations for the observed negative correlation between stock yields and inflation.

Tax Effects

The inverse relationship between unanticipated inflation and nominal yields could be due to an increase in effective corporate or personal income taxes with inflation. However, the empirical evidence does not support this hypothesis. A number of studies find that the average rate of taxation of corporate profits does not increase over this period. Studies by Fama[72] and Gonedes[73] find that the net effects on profits of historical cost accounting, the deductibility of nominal interest payments, and more liberal depreciation are negligible. Myron Gordon finds that over the years 1960 to 1980 the net effects of taxes on corporate profits should have *increased* the market value of equity.[74] Summers' results, discussed above, support this finding. Hasbrouck indicates that negative historical cost depreciation and inventory valuation effects reach limiting points as inflation increases, while the positive effect of nominal interest rate deductibility grows.[75] Leaving aside liberalized depreciation allowances, Hasbrouck finds in a simulation analysis that at higher than 10 percent inflation rates, the positive effect dominates. In sum, there is little evidence that corporate tax effects explain the negative correlation of inflation with real stock returns.

Similarly, there is no strong evidence to support the hypothesis that the negative correlation is due to the personal income tax consequences of inflation. The hypothesis that they do depends on a positive impact on required before-tax yields. If it is assumed that inflation does not change the required after-tax rate of return on stocks, then the before-tax rate of return must increase. For the before-tax rate to rise, the holding period rate of return must decline. (This is because stock market prices must decline to raise the future real rate of return, given an unchanged real earnings stream.) However, if the before-tax rate of return on stocks increased because of the rise in the effective personal income tax, the before-tax, risk-free rate of return would presumably also rise; and the evidence of other studies, cited above, shows that an increase in the expected rate of inflation either leaves the before-tax, risk-free rate of return unchanged or reduced. Moreover, as indicated by Miller, the effective personal income tax rate on equities may be close to zero.[76] Also, a rise in the effective personal income tax rate lowers the before-tax corporate cost of capital.[77] The implication is that with higher personal income tax rates, stock prices might rise. Finally, as shown by Friend and Hasbrouck, any conclusions on net effects are highly sensitive to assumptions on tax rate and other parameter values.[78] It appears that neither the corporate nor the personal consequences of inflation can contribute to an explanation of the observed inverse relationship of stock market real returns to inflation.

Distribution Effects

The theoretical discussion above also showed that unanticipated inflation has distribution effects. Debtors gain from unanticipated inflation and lenders lose. Individual firms may be net debtors or lenders depending on their holdings. If firms taken together are net lenders (debtors), this may result in a negative (positive) correlation of unanticipated inflation with real stock returns. French, Ruback, and Schwert analyze the effects of unanticipated inflation on the stock returns of firms with different nominal contracting positions.[79] They include in their determination of nominal contracting positions data on a short-term monetary position (i.e., cash and accounts receivable minus current liabilities) and a long-term monetary position (i.e., long-term debt minus preferred stock) and an estimate of the depreciation tax shield, which is negatively affected by inflation. They find "little evidence that stockholders of firms with relatively large net monetary liabilities benefited from unexpected inflation relative to the stockholders of firms with net monetary assets during the 1947–79 period."[80] They attribute their surprising findings to their lack of data on some nominal contracts (e.g., labor, pensions, raw materials, and final product). The evidence is consistent with firms hedging against unexpected inflation, by combining a set of contracts, so that stock values are unaffected by unexpected inflation. In any case, these results cannot support the attribution of the observed negative real stock returns-inflation correlation to distribution effects.

Money Illusions

Thus, empirical evidence suggests that neither distribution nor tax effects contribute to the negative response of real stock returns to unanticipated inflation, although, money, demand, and supply shocks may do so. The negative relationship between *anticipated* inflation and expected real equity yields cannot be explained by distribution effects, tax effects, or short-run shocks. Lags in the adjustment of the market to expected inflation information may explain some part of a continuing negative impact of past inflation on real yields. It is reasonable, given bounded rationality, that available information is not immediately incorporated into stock market yields. However, pervasive money illusion is unlikely to be a full explanation of the negative relationship between anticipated inflation and expected real equity yields, at least in recent decades. Indeed, direct tests of investor irrationality in the post–World War II period do not confirm money illusion. Davidson and Froyen show that the stock market efficiently uses information on money growth rates in their 1971 through 1976 sample period.[81] Gordon shows that the Modigliani and Cohen hypothesis, if applied to the 1960 to 1980 period, would explain too much of the decline in stock values.[82]

Notes

[1] See Eugene F. Fama and G. W. Schwert, "Asset Returns and Inflation," *Journal of Financial Economics* 5, no. 2 (November 1977), pp. 115–46; and Jeffrey F. Jaffe and Gershon Mandelker, "Inflation and the Holding Period Returns on Bonds," Rodney L. White Center for Financial Research, University of Pennsylvania, Working Paper No. 8-75.

[2] In the United States, cash holdings of individuals and noninterest earning

reserves of banks amount to less than 2 percent of the value of the capital stock. Even under the most extreme assumptions that (1) inflation and the nominal interest rate reach sufficiently high levels that money holdings were reduced to zero and that (2) capital increased to maintain wealth constant, the real interest rate would only decline by six basis points, as noted by Lawrence Summers. Thus, the real interest rate should be negligibly affected by anticipated inflation through the wealth-shift effect. See Lawrence H. Summers, "The Nonadjustment of Nominal Interest Rates: A Study of the Fisher Effect," in *Macroeconomics, Prices, and Quantities: Essays in Memory of Arthur M. Okun*, ed. James Tobin (Washington, D.C.: Brookings Institution, 1983).

[3] See Eugene F. Fama, "Short-Term Interest Rates as Predictors of Inflation," *American Economic Review* 65 (June 1975), pp. 269–82.

[4] See Steven C. Leuthold, "Interest Rates, Inflation and Deflation," *Financial Analysts Journal* (January–February 1981), pp. 28–41.

[5] See Summers, "The Nonadjustment of Nominal Interest Rates: A Study of the Fisher Effect."

[6] See Robert J. Shiller and Jeremy J. Siegel, "The Gibson Paradox and Historical Movements in Real Interest Rates," *Journal of Political Economy* 85 (October 1977), pp. 891–907.

[7] See Summers, "The Nonadjustment of Nominal Interest Rates: A Study of the Fisher Effect."

[8] Summers relies on a study by Martin Feldstein and Lawrence Summers, "Inflation and the Taxation of Capital Income in the Corporate Sector," *National Tax Journal* 32 (December 1979), pp. 445–70. Also see studies cited below which indicate a negligible effect.

[9] See reference above for an explanation.

[10] See Roger H. Gordon and Burton G. Malkiel, "Corporation Finance," in *How Taxes Affect Economic Behavior*, ed. Henry J. Aaron and Joseph A. Pechman (Washington, D.C.: Brookings Institution, 1981), pp. 131–92.

[11] See reference above for further discussion.

[12] Ibid.

[13] For a derivation of a model that can lead to a unitary effect, see Jeffrey F. Jaffe, "Inflation and Miller's Model of Capital Structure," Rodney L. White Center for Financial Research, The Wharton School, University of Pennsylvania, Working Paper No. 10-83.

[14] Ibid.

[15] See James A. Wilcox, "Interest Rates, Expected Inflation, and Supply Shocks—Or Why Real Interest Rates Were So Low in the 1970s," National Bureau of Economic Research Working Paper. Prepared for the NBER Conference on Inflation and Financial Markets, Cambridge, Mass., May 15, 1981.

[16] Summers also attempts to model changes in the marginal productivity of capital, but the proxies used may not be adequate.

[17] The survey used is of a group of business, government, labor, and academic economists (conducted by Joseph Livingston of the *Philadelphia Inquirer*). Average forecasts lagged inflation.

[18] See discussion above.

[19] Wilcox finds that a 1 percent increase in expected inflation drives interest rates up by approximately .8 of a point. Given the standard error of a .08, this coefficient supports the hypothesis that expected inflation of 1 percent leads to a 1 percent increase in interest rates, although only at the 90 percent confidence level. However, some supply-shock proxies support a unitary response at the 95 percent confidence level.

[20] See N. B. Gultekin, "Stock Market Returns and Inflation: Evidence from Other Countries," *Journal of Finance*, forthcoming.

[21] See Zvi Bodie, Alex Kane, and Robert McDonald, "Inflation and the Role of Bonds in Investor Portfolios," National Bureau of Economic Research Working Paper No. 1091, March 1983. It is possible that shorter duration bonds became more desirable as the risk of holding equity or long-term bonds increased and that this depressed the expected real return on these instruments. However, the lower than unitary response found for bonds of all durations in Summers' work throughout the 1970s cannot be explained by uncertainty effects.

[22] In a survey of the impact of inflation, Reilly cites a number of studies that show this. His year-by-year discussion of U.S. stock price movements during 1966 through 1973 points to the inverse impact of changes in the inflation rate, given earnings. See Frank K. Reilly, "Companies and Common Stocks as Inflation Hedges," New York University, Graduate School of Business Administration, Center for the Study of Financial Institutions, *The Bulletin*, Bulletin 1975–2.

[23] In a comprehensive historical survey, Cagan analyzes stock and CPI data from the 24 countries that reported both sets of data. He finds that, over the years 1939 to 1950, deflated stock values (the rate of change in stock prices minus the rate of change in prices) were negative in 21 of the 24 countries. In the period 1950 through 1969, stocks did well, with positive deflated stock values in 17 of 24 countries, and if dividends are included, in 21 of 24 countries. See Phillip Cagan, "Common Stock Values and Inflation—The Historical Record of Many Countries," *National Bureau Report Supplement* (New York: National Bureau of Economic Research, March 1974).

[24] See Jeffrey Jaffe and Gershon Mandelker, "The Fisher Effect for Risky Assets," *Journal of Finance* 31 (May 1976), pp. 447–58; and Charles R. Nelson, "Inflation and Rates of Return on Common Stock," *Journal of Finance* 31 (May 1976), pp. 471–83.

[25] In his comprehensive study, described further below, Gultekin finds a lack of positive relationship between unanticipated inflation and stock returns in the majority of 26 countries investigated between 1958 and 1979.

[26] See Jaffe and Mandelker, "The Fisher Effect for Risky Assets."

[27] Nelson finds significantly negative coefficients for the following set of regressions:

$$Rmt = a + b\Delta_{t+i}$$

where i varies between $+4$ and -6. A negative coefficient when $i \geqslant 1$ is understandable as it merely suggests that the market predicts future inflation. However, the negative coefficient when $i \leqslant -1$ is evidence of inefficiency, since the result implies that past information can be used to predict future returns on securities.

Nelson next uses the results for the 1953–71 period to make predictions of inflation rates and market returns over the period from January 1973 to June 1974. He finds that his model can be used to form trading rules which outperform the buy and hold stock market strategy, assuming no transaction costs. See Nelson, "Inflation and Rates of Return on Common Stock."

Bodie performs regressions similar to those mentioned above in order to calculate the ability of common stocks to serve as an inflation hedge. Because of the perverse results from the regressions, Bodie concludes that a short position in stocks over the period from 1953–71 would have served as an effective hedge. See Zvi Bodie, "Common Stocks as a Hedge against Inflation," *Journal of Finance* 31 (May 1976), pp. 459–70.

The post-1953 period has been investigated more fully than earlier periods because of the substantial upgrading of the CPI index during 1953. However, studies examining prior periods have not uncovered any positive relationship between actual returns on stocks and inflation. For example, Lintner presents evidence that, over the period 1934–48, $Rmt - Rt$ is negatively related to inflation. See J. Lintner, "Inflation and Security Returns," *Journal of Finance* 30, no. 2 (May 1975).

Friend and Hasbrouck reach similar conclusions for the United States in a study that uses data as far back as 1926. See I. Friend and J. Hasbrouck, "Effect of Inflation on the Profitability and Valuation of U.S. Corporations," in *Saving, Investment and Capital Markets in an Inflationary Economy,* ed. M. Sarnat and G. Szego (Cambridge, Mass.: Ballinger, forthcoming).

Finally, in the most comprehensive recent study, Gultekin examines inflation and stock returns in 26 countries, from 1947 to 1979, using lagged inflation rates and short-term interest rates as proxies for expected inflation and finds regression coefficients that are predominantly negative. See N. B. Gultekin, "Stock Market Returns and Inflation: Evidence from Other Countries."

[28] Indeed, the anticipated inflation results can be explained by the Modigliani and Cohn arguments that investors consider higher nominal interest payments an increased expense (rather than early repayment of capital) and that they capitalize profits at nominal rather than real rates of return. See Franco Modigliani and Richard Cohn, "Inflation, Rational Valuation and the Market," *Financial Analysts Journal* 35 (March–April 1979).

[29] Unanticipated inflation was shown to result from supply, demand, and money shocks. In each case the impact on inflation and real profit growth is an inverse one. At base, the inverse outcome derives from the inverse relation between real output growth and inflation in the quantity theory equation. See Theodore E. Day, "Real Stock Returns and Inflation," *Journal of Finance* 35, no. 2 (June 1984), pp. 493–502, for a formal derivation of these results.

[30] In themselves, shocks cannot explain the inverse relationship of yields to *expected* inflation, nor can tax and distribution effects unless there is a slow perception of their negative impact over time. This is discussed further below.

[31] If inflation is expected over period t to period $t + 1$, and if, as a result, real earnings are expected to be lower, stock prices should be depressed at the beginning of period t, so that real holding period returns over this period are not affected. Expected inflation should have no impact on the realized return.

[32] In addition, an increase in expected inflation is associated with declines in future output and earnings growth if fiscal or monetary stimulus is eventually followed by a contractionary monetary policy. Chapter 1 presents evidence for a political cycle, which would result in this pattern. The pursuit of a polit-

ical cycle is also consistent with evidence of an increase in the variance of earnings, which is discussed below.

[33] See Eugene F. Fama, "Stock Returns, Real Activity, Inflation, and Money," *American Economic Review* 71, no. 4 (September 1981), pp. 545–65. Fama relies on positive and negative supply shocks as the cause for the negative relation between inflation and real activity, with monetary policy constant. In addition, Fama's argument uses the strict rational expectation assumption that prices adjust fully and immediately to monetary changes. However, his statistical results are consistent either with this assumption or the interaction of supply shocks (or indeed demand shocks) with long-term nominal contracts. Fama notes (p. 550) that the finding of significant lagged money supply is not consistent with the maintained strict rationality assumption. However, it is consistent with the nominal contracts. Demand as well as supply shocks can produce a negative correlation between inflation and real activity. Due to fiscal stimulus, for example, real activity expands initially, followed by accelerated inflation and slower growth. Then, assuming corrective monetary policy, real output declines, followed by a decline in inflation and renewed real output growth.

In regressions to explain real stock returns, Fama uses the after-tax average real rate of return as capital, the future change in the capital expenditure rate, and growth rates of industrial production and real GNP. The rate of change in real GNP is found to explain most of the variation in real stock returns and the other variables are dropped.

[34] Fama continues to find, in monthly and quarterly regressions, a reliable negative relation between stock returns and unexpected inflation. More troubling for the hypothesis of rational expectations, the significantly negative coefficient on the monetary base variable (which grew over this period and which is highly correlated with expected inflation) indicates that there may be an omitted explanation for the decline in stock market yields.

[35] See Friend and Hasbrouck, "Effect of Inflation on the Profitability and Valuation of U.S. Corporations." They attempt to explain the observed negative coefficient obtained in the United States in terms of assumptions of the Fisher hypothesis which could be violated. Specifically, they attempt to see whether the adverse effect of inflation on realized market return is due to a negative effect on expected cash flow or to an increase in real risk. To investigate the first possibility, three different measures of expected cash flow are examined—dividends per share, reported book earnings per share, and estimated economic earnings per share.

The economic earnings series is the most meaningful one to examine, since it looks directly at the impact of inflation without being clouded by accounting methods (as book earnings would be) and by dividend policies. In some of the regressions, *current* inflation is found to have a positive and significant effect on earnings due, perhaps, to a wage lag effect. Overall, however, the study finds a significant 11 percent depressant effect (measured as the sum of the coefficients for contemporaneous and lagged inflation over five years) on real economic earnings, as a result of one percentage point sustained increase in the annual rate of inflation. (A sustained inflation rate of 1 percent depresses dividends and book earnings by approximately 5 percent.)

The depressant effect may be due to negative output effects associated with inflation, due to money, demand, and supply shocks. Friend and Hasbrouck test for the impact of output effects by including the Federal Reserve Board total industrial production index as a measure of real output fluctuations. They find that its coefficient is positive and significant in explaining real earnings, as expected. Current and past inflation variables remain significant, although their depressant effect is reduced from 11 to 9 percent.

The remaining depressant effect may be the result of inefficiencies due, in part, to more variable prices. In addition, increased relative raw material prices, real wage cost increases (due, perhaps, to indexation), and continuing negative output effects may accompany the initial unanticipated and ongoing inflation. In the United States, especially since the mid-1960s, there is some evidence that these effects accompanied increased inflation, as discussed in Chapter 1.

[36] Other studies have found a decline in the real rate of return on capital in the 1970s, perhaps from 12 to 20 percent. See Robert S. Pindyck, "Risk, Inflation, and the Stock Market," Massachusetts Institute of Technology, Alfred P. Sloan School of Management, Working Paper No. 1423-83, January 1983, revised April 1983; and other studies cited therein.

[37] See Pindyck, "Risk, Inflation, and the Stock Market," p. 15.

[38] Pindyck thus attributes the decline in real share values to a combination of an increase in risk and a decrease in the expected real rate of return, with the relative importance depending on the investor's risk aversion. If, as is estimated by Friend and Blume, the index of risk aversion exceeds two, the major portion of the decline in share values may be attributed to an increase in risk. See Irwin Friend and Marshall E. Blume, "The Demand for Risky Assets," *American Economic Review*, December 1975, pp. 900–922.

Friend and Hasbrouck's work also confirms an increase in the required rate of return due to an increase in the variance of return of the market portfolio (see note 35). To approximate the impact of inflation on the required return, their study regresses the earnings price (E/P) ratio on the rate of inflation. While the earnings price ratio is likely to be an inadequate measure of required return for individual stocks, it is a more satisfactory measure for stocks as a whole. The results seem to indicate that inflation increases real required returns. They are not, however, conclusive in view of the inadequacy of the E/P ratio for estimating required returns.

The authors use the capital asset pricing model as a second method for estimating the effect of inflation on real required returns, since this does not require direct estimates of required returns. The results are found to be very sensitive to the values of parameters assumed. However, there is a clustering of results around the conclusion found by regressing E/P on inflation—an increase in the cost of equity capital with inflation.

[39] There has been far less study of inflation's impact on other real assets, such as real estate. A study by Fama and Schwert shows that the rate of return in real estate hedges both unanticipated and anticipated inflation. See Fama and Schwert, "Asset Returns and Inflation," pp. 115–46. The hedging ability of real estate, in contrast to equities, may be due to the lesser dependence of its yields on short-run real income growth fluctuations and on material input costs and cost variability, which may lower equity returns with unanticipated inflation. Money illusion may play a larger part in equity markets, at least in the past. In addition, positive tax effects are clearly important in this market. Summers and Poterba provide confirming evidence that homebuyers have taken account of the real cost reductions, due to the deductibility of nominal

interest rates, in their buying decisions and that their homebuying behavior displays no money illusion. See Lawrence H. Summers, "Capital Taxation and Accumulation in a Life Cycle Growth Model," *American Economic Review* 71 (September 1981); and James M. Poterba, "Inflation, Income Taxes, and Owner-Occupied Housing," National Bureau of Economic Research Working Paper No. 553, 1980. There is some evidence that commodities are, in contrast to equities, an inflation hedge, although they could not be relied on to provide an inflation indexed income stream.

[40] See R. G. Ibbotson and R. A. Singuefield, "Stocks, Bonds, Bills, and Inflation: The Past and the Future," Financial Analysts Research Foundation, 1982. Updates published annually as *Stocks, Bonds, Bills and Inflation Yearbook* (Chicago: R. G. Ibbotson Associates, 1984).

[41] See Benjamin M. Friedman, "The Substitutability of Debt and Equity Securities," Nation Bureau of Economic Research Working Paper No. 1130, May 1983.

[42] The persistent finding of significance for coefficients of the expected inflation rate (or for variables that may proxy this, such as a time trend or growth in the money base) in stock and bond regressions indicates that the hypothesis of the existence of some residual money illusion cannot be rejected. The evidence also is consistent with a diminishing impact of money illusion over time.

[43] The initial demand shocks of the mid- and late-1960s (associated with increased military and domestic spending) resulted in an increase in inflation and interest rates. However, from the mid-1960s to the end of the 1970s (although government spending and the deficit continued to increase), excessive monetary expansion depressed interest rates, on average. Excessive monetary expansion in the 1970s was due, in part, to the unrecognized lowered rate of potential output growth, which also directly decreased real yields. Most critically, the OPEC and agriculture supply shocks of 1973–74 and 1979 depressed the rate of potential output growth, the underlying rate of return on capital, and bond and equity yields, at the same time that they induced unanticipated inflation. These shocks were accompanied by temporary short-term interest rate surges, due to exogenous price rises and the resulting liquidity shortage as shown in Table 5–4. Average short-term real interest rates, however, throughout this period, were, as Tables 5–1 and 5–5 indicate, low due to excessive monetary expansion (relative to lowered potential output growth), low underlying rates of return (associated with supply shocks), and money illusion.

[44] Throughout the post–World War II period, the monetary expansion and inflation processes were autoregressive, with inflation followed by similar inflation, as shown by the 68 percent serial correlation of inflation in Table 5–2. A portion of accelerations in inflation, due to shocks, was made a part of "permanent" inflation, as rates of monetary expansion adjusted upward over time, at least to some extent.

[45] Returns on short-term debt, commodities, and real estate are not decreased by either unanticipated increases in anticipated inflation or accompanying increased money and real risks; thus they are superior inflation hedges. Moreover, positive tax effects due to leveraging and seeming lack of money illusion in these markets may help to make these investments less vulnerable to inflation. They may be vulnerable, however, to unanticipated inflation, depending on the source of the shock that causes the unexpected inflation. The real return on short-term debt falls with the excess liquidity and the unanticipated infla-

tion of a money shock. The real return on real estate and commodities falls with declines in real income growth, arising out of a supply shock, although, depending on the source of the shock, some commodity values may not decline. Since it is impossible to know which shock is coming before its occurrence, an undiversified portfolio of either short-term debt or commodities and real estate will be harmed eventually by one or another shock, while a diversified portfolio may be harmed (to a lesser extent) by both of these (money and supply) shocks. There is no necessary offsetting benefit to short-term debt due to a supply shock nor to commodities due to an excess liquidity shock. A recent study by Joel Poplin et al. ("Inflation, Portfolio Balancing and Pension Indexation," final Report submitted to U.S. Department of Labor, Contract No. J-9-P-1-0076, March 1983) shows that, due to these negative effects of unanticipated inflation on real yields, it would not have been economically feasible to index an average real rate of return using hedging assets over the 1960s and 1970s.

[46] See Bodie, "Common Stocks as a Hedge against Inflation." Note 45 describes why indexing an average yield, even of such inflation pensions, is not riskless.

[47] The costs of pensions, as the following chapters indicate, are ultimately borne by workers, since it is from workers' income that a higher or lower dollar amount is taken (depending on real rates of return) to fund pension benefits.

[48] See Ibbotson and Singuefield, "Stocks, Bonds, Bills, and Inflation."

[49] See Howard Winklevoss, *Pension Mathematics* (Homewood, Ill.: Richard D. Irwin, 1977. Published for the Pension Research Council, Wharton School, University of Pennsylvania).

[50] See R. W. Hafer and S. E. Hein, "Evidence on the Temporal Stability of the Demand for Money Relationship in the United States," *Federal Reserve Bank of St. Louis Review*, December 1979, pp. 3–14.

[51] The evidence of a minor overall impact of demand shocks on both interest rates and inflation in the postwar U.S. economy is substantiated in other empirical studies. See Richard W. Lang, "The 1975–76 Federal Deficits and the Credit Market," *Federal Reserve Bank of St. Louis Review*, January 1977, pp. 9–16. Historically, unprecedented structural deficits of the recent period (combined with strong nondurable and durable consumption demand and lack of credit controls in a deregulated market) may have been of more importance in interest rate and one-shot inflation increases. See Michael J. Hamburger and Burton Zwick, "Checking Inflation in Spite of a Deficit," *Business Week*, March 23, 1981, pp. 12–15.

[52] See Wilcox, "Interest Rates, Expected Inflation, and Supply Shocks—Or Why Real Interest Rates Were So Low in the 1970s."

[53] It is more difficult to construct models to test for general equilibrium interest rate effects deriving from supply shocks than demand shocks, especially since, unlike demand shocks, in each case of supply-shock inflation there are a variety of possible real and liquidity interest rate outcomes. The liquidity effect that accompanies supply-shock inflation may be positive or negative, depending on whether exogenous price level or output declines predominate. In addition, the accompanying effects on the marginal productivity of capital may be positive or negative. Complicating the testing possibilities, the marginal productivity of capital is affected by both demand and supply shocks. In studies that do incorporate a measure of the marginal productivity of capital in a

test for the variables that determine interest rates, the marginal productivity of capital does vary positively with and explain a small portion of interest rate variation. For example, see Summers, "The Nonadjustment of Nominal Interest Rates: A Study of the Fisher Effect."

[54] See R. W. Hafer and S. E. Hein, "Monetary Policy and Short-Term Real Rates of Interst," in *Federal Reserve Bank of St. Louis Review* 64, no. 3 (March 1982). There is controversy over whether prices adjust immediately. If so, ex post (rather than ex ante) real interest rates are temporarily lowered (raised) through unanticipated inflation (disinflation). This is the strict rational expectations explanation of the impact of money shocks on interest rates. Alternatively, assuming lags in price and wage adjustment, a positive (negative) money shock lowers (raises) ex ante real interest rates temporarily, before prices adjust, due to an excess (shortage) of liquidity. The existence of contracts can explain the continuing impact of a money shock even after its inflationary effect is anticipated.

Richard Startz models a strict view of rational expectations, in which ex ante interest rates are invariant to anticipated inflation and inflation is anticipated rationally. Thus, only unanticipated inflation causes deviations in real interest rates. Moreover, in real markets, assuming this strict view, only unanticipated inflation causes unemployment (or output) to deviate from its full-employment rate. Startz tests for the validity of the strict rational expectations hypothesis by combining the predicted interest rate effect with the predicted Phillips curve effect. On his evidence, the strict rational expectation hypothesis can be rejected. See Richard Startz, "Unemployment and Real Interest Rates: Econometric Testing of Inflation Neutrality," *American Economic Review*, forthcoming.

[55] See Meiselman, D., *The Term Structure of Interest Rates* (Englewood Cliffs, N.J.: Prentice-Hall, 1962).

[56] See William E. Gibson, "Price Expectations Effects on Interest Rates," *Journal of Finance* 25, no. 1 (March 1970), pp. 19–34.

[57] The study by William P. Yohe and Denis S. Karnosky of the years 1952–69 divides the period into two subperiods and finds that the total price expectations effect was much larger during the second period than during the earlier period. See Yohe and Karnosky, "Interest Rates and Price Level Changes, 1952–1969," *Federal Reserve Bank of St. Louis Review* 51, no. 12 (December 1969), pp. 18–38.

[58] See Martin Feldstein and Otto Eckstein, "The Fundamental Determinants of the Interest Rate," *Review of Economics and Statistics*, November 1970, pp. 363–75.

[59] See Jan Walter Elliot, "Measuring the Expected Real Rate of Interest: An Exploration of Macroeconomic Alternatives," *American Economic Review*, June 1977, pp. 429–44.

[60] Ibid.

[61] See W. W. Brown and G. J. Santoni, "Unreal Estimates of the Real Rate of Interest," *Federal Reserve Bank of St. Louis Review*, January 1981, pp. 18–26, and chap. 2, note 33, for a discussion of how an increase in the real interest rate induces an upward bias in the CPI and PCE measurement of inflation. If this upwardly biased measured inflation rate is then subtracted from the nominal inflation rate to determine the real interest rate, the measurement of the real interest rate that results will be biased downward. Thus, when the real

interest rate is rising, commonly used price indexes will overestimate the price rise and underestimate the interest rate rise, with the reverse holding when the interest rate falls.

[62] See Fama, "Short-Term Interest Rates as Predictors of Inflation," pp. 269–82.

[63] Fama's results are duplicated in a later study with Michael Gibbons in which the assumption of a constant real interest rate is dropped. Instead, it is assumed that the expected real rate of interest is invariant to the inflation rate. See Eugene F. Fama and Michael R. Gibbons, "Inflation, Real Returns and Capital Investment," University of Chicago, Graduate School of Business, Working Paper, 1980.

[64] Ibid.

[65] See E. F. Fama, "Interest Rates and Inflation: The Message in the Entrails," *American Economic Review,* June 1977, pp. 487–96.

[66] See D. Joines, "Short-Term Interest Rates as Predictors of Inflation: Comment," *American Economic Review,* June 1977, pp. 476–77.

[67] See C. R. Nelson and G. W. Schwert, "Short-Term Interest Rates as Predictors of Inflation: On Testing a Hypothesis that the Real Rate of Interest Is Constant," *American Economic Review,* June 1977, pp. 478–86.

[68] See Patrick J. Hess and James L. Bicksler, "Capital Asset Prices versus Time Series Models as Predictors of Inflation: The Expected Real Rate of Interest and Market Efficiency," *Journal of Financial Economics* 2 (December 1975), pp. 341–60.

[69] See J. A. Carlson, "Short-Term Interest Rates as Predictors of Inflation: Comment," *American Economic Review,* June 1977, pp. 469–75.

[70] Fama, "Interest Rates and Inflation: The Message in the Entrails."

[71] Ibid. The previous results establish a strong positive relationship between the anticipated rate of inflation and the short-term interest rate, at the very least, for the period under consideration. Other authors have investigated the dependence between the anticipated rate of inflation and the returns to longer term bonds over this period. Both Fama-Schwert and Jaffe-Mandelker have examined the following sets of regressions:

$$Rbxt = a + bE(R)_t$$

where $Rbxt$ is the holding period return over period t on a bond with maturity of one month. Maturities from two months to 20 years were used in the studies. Given Fama's results, expected inflation was measured first by R_t. The coefficient, b, is insignificantly different from 1 in all the regressions. These results suggested that the joint hypothesis of (1) the expected holding period returns on bonds are invariant to inflation and (2) the market is efficient cannot be rejected. Thus, using the terminology of Jaffe-Mandelker, the "generalized Fisher effect" cannot be rejected. As a check on the regression equation, Jaffe-Mandelker also ran the following set

$$Ybxt = a + b_1\Delta_{t-1} + b_2\Delta_{t-2} + b_3\Delta_{t-3} + b_4\Delta_{t-4}$$

where $Ybxt$ is the real holding period return over period t on a bond with maturity x. The coefficients b_1 through b_4 are insignificantly different from zero in almost all regressions, again suggesting that the generalized Fisher effect cannot be rejected. See Fama and Schwert, "Asset Returns and Inflation," pp. 115–46; and Jaffe and Mandelker, "Inflation and the Holding Period Returns on Bonds."

[72] See Fama, "Stock Returns, Real Activity, Inflation and Money," p. 554 and note 3.

[73] See N. J. Gonedes, "Evidence on the 'Tax Effects' of Inflation under Historical Cost Accounting Methods," Rodney L. White Center, The Wharton School, University of Pennsylvania, Working Paper 3-80, 1980.

[74] See Myron J. Gordon, "The Impact of Real Factors and Inflation on the Performance of the U.S. Stock Market from 1960 to 1980," *Journal of Finance* 38, no. 2 (May 1983).

[75] See Joel Hasbrouck, "Three Essays on Inflation and Capital Markets," Ph.D. dissertation, University of Pennsylvania, 1981.

[76] This is because high-dividend stocks are chosen by tax-exempt and low-income investors and low-dividend stocks yield their return in capital gains that are realized and taxed infrequently. See Merton Miller, "Debt and Taxes," *Journal of Finance* 32 (May 1977), pp. 261–75.

[77] Ibid.

[78] See Irwin Friend and Joel Hasbrouck, "Inflation and the Stock Market: Comment," *American Economic Review* 72 (March 1982), pp. 237–42.

[79] See Kenneth R. French, Richard S. Ruback, and G. William Schwert, "Effects of Nominal Contracting on Stock Returns," *Journal of Political Economy* 91, no. 1 (February 1983), pp. 70–96.

[80] Ibid., p. 96.

[81] See Lawrence S. Davidson and Richard T. Froyen, "Monetary Policy and Stock Returns: Are Stock Markets Efficient?" *Federal Reserve Bank of St. Louis Review* 64, no. 3 (March 1982), pp. 3–12.

[82] See Gordon, "The Impact of Real Factors and Inflation on the Performance of the U.S. Stock Market from 1960 to 1980."

Bibliography

ABLE, ANDREW B. "Investment and the Value of Capital." Federal Reserve Bank of Boston, Report No. 65, December 1978.

BALBACH, RACHEL. "The Effects of Changes in Inflationary Expectations." *Federal Reserve Bank of St. Louis Review* 59, no. 4 (April 1977).

BENNINGA, SIMON, and ARIS PROTOPAPADAKIS. "Real and Nominal Interest Rates under Uncertainty: The Fisher Theorem and the Term Structure." The Wharton School, University of Pennsylvania, July 1982.

BIERWAG, G. O., and M. A. GROVE. "A Model of the Term Structure of Interest Rates." *Review of Economics and Statistics.*

BODIE, ZVI. "Common Stocks as a Hedge against Inflation." *The Journal of Finance* 31 (May 1976).

_______ . "Inflation Risk and Capital Market Equilibrium." *The Financial Review* 17 (May 1982).

_______ . "Purchasing Power Annuities: Financial Innovation for Stable Real Retirement Income in an Inflationary Environment." National Bureau of Economic Research, Working Paper No. 442, February 1982.

BODIE, ZVI; ALEX KANE; and ROBERT MCDONALD. "Inflation and the Role of Bonds in Investor Portfolios." National Bureau of Economic Research, Working Paper No. 1091, March 1983.

_______ . "Why Are Real Interest Rates So High?" National Bureau of Economic Research, Working Paper No. 1141, June 1983.

BRENNER, MENACHEM, and DAN GALAI. "The Empirical Relationship between Inflation and Financial Assets' Returns in an Inflation-Intensive Capital Market." Hebrew University, December 1976.

BROWN, W. W., and G. J. SANTONI. "Unreal Estimates of the Real Rate of Interest." *Federal Reserve Bank of St. Louis Review* 63, no. 1 (January 1981).

CAMPBELL, JOHN Y., and ROBERT J. SHILLER. "A Simple Account of the Behavior of Long-Term Interest Rates." National Bureau of Economic Research, unpublished manuscript, September 1983.

CHEN, A. H., and A. J. BONESS. "Effects of Uncertain Inflation on the Investment and Financing Decisions of a Firm." *The Journal of Finance* 30, no. 2 (May 1975).

COX, JOHN C.; JONATHAN E. INGERSOLL; and STEPHEN A. ROSS. "A Re-Examination of Traditional Hypotheses about the Term Structure of Interest Rates." *The Journal of Finance* 36, no. 4 (September 1981).

CUKIERMAN, ALEX, and PAUL WACHTER. "Differential Inflationary Expectations and the Variability of the Rate of Inflation: Theory and Evidence." *American Economic Review* 69, no. 4 (September 1979).

DAEHONG, CHANG. "A Research Proposal on 'Intertemporal Equilibrium in Assets Markets under Uncertainties.'" February 5, 1982.

DAY, THEODORE, E. "Real Stock Returns and Inflation." *The Journal of Finance* 35, no. 2 (June 1984).

ELTON, EDWIN; MARTIN GRUBER; and JOEL RENTZLER. "Equilibrium Returns on Assets under Inflation." Salomon Brothers Center for the

Study of Financial Institutions, New York University, Working Paper No. 241, August 1981.

FAMA, EUGENE F. "Multi-Period Consumption Investment Decision." *American Economic Review* 60, no. 1 (March 1970).

_______. "Short-Term Interest Rates as Predictors of Inflation." *American Economic Review* 65, no. 3 (June 1975).

_______. "Inflation Uncertainty and Expected Returns on Treasury Bills." *Journal of Political Economy* 84 (June 1976).

_______. "Stock Returns, Real Activity, Inflation and Money." *American Economic Review* 71 (September 1981).

FAMA, EUGENE, and G. William Schwert. "Asset Returns and Inflation." *Journal of Financial Economics* 5, no. 2 (November 1977).

FELDSTEIN, MARTIN. "Private Pensions and Inflation." Prepared for the Annual Meeting of the American Economic Association, Denver, Colorado, September 6, 1980.

_______. "Inflation and the Stock Market." *American Economic Review* 70 (December 1980).

FELDSTEIN, MARTIN, and L. SUMMERS. "Inflation and the Taxation of Capital Income in the Corporate Sector." *National Tax Journal* 32 (December 1979).

FISCHER, STANLEY. "The Demand for Index Bonds." *Journal of Political Economy* 83, no. 3 (1975).

_______. "Investing for the Short and Long Term." National Bureau of Economic Research, Working Paper No. 992, June 1982.

FISHER, IRVING. *The Theory of Interest.* New York: Macmillan, 1930.

FRENCH, KENNETH R.; RICHARD S. RUBACK; and G. WILLIAM SCHWERT. "Effect of Nominal Contracting on Stock Returns." *Journal of Political Economy* 91, no. 1 (February 1983).

FRIEDMAN, BENJAMIN M. "The Substitutability of Debt and Equity Securities." National Bureau of Economic Research, Working Paper No. 1130, May 1983.

FRIEDMAN, MILTON, and ANNA J. SCHWARTZ. *Monetary Trends in the United States and the United Kingdom: Their Relation to Income, Prices and Interest Rates, 1867–1975.* Chicago: University of Chicago Press, 1982.

FRIEND, IRWIN, and MARSHALL E. BLUME. "The Demand for Risky Assets." *American Economic Review* 65, no. 5 (December 1975).

FRIEND, IRWIN, and JOEL HASBROUCK. "Inflation and the Stock Market: Comment.'" *American Economic Review* 72, no. 1 (March 1982).

———. "The Effect of Inflation on the Profitability and Valuation of U.S. Corporations." In *Saving, Investment and Capital Markets in an Inflationary Economy*, ed. M. Sarnat and G. Szego. Cambridge, Mass.: Ballinger Publishing, forthcoming.

FRIEND, IRWIN; YORAM LANDSKRONER; and ETIENNE LOSQ. "The Demand for Risky Assets under Uncertain Inflation." *The Journal of Finance* 31, no. 5 (December 1976).

GONEDES, NICHOLAS J. "Evidence of 'Tax Effects' of Inflation under Historical Cost Accounting Methods." *Journal of Business* 54 (April 1981).

GORDON, MYRON J. "The Impact of Real Factors and Inflation on the Performance of the U.S. Stock Market from 1960 to 1980." *The Journal of Finance* 38, no. 2 (May 1983).

GORDON, MYRON J., and PAUL J. HALPERN. "Bond Share Yield Spreads under Uncertain Inflation." *American Economic Review* 66, no. 4 (September 1976).

GULTEKIN, N. BULENT. "Stock Market Returns and Inflation: Evidence from Other Countries." *The Journal of Finance*, forthcoming.

HAFER, R. W., and SCOTT E. HEIN. "Monetary Policy and Short-Term Real Rates of Interest." *Federal Reserve Bank of St. Louis Review* 64, no. 3 (March 1982).

HASBROUCK, JOEL. "Inflation, Stock Valuation and Market Returns, Part I: The Impact of Inflation upon Corporate Dividends and Earnings." Unpublished manuscript, University of Pennsylvania, 1980.

———. "Inflation, Stock Valuation and Market Returns, Part II: The Impact of Inflation upon Stock Returns and Prices." Unpublished manuscript, University of Pennsylvania, 1980.

HUANG, ROGER D. "Volatility of Exchange Rates, Interest Rates Parity, and the Monetary Approach to Exchange Rate Determination: Test of Market Efficiency." Ph.D. dissertation, University of Pennsylvania, 1979.

IBBOTSON, ROGER G., and REX A. SINGUEFIELD. "Stocks, Bonds, Bills and Inflation: Year-by-Year Historical Returns (1926–1974)." *Journal of Business* 49 (1976).

JAFFE, JEFFREY F. "Inflation and Miller's Model of Capital Structure." Rodney L. White Center for Financial Research, University of Pennsylvania, Working Paper No. 10, 1983.

JAFFE, JEFFREY F., and GERSHON MANDELKER. "Inflation and the Holding Period Returns on Bonds." Rodney L. White Center for Financial Research, University of Pennsylvania, Working Paper No. 8, 1975.

———. "The Fisher Effect for Risky Assets: An Empirical Investigation." *The Journal of Finance* 31 (May 1976).

JONES, EMERSON PHILIP, JR. "Intertemporal Financial and Monetary Equilibrium." Ph.D. dissertation, Massachusetts Institute of Technology, 190.

KESSEL, REUBIN, and ARMEN ALCHAIN. "The Meaning and Validity of the Inflation Induced Lag of Wages behind Prices." *American Economic Review* 50 (March 1960).

———. "Effects of Inflation." *Journal of Political Economy* 70 (December 1962).

LEUTHOLD, STEVEN C. "Interest Rates, Inflation and Deflation." *Financial Analysts Journal*, January–February 1981.

LINTNER, JOHN. "Inflation and Security Returns." *The Journal of Finance* 30, no. 2 (May 1975).

LOGUE, DENNIS E., and THOMAS D. WILLETT. "A Note on the Relation between the Rate and Variability of Inflation." *Economics* 43 (May 1976).

LONG, JOHN B., JR. "Stock Prices, Inflation and the Term Structure of Interest Rates." *Journal of Financial Economics* 1 (1974).

LONG, MICHAEL S., and ILEEN B. MALITZ. "Investment Patterns and Financial Leverage." National Bureau of Economic Research, Working Paper No. 1145, June 1983.

MANKIW, N. GREGORY. "Consumer Durables and the Real Interest Rate." National Bureau of Economic Research, Working Paper No. 1148, June 1983.

MODIGLIANI, FRANCO, and RICHARD COHN. "Inflation, Rational Valuation and the Market." *Financial Analysts Journal* 35 (March–April 1979).

MODIGLIANI, FRANCO, and MERTON H. MILLER. "The Cost of Capital, Corporation Finance, and the Theory of Investment." *American Economic Review* 48 (June 1958).

———. "Corporation Income Taxes and the Cost of Capital: A Correction." *American Economic Review* 53 (June 1963).

MUNDELL, ROBERT. "Inflation and Real Interest." *Journal of Political Economy* 71, no. 3 (June 1963).

NELSON, CHARLES R. "Inflation and the Rates of Return on Common Stocks." *The Journal of Finance* 31, no. 2 (May 1976).

PAULUS, JOHN D. "How High Are Bond Rates?" Morgan-Stanley Economic Research Essay, *Economic Perspectives*, June 23, 1983.

PEAT, MARWICK, MITCHELL, et al. "1980 Survey of Investment Performance."

_______ . "Surveys of Economic and Capital Market Expectations for 1980 and the Next Twenty Years."

PINDYCK, ROBERT S. "Risk, Inflation and the Stock Market." Massachusetts Institute of Technology, Working Paper No. 1423-83, revised April 1983.

REILLY, FRANK K. "Companies and Common Stocks as Inflation Hedges." *The Bulletin of the New York Graduate School of Business Administration*. 1975.

SAMPLETON, RICHARD C., and MARTI G. SUBRAHMANY. "Uncertain Inflation, Exchange Rates and Bond Yields." Salomon Brothers Center for the Study of Financial Institutions, New York University, Working Paper No. 210, April 1980.

SANTOMERO, ANTHONY M. "A Note on Interest Rates and Prices in General Equilibrium." *The Journal of Finance* 28, no. 4 (September 1973).

SANTONI, G. J., and COURTENAY C. STONE. "Navigating through the Interest Rate Morass: Some Basic Principles." *Federal Reserve Bank of St. Louis Review* 63, no. 3 (March 1981).

_______ . "The Fed and the Real Rate of Interest." *Federal Reserve Bank of St. Louis Review* 64, no. 10 (December 1982).

SARGENT, THOMAS J. "Interest Rates and Prices in the Long Run: A Study of the Gibson Paradox." *Journal of Money, Credit and Banking* 5 (February 1973).

SAUNDERS, ANTHONY, and RICHARD B. TRESS. "Inflation and Stock Market Returns: Some Australian Evidence." Salomon Brothers Center for the Study of Financial Institutions, New York University, Working Paper No. 173, June 1979.

SCHWERT, G. WILLIAM. "The Adjustment of Stock Prices to Information about Inflation." *The Journal of Finance* 36, no. 1 (March 1981).

SHILLER, ROBERT J. "The Volatility of Long-Term Interest Rates and Expectations Models of the Term Structure." Federal Reserve Bank of Philadelphia, 1978.

SHILLER, ROBERT J., and JEREMY J. SIEGEL. "The Gibson Paradox and Historical Movements in Real Interest Rates." *Journal of Political Economy* 85 (October 1977).

SHILLING, JAMES D., and C. F. SIRMANS. "Interest Rate Uncertainty, Default Risk and Yield Spreads: An Examination of Fixed and Adjustable Rate Mortgages." Louisiana State University, May 1984.

STARTZ, RICHARD. "Unemployment and Real Interest Rates: Econometric Testing of Inflation Neutrality." *American Economic Review,* forthcoming.

SUMMERS, LAWRENCE H. "The Nonadjustment of Nominal Interest Rates: A Study of the Fisher Effect." In *Macroeconomics, Prices and Quantities: Essays in Memory of Arthur M. Okun,* ed. James Tobin. Washington, D.C.: Brookings Institution, 1983.

TAYLOR, JOHN B. "On the Relationship between the Variability of Inflation and the Average Inflation Rate." Prepared for the Carnegie-Rochester Conference, Carnegie-Mellon University, November 14, 1980.

VAN HORNE, JAMES C., and WILLIAM F. GLASSMORE, JR. "The Impact of Unanticipated Changes in Inflation on the Value of Common Stocks." *The Journal of Finance* 27, no. 5 (December 1972).

WACHTER, MICHAEL L., and SUSAN M. WACHTER. "The Setting for a Pro-Growth Strategy." In *Removing Obstacles to Economic Growth,* ed. Michael L. Wachter and Susan M. Wachter. Philadelphia: University of Pennsylvania Press, 1984.

WACHTER, SUSAN M. "Discussion of 'The Impact of Real Factors and Inflation on the Performance of the U.S. Stock Market from 1960 to 1980' by Myron J. Gordon." *The Journal of Finance* 38, no. 2 (May 1983).

WILCOX, JAMES A. "Interest Rates, Expected Inflation and Supply Shocks—Or Why Real Interest Rates Were So Low in the 1970s." National Bureau of Economic Research Working Paper. Prepared for the NBER Conference on Inflation and Financial Markets, Cambridge, Mass., May 15, 1981.

YOHE, WILLIAM P., and DENNIS S. KARNOSKY. "Interest Rates and Price Level Changes, 1952–1969." *Federal Reserve Bank of St. Louis Review* 51, December 1969.

YOUNG, JUNE KWON. "Capital Asset Pricing Model under Uncertain Inflation with Stochastic Consumption and Investment Opportunities." Preliminary draft, University of Pennsylvania, 1982.

PART THREE

Demand for Savings and Pensions under Inflation

Pensions are a form of savings. Thus, the factors that influence overall savings are likely to influence pensions. However, pensions differ from other forms of savings in several important respects:

1. They are savings for retirement, specifically.
2. They are advantaged by their special tax treatment.
3. They are not guaranteed due to inflation, the lack of vesting and portability, and the threat of bankruptcy.
4. They are "purchased" by combined employee group and employer decision, not by the individual.

For these reasons, demand for pensions will be determined differently than demand for overall savings.

Part Three explores the factors that influence the demand for savings and pensions in an inflationary environment. We describe the fundamentals of savings behavior to show their interaction with inflation and to provide a background for analyzing government policy in Part Four.

Chapter 6 examines the factors that determine overall rates of savings. The first section describes the life-cycle savings model; the second section, the impact of bequests, interest rates, demographics, and uncertainty; the third section, the substitutability among forms of savings; the fourth section, the impacւ of Social Security; and the last section, the impact of inflation.

Chapter 7 investigates the determinants of the demand for pensions on the part of employee groups and employers and inflation's impact on the demand for the overall amount and the form of pensions.

6 General Factors Influencing the Demand for Savings: Theory and Evidence

This chapter examines the theory and evidence on what motivates people to save. According to economic theory, rational households save to maximize their well-being through increased future consumption possibilities. Whether households do save in a manner consistent with theory must be addressed with empirical evidence. Some households may be myopic and may save too little to maintain their desired retirement living standard. Other households, while rational, may have insufficient income to provide themselves with old age income security that is minimally adequate in society's view.

The chapter is organized as follows: The first section briefly discusses the theoretical determinants of rational savings behavior, the second section evaluates empirical evidence on each of these determinants and the overall issue of rationality, the third and fourth sections consider the theoretical issues and empirical evidence on the substitutability among the various forms of savings, and the last section discusses the impact of inflation on optimal and actual savings behavior.

The Theoretical Determinants of Savings Behavior

People can do only two things with their (after-tax) income: they can consume or they can save. Thus, an analysis of saving behavior is implicitly equivalent to an analysis of consumption. In fact, the primary motive for saving *now* is to be able to consume more later. If this motive is interpreted broadly, people save for two reasons:

1. Savings enable people to smooth out fluctuations in income to avoid "feast and famine" extremes in their living standards, finance large purchases, deal with emergencies, and provide for their retirement.
2. Savings enable the accumulation of wealth and bequests so that current and future generations can consume more than otherwise.

The use of saving to smooth planned consumption and earnings is formalized in the life-cycle theory of consumption and saving introduced by Modigliani, Brumberg, and Ando.[1] To illustrate with a simplified example, assume a worker will live only "three periods," neither receiving nor leaving a bequest, with an assumed 0 percent rate of return. Table 6–1 shows a typical earnings pattern that starts out at a low income level but advances to a higher income level before retirement. Since the worker prefers a stable consumption pattern, consumption will be $8 per period with lifetime earnings of $24 ($24/3 = $8). Notice that this earnings pattern implies that a worker dissaves when young and again when old. It also implies that middle-aged workers at the height of their earning power will consume relatively little of their earnings. The theory implies that if the population is stable with no economic growth, there will be no net savings economywide because the dissaving by the old and young match the savings by the middle-aged. Both a growing population and a growing per capita wage rate result in a positive savings rate.

The life-cycle theory does not require the stringent simplifying assumptions of the example. Initial endowments, bequest wishes, varying time preferences, positive interest rates, uncertainty including uncertain lifetimes, more complicated lifetime earnings patterns, and heavy consumption needs during family formation years only make the computations more complex. Similarly, it is also likely that "permanently" relatively poor wage earners save less than relatively wealthy recipients of property income, both because of some impact of income level on

TABLE 6–1
Example of Life-Cycle Consumption Behavior

Period	*Income*	*Consumption*	*Savings*
1	4	8	−4
2	20	8	+12
3	0	8	−8
Total	24	24	0

optimal savings rates and because those with a high propensity to save are more likely to be wealthy.

To incorporate the role of these factors, it is useful to derive the hypothesis in a utility-maximizing framework. This assumes that individuals "plan" consumption, savings, and retirement to maximize expected lifetime welfare. However, the theory does not require that individuals precisely or consciously plan out their retirement and savings behavior or that their plans remain unchanged. Rather, it means that individuals, in a world of imperfect and costly information, broadly take account of their expected lifetime income as opposed to focusing on current income only.

Studies by Ando, Modigliani, and Brumberg show how the life-cycle theory can be used to derive a consumption demand function by maximizing utility subject to a multiperiod wealth constraint.[2] Since savings equals income minus consumption, the same procedure then can be used to derive the demand for savings. The model assumes that there is no uncertainty over age of retirement or of death. The motivation for the demand for pensions (or annuities) is introduced when the effects of an uncertain lifetime are added.

Lifetime utility is assumed to be a function of consumption (C) in all years and of the bequest (B) which is left at death. Thus, individual (i) maximizes the following utility function:

(6.1) $$U_i = U_i\,(C_0, \ldots, C_n, B)$$

This is subject to a wealth constraint which states that a person's wealth at any time equals initial wealth W_0 (multiplied by an appropriate growth rate to reflect interest accumulation) plus the difference between income and expenditure for that period.

Thus:

(6.2)
$$\begin{aligned} W_{t,i} &= W_{t-1}(1 + r) + (Y_t - C_t) \\ t &= 1, \ldots, T, \ldots, N \\ B &= W_n \end{aligned}$$

where

N = Number of years in adult life (i.e., working plus retirement years)
T = Retirement age (i.e., working years)
W = Wealth, W_0 = Initial wealth
r = Real interest rate
Y = Annual wage

Rearranging the resulting first-order conditions results in consumption (C_i) and savings (S_i) demand functions for individual (i) of the forms:

(6.3)
$$C_i = C_i, (Y_t, \ldots, Y_n, T, N, W_0, r)$$

(6.4)
$$S_i = S_i, (Y_t, \ldots, Y_n, T, N, W_0, r)$$

Thus, C_i and S_i depend on income, wealth, age of retirement, age of death, and the interest rate. The functional forms of Equations 6.3 and 6.4 differ across individuals and for the same individual at different points of time as tastes vary.

Individuals differ in their rate of time preference, and time preferences change over time for the same individual. With a higher rate of time preference, the demand for savings is less, all else equal, since the individual values current income more than future income. In equilibrium, individuals adjust their savings rate and demand for retirement income to equate their rate of time preference to the real interest rate, r. For example, one household, at a given rate of return, may choose to smooth consumption completely by replacing preretirement consumption out of income with equivalent consumption out of savings after retirement. This household's consumption replacement rate (CRR) equals one. A household with a higher rate of time preference at the same interest rate will choose a lower savings rate and a lower CRR.[3]

In addition, individuals will vary in the amount of bequests, if any, that they wish to leave for future generations and in their degree of risk aversion and consequent need to save for uncertain emergencies. They will also vary in their lifetime earnings patterns, expected retirement age and longevity, presence and age of children, taste for consumption intensive leisure time activities, and so on. Thus, desired savings and pensions differ among individuals with the same wealth and income. For all individuals, theory predicts that savings are a positive function of income, both current and future. Lifetime savings are directly related to lifetime income so that the savings rate out of (what economists term) permanent income is constant. As a result, the desire to save out of current income, Y_t, depends positively on the dispersion between current and expected future income. A temporary increase in income in a good year results in an increased savings rate. All else equal, high transitory income yields high savings in that year.

The demand for retirement savings can be derived from the life-cycle framework, assuming a certain lifetime. (The following chapter extends the model to derive the demand for pensions, given an uncertain lifetime.) For ease of exposition, assume (as Modigliani and Brumberg and Ando and Modigliani do) that: (1) $r = 0$, so that current saving translates exactly into future consumption possibilities; and (2) $W_0 = B = 0$ (individuals are born with no wealth and leave no bequest), so that lifetime consumption must equal lifetime income. Or, in symbols:

(6.5) $$C \cdot N = Y \cdot T$$

where the left side is adult lifetime consumption as represented by consumption per year multiplied by the number of years in adult life. The right side is adult lifetime income as represented by annual income multiplied by the number of working years. Rearranging:

(6.6) $$C = \frac{T}{N} Y$$

Thus, planned consumption in all periods is related to income by the factor $\frac{T}{N}$, which is the fraction of adult life spent working.

Since saving equals income less consumption:

(6.7) $$S = Y - C = Y - \frac{T}{N} Y = \left(1 - \frac{T}{N}\right) Y$$

FIGURE 6–1
Life-Cycle Savings and Dissavings

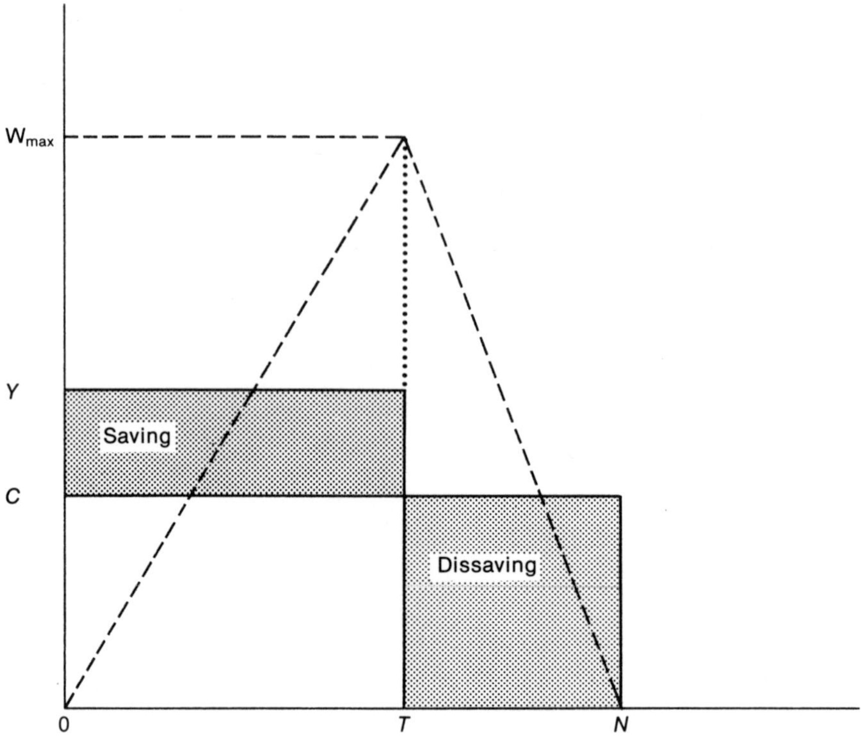

SOURCE: Franco Modigliani, "The Life-Cycle Hypothesis of Saving, the Demand for Wealth, and the Supply of Capital," *Social Research* 33 No. 2.

Or, equivalently,

$$\frac{S}{Y} = 1 - \frac{T}{N} = \frac{N - T}{N} \tag{6.8}$$

Thus, workers should equate their savings rate to the proportion of their adult years spent in retirement. In other words, the portion of income saved every year before retirement corresponds to the portion of adult life spent in retirement. If, for example, work begins at age 20 and ends at age 65 with 15 years expected retirement, the savings rate should be the ratio of retirement to adult years, or 25 percent. After retirement, dissaving occurs at the rate of $\frac{T}{N}$ Y dollars per year. It is the process of saving before retirement and dissaving after retirement that allows consumption to be kept at a constant level.

Figure 6–1 summarizes this discussion. Note that the areas of the two shaded blocks are equal (preretirement saving equals postretirement dissaving). The diagram also shows what happens to wealth over a lifetime. It increases steadily until retirement, since it is constantly being augmented with fresh saving. At the time of retirement the stock of wealth begins to be drawn down as dissaving occurs. Finally, at death, $W = 0$ just as it had at birth. The earning and consumption patterns of Figure 6–1 are schematic. In particular, as noted, it is assumed that there are no desired bequests, that the interest rate is zero, that there is no need to borrow or to vary consumption to income ratios except for retirement, and that there is no uncertainty. As the following sections show, in general, individual savings rates will be influenced by each of these factors, and the economywide savings rate will be affected by population and per capita real income growth rates as well.

Empirical Evidence on Savings Determinants

Life-Cycle versus Altruistic Motives

Once complicating factors are allowed, the theories of rational life-cycle savings behavior include many possibilities. Rational households, under the modified life-cycle theory, may save little if their time preference is high. For example, low and even moderate income households may have such large current consumption needs that saving for the future dims in importance. Other equally rational households may save a large proportion of their income throughout their working years and not dissave at all during retirement, for example, if they are very risk averse. Moreover, it is quite possible that a substantial proportion of households' behavior cannot be described by models of rational behavior. Many households may be myopic and have neither the foresight nor the requisite information to accumulate savings for retirement that in retrospect they view as adequate.

This section examines the empirical evidence on household saving behavior, although, as we will see, the range of possibilities, the many complicating factors, and the lack of data preclude definitive tests of these theories and make predicting household savings rates difficult.

The other major motivation to explain savings behavior besides life-cycle savings has been termed *altruistic behavior*. Altruistic households, by definition, "plan not only over their own entire lifetimes, but actually over the lifetimes of their children as well. In fact, as long as parents care about the welfare of their children, the planning horizon immediately becomes infinite as long as there are no breaks in the family tree."[4]

If altruistic families have a desired bequest goal, which is a function of their own consumption levels, they would save more than others for a given planned retirement. Moreover, they would dissave less in retirement and leave bequests to their children. Of course, bequests may be unplanned or the secondary result of assets held against emergencies and thus their existence is not in itself evidence of altruistic behavior.

In general, the aggregate empirical results are consistent with life-cycle, altruistic, or myopic savings behavior. Because aggregate results do not provide information on age-income profiles and savings behavior, they do not indicate what proportion of families exhibit a significant bequest motive or myopia. Determining the motivation of individual savings behavior requires time-series panel data, which would follow the savings decisions of individual households over time and relate these decisions to household characteristics.

Absent these data, Kotlikoff and Summers use age-specific data to present evidence that an extreme view of the life cycle, in which there is no bequest motive, does not hold. Longitudinal data on earnings and consumption profiles for males and females, age 18 in 1910 through age 82 in 1974 and age 18 in 1940 through age 52 in 1974 in Figure 6–2, indicate that, on average, consumption moves with earnings until late middle age when earnings exceed consumption until retirement, at which point consumption is maintained by dissaving. Figure 6–2, with inclusive lifetime data, demonstrates the smoothing function of savings. But the data embodied in these figures also provide indirect evidence that the bequest motive of saving is as important as the life-cycle smoothing motive in explaining aggregate U.S. wealth holdings. As noted by Kotlikoff and Summers, half of aggregate U.S. wealth must be accumulated for bequest rather than for life-

FIGURE 6–2
Average Age-Earnings and Age-Consumption Patterns

a. Sum of male and female longitudinal average earnings and average consumption profiles, age 18 in 1910—age 82 in 1974.

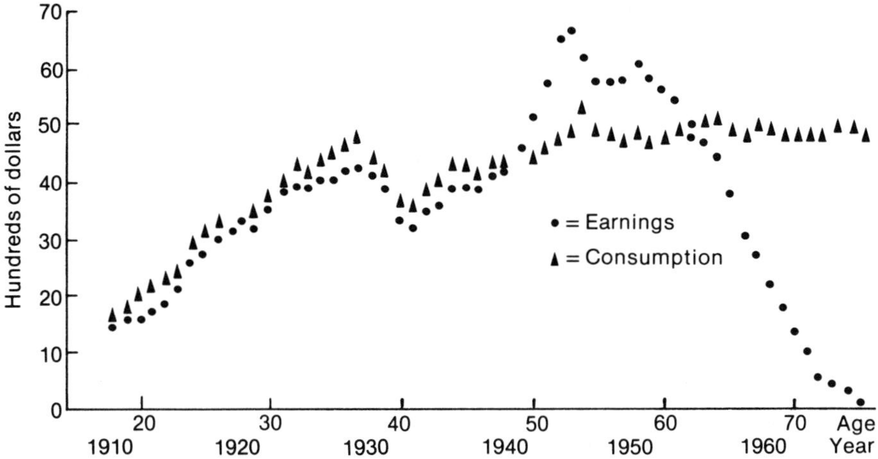

b. Sum of male and female longitudinal average earnings and average consumption profiles, age 18 in 1940—age 52 in 1974.

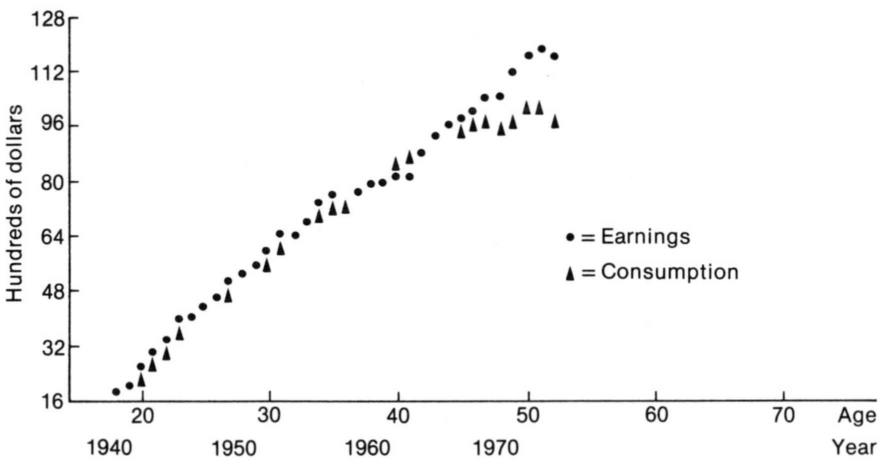

SOURCE: Laurence J. Kotlikoff and Lawrence H. Summers, "The Role of Intergenerational Transfers in Aggregate Capital Accumulation," *Journal of Political Economy* 89, no. 4 (August 1981), pp. 706–32.

cycle purposes, since the savings hump shown in Figure 6–2 cannot be responsible for more than one half of U.S. wealth.[5] Data on the median estate size show, however, that the non-wealthy do not primarily save for intergenerational transfer purposes. Thus, on the basis of this evidence, for the wealthy the bequest motive is major.

Studies that examine dissaving during retirement also confirm that the strict life-cycle model is inconsistent with the data. If assets are broadly defined to include expected pensions, Social Security benefits, and expected earnings, dissaving is found during retirement, although less than predicted by a strict life-cycle model.[6]

Evidence from cross-sectional data also suggests some dissaving out of discretionary (nonsocial security or pension) wealth. Bureau of the Census 1983 data indicate that the mean amount of financial assets of households with head of household aged 65 to 75 was $65,000.[7] In 75 and older households financial assets decline to $37,000. However, median statistics suggest that for most elderly households dissaving, if any, occurs almost completely out of pensions and Social Security wealth. Median assets decline, although insignificantly, from $11,400 to $10,350 over these age groups. These latter statistics also reveal the considerable polarization of financial assets between asset-wealthy and asset-poor households.

The strict altruism model is not consistent with the data either. A test of the strict altruism model is performed by Boskin and Kotlikoff.[8] They note that in this model aggregate consumption depends only on aggregate resources, not on the age distribution. However, they find that age distribution does influence savings rates somewhat, as predicted by the life-cycle model.[9] Cross-sectional studies across countries by Leff[10] and Modigliani, also show that age distribution affects national savings rate, as predicted by life-cycle models.[11] For the United States, Boskin and Lau estimate variable savings rates by age cohort with savings varying from about 2 percent of disposable income for households in their 20s to about 7 percent for those in their 50s.[12] Thus, although much is unknown about the determinants of the U.S. savings rate, one third of the decline in the U.S. savings rate from the mid-1970s to the early 1980s is explainable by the decline in the average age of U.S. households, a finding that is inconsistent with the strict altruistic model.

The overall evidence on the motivation for savings in the United States remains ambiguous. We do not know what proportion of households do not save due to myopia or to insufficient income. The limited existing aggregate evidence is consistent with disparate behavior among households. Over their lifetimes, most households of average wealth may be life-cycle or myopic savers, while some households, perhaps disproportionately the wealthy, may save for bequests. Empirical testing that could support or reject such hypotheses would require time-series panel data. Nonetheless, the data are likely to confirm that families differ and that individually they may display life-cycle, altruistic, or myopic behavior.

Interest Rates

Although the theoretical effect of changes in income, wealth, and demographics on savings in life-cycle and altruistic models is clear, the effect of changes in interest rates is not. In broad terms, this is because any interest rate movement combines two effects. On the one hand, a rise in interest rates implies that the same future consumption can be supported by less savings today. This is an *income effect*. On the other hand, a rise in interest rates is an inducement to save more today, since the wealth gain tomorrow will be greater. This is a substitution effect. The two effects on savings operate in opposite directions.

In a pure life-cycle model, the two effects can be shown to offset each other. To illustrate, compare two periods, one with a zero real interest rate and the second with a 4 percent real rate. For ease of exposition, individuals are assumed not to work but to consume out of wealth at a rate that smooths consumption. Since new savings of $1.00 can be invested to earn $1.04 in the future (rather than $1.00), the cost of today's consumption in terms of tomorrow's consumption has increased. Thus, there is an incentive to increase tomorrow's consumption at the expense of today's. However, total lifetime income out of wealth now will be higher, and it is possible to increase both today's and tomorrow's income and consumption by 4 percent. If the goal is to smooth consumption, the option of an increased savings rate will not be taken because consumption would decrease now while future consumption would increase. Similarly, while previously planned retirement consumption could be achieved with a lower savings rate and a higher real current consumption, this option will not be taken because this would increase consumption now while future consumption would remain at the fixed lower level. If the savings rate remains constant, the higher productivity of capital allows increased consumption now and in the future, so that each year provides an equal share of lifetime utility. The gain to overall lifetime welfare (allowed by the interest rate increase) is maximized by an unchanged savings rate.

In technical terms, the interest elasticity of the savings rate depends on the elasticity of substitution between present and future consumption. When this is one, we are in the Cobb-Douglas case in which the share of total utility provided by the two goods, present consumption and future consumption, remains the same. Thus, the theoretical implication of this version of the life-cycle theory is clear. The savings rate is independent of the interest rate.

Of course, modified life-cycle models, which do not constrain consumers' utility functions in this way, may be consistent with positive, zero, or negative interest elasticities, depending on whether substitution or wealth effects predominate.

Moreover, the theory, as derived thus far, assumes no need or desire to borrow. Once financial assets are accumulated, they can be sold to finance the purchase of consumer durables or other consumption or to invest in human capital. However, households that lack sufficient assets to make these purchases out of savings at the time when they are needed, borrow. If a household is constrained in its borrowing by the present value of its future income, the real interest rate determines how much it can borrow. For example, for a home-buying family with a given income and without assets beyond the requisite down payment, an interest rate rise reduces the amount of a mortgage loan that a financial institution will grant (since mortgage expenditures should not exceed a certain percentage of income to minimize defaults). Given real income, a higher real interest rate decreases the amount that can be borrowed and, thereby, lowers consumption. Since consumption is generally a large proportion of income, a small variation in consumption may affect overall savings rates substantially.

The net effect of changes in interest rates on savings is an empirical question. The empirical evidence does not provide a single, clear-cut answer as to the direction of this effect. The theory does indicate, however, that a "compensated" interest rate change, which by definition only has a substitution effect, raises the savings rate. With a compensated increase in interest rates, wealth and lifetime earnings remain constant; thus, there is no income effect to offset the substitution effect. A compensated interest rate increase could be accomplished through government policy in which, for example, a decrease in after-tax interest rates is accompanied by an increase in income taxes. This should have a positive effect on the savings rate, although the size of the effect is not known.[13]

Uncertainty

We have so far assumed no uncertainty. But people are concerned not only about the rewards that they expect from their investments but also with the risks that they assume in seeking the rewards. People prefer a stable consumption pattern. Thus, they tend to be "risk averse"—they demand compensation for bearing risk. Casual empiricism suggests that this is true; it certainly is consistent with cliches such as, "don't put all your eggs in one basket" and the fact that people *do* diversify their holdings of investments.[14]

Econometric evidence supports a finding that investors in general are relatively risk averse and that risk aversion is independent of the level of wealth.[15] In a 1983 survey of the purposes of savings, most respondents mentioned emergencies.[16]

The major purpose of life-cycle savings is to smooth variations in earnings. Thus, savings out of unanticipated income increases are greater than out of permanent income.[17] Due to relatively high risk aversion, rational savers will respond to increased uncertainty in their lifetime wealth (due, for example, to an increased riskiness of investment in the economy) by saving a higher proportion of their lifetime income.[18] In particular, although empirical evidence is mixed, theory supports an increase in the savings rate in response to an increase in inflation uncertainty.[19]

Summary

Empirical evidence generally supports the expected theoretical effects of demography, income, and wealth on savings behavior. Yet, in the absence of cross-section panel data, we do not know the percentage of households that are saving for life-cycle or bequest purposes. We also do not know how many households are myopic or too poor to save for minimally adequate retirement income out of their own resources.

Nor do we know the role of interest rates and uncertainty in determining savings rate behavior. Theory clearly indicates that an increase in uncertainty should increase savings, given the empirically observed levels of risk aversion; yet the empirical evidence cannot confirm that this occurs. Neither theory nor empirical evidence can give a clear picture of the direction of the impact of interest rates.

Given this lack of knowledge and the large number of factors at work, it is difficult to explain or to predict savings rates out of disposable income. Savings rates were unusually high in the United States in the 1970s in a period of unanticipated inflation, which contributed to low real interest rates and high uncertainty. Savings rates were unusually low in the early 1980s in a period of moderating inflation, high real interest rates, and diminished uncertainty. Demographic factors undoubtedly contributed to this savings rate shift, with baby boomers moving into their heavy-spending, family-formation years, as the average age of U.S. households declined. Diminishing uncertainty may have contributed to lower savings rates. Although there is no firm empirical evidence on this, such behavior conforms to theory. The role of interest rates is even less clear. It is possible that individuals may have saved more in the 1970s because interest rates were low in an effort to build up their life-cycle and bequest wealth, with behavior reversed in the early and mid 1980s. Some of the decline in savings in this latter period is likely to be explained by the lower contribution rates required of private pensions to fund retirement plans given high real and nominal interest rates.

In any case, as the population ages, savings out of disposable income should rise, due to individual choices of rational households who will be moving out of their family-formation years and into their preretirement years. The extent to which the government can and should intervene to assure retirement income security depends on the rationality of individual households and, in particular, whether this increased personal retirement savings materializes. Resurgent inflation (together with diminished roles for indexed Social Security and Medicare benefits and an expanded role for nominal pensions) may endanger the retirement income security of myopic households.

The following sections consider the role of different savings vehicles in household wealth, the degree that government can influence these shares and the overall level of wealth, and the influence of inflation on savings. Appropriate government policies under various possible scenarios are considered in Part Four.

Substitutability among Different Forms of Savings

Although evidence for a significant impact of rates of return on overall savings is lacking, there is substantial evidence that rates of return affect the choice of savings instruments.[20] To the extent that various forms of savings are not perfect substitutes for each other, an increase in a particular form of savings will to some degree increase the overall amount of savings. The following considers the substitutability of various forms of savings. We focus on private pensions, housing, government savings (or dissavings), and Social Security.[21]

Private Pensions

The following chapter examines the factors that influence the demand for pensions and how they differ from determinants of overall savings. This section briefly discusses the substitutability of pensions and the impact of the quantity of pensions on the overall demand for savings.

Major tax advantages have been granted to pensions in the post–World War II period. The life-cycle model implies that households can take advantage of these favored tax provisions by shifting the form of their savings and, at the same time, offset pension benefits by reducing their discretionary savings from current income by borrowing or by consuming out of wealth.

The growth of pensions, however, does not seem merely to have substituted for savings in other forms. Indeed, an early survey by Cagan suggested the contrary.[22] Private pension coverage appeared to increase household savings efforts. Explanations for this behavior have included the ideas of a "recognition effect" and a "goal feasibility" effect. In addition to these psychological explanations, Munnell suggested that the Cagan study suffered from data and methodological problems.[23] Munnell refined Cagan's study and found, in contradiction to Cagan's results, that individuals covered by pension plans saved less in other forms.

Munnell also examined, in the context of a life-cycle model, data from a series of Bureau of the Census data for 1966 to 1971 of employed male heads-of-households who were aged 45–59 in 1966.[24] She concluded that both private pension plans and expected Social Security benefits had a significant negative impact on household saving. For 1973, Munnell estimated the effect to be a $13 billion reduction in household saving, compared to total contributions to private pensions of $21 billion. Some suggested that this less than one-to-one trade-off may be due to lack of vesting and other uncertainties associated with private pension plans. In addition, pensions are not bequeathed, and imperfect capital markets prevent their easy use as collateral in borrowing, say, for emergencies. Moreover, tax advantages granted pension savings, as intended, may well encourage pension savings among those who otherwise would save less or not at all. Thus, for some, pensions are imperfect substitutes for other savings; and for others, pensions result in savings that otherwise would not occur. For these reasons, pensions are likely to stimulate savings for a given retirement age. In addition, workers covered by private pension plans have an incentive to retire earlier; thus, their shorter working life induces them to save more. According to these theories, pensions are likely to reduce savings in other forms, but not proportionately. The result of pension savings is increased savings overall.

A conclusion that pensions add to overall savings, however, cannot be based on theoretical arguments, because two other aspects of pensions may lower savings and one other has an indeterminate effect. Exaggerated views of pension benefits may cause individuals to overestimate their pension wealth and consequently to reduce other savings more than proportionally. And, even with a correct estimate of pension wealth, decreased uncertainty due to the annuity form of pensions can be shown to reduce required life-cycle savings. In addition, the lower after-tax cost of pensions may result in lower or higher combined pension and discretionary savings than otherwise, depending on the relative strength of income and substitution effects.

Thus, while the weight of theoretical debate may seem to argue for a net contribution of pensions wealth to savings, ultimate resolution of the issue and estimate of the size of the net contribution depend on empirical verification. Nonetheless, recent results continue to confirm that pensions add to overall savings. A recent study by M. Kurz suggests that Munnell's earlier findings underestimate the amount pensions add to savings.[25] Kurz finds that $1 of additional pension wealth may expand overall savings by 7 to 8 cents. In sum, theory and empirical evidence suggest that for a given retirement period individuals substitute pensions for other savings, although given that they are unlike other financial assets, the substitution is not complete.

Housing

For most U.S. households, the bulk of the wealth is in housing and consumer durables. These are clearly not a perfect substitute for other forms of savings. Investment in owner-occupied housing and other consumer durables provides a return in the form of an in-kind flow-of-services rather than in cash. In addition, housing differs from other investments in its illiquidity. Nonetheless, purchase of this flow-of-services requires an investment similar to any financial investment, and, in theory, households would optimize by equilibrating after-tax rates of return between housing and other investments.

Supportive evidence is found in a number of empirical studies[26] with recent evidence suggesting that per capita U.S. housing investment increased in response to an increase in its relative after-tax yield in the 1970s.[27] By 1983, 77.3 percent of U.S. householders between the ages 65 and 75 owned their homes 95 percent debt free.[28] Increased real interest rates of the 1980s may diminish the percentage of wealth in housing somewhat. However, the large percentage of retirees who are homeowners is not likely to decrease and may increase as per capita income grows. Indeed, if tax law changes, so that one-family houses become one of the few tax-exempt investments, other than pensions, the percentage of wealth in housing may increase along with the percentage of homeownership.

Government and Taxes

The high degree of substitutability that apparently exists between corporate savings and personal household savings raises the question of whether similar substitutability exists between household consumption and taxes and between investment and government deficits. If so, government tax and spending policy may have little or no effect on the economy's savings rate.

Government transfers and consumption may substitute for private consumption, so that an increase in government transfers and consumption would result in a matching decrease in private spending. Moreover, if such government spending were financed by deficits, which taxpayers viewed as liabilities that they or their descendants had to repay, they may save more to balance the increase in liabilities. Taxpayers would compensate for increased deficit spending by saving more if they integrated the welfare of future taxpaying generations into measures of their own well-being in an extension of altruistic savings models.

Empirical evidence, however, seems to indicate that these conditions do not hold. The data do not support a substitutability of government consumption for private household consumption[29] nor do they support the purely altruistic model of complete welfare integration across generations.[30] As a result, government deficit-financed spending results in lower saving, while the optimal life-cycle savings rate (with or without bequests) out of disposable income remains unchanged.

Government tax policy also affects savings. In particular, the income tax double-taxes savings, first with a tax on wage income and second, with a tax on the interest of that portion of wage income that is saved. The flow-of-service return on consumption is, of course, not taxed. The result is that investment and future consumption may be discouraged, since investors and savers receive less than the full marginal product of their investment. A policy that increases the marginal after-tax interest rate without increasing income, such as a consumption tax, should increase savings for two reasons: First, there is a pure substitution effect as discussed above and, second, those with higher propensities to save are taxed less than others. However, the size of these effects is unknown.

The accumulation of wealth may be increased by changing other aspects of the structure of tax policy, for example, by lowering marginal while maintaining average income tax rates. In general, those government policies that promote full employment and economic growth, increase savings and wealth accumulation, although not the savings rate.

Evidence that pension savings do not substitute one-for-one for other savings implies that the government is also able to affect the overall savings rate by encouraging savings in specific forms.[31] In addition, expected Social Security benefits may affect savings rates, as the following section indicates.

Social Security

In the life-cycle savings model, expected Social Security benefits would serve the same purpose as benefits from private pension plans. Accordingly, we would expect a similar reduction in household savings. However, in the United States Social Security has been "pay-as-you-go" financed—there is no government savings to offset the induced reduction in household savings. Social Security assessments are a tax that reduces disposable income and, hence, reduces private savings. The promised future benefits have a "wealth effect" and further depress private savings.

From the point of view of an individual, accrued OASDI benefits are "wealth" just as are accrued pension benefits, so the greater the expected Social Security benefits, the less personal saving may be. From a macroeconomic perspective, however, OASDI contributions add nothing to the availability of capital because there is no pool of financial assets to back up the system.

Instead, money is merely transferred from workers to retirees. Thus, contributions to and benefits from Social Security and private pension plans (as well as the accumulation of personal savings) may appear to individuals as economic substitutes and enter utility functions similarly. If so, expected Social Security wealth may produce an equivalent decline in actual wealth accumulation.

Social Security benefits, however, are not likely to be perfect substitutes for fungible assets for at least four reasons. First, they are determined by legislation rather than by contract. Second, they are not actuarially fair and thus alter persons' lifetime budget constraints. Third, they are intergenerational transfers, which may induce altruistic families to save more in order to leave a larger bequest. Compensatory savings may be a consequence of a pay-as-you-go Social Security system in which a family's future benefits will be paid for by taxes imposed on the next generation, including their own children. Fourth, Social Security benefits may simply result in less dissaving in retirement, enabling maintenance of an emergency savings fund. Fifth, those who receive Social Security benefits might not have saved in any case due to low income or myopia. To the extent these factors are operative, the substitution effect of Social Security on savings is reduced, possibly to zero. In addition, there may be a positive effect on savings through induced savings for an earlier retirement, since evidence indicates that Social Security benefits have lengthened the retirement period. Thus the trade-off between Social Security and private savings is necessarily an empirical question.

This trade-off was estimated to be near one-to-one in Feldstein's original time-series study of U.S. savings during 1929–71 (excluding 1941–46), i.e., the marginal propensity to consume Social Security "wealth" was approximately the same as for other wealth.[32]

A study by Munnell only partially confirms these results.[33] In addition to Feldstein's explanatory variables, she includes the retirement rate of men over age 65, so that the coefficient of gross Social Security wealth reflects only the pure asset substitution effect. The results imply that the "induced retirement effect" does substantially offset the "pure asset substitution effect." The remaining net substitution effect, however, is enough to cause some loss to the capital stock.

Other studies have shown substitution effects that are either much smaller than Feldstein's results or nonexistent.[34] Moreover, a study of Leimer and Lesnoy found a computational error in Feldstein's results that, when corrected, resulted in a finding of an insignificant wealth effect.[35] However, Feldstein redid his estimates in 1982 for a longer period and found a similar substitution effect.[36] The entire enterprise of testing for the effect of Social Security using time-series data has been questioned recently, due to the multiplicity of possible results. As Auerbach and Kotlikoff show in a simulation analysis, both the magnitude and direction of the impact of Social Security on wealth are highly sensitive to the sample period and to the timing of the phasing in of unfunded Social Security benefits.[37] One cross-section study shows that Social Security does decrease the accumulation of wealth by single male heads of households one-for-one but not for others.[38] Thus, the available empirical evidence does not resolve the issue of the impact of Social Security on savings but does suggest some significantly less than one-for-one negative effect.

Inflation's Impact on Savings

In the life-cycle theory, the savings rate that individuals optimally choose is derived in terms of real consumption and real income flows. Thus, neutral inflation has no effect on the optimal savings rate. The real interest rate, demographic structure of the economy, and uncertainty are unchanged by neutral inflation, as are individuals' rates of time preference, relative risk aversion, and desired real bequests. Individuals should see through the veil of neutral inflation and not change their desired or actual savings rate or their forms of saving.

While in theory it is possible that inflation is neutral in the long run, empirical evidence indicates that this is not the case. First, increased real and inflation uncertainty seem to accompany higher levels of inflation. If empirical evidence on risk aversion is accurate, savers should respond to increased variance of returns on their wealth by saving more. Second, an increase in the long-run inflation rate may be accompanied by a decline in the after-tax interest rate.[39] Savers may respond by saving less until the interest rate rises or by saving more to compensate for the decline in the value of their assets. Third, shifts should occur in the asset and liability composition of wealth toward tax-advantaged investments, such as pensions and housing, and to tax-deductible debt as individuals and firms respond to the interaction of the tax system and long-term inflation. Fourth, sustained inflation may affect actual savings as opposed to optimal savings behavior through persistent money illusion.

Empirical studies cannot confirm any impact of increased uncertainty or lowered after-tax returns on savings behavior due to the inflation of the 1960s and 1970s. However, there is strong evidence of shifts to tax-advantaged forms of savings and to debt.

We have seen that the inflationary experience of the 1960s and 1970s was, to a large extent, unanticipated. Persistent money illusion may have contributed to the negative real rates of return on most assets over this period, although increases in sustained inflation and supply shocks also contributed to the deterioration of nominal and equity asset values. Empirical evidence, however, suggests that, on average, the impact of this inflationary experience on the income of the elderly was not negative.

Indeed, on the basis of a recent study, Michael D. Hurd and John B. Shoven conclude that, contrary to the popular view, the wealth and income of the elderly were not hurt by inflation over the 1970s.[40] Statistics compiled by Hurd and Shoven on relative per capita real income and reproduced in Table 6–2, indicate that elderly households had on average 56 percent as much disposable income as the average household in 1970, and that by 1978 this had grown to 63 percent. Per capita elderly income was 1.16 percent of nonelderly income in 1970 and grew to 1.21 percent in 1978.

The source of this result was the growing contribution of indexed Social Security and Medicare benefits to the elderly's income over this period. This is reflected dramatically in the time-series income composition tables compiled by Hurd and Shoven. Table 6–3 shows that over the period 1963 to 1978 Social Security's share of the elderly's income increased from 27 percent to 30 percent and Medicaid/Medicare from 2 percent to 16 percent, while earnings declined from 29 percent to 18 percent of total income.

Hurd and Shoven also compiled statistics on the elderly's wealth composition. Assets of 8,164 households whose ages

TABLE 6–2
Incomes of the Elderly and the Entire Population

	1970	1972	1975	1976	1977	1978
A. Elderly						
1. Total income of elderly ($ billions)	$78.129	$97.748	$138.897	$152.922	$169.114	$194.425
2. Number of households (000)	12,983	13,771	15,014	15,168	15,531	16,120
3. Per household ($)	$6,018	$7,098	$9,251	$10,082	$10,888	$12,061
4. Number of persons (000)	20,087	20,949	22,420	22,947	23,507	24,064
5. Per capita ($)	$3,890	$4,666	$6,195	$6,664	$7,194	$8,079
6. Real per household (1967 = 100; $)	$5,175	$5,665	$5,739	$5,913	$5,999	$6,172
7. Real per capita (1967 = 100; $)	$3,345	$3,724	$3,845	$3,908	$3,964	$4,135
B. Entire population						
8. Personal disposable income ($ billions)	$685.9	$801	$1086.7	$1184.5	$1305.1	$1458.4
9. Number of households (000)	63,450	66,700	71,120	72,900	74,142	76,030
10. Per household ($)	$10,810	$12,009	$15,280	$16,248	$17,603	$19,182
11. Number of persons (000)	204,878	208,837	213,559	215,142	216,863	218,717
12. Per capita ($)	$3,348	$3,835	$5,088	$5,506	$6,018	$6,668
13. Real per household (1967 = 100; $)	$9,295	$9,584	$9,479	$9,530	$9,699	$9,817
14. Real per capita (1967 = 100; $)	$2,879	$3,061	$3,156	$3,229	$3,316	$3,412
C. Income ratios						
15. Per household	.56	.59	.61	.62	.62	.63
16. Per capita	1.16	1.21	1.22	1.21	1.20	1.21

SOURCE: *Statistical Abstract of the United States*, various years. Compiled by Michael D. Hurd and John B. Shoven, "The Economic Status of the Elderly," in *Financial Aspects of the United States Pension System*, ed. Zvi Bodie and John B. Shoven (Chicago: University of Chicago Press, 1983).

TABLE 6–3
Shares of Aggregate Income of Aged Units 65 and Older: Percentage Distribution from Particular Sources of Income

Source	*1963*[a]	*1967*[b]	*1976*[c]	*1978*[d]
Retirement pensions:	35%	39%	43%	41%
Social Security	27	29	31	30
Railroad retirement	<1	<1	1	1
Government employee pensions	5	6	5	5
Private pensions or annuities	3	4	6	5
Veterans benefits	4	3	<1	<1
Earnings	29	25	18	18
Income from assets	14	13	14	15
Housing services	7	8	7	7
Medicaid/Medicare	2	7	15	16
Public assistance	5	3	2	2
Other	4	3	2	2
Mean income (excluding housing services and Medicaid/ Medicare)[e]	$3,504	$4,306	$8,708	$10,291
Mean housing services[f]	$297	$387	$726	$919
Mean Medicaid/Medicare[g]	$69	$330	$1,613	$2,081
Mean total income	$3,870	$5,023	$11,047	$13,291

SOURCE: Compiled by Michael D. Hurd and John B. Shoven, "The Economic Status of the Elderly," in *Financial Aspects of the United States Pension System*, ed. Zvi Bodie and John B. Shoven (Chicago: University of Chicago Press, 1983), from the following:

[a]Lenore A. Epstein, "Income of the Aged in 1962: First Findings of the 1963 Survey of the Elderly," *Social Security Bulletin*, March 1964, pp. 3–24.

[b]U.S. Department of HEW, Social Security Administration, *Demographic and Economic Characteristics of the Aged: 1968 Social Security Survey*, SSA Research Report No. 45 75-11802.

[c]U.S. Department of HEW, Social Security Administration, *Income of the Population Aged 55 and Over: 1976*, SSA Publication No. 13-11865, Staff Paper No. 35, December 1979.

[d]1978 *Survey of the Elderly.*

[e]U.S. Bureau of the Census, *P-60 Series*, various reports.

[f]U.S. Bureau of the Census, *Annual Housing Survey: Part C Financial Characteristics of the Housing Inventory*, 1973–1979.

[g]*Statistical Abstract of the United States*, various years.

were 58–63 in 1969 were studied using data from the 1969 Retirement History Survey of the Social Security Administration. Results are reproduced in Table 6–4. Seventy percent of the average retired couples' wealth and 60 percent of the upper tenth's wealth is in the form of indexed social transfer payments and housing, which are largely invulnerable to inflation.

The Hurd and Shoven study shows the relative inconsequence of inflation over the 1970s, given the high proportion of the elderly's wealth derived from Social Security and Medicare benefits. However, the recent Social Security changes, along with potential cutbacks in Medicare (to deal with the elderly population bulge, when the baby boom retires in the next century), may make the balance sheet of the average elderly couple of the future closer to that of the 90 percent tail than to the average of the 1969 statistics. This group is vulnerable to an unanticipated increase in the inflation rate.

Using data on wealth composition of the 90 percent tail provided in Table 6–4, 40 percent of wealth is vulnerable to inflation if stocks are included in this category, as they should be, according to the empirical results examined below.[41] In addition, as the following chapter on pension demand discusses, retirement income security may become more fragile as the asset share of nominal pensions grows and as pensions are increasingly invested in nominal instruments with high risk-reflective yields (which, due to real value decline with increased inflation, may make compensatory ad hoc payments less likely). Thus, in the future, the composition of wealth of the elderly is likely to be more vulnerable to an unanticipated increase in the inflation rate than over the decade of the 1980s.

In response to increased vulnerability to an unanticipated rise in inflation, risk-averse savers should optimally save more as a buffer. Yet there is little evidence that this has happened in the past. In addition, while the evidence points to a decline in money illusion in the post–World War II period, nonetheless it is likely that some households still display money illusion, mistaking high nominal returns for guaranteed "millionaire" postretirement status. The household with a small amount of savings is likely to be most vulnerable to money illusion since information gathering is likely to be relatively expensive. Money illusion

TABLE 6–4

Balance Sheet of the Elderly, 1969 (mean values for various elderly populations)

Assets (Liabilities)	All	Nonfarm	All 10 Percent Wealth Tail	All 90 Percent Wealth Tail	All Couples	All Singles	All Male Singles	All Female Singles
1. Number	$ 8,164	$ 7,200	$ 816	$ 816	$ 5,452	$ 2,712	$ 628	$ 2,084
2. Social Security	21,957	22,198	4,998	29,081	27,067	11,683	12,531	11,427
3. Medicare/ Medicaid	7,087	7,022	5,064	8,040	8,225	4,797	3,828	5,090
4. Net physical assets	21,779	16,789	(427)	108,670	27,513	10,253	11,223	9,961
5. Bonds	807	822	28	3,613	897	627	995	516
6. Stocks	5,247	5,051	79	41,800	6,839	2,046	2,635	1,869
7. Loan assets	841	674	36	5,457	1,018	486	642	439
8. Bank accounts	4,774	4,583	404	18,575	5,275	3,770	4,039	3,688
9. Public and private pensions	6,645	7,034	326	23,027	7,670	4,585	6,574	3,985
10. PV transfers	338	345	593	701	333	348	350	347
11. Nonphysical asset debts	(388)	(318)	(243)	(1,572)	(499)	(167)	(360)	(108)
12. Wealth	69,087	64,200	10,858	236,392	84,338	38,428	42,455	37,214

SOURCE: 1969 *Retirement History Survey*, Social Security Administration.

may exaggerate the effects of myopia in households without the desire or ability to save to maintain postretirement consumption standards. These issues are considered in the evaluation of government pension regulation policy under different inflation scenarios in Part Four.

Notes

[1] For example, see Albert Ando and Franco Modigliani, "The 'Life Cycle' Hypothesis of Saving: Aggregate Implications and Tests," *American Economic Review*, March 1963; and Franco Modigliani and Richard Brumberg, "Utility Analysis and the Consumption Function: An Interpretation of Cross-Section Data," in *Post Keynesian Economics*, ed. Kenneth K. Kurihara (New Brunswick, N.J.: Rutgers University Press, 1954).

[2] Ibid.

[3] If the rate of return declines, both households' rates of time preference will exceed the new lower rate of return. More current income will have to be sacrificed to achieve the same amount of retirement consumption. Thus, all else equal, both households will increase their current consumption and will reduce both their savings rate and planned CRR until an extra dollar of future consumption is worth the extra cost in terms of current consumption, and their rate of time preference is brought into equality with the new lower rate of return. As discussed below, this assumes a "compensated" interest rate decline.

[4] See R. J. Barro, "Are Government Bonds Net Wealth?" *Journal of Political Economy* 82 (November–December 1974), pp. 1095–1117, for the seminal article. Altruistic behavior can also be explained as a selfish trade-off for services rendered during retirement or as a private insurance arrangement in which, in the absence of perfect annuity markets, children promise to support parents, if they are long-lived. In return, parents bequeath their wealth to their children if they are short-lived. See Laurence J. Kotlikoff and A. Spivak, "The Family as an Incomplete Annuity Market," *Journal of Political Economy* 89, No. 2 (April 1981), pp. 372–91.

[5] To arrive at this estimate, Kotlikoff and Summers use data on female and male earnings and consumption profiles. They find, "For males, earnings profiles greatly exceed consumption profiles over most of the life cycle. For females, however, the opposite is true. Life-cycle wealth starts out negative and remains negative over all ages . . . the male excess of earnings over consumption is essentially offset by the female excess of consumption over earnings" (p. 724). Summing male and female profiles together, the hump in savings that occurs in late middle years is shown, in the study's theoretical framework, to account for only one half of U.S. wealth holdings. Unfortunately, a mathematical error in the derivation of the formulas caused them to misestimate and report an even lower number. See Laurence J. Kotlikoff and Lawrence H. Summers, "The Role of Intergenerational Transfers in Aggregate Capital Accumulation," *Journal of Political Economy*, August 1981.

[6] See S. A. Blinder, R. H. Gordon, and D. E. Wise, "Social Security, Bequests and the Life-Cycle Theory of Savings: Cross-Sectional Tests," National Bureau of Economic Research Working Paper No. 619, 1980. The findings that "the aged do not run down their wealth during their lifetime" in a study by Thad W. Mirer, "The Wealth-Age Relation among the Aged," *American Economic Review*, June 1979, provide additional evidence on this.

Simulation-based studies find a higher percentage of life-cycle savings and imply that life-cycle savings could explain almost all of the capital to income ratio in the U.S. See J. Tobin, "Life-Cycle Saving and Balanced Growth," in *Ten Essays in Honor of Irving Fisher*, ed. W. Fellner (New York: John Wiley & Sons, 1967); and also J. Tobin and W. Dolde, "Monetary and Fiscal Effects on Consumption," *Consumer Spending and Monetary Policy: The Linkages*, Federal Reserve Bank of Boston, Conference Series No. 3, 1971.

[7] Financial assets include all liquid assets, also stocks, bonds, and all similar assets. Data are based on a Bureau of the Census study of a representative sample of 60,000 households and were processed by the Consumer Research Center of the Conference Board as reported in a study by Fabian Linden, "Midlife and Beyond, The $800 Billion Over-Fifty Market," 1985.

[8] See M. Boskin and L. Kotlikoff, "Public Debt and U.S. Saving: A New Test of the Neutrality Hypothesis," Carnegie-Rochester Conference Series, Summer 1985.

[9] The distribution of age groups in the population should have an impact on aggregate savings. In general, the implications of population and economic growth for required life-cycle savings are well understood. Actuaries predict Social Security funding requirements, based on assumed rates of population and per capita income growth. See Robert J. Myers, *Social Security*, 3rd ed. (Homewood, Ill.: Richard D. Irwin, 1985.)

[10] See Nathaniel Leff (1969). Leff's sample of 1964 data included 47 less developed countries, 20 Western developed countries, and 7 Eastern European countries. He regressed the logarithm of per capita savings (and savings as a percentage of income) against per capita income, rate of growth of income, and dependency ratios:

$$D_1 = \text{Percentage of population aged 14 years and less}$$
$$D_2 = \text{Percentage of population aged 65 years or more}$$
$$D_3 = D_1 + D_2$$

He found that the coefficients of these dependency ratios were significantly negative, thus both supporting the life-cycle model and showing the importance of demographics on savings.

[11] See Modigliani (1970). Modigliani used data from 36 countries (at various stages of development) for data from 1952–60; his results were very similar to Leff's.

[12] See Boskin and Lau (1984).

[13] For some estimates see *Savings and Capital Formation: The Policy Options*, ed. F. Gerard Adams and Susan M. Wachter (Lexington, Mass.: D. C. Heath, 1985).

[14] Similarly, people are willing to pay to reduce their risk (e.g., insurance). Perhaps the only exception to this "rule" is gambling in unfair games—that is

in games with a negative expected return due to "the house percentage." But here, part of the return is psychological—"entertainment" of sorts.

[15] In economic terms, utility functions are convex. Risk aversion is reflected in the elasticity of the marginal utility of wealth. If utility increases by more than the percent increase in wealth, individuals are risk tolerant; if utility increases by less than the percent increase in wealth, individuals are risk averse. Risk aversion can be measured as the added expected return an investor requires as compensation for taking on one more unit of variance. If no increase is required, investors are said to be risk neutral and their index of risk aversion is zero. If the percentage increase in expected return required equals the percentage increase in variance, investors are said to have an index of risk aversion of one. High-risk averters require a greater increase in expected return, and their index of risk aversion is greater than one. (Among other things, this assumes that expected return and variance indicate all the relevant aspects of uncertainty. See Benjamin Friedman, "The Substitutability of Debt and Equity Securities," NBER Working Paper No. 1130, May 1983, p. 5 and note 5, for a discussion of the theory and empirical evidence supporting the relevance of these assumptions in general.) In their study of U.S. household assets, Friend and Blume find evidence of an index of risk aversion of approximately two. Grossman and Shiller find evidence of greater risk aversion. See Irwin Friend and Marshall E. Blume, "The Demand for Risky Assets," *American Economic Review* 65 (December 1975), pp. 900–923; and Sanford J. Grossman and Robert J. Shiller, "The Determinants of the Variability of Stock Market Prices," *American Economic Review* 71 (May 1981), pp. 222–27.

[16] The next most mentioned category for discretionary (non–Social Security or pension) savings was for retirement with education, durable goods, and buying a home also mentioned frequently. See Robert B. Avery, Gregory E. Elliehausen, and Thomas A. Gustafson, "Pensions and Social Security in Household Portfolios," in *Savings and Capital Formations: The Policy Options*, ed. Adams and Wachter.

[17] The models considered in the previous section were constructed to describe an economy without uncertainty. Once uncertainty and risk aversion are added, it can be shown that individuals (given the relatively high risk aversion that empirical studies imply) will consume more out of wealth, if the real interest rate increases.

This assumes a constant relative risk aversion that exceeds one, which the empirical evidence, cited in the previous note, supports. See Robert C. Merton, "Lifetime Portfolio Selection under Uncertainty: The Continuous-Time Case," *The Review of Economics and Statistics* 51, no. 3 (August 1969), pp. 247–57. Also see Emerson Philip Jones, Jr., "Intertemporal Financial and Monetary Equilibrium," Ph.D. dissertation, Massachusetts Institute of Technology, 1980. Even with uncertainty, assuming an index of risk aversion of one, the strict life-cycle model still predicts a constant consumption rate, that is, a zero elasticity of the savings rate to interest rates.

[18] An increase in the riskiness of investment has two effects which operate in different directions. On the one hand, a relatively certain future income requires a higher savings rate, with an increased level of risk. On the other hand, since the cost in terms of current consumption of a certain future consumption has increased, the desired level of certain future consumption may fall and the savings rate may decline. For observed risk aversion levels, the first effect pre-

dominates. For a theoretical deviation of this result, assuming constant relative risk aversion, see Merton, "Lifetime Portfolio Selection under Uncertainty: The Continuous-Time Case."

[19] See David M. Modest, "Uncertainty and Optimal Consumption: Theory and Evidence," mimeographed, Cambridge, Mass.: Massachusetts Institute of Technology, January 1981.

[20] See John B. Shoven, "Saving in the U.S. Economy," in *Removing Obstacles to Economic Growth*, ed. Michael L. Wachter and Susan M. Wachter (Philadelphia: University of Pennsylvania Press, 1984), pp. 187–223. Broad categories of saving are not likely to be perfect substitutes for each other. Thus, government policy may be able to encourage savings by tax advantages for broad categories of investment. On the other hand, narrowly defined savings vehicles may be close substitutes, so that savings merely shift rather than grow as a result of tax advantages granted to these vehicles. Through the 1970s, the share of all wealth in tax-exempt assets increased with the rise in their after-tax return differential with the result that by the early 1980s in the United States slightly less than 50 percent of savings was in tax-exempt forms, with more than 30 percent of savings through private pension plans, IRAs, Keogh plans, and cash value insurance plans, and about 20 percent in newly constructed housing.

[21] The evidence for substitutability is of course greatest for various forms of financial savings, for example, corporate stock. Although ownership of corporate stock is concentrated among the wealthy, it accounts for a large share of gross financial savings. Because of its relative liquidity, theory implies that corporate stock should be a close substitute for personal savings. Empirical studies suggest that corporate savings are a close but not perfect substitute.

[22] See Philip Cagan, *The Effect of Pension Plans on Aggregate Saving: Evidence from a Sample Survey*, (New York: Columbia University Press, 1965).

[23] See A. Munnell, *The Effect of Social Security on Personal Saving* (Cambridge, Mass.: Ballinger Publishing Co.: 1974).

[24] David and Scadding's study provides empirical evidence to support the idea that corporate savings are a perfect substitute for household savings. During the past 70 years, they found that the ratio of *gross* (inclusive of depreciation) private savings to GNP remained stable, whereas its components (i.e., personal and corporate saving rates) varied considerably. (See Paul A. David and J. L. Scadding, "Private Savings: Ultrarationality, Aggregation, and 'Denison's Law,'" *Journal of Political Economics* 82 (1974), pp. 225–49.

[25] For single male heads of families a $1 increase in pension wealth results in the equal decumulation of nonpension wealth. However, for single females there is no impact on decumulation of other wealth, and for two-headed families, the receipt of $1 of pension wealth results in only partial decumulation by 29 cents of other wealth. See Mordecai Kurz, "The Life-Cycle Hypothesis and the Effects of Social Security and Private Pensions on Family Saving," Institute for Mathematical Studies and the Social Science Technical Paper No. 335. (Palo Alto: Stanford University, 1981).

[26] Friend and Jones report a high degree of substitutability between consumer durables and other forms of savings. See Irwin Friend and Robert Jones, "The Concept of Saving," in *Consumption and Saving*, Vol. 2, Study of Consumers' Expenditures (Philadelphia: University of Pennsylvania Press, 1960).

In addition, there is a variety of evidence that housing's favorable federal income tax treatment, which has raised its relative after-tax yield, has resulted in its substitution for other forms of savings. (The federal income tax allows deductions of interest payments, plus no taxes are paid on implicit rent. Other consumer durables also gain from these pensions. Capital gains taxes provisions on owner-occupied housing are also liberal, with rollover provisions and no tax at all on $100,000 in capital gains after the owner reaches age 55.)

Harvey Rosen's cross-section evidence, drawn from a study of U.S. families from 1970, suggests that U.S. housing demand would be 15 percent less without the favorable federal income tax treatment of homeownership. See H. S. Rosen, "Housing Decisions and the U.S. Income Tax," *Journal of Public Economics* 11 (February 1979), pp. 1–23. In addition, cross-country comparisons, as of 1970, indicate that U.S. investment in housing relative to overall investment exceeded that of seven out of eight industrialized economies studied in which housing is less tax advantaged. Laurits R. Christensen, Dianne Cummings, and Dale W. Jorgenson, "Economic Growth 1947–73: An International Comparison," in *New Developments in Productivity Measurement and Analysis,* Studies in Income and Wealth 44, ed. John W. Kendrick and Beatrice N. Vaccara (Chicago: University of Chicago Press, 1980). U.S. relative investment in housing and consumer durables exceeded that of Canada, Germany, Japan, the United Kingdom, France, and the Netherlands. Only Italy had a slightly higher ratio of housing investment.

[27] See Douglas B. Diamond, Jr., "Taxes, Inflation, Speculation and the Cost of Homeownership," *AREUEA Journal* 8 (1980)—indicates that over the 1970s, inflation combined with the tax deductibility of nominal interest rates resulted in increases in the after-tax rate of return and in the demand for housing. The ratio of residential construction to nonfarm plant and equipment expenditures rose from 36 percent in 1965 to 1970 to 41 percent in 1971 to 1978. See Marshall E. Blume, Jean Crockett, and Irwin Friend, "Stimulation of Capital Formation: Ends and Means," in *Towards a New U.S. Industrial Policy?* ed. Michael L. Wachter and Susan M. Wachter (Philadelphia: University of Pennsylvania Press, 1981). As shown by the Diamond study, a substantial part of the rise in the after-tax rate of return of investment in housing was through a decline in after-tax mortgage costs, with the expected result that the housing demand increase was accompanied by an even greater increase in mortgage financing. Over the short run, debt financing, which would have gone to finance plant and equipment, was drawn to housing. Over the long run, as mortgages are repaid, homes become equity financed.

[28] Fabian Linden, "Midlife and Beyond: The $800 Billion Over-Fifty Market," 1985.

[29] Alternatively, tax-financed government spending may be for public investment; however, the evidence is that by and large this has not been the case. (See Blume, Crockett, Friend, "Stimulation of Capital Formation: Ends and Means," pp. 41–94, and articles cited.)

In addition, tax-financed transfers tend to be from those with relatively low time preference rates (and correspondingly low marginal propensities to consume) to those with high time preference rates. (See Laurence J. Kotlikoff, "Taxation and Savings—A Neoclassical Perspective," NBER Working Paper No. 1302, March 1984, and articles cited.)

[30] See, in particular, tests of the strict altruism model on which this depends, performed by Boskin and Kotlikoff, discussed above, and note 11.

[31] See Friend and Jones, "The Concept of Savings," in *Consumption and Saving* for further evidence on this.

[32] In this study Feldstein estimated a life-cycle type consumption function in which "gross Social Security wealth" appeared as an explanatory variable, as follows:

$$\underset{(31)}{C = 238} + \underset{(.047)}{.530YD} + \underset{(.035)_{-1}}{.120YD} + \underset{(.074)}{.356RE} + \underset{(.004)_{-1}}{.014W} + \underset{(.006)}{.021SSWG}$$

where

C = Consumption
YD = Disposable income
RE = Retained earnings
W = Private wealth
$SSWG$ = Gross Social Security wealth

Standard errors in parentheses; −1 refers to a one-period lag. The coefficient of *SSWG* is significant at any reasonable level and implies an initial reduction of savings by $2.10 for a $100 increase in *SSWG*. Feldstein's findings imply that a wealth substitution effect dominates any induced retirement effect. Using these results, Feldstein estimates that the long-run capital stock in the United States is lowered by 38 percent because of Social Security, with a corresponding 20 percent drop in GNP. See Martin Feldstein, "Social Security, Induced Retirement, and Aggregate Capital Accumulation," *Journal of Political Economy* 82 (September–October 1974), pp. 905–26.

[33] See Alicia Munnell, *The Impact of Social Security on Personal Saving* (Cambridge, Mass.: Ballinger, 1974).

[34] See R. J. Barro, *The Impact of Social Security on Private Savings* (Washington: American Enterprise Institute, 1978); and M. R. Darby, *The Effect of Social Security on Income and the Capital Stock* (Washington: American Enterprise Institute, 1979).

[35] See D. Leimer and S. Lesnoy, "Social Security and Private Saving: New Times Series Evidence," *Journal of Political Economy* 90 (1982), pp. 606–29.

[36] See M. S. Feldstein, "Domestic Saving and International Capital Movements in the Long Run and the Short Run," National Bureau of Economic Research Working Paper No. 947, 1982.

[37] See Alan J. Auerbach and L. J. Kotlikoff, "Investment versus Savings Incentives: The Size of the Bang for the Buck and the Potential for Self-Financing Business Tax Cuts," in *The Economic Consequences of Government Deficits*, ed. L. H. Meyer (Boston: Kluwer-Nijhoff Publishing, 1983), pp. 121–54.

[38] See M. Kurz, "The Life-Cycle Hypothesis and the Effects of Social Security and Private Pensions on Family Savings." Also see M. Feldstein and A. Pellechio, "Social Security and Household Wealth Accumulation: New Microeconomic Evidence," *Review of Econmics and Statistics* 61 (1979), pp. 361–68; and L. J. Kotlikoff, "Testing the Theory of Social Security and Life-Cycle Accumulation," *American Economic Review* 69, no. 3 (June 1979), pp. 396–410.

[39] Several factors may contribute to a decline in the after-tax (shadow) risk-free real interest rate. First, increased inflation uncertainty and real risk may decrease the marginal efficiency of investment. Second, as the Munnell hypothesis asserts, a decline in the real interest rate may occur through a com-

positional shift in savings from monetary to nonmonetary savings. Third, an increase in uncertainty may increase the savings rate which, all else equal, would lower the shadow risk-free rate. Fourth, the taxation of nominal interest rates, as though they were real, reduces the after-tax interest rate. (See Chapter 4 for further discussion.) However, theoretical and empirical evidence on savers' reaction to any decline in the after-tax interest rate is unknown. Savers may respond by lowering their savings rate until the interest rate rises, or they may raise their savings rate to compensate for the resulting decline in their wealth. Under the infinite generation bequest model, individuals would lower their savings rate. However, in the strict life-cycle model, savings for income smoothing would not be affected, except if high relative risk aversion caused individuals to save more.

[40] See Michael D. Hurd and John B. Shoven, "The Economic Status of the Elderly," in *Financial Aspects of the United States Pension System*, ed. Zvi Bodie and John B. Shoven (Chicago: University of Chicago Press, 1983).

[41] Long-term empirical evidence for the United States suggests that an increase in the sustained inflation rate is accompanied by a decrease in real earnings, perhaps due to indirect negative effects on real profits of increased inflation uncertainty. See I. Friend and J. Hasbrouck, "Effect of Inflation on the Profitability and Valuation of U.S. Corporations," in *Saving, Investment and Capital Markets in an Inflationary Economy*, ed. M. Sarnat and G. Szego (Cambridge, Mass.: Ballinger, forthcoming). The authors find that a 1 percent sustained increase in the inflation rate is associated with about a 14 percent reduction in real economic earnings. See Chapter 4 for a discussion of the results of this study.

Bibliography

ADAMS, G. F., and S. M. WACHTER. *Savings and Capital Formation: The Policy Options*. Lexington, Mass.: D. C. Heath, 1985.

ANDO, A., and F. MODIGLIANI. "The Life-Cycle Hypothesis of Saving: Aggregate Implications and Tests," *American Economic Review* 53 (March 1963), pp. 55–84.

ATKINSON, A. B. "The Distribution of Wealth and the Individual Life Cycle." *Oxford Economic Papers* 23 (July 1971).

AUERBACH, A. J. "Saving in the U.S.: Some Conceptual Issues." In *The Level and Composition of Household Saving*, ed. P. Hendershott. Cambridge, Mass.: Ballinger, 1985.

AUERBACH, A. J., and L. J. KOTLIKOFF. "An Examination of Empirical Tests of Social Security and Savings." Cambridge, Mass.: National Bureau of Economic Research Working Paper No. 730, August 1981.

_______ . "Investment versus Savings Incentives: The Size of the Bang for the Buck and the Potential for Self-Financing Business Tax Cuts." In *The Economic Consequences of Government Deficits,* ed. L. H. Meyer. Boston: Kluwer-Nijhoff Publishing, 1983, pp. 121–54.

BARRO, R. J. "Are Government Bonds Net Wealth?" *Journal of Political Economy,* November–December 1974, pp. 1095–1117.

_______ . *The Impact of Social Security on Private Savings.* Washington, D.C.: American Enterprise Institute, 1978.

BARTH, J. R.; G. IDEN; and F. S. RUSSEK. "Do Federal Deficits Really Matter?" *Contemporary Policy Issues* 3 (Fall 1984–1985), pp. 79–85.

BERNHEIM, B. D. "Dissaving after Retirement: Testing the Pure Life-Cycle Hypothesis," Cambridge, Mass.: National Bureau of Economic Research Working Paper No. 1409, July 1984.

BERNHEIM, B. D., and J. B. SHOVEN. "Pension Funding and Saving," Cambridge, Mass.: National Bureau of Economic Research Working Paper No. 1622, May 1985.

BLINDER, S. A.; R. H. GORDON; and D. E. WISE. "Social Security, Bequests and the Life-Cycle Theory of Savings: Cross-Sectional Tests." Cambridge, Mass.: National Bureau of Economic Research Working Paper No. 619, 1980.

_______ . "Social Security, Bequests, and the Life-Cycle Theory of Saving: Cross-Sectional Tests." In *The Determinants of National Saving and Wealth,* ed. F. Modigliani and R. E. Hemming. New York: St. Martin's Press, 1983.

BLUME, MARSHALL E.; JEAN CROCKETT; and IRWIN FRIEND. "Stimulation of Capital Formation: Ends and Means." In *Towards a New Industrial Policy,* ed. Michael L. Wachter and Susan M. Wachter. Philadelphia: University of Pennsylvania Press, 1981.

_______ . "Stock Ownership in the United States: Characteristics and Trends." *Survey of Current Business,* November 1984.

BLUME, MARSHALL, and IRWIN FRIEND. "The Demand for Risky Assets." *American Economic Review* 71 (May 1981).

BLUME, MARSHALL, and JEREMY SIEGEL. "Personal Saving: Theory and Evidence." In *Saving, Investment and Capital Formation in an Inflationary Economy,* ed. Marshall Sarnat and Giorgio Szego. Cambridge, Mass.: Ballinger, 1982.

BOSKIN, M., and L. KOTLIKOFF. "Public Debt and U.S. Savings: A New Test of the Neutrality Hypothesis." Carnegie-Rochester Conference Series, Summer 1985.

BOSKIN, M., and L. LAU. *An Analysis of Post-War U.S. Consumption.* Cambridge, Mass.: National Bureau of Economic Research, 1985.

CAGAN, PHILLIP. *The Effect of Pension Plans on Aggregate Savings: Evidence from a Sample Survey.* New York: Columbia University Press, 1965.

CHRISTENSEN, D. C., and D. W. JORGENSON. "Economic Growth in 1947–73: An International Comparison." In *New Developments in Productivity Measurement and Analysis,* ed. J. W. Kendrick and B. V. Vaccara. Studies in Income and Wealth, Vol. 44. Chicago: University of Chicago Press, 1980.

DARBY, M. P. *The Effect of Social Security on Income and the Capital Stock.* Washington, D.C.: American Enterprise Institute, 1979.

DAVID, P. A., and J. L. SCADDING. "Private Savings: Ultrarationality, Aggregation, and 'Denison's Law.'" *Journal of Political Economy* 82 (March–April 1974).

DE MAGISTRIS, R., and C. J. PALASH. *New York Federal Reserve Bank Review,* 1984.

DIAMOND, DOUGLAS B. "Taxes, Inflation, Speculation and the Cost of Homeownership." *AREUEA Journal* 8 (1980).

DOLDE, W., and J. TOBIN. "Monetary and Fiscal Effects on Consumption." *Consumer Spending and Monetary Policy: The Linkages.* Federal Reserve Bank of Boston, Conference Series No. 3, 1971.

FELDSTEIN, M. S. "Domestic Savings and International Capital Movements in the Long Run and the Short Run." Cambridge, Mass.: National Bureau of Economic Research Working Paper No. 947, 1982.

———. "Social Security, Induced Retirement, and Aggregate Capital Accumulation." *Journal of Political Economy,* 1974, pp. 905–26.

———. "Does the U.S. Save Too Little?" *American Economic Review* 67, no. 1 (February 1977), pp. 116–21.

———. "Do Private Pensions Increase National Savings?" *Journal of Public Economics* 10, no. 3 (December 1978), pp. 277–93.

———. "Government Deficits and Aggregate Demand." *Journal of Monetary Economics* 9, no. 1 (January 1982), pp. 144–49.

FELDSTEIN, M. S., and A. PELLECHIO. "Social Security and Household Wealth Accumulation: New Microeconomic Evidence." *Review of Economics and Statistics* 61 (1979), pp. 361–68.

FELDSTEIN, M. S., and L. SUMMERS. "Inflation and the Taxation of Capital Income in the Corporate Sector." *National Tax Journal* 32 (December 1979), pp. 445–70.

FRIEND, IRWIN, and JOEL HASBROUCK. "Comment on Inflation and the Stock Market." *American Economic Review*, March 1982, pp. 237–42.

———. "Effect of Inflation on the Profitability and Valuation of U.S. Corporations." In *Saving, Investment and Capital Markets in an Inflationary Economy*, ed. M. Sarnat and G. Szego. Cambridge, Mass.: Ballinger, forthcoming.

———. "Saving and After-Tax Rates of Return." *Review of Economics and Statistics*, November 1983, pp. 537–43.

FRIEND, IRWIN, and ROBERT JONES. "The Concept of Saving." In *Consumption and Saving* 2, ed. I. Friend and R. Jones. Philadelphia: University of Pennsylvania, 1960.

HÚRD, M. D., and J. B. SHOVEN. "The Economic Status of the Elderly." In *Financial Aspects of the United States Pension System*, ed. Zvi Bodie and John B. Shoven. Chicago: The University of Chicago Press, 1983.

KING, M., and L. DICKS-MIREAUX. "Asset Holdings and the Life Cycle." *Economic Journal* 92 (1982), pp. 247–67.

KOTLIKOFF, LAURENCE J. "Taxation and Savings: A Neoclassical Perspective." *Journal of Economic Literature*, December 1984.

———. "Testing the Theory of Social Security and Life-Cycle Accumulation." *American Economic Review* 69, no. 3 (June 1979), pp. 396–410.

KOTLIKOFF, LAURENCE J., and A. SPIVAK. "The Family as an Incomplete Annuities Market." *Journal of Political Economy* 89, no. 2 (April 1981), pp. 372–91.

KOTLIKOFF, LAURENCE J., and L. SUMMERS. "The Role of Intergenerational Transfers in Aggregate Capital Accumulation." *Journal of Political Economy* 89 (August 1981), pp. 706–32.

KURZ, MORDECAI. "The Life-Cycle Hypothesis and the Effects of Social Security and Private Pensions on Family Saving." Institute for Mathematical Studies and the Social Science Technical Paper No. 335. Palo Alto, Calif.: Stanford University, 1981.

LEIMER, DEAN, and SELOG LESNOY. "Social Security and Private Saving." *Journal of Political Economy*, June 1982, pp. 606–29.

———. "Social Security and Private Saving: An Examination of Feldstein's New Evidence." ORS Working Paper No. 31. Washington, D.C.: U.S. Department of Health and Human Services, Social Security Administration, 1983.

———. "Social Security and Private Saving: Theory and Empirical Evidence." *Social Security Bulletin*, January 1985.

MERTON, ROBERT C. "Lifetime Portfolio Selection under Uncertainty: The Continuous-Time Case." *The Review of Economics and Statistics* 51, no. 3 (August 1969), pp. 247–57.

MIRER, THAD W. "The Wealth Age Relation among the Aged." *American Economic Review*, June 1979, pp. 435–43.

MODEST, DAVID M. "Uncertainty and Optimal Consumption: Theory and Evidence." Mimeographed, Cambridge, Mass.: MIT Press, January 1981.

MODIGLIANI, FRANCO, and R. BRUMBERG. "Utility Analysis and the Consumption Function: An Interpretation of Cross-Section Data." In *Post-Keynesian Economics*, ed. K. E. Kurihara. New Brunswick, N.J.: Rutgers University Press, 1954.

MODIGLIANI, FRANCO, AND ARLIE STERLING. "Determinants of Private Saving with Special Reference to the Role of Social Security—Cross-Country Tests." In *The Determinants of National Saving and Wealth*, ed. F. Modigliani and R. E. Hemming. New York: St. Martin's Press, 1983.

MUNNELL, ALICIA. *The Impact of Social Security on Personal Savings*. Cambridge, Mass.: Ballinger, 1974.

MYERS, ROBERT J. *Social Security*, 3rd ed. Homewood, Ill.: Richard D. Irwin, 1985.

ROSEN, H. S. "Housing Decisions and the U.S. Income Tax." *Journal of Public Economics* 11 (February 1979).

SHOVEN, J. B. "Saving in the U.S. Economy." In *Removing Obstacles to Economic Growth*, ed. M. L. Wachter and S. M. Wachter. Philadelphia: University of Pennsylvania Press, 1984.

SUMMERS, L. H. "Capital Taxation and Accumulation in a Life-Cycle Growth Model." *American Economic Review* 71 (September 1981), pp. 533–44.

———. "Tax Policy, the Rate of Return, and Saving." Cambridge, Mass.: National Bureau of Economic Research Working Paper No. 995, September 1982.

———. "The After-Tax Rate of Return Affects Private Savings." *American Economic Review* 74, no. 2 (May 1984), pp. 249–53.

TANNER, ERNEST J. "Fiscal Policy and Consumer Behavior." *Review of Economics and Statistics* 61 (May 1979), pp. 317–21.

TOBIN, J. "Life-Cycle Saving and Balanced Growth." *Ten Essays in Honor of Irving Fisher,* ed. W. Fellner. New York: John Wiley & Sons, 1967.

The Demand for Pensions and the Impact of Inflation

7

Introduction

Widespread pension coverage in the United States is a post–World War II phenomenon. For much of this period—until the mid-1960s—nominal pensions provided retirees, de facto, a nearly constant real income.

Inflation has three effects on nominal pensions. First, the expected value of total pension receipts declines unless the initial level of benefits has been raised. Second, the real level of pension benefits declines over time. These two effects are illustrated in Table 5–6. As shown, with inflation real benefits decline with number of years after retirement, and at any age higher rates of inflation have a more than proportionately negative impact. The third effect results from the increased inflation uncertainty that accompanies higher rates of inflation. While pension benefits that grow at the anticipated inflation rate would eliminate the first two effects, the third effect of inflation could be eliminated only if benefits fluctuated with actual inflation.

An inflation-indexed pension could ensure a constant real postretirement income in an inflationary environment. To examine the demand for an inflation-indexed pension and, more generally, inflation's impact on pension demand, requires an understanding of the fundamental functions that a pension serves.

Pensions are a form of tax-deferred savings that can help to provide an optimal lifetime income stream and can be part of an optimal employee compensation scheme. As a public good, pensions can reduce social transfer payments (largely in the form of Social Security benefits) necessary to maintain socially acceptable minimum standards of living. Tax dollars lost due to pensions' tax deferral may accomplish this by encouraging pension savings by myopic and relatively low-income individuals that would otherwise not occur. Part Four analyzes why it may be efficient for society to encourage pension demand. This chapter focuses on the factors influencing private demand for pensions and the likelihood that inflation will lead to a demand for partial or full indexing of pensions.

Because pensions are received as deferred employment compensation, they are not, for the most part, demanded explicitly by individuals.[1] Nonetheless, the receipt of a pension involves current wage versus future retirement income trade-offs, which generally require current wages that are lower than otherwise.

Within the limitation that purchase is typically through the agency of a firm, a pension is an asset, like other assets, with a risk-return trade-off and demand based on risk and return. Pensions differ among themselves in these characteristics, most broadly in whether they are defined benefit or defined contribution plans, but they can also be viewed as a class of savings assets and differentiated in important respects from the other major forms of savings: individual annuity contracts, personal savings, and housing.

Pensions are most similar to individual annuity contracts. Pension benefits, like payments under deferred annuity contracts, do not begin at once; rather, they are held in abeyance until retirement and usually terminate at the death of the holder or the holder and beneficiary. Most pensions and individual annuity contracts are structured to ensure a constant stream of future nominal income. However, pensions differ from annuities in two respects. First, pensions receive more favorable tax treatment. Second, unlike individual annuity contracts, which are directly purchased, pensions are part of an employment compensation package. Firms may use pensions to hold skilled employees and to provide long-term performance incentives. While the price paid for a pension is generally lower current wages, the firm's after-tax cost of and productivity gain in supplying a pension affect the price to the employer and, ultimately, to the employee.

These two factors also differentiate pensions from other (nonannuity) personal savings vehicles. In addition, while all savings forms involve giving up current consumption for future income, pensions (like individual annuity contracts) help provide a constant future income and thus have an insurance component as well as a savings component.

Indeed, a primary factor in pension demand has been the ability of pensions to allow consumers to maintain an even stream of consumption over their lives and so reduce uncertainty. Evidence indicates that pensions and housing provide the bulk of the savings of the nonwealthy. Thus, most individuals must rely on pensions and housing together with Social Security and Medicare benefits to provide income security in retirement.

Inflation may substantially erode the ability of nominal pensions to provide a level expected real income. Social Security and Medicare benefits, on the other hand, are indexed to inflation, and in-kind housing services are not affected by inflation.[2] Indexed Social Security benefits reduce the need for indexed private pensions, as do in-kind housing services and Medicare benefits. Thus, part of the explanation for the lack of widespread indexing is that an individual's need for indexed retirement income is to a large degree fulfilled by Social Security and Medicare benefits and widespread homeownership. In addition, cost factors are likely to preclude a demand for full indexing and to discourage a demand for inflation-hedging "performance" indexing. Further, liquidity constraints, bequest motives, money illusion, and myopia may all contribute to a continued demand for nominal pensions. This chapter considers these issues by examining the factors that influence the demand for pensions and inflation's impact on these factors.

The chapter develops the demand for pensions through a life-cycle model, modified to include the role of uncertain longevity, price (or cost) of pensions, taxes, and the firm's demand for pensions as part of an optimal compensation scheme. The first section provides a broad discussion of pension coverage and growth over time and the influence of demographics on this growth. The second section explains the basic demand for pensions through the life-cycle approach in which an assured form of retirement income is desired, given uncertain longevity. In the third section there is an examination of the impact of favorable tax provisions on pension demand. The fourth section discusses employer demand for pensions. The last section analyzes the demand for inflation-hedging pensions as influenced by the household's process of portfolio optimization, the nature of the employment contract, and the provision of indexed Social Security benefits.

The chapter concludes that fully neutral inflation need not affect pension demand in real terms. Neutral inflation essentially induces a "tilt" problem. Pension payments need only be tilted to increase at the expected inflation rate to be equivalent to nominal pension payments in a world of no anticipated inflation. Nonetheless, in an inflationary environment, a tilted pension may not be preferred to a nominal pension. Rational employees with liquidity constraints or bequest motives and myopic employees may value the early receipt of pension dollars afforded by a constant nominal pension. Neutral inflation, however, does allow pensions to be tilted to compensate for the expected loss of value, at no extra cost. This assumes that inflation has always been at its anticipated level. If not, there may be a transition problem. If an increase in inflation has been anticipated by capital markets so that the nominal returns to the pension fund assets have increased with inflation, pension sponsors may have decreased contribution rates or raised nominal pension levels. If so, the movement to an inflation-adjusted pension will necessitate lowering the initial real payment levels in order to build in a positive tilt.

Neutral inflation is unlikely. Theory and empirical evidence indicate that increased inflation uncertainty accompanies increased inflation rates. Tilting pensions to the anticipated inflation rate does not deal with the heightened risk of an increase in inflation. Moreover, a tilted income stream at the anticipated inflation rate may provide an undesired tilt in real income if the actual inflation rate falls beneath the anticipated rate.

To protect retirees from uncertain inflation at no extra risk or cost to pension sponsors requires variable annuity pensions that are funded with inflation-hedging assets. Such pensions would provide a nearly constant real income stream and, thus, could duplicate the role of nominal pensions in an environment of long-term price stability. However, the real rate of return of a portfolio designed to hedge inflation is lower than that of pension portfolios not designed to provide such protection. The alternative of full indexation is not likely since no portfolio, in the absence of indexed government bonds, could guarantee a real return that would not decline with unanticipated inflation. The additional costs of less than fully indexed pensions would be passed on to employees in the long run.

In spite of their higher cost, a demand for variable annuity pensions might evolve if there were sustained high inflation, especially with a diminished role for Social Security and Medicare and increased longevity.[3]

There remains, however, the issue of whether individuals would choose an expected flat real payment stream or whether they have been constrained to do so in a world of long-run price stability. Myopic individuals, as well as those with liquidity constraints and bequest motives, may prefer high initial and subsequently declining benefits that result from nominal pensions and high rates of expected inflation. Moreover, money illusion may conceal the impact of inflation. New laws may be required if public goals are served by flat rather than declining real retirement income.[4] The implications of these issues for public policy are discussed in Part Four.

Pension Growth[5]

In the post–World War II period, our nation has become increasingly reliant on pensions to provide old age income security. In 1950 almost one third of the elderly lived with their children. This declined to 9 percent in 1970. By 1980, children's contributions were less than 1 percent of the elderly's income. Social Security, Medicare, and pension benefits provide by far the major portion of nonearned income for most of the nation's elderly. Over the same period, the expected duration of retirement for male workers grew from 5.93 years to 11.47 years. This was due to a combined increase in life expectancy and a decrease in years worked of about three years each.

The three major factors identified as influencing pension demand—life-cycle savings, optimal employment compensation, and tax advantages—all may have had a part in the growing importance of pensions and retirement. An increased demand for leisure, and specifically retirement, with per capita income growth, an increased need for labor force planning and management with industrial and service sector expansion, and increased tax advantages of tax sheltered income with the higher average federal income tax rates all may have played a role. In addition, while Social Security and private pensions can substitute for each other in the provision of a given amount of retirement income, the financial attractiveness to firms of sheltering workers' wages is heightened because increased Social Security benefits can be integrated into pension plans, as discussed below. Thus, federal income tax rates, per capita income, planned retirement, service and manufacturing employment, and private and public pensions all have grown together.

In 1980, almost 30 percent of elderly households received pension benefits representing, on average, 31.39 percent of their total income. In 1979, coverage of private workers was almost 50 percent, while 90 percent of state and local government workers were covered. Thus, the proportion of elderly households receiving pensions will increase in the coming decades.

The average replacement rate of preretirement income provided by pensions in 1978 was 18.3 percent for a hypothetical worker with 35 years of service (who earned an average real income of $19,952). The replacement rate varied considerably among workers depending on, among other factors, whether the retiree was covered under a defined benefit or defined contribution plan and the amount of preretirement income. The average income worker retiring in 1978 with 35 years of service covered by a defined contribution plan received a pension that replaced 14.8 percent of preretirement income, while the average worker covered by a defined benefit pension received 18.6 percent of preretirement income. (Although 65 percent of plans were defined contribution plans in 1980, these were mostly the smaller plans, and 75 percent of workers were covered by defined benefit plans.) Average replacement rates for typical workers with fewer years of service were lower.

The income level of pension recipients also affects the replacement rate provided by private pension plans, especially rel-

FIGURE 7–1
Fertility Rate, 1930–1976

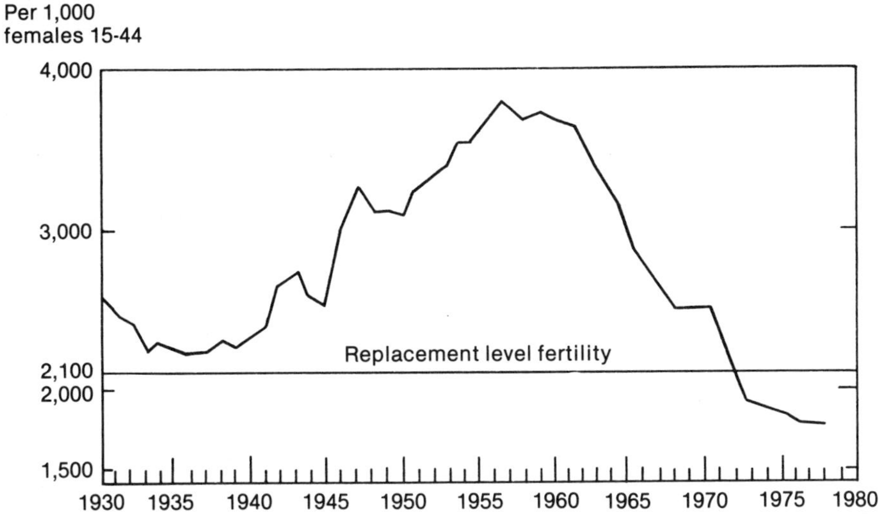

SOURCE: U.S. Bureau of the Census, "Estimates of the Population of the United States and Components of Change: 1940 to 1976," *Current Population Reports*, Series P-25, No. 706 (Washington, D.C.: U.S. Government Printing Office, 1977).

ative to Social Security benefits. The Internal Revenue Service requires that pension plans not discriminate in favor of highly paid workers. However, they permit firms to integrate the benefits that their plan provides with Social Security benefits. This integration offsets Social Security's provisions of higher replacement rates for lower income workers. Thus, a hypothetical worker retiring in 1978 with 35 years of service and a final salary of $40,000 (1980 dollars) would receive a pension that would replace 38.99 percent of this salary, while a worker with a $10,000 final salary would receive a pension that would replace 21.16 percent of this salary.

The role of private pension benefits relative to Social Security and Medicare benefits is likely to increase in the long term with the changing population structure. The absolute amount of real resources devoted to pensions also will increase.

Figure 7–1 shows the U.S. fertility experience from 1930 to 1980. It is close to bell-shaped. Fairly low prewar levels were replaced by the baby boom of 1946–66, which was followed by the very low, subreplacement growth exhibited up to the present.

FIGURE 7–2
Dependency Ratios

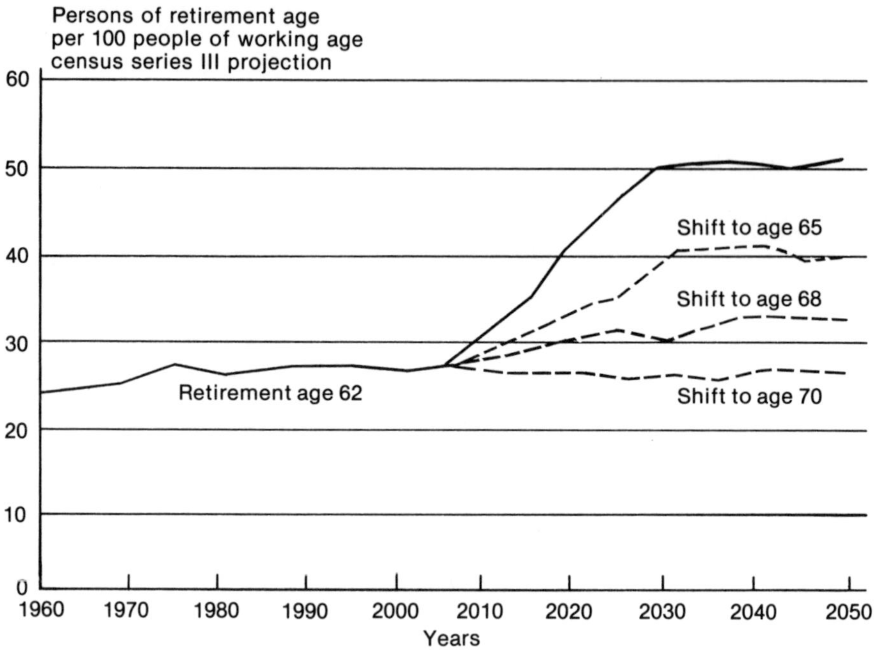

SOURCE: CMB Technical Staff paper by Douglas Norwood.

Thus, the 65-plus population can be expected to increase at a slower rate over the next few decades due to the low number of 1920–40 births. But when those of the postwar baby boom start to enter retirement years, sometime early in the next century, we can expect a huge growth in the 65-plus population, augmented due to increased longevity. This will level off around 2040, when those born after 1970 begin to control the 65-plus group.

One fruitful way to look at these demographic phenomena is through dependency ratios, which show the number of people of retirement age per 100 people of working age. Figure 7–2 shows the rise in the ratio under alternative retirement age scenarios. Note the large jump if minimum retirement age stays at 62.

The pay-as-you-go financing of the Social Security system has made it highly susceptible to the upcoming high dependency ratios. Reduction in after-tax Social Security benefits for those who retire at age 65, along with Social Security tax increases and other changes adopted in 1983, have solved the projected funding crisis as discussed in Part Four. However, Medicare Part A hospital benefits may also have to be reduced or taxes further raised. Medicare Part B supplemental medical insurance benefits may also have to be reduced, or the premiums paid by retired workers may rise more than the CPI. A reduction in after-tax OASDHI benefits would tend to increase the demand for pensions.

On the employer side, the baby boom labor glut may increase employer provision of pensions because employers may want to use pension policy to make room for the large cohort of 30- to 40-year-olds. As that cohort enters the retirement years in the next century, however, such a trend could reverse. There will be a *shortage* of working age people, so their relative wage will rise. This will decrease the motivation of employers to retire their older workers and may advance the average age of retirement. Nonetheless, increases in longevity, the number of the elderly, the pension share of retirement income, and the percentage of the elderly receiving pensions all should increase through the middle of the next century, with the result that the overall demand for pensions also increases.

Pensions in a Life-Cycle Framework: The Reduction of Actuarial Uncertainty

One way to explain pension demand is within the framework of the life-cycle model introduced in Chapter 6. In the life-cycle theory, pension demand derives from the desire to reduce income uncertainty in retirement. The life-cycle model also has implications for the demand for pensions under inflation: The desired pension is proportionally related to preretirement income and, in real terms, is unaffected by neutral inflation.

Due to the assumption of certainty over length of life, the life-cycle theory of savings motivates a demand for savings but not a demand for savings in the form of pensions.[6] In the life-cycle model, as described above, a person works T years for income Y and dies after N years; since there is no uncertainty involved, consumption can be undertaken in such a way as to enable a perfectly constant consumption stream over the individual's life along with any desired bequest.

With a zero real interest rate, the desired savings rate $\left(\frac{S}{Y}\right)$ is chosen to equal the desired retirement length as a proportion of adult lifetime $\left(\frac{N}{T + N}\right)$ to assure constant life-time consumption. Lower desired postretirement consumption allows a lower savings rate. The desired savings rate increases if precautionary savings or bequests are desired.

With certainty assumed, retirement consumption and length can be planned together with pre- and postretirement savings to maximize lifetime welfare. Whether many households do engage in such planning is not known, however. Some households may be myopic and may not plan or save at all unless forced to do so. In a sense, they do not identify with their older selves and thus cannot plan or do not wish to plan for their consumption in their older years when they are likely to wish to retire. Other households may have a high relative time preference and rationally decide not to save for retirement because they lack sufficient income even for pressing current needs. In any case, certainty over retirement length allows those who can and wish to plan savings for retirement to do so.

In the real world, of course, there is uncertainty over years in retirement as well as uncertainty over the period of savings accumulation. To indicate uncertainty, N and T can be viewed as normally distributed random variables with means $E(N)$ and $E(T)$ and standard deviations σ_N^2 and σ_T^2. An individual thus *expects* to retire after $E(T)$ years and die after $E(N)$ years, but the dates are not certain. With an uncertain lifetime, individuals can no longer plan to exhaust their savings with precision. They will generally have to maintain higher savings than otherwise to self-insure against the risk of unanticipated longevity or accept a postretirement standard of living that is reduced by an uncertain amount, depending on longevity.

Pensions can substitute for certainty over retirement length. With pensions, individuals can plan their retirement savings as if they were certain about N and T. Pensions suppliers can use actuarial assumptions to allow a group of savers to save according to expected group longevity. As a result, retirement consumption and any desired bequests can be planned by individuals who can then save less. Kotlikoff finds that a group of individuals without a bequest motive would have to leave at least one third of their wealth in estates, if there were no annuities, to insure against long life expectancy.[7]

Pensions can do this at a lower cost than individual annuity contracts because they are not purchased by individuals but by groups. This avoids the adverse selection problem which raises the cost of individual annuity contracts because those individuals who choose these contracts are likely to view themselves as living to a relatively old age.[8]

Thus, a factor in the demand for pensions is their ability to provide a guaranteed income flow throughout retirement at a lower cost than individual annuity contracts. Risk-averse individuals are willing to pay a premium to trade a risky situation for a less risky one and, thus, are willing to pay for the costs of providing pensions to reduce longevity risk. The greater the dispersion between $E(N)$ and $E(T)$, the greater σ_N^2 and σ_T^2, and the greater the level of risk aversion (V), the greater is the demand for pensions.

The factors that determine the individual's demand for pensions can be summarized symbolically as:

$$Q_i = f_i(W, Y, E(T), E(N), \sigma_T^2, \sigma_N^2, V, P_p) \tag{7.1}$$

where P_p is the price of pensions, so far determined by the price of insurance, administrative costs, and the real interest rate, r.[9] Pension demand must be an inverse function of the price of pensions:

$$\frac{Q_p}{P_p} < 0$$

In addition, pension demand is a positive function of real wealth, W, real income, Y, and the actuarially expected retirement period $E(N) - E(T)$.

Because the demand function in Equation 7.1 is specified in real terms, it is unaffected by neutral inflation. Individuals demand the same expected real pensions at all inflation rates. Demand for pensions in dollars increases at the neutral anticipated inflation rate. Moreover, there would not only be constancy in real pensions amount in total but also in the expected real size of the stream of pensions in each period. Under the life-cycle model, neutral inflation should create a demand for pension benefits that grow at the expected inflation rate. Since neutral inflation is fully anticipated, the demand for inflation-proofed defined benefit pensions can, in this case, be funded by a long-term bond portfolio with no risk to the pension sponsor.

The world described thus far lacks employers, taxes, Social Security, and uncertainty over Q_i, r, and P_p. Moreover, as so far described, demand for a pension is equivalent to a demand for an annuity to reduce longevity risk by those who wish to plan for their retirement. It is clear that the demand for pensions is not only a response to this need. Tax laws and, to a lesser extent, employer demand for an optimal compensation mechanism are the two other factors that contribute to pension demand, with Social Security benefits discouraging the demand for private pensions.

The following sections modify the pension demand function (Equation 7.1) to include the tax treatment of pensions (*Tax*), employers' demand and costs as they affect P_p, expected Social Security benefits (*SS*), and the variance in real pension income (σ_Q^2). Including these factors, the individual's demand for pensions is rewritten as:

$$\textbf{(7.2)} \quad Q_i = f_i(W, Y, E(T), E(N), \sigma_T^2, \sigma_N^2, V, P_p, \sigma_Q^2, SS, Tax)$$

Neutral inflation will leave the demand for pensions, as expressed in Equation 7.2, unchanged in real terms, assuming that Social Security benefits and taxes are indexed, and that the only motive for savings is life-cycle income smoothing. The demand for defined nominal benefit plans is transformed by neutral inflation into a demand for defined indexed benefit plans. The demand for defined contribution plans also remains unchanged in real terms. As discussed in the following, nonneutral inflation, however, does affect the real demand for pensions, as expressed in Equation 7.2, and even neutral inflation affects pension demand, assuming other motives for pensions besides life-cycle income smoothing. Nonneutral inflation raises the price of and is likely to decrease the demand for inflation-hedging pensions. In addition, if pension savings are motivated by tax advantages or employer demand, nominal pensions that decline over time in real terms may be preferred to inflation-hedging pensions.

Taxes

Favorable tax treatment is a critical factor in the demand for pensions. Pension plans have undergone tremendous growth in the decades following the 1930s, and this growth has been heavily influenced by tax considerations. Beginning in 1921, a series of federal revenue acts containing favorable tax inducements were passed, the most important of which was the Revenue Act of 1942. This act, which came at a time of increasing personal and corporate taxes, initiated a number of tax incentives for pensions, which are discussed below in their current form. In 1980, the annual tax revenue losses to the U.S. government due to these tax incentives were estimated to be $36.7 billion or $229 per adult American. Per retiree, these tax advantages account for 20 to 40 percent of their private pension income.[10]

Employer contributions are fully tax deductible so long as they represent "ordinary and necessary business expenses," are made within the IRS-prescribed deductibility period, and are within the annual IRS deduction limits.[11] This factor contributes to the demand for pensions in a passive way. Since employer Social Security and wage contributions are also tax deductible, pension contributions would be at a serious disadvantage if they were not.

Income from the assets of a qualified plan is tax deferred. (In particular, the legal rules for qualified pensions prevent discriminating among different classes—for example, by wages—of employees.[12]) Tax deferral of earnings is a distinct benefit, and it is not matched by similar treatment regarding Social Security or wages. For example, an employer can set up a pension fund that earns income which is then added to the fund, thereby increasing future employee benefits by the full amount of the interest income. In contrast, if the employer sets aside a "wage fund" to be used to pay employees at some future date, the wage fund would earn interest, but part of it would be taxed away. Thus, under existing tax law, pension plans are a more cost-effective way of compensating employees than are current wages.

The favorable tax treatment of pension benefits is advantageous to most employees for a third reason. The taxation of pensions income earned in the current working period is deferred until retirement when an individual's tax bracket is likely to be lower.[13]

From the preceding discussion, we can isolate three tax factors that affect pension demand. The first is the tax deductibility of employer contributions relative to Social Security and wages. Because all three are fully deductible, the effects cancel out. The second is the difference between applicable federal income tax rates on standard interest income and pension fund interest income. The greater this difference, the greater the demand for pensions. The third is the difference in an employee's working versus retirement period federal income tax bracket.

Thus, the partial demand function occurs:

(7.3) $$Q = f[Tax(D_s, D_w, D_p, t_i - t_{ip}, med, dbrak)]$$

where

D_s	=	Percent tax deductibility of employer Social Security contributions
D_w	=	Percent tax deductibility of employer wage payments
D_p	=	Percent deductibility of employer pension contributions
$t_i - t_{ip}$	=	(Effective) tax rate on interest income less tax rate on pension fund interest income
med	=	Median income tax bracket
$dbrak$	=	Difference in working versus retirement period median tax brackets.

One implication of the above is that "tax bracket creep" due to inflation should increase the demand for pensions, other things held constant. A second implication is that even if tax brackets are indexed, inflation should in itself increase the demand for pensions, since $(t_i - t_{ip})$ increases with higher nominal yields.

However, since demand for pensions may be motivated primarily by tax advantages, the demand for pensions (though increased) may continue to be in the form of *nominal* pensions. With low or no inflation, individuals may be constrained to choose a de facto real annuity in order to take advantage of favorable tax provisions, in spite of their preference for more flexibility in the time allotment of their expenditures than is possible with existing pensions under current tax law. With inflation, nominal pensions provide more flexibility.

Individuals who are constrained to save in the form of de facto real annuities, under no inflation, fall into two groups. The first constrained group consists of those who plan their savings in part to smooth lifetime income; nonetheless, they would wish to have more flexibility than pensions allow due to their preference for liquidity or bequest motives. Some individuals might prefer to spend more early in retirement (especially those with limited survival expectations) or to leave a larger bequest or, in general, to have the option of spending or not spending their savings at any given point.[14]

The second constrained group is those who cannot save or do not wish to save for retirement due to myopia or lack of sufficient current income. There may be a public interest in constraining these groups to save to shelter them from the consequences of their own myopia and to meet what society views as minimum retirement income needs.[15]

Under the life-cycle motive for pension demand, as noted above, neutral inflation would result in an unchanged real demand for pensions. With neutral inflation, individuals who are saving for retirement will demand pensions indexed to the anticipated inflation rate. Given the nonneutral tax system, the tax advantages of pensions grow with anticipated inflation. Thus, otherwise neutral inflation should increase the demand for indexed pensions in real dollars under a life-cycle model. However, if the primary motivation for pensions is that they shelter income from taxes, the demand for pensions, while higher, will continue to be in the form of nominal pensions which decline in real value over time. Such pensions allow more income earlier in retirement. A tilted real income flow, due to the greater flexibility in time allotment of expenditures that is allowed, will be preferred in both myopic households and rational households who are not saving to smooth income over the life cycle. To the extent an income flow is tilted to early retirement years, the constraint embodied in a constant annuity is eroded.

It is not a public policy concern if rational households, who have adequate retirement income, make use of this greater flexibility to change the tilt of their consumption. In any case, a tax law change to allow investment of excess income flow would enable these households to compensate for the forward tilt of inflation. However, a public policy concern for myopic households or households with retirement income, rendered inadequate by inflation, is a public policy concern. These households are not likely to be helped by tax laws to encourage reinvestment both because their tax bracket is zero or low and because their trade-off between greater overall income and greater current income will favor the latter.

It is possible that the substantial tax advantages given to pensions were granted as a way of sheltering income used for savings from the increased income tax rates of the post–World War II period to increase the overall savings rate. However, economists still do not know whether such provisions would have this effect. It is also possible that tax advantages were given to shelter income from higher taxes, thus lowering the overall effective tax rate. However, the fact that these advantages were given only to qualified pensions as opposed to all savings or pension vehicles suggests that there was another public policy concern embodied in pension law: The concern was to make sure that all workers—whether rational, able, and willing to save on their own or myopic, poor, and unwilling to do so—would have sufficient retirement savings, especially the latter since the former would do so on their own.

This goal has been supported by nominal pensions in the absence of chronic inflation. Sustained inflation at the double-digit levels that were reached in the United States in the 1970s and that are chronic elsewhere would preclude continued achievement of this goal through nominal defined benefit pensions. Individuals whose pension demand is motivated by tax advantages may not seek to change pensions into a form that could maintain real income, even if inflation were neutral.

As we shall see, nonneutral inflation (that we can realistically expect) is likely to exert an additional negative influence on the demand for inflation-indexed pensions through a cost increase. Before discussing this, we turn to the third factor likely to play a role in explaining the demand for pensions: optimizing employee productivity.

Employer Demand

Employers are not required to provide pensions. Other than the tax considerations and the avoidance of adverse selection which make pensions an attractive employee benefit, we have not specifically discussed employer demand.

Firms are motivated to provide pensions, even in the absence of tax considerations and an annuity demand on the part of their employees, as part of optimal wage contracts that can raise employee productivity and the firm's net worth. First, because the productivity of older employees is likely to decline, efficiency considerations require retirement or wage decreases. The latter solution is likely to interfere with the morale of the existing work force, as would the former without a pension. Adequate pensions allow the severance of employment contracts without adverse effects on morale. Moreover, the structure of pension plans can be used to encourage retirement within specified "age-windows."

Second, with a defined benefit pension, the employee earns a pension that is heavily influenced by final salary, which is itself determined by work efforts and results throughout the working period. An implicit contract is created in which the firm rewards long-term effort and results.

Long-term implicit contractual relationships may encourage worker diligence by paying less than the worker is worth when young and more when old. This provides an incentive to not jeopardize the future receipt of wages and to work for long-term results, thus decreasing managers' short-term worker surveillance cost. Pensions based on final pay emphasize this forward tilt of compensation and provide an incentive to retire in spite of the higher wage relative to the productivity pattern of the later employment years. This holds for the defined contribution pension as well, but to a lesser extent (since the pension amount in this case is heavily influenced by variable investment performance).[16]

Third, employers make substantial investments in recruiting and training employees. If employees leave prematurely, the employer's investment may be partially or entirely wiped out. Thus, unit benefit pension plans based on years of service, nonportable plans, and nominal pensions decrease unwanted labor mobility and ensure a return on firms' specific training of young workers.

Fourth, moral obligation to reward employees for faithful service is also a factor in employer demand. In addition, pension plans promote a healthy working climate and build a good corporate image.[17]

Fifth, pension plans allow employers to tailor retirement of cohorts of workers to their wage relative to earlier cohorts.

In sum, pension plans provide a dignified means of allowing retirement and encourage productivity throughout the working years. This permits firms to increase their net worth and pay higher wages than otherwise.

Firms can continue to achieve most of these goals with nominal pensions with inflation. What matters in achieving most of these goals is the expected value of the pension to employees. Even though the real value of nominal pensions declines over time with inflation, this decline may be anticipated by employer and employee alike. If anticipated, the expected value of pensions need not be affected by inflation since initial benefits can be adjusted upwards.

Encouraging productivity through long-term awards is equally well accomplished with a high initial pension which then declines as with a constant pension. Similarly, encouragement of early or delayed retirement can be accomplished by more or less remunerative pensions in expected value terms, depending on when retirement is taken, hence, subsidizing the former or latter. Again the expected value is likely to be more important than the tilt of the pension. Retention of skilled employees is enhanced by inflation because the nominal pension remains fixed at the point when employment is terminated and, thus, erodes until the age of normal retirement, with inflation.

Given that these ends are accomplished either by nominal or indexed pensions, employers may respond to employee interest by continuing to provide nominal pensions even with anticipated inflation if rational employers prefer them. This may be the case due to the higher cost of indexed pensions and the provision of indexed Social Security benefits which substitute for indexed pensions, or due to the forward real tilt and increased expenditure flexibility that nominal pensions allow under inflation.

A problem arises, however, if employees prefer nominal pensions due to myopia or money illusion. If so, the firm's moral obligation to workers is not discharged. Moreover, impoverished older employees may undermine the morale of the existing work force. With double-digit inflation, retirement benefits are rapidly eroded, and elderly retirees may find themselves with their pension effectively wiped out, with no planned alternative to compensate for this loss of income.

Employers have an obvious financial incentive to respond to the demand for nominal pensions on the part of workers who are myopic or who suffer from money illusion since such pensions are less costly, especially so in the case of money illusion. Workers with money illusion may not have to be compensated for a decline in the value of their pensions, because it is unanticipated. Thus, firms may profit from an increase in inflation if capital markets in general respond to an increase in inflation with some adjustment in nominal returns, while workers do not anticipate inflation's impact on pensions, at all or by a lesser amount.

With an anticipated increase in inflation, nominal pensions of the same initial (and continuing) levels are less costly. The decrease in expected value to retirees of these pensions due to anticipated inflation is mirrored in an equal decrease in cost to firms. If workers anticipate the inflation decline, in the long run the cost decrease is passed on to workers in the form of higher current compensation. But in the short run, there may be a gain to the firm, assuming that current or future workers do not react to a decrease in pensions by demanding higher current wages. The gain is extended in time if workers do not recognize the impact of inflation on pension value, so that in choosing employment they are misled by high initial pension value.

Even if money illusion is not a problem, myopic workers fully knowing that their pensions will decline in value may prefer these pensions to a constant real expected pension. Though for different reasons, both rational and myopic employees may prefer nominal pensions, while those deceived by money illusion are unaware of their lowered lifetime compensation. As a result, firms may find their total wage bill lower than otherwise if nominal rather than inflation-indexed pensions are offered.

Pension Demand with Inflation

The demand for any good, even for one such as a pension that is generally demanded by a group of individuals through the agency of a firm, is a function of its price. Demand is also affected by the "representative" individual demander's income, wealth, and risk-aversion characteristics. The price of a pension that is expected to yield a given income stream in a competitive industry is, in the long run, the wage decrease due to the pension. In the short run, the price of the pension may be shared by the firm's owners in the form of lower profits as well. Given the favored tax treatment of pensions, part of the price also rests on taxpayers.

The next sections consider: the impact of inflation uncertainty on the price and demand for a pension; who, other than taxpayers, pays for pensions and how inflation affects the expected value and cost of pension liabilities; the construction and cost of inflation-hedging alternatives to nominal pensions; and the impact of inflation on the form of the demand for pensions.

Uncertainty and the Demand for Pensions

The demand for pensions is in part a response to the desire to smooth lifetime consumption by eliminating longevity risk. In a world of certain inflation, nominal pensions eliminate this risk. With uncertain inflation, nominal pensions no longer perform this function. Pension plans that guarantee constant nominal income flows result in constant real income in a period without inflation. With inflation, the expected real benefit flow declines over time. Moreover, the risk of unanticipated inflation rests on the employee. Thus, inflation should lead to the demand for modified pension instruments that continue to insure against longevity risk by assuring an inflation-indexed lifetime income stream.

A nominally fixed pension may be viewed as a nominally fixed long-term bond. As such, firms can fund pensions with no risk by investing in long-term noncallable bonds of similar maturity. Firms can choose a mixed funding strategy to attempt to achieve a greater return. The mixed funding strategy may produce an investment return which is less vulnerable to unanticipated inflation. This facilitates ad hoc pension adjustments, assuming the firm grants these based in part on the fund's performance. There is no contractual assurance, however, that ad hoc benefit increases will be granted.[18] Thus, they cannot assure income smoothing.

It is possible to construct graduated payment pensions to prevent an expected real decline in benefits. Built-in benefit growth at a predetermined contractual rate can be provided at no extra cost or risk, assuming neutral inflation. However, both the underlying causes of increased inflation and the empirical evidence indicate that greater inflation uncertainty accompanies higher anticipated inflation rates. The result is that graduated pension plans are riskier than nominal level plans in the absence of inflation. The risk increase is borne by retirees. If inflation increases above the built-in graduated rate, retirees' real benefits decline. If inflation decreases, the positive tilt may produce too little income in the early years of retirement and too much income in the later years.

While noncallable U.S. government debt instruments exist and, thus, can serve to immunize graduated nominal liabilities, they are offered at significantly lower yields than generally callable private market debt. The higher return compensates for the risk that if anticipated inflation and nominal interest rates fall, the debt is recalled and interest is no longer paid at the higher previously contracted rate used to fund the graduated pension. Thus, the retiree experiences increased risk and higher costs with tilted pensions.

Inflation-hedging variable annuity pensions that can insure retirees against inflation uncertainty need impose no additional risk or cost on the sponsor, but they are more expensive than nominal pensions because of the lower real yield of an inflation-hedging portfolio. Zvi Bodie shows that the real rate of return on the efficient portfolio to hedge inflation is approximately zero, using average historical data.[19] As the following section indicates, in the long run, this cost increase is borne by pension recipients.

Who Pays for Pensions?

What determines the cost of a pension plan, and who pays for it? Does the employee always pay for the greater cost of inflation-hedging pensions? This is a complicated question. One complicating factor, among others, is that the burden of the short-run and long-run cost differs. The short-run cost may fall on the employer and the employee, while the long-run cost generally falls on the employee.

In addition, the long-run cost of a pension plan cannot be known when the plan is in operation because of the uncertainty regarding future demographic trends and interest rates. Only after the plan has been terminated and all benefits and other expenses have been paid will the exact cost be known. It is traditionally calculated as:

$$\text{(7.4)} \quad \text{Pension cost} = \text{Total benefits} + \text{Administrative expenses} - \text{Interest income}$$

While a plan is in operation, or before it is started, cost must be estimated using actuarial assumptions. Of course, different assumptions produce different cost estimates. One must keep in mind that they are estimates and that the ultimate cost remains unknown.

Having estimated the total plan cost, actuarial cost methods must be used to spread it over future years. This is much like the concept of depreciation: Regardless of the method that is used, the ultimate cost remains the same in dollar terms but not necessarily in present value terms.

A common actuarial cost method is the "projected benefit method," which projects all benefits that will be earned until retirement and spreads their cost evenly over some future period. This method generates a level cost stream. It expresses pension cost as a constant percentage of salary.[20]

The pension cost in the short run is borne by the employer in the form of a lower profit margin, the employee in the form of lower wages, or both. In the long run, employee groups that are given increased pensions will have to take more of their total compensation in the form of pensions and less in the form of wages. This happens because a firm competes with other firms in its industry.[21] If the firm's total compensation costs go up as a result of the pension increase, the firm will suffer losses unless the firm passes on the costs in the form of higher prices. This is not an option in a competitive setting, since buyers will purchase goods from other firms whose prices have not gone up.[22] Thus, higher pensions are generally not, in the long run, passed on to consumers in the form of higher prices, but rather result in a change in the form of compensation.[23]

Further, for pensions to be viable in the long run, they must be chosen by workers in spite of their cost in terms of lower current wage compensation. Workers may wish to take more of their compensation in the form of pensions and less in the form of wages to pay lower taxes, as discussed above. If so, firms that do not offer tax-qualified pension plans will be at a competitive disadvantage and will have to offer higher total compensation packages.[24] Firms that do offer pensions can pay lower total compensation by trading off their employees' current earnings for tax-deferred income.

Although in the long run employees pay for pensions, in the short run the firm's profits may be decreased by a pension plan increase. In this case, the cost of the pension plan increase is shared by the firm and the workers. Depending on the nature of the pension plan, the firm bears more or less risk in its short-run implementation; however, in the long run, increased costs generally are paid for by the employee.

Regardless of who bears the largest burden, a price rise negatively influences the demand for pensions. A price rise can occur because of increased benefit costs, increased administrative expenses, or decreased interest rates. Thus the partial demand function occurs:

(7.5) $$Q_p = f[P_p(B, AD, r_p)]$$

where

B = Total benefits
AD = Administrative expenses
r_p = Interest rate on fund assets.

In addition, pensions may affect employees' productivity and employers' profitability, which indirectly lower benefit costs. As before, neutral inflation affects none of these variables in real terms.

If inflation is neutral so that real returns are unchanged, and if pensions paid to workers are adjusted by the neutral inflation rate, the cost of pensions remains unchanged by inflation. Assuming for the moment that real returns are unchanged, the impact of inflation on the real value and cost of pensions depends on how pension liabilities are viewed.

There are two theories of the nature of pension obligations. In the legal view, firms are obligated only to pay nominal accrued liabilities. Thus, the higher the inflation, the lower the real cost of pension obligations. On the other hand, firms may be viewed as having implicit contracts with workers to pay them real pensions that are proportional to their final wages if they remain at work until retirement. In this view, unless the worker or plan is terminated or the firm fails, workers are paid their real pensions.

Ippolito finds that firms fully fund their pensions according to this second criterion, except for unionized firms which underfund their pensions.[25] He accepts the implicit contract view and explains unionized firms' behavior as an exception due to the need to give unionized workers a stake in their firms' continuing viability, since they can cause their firms to fail. Ippolito also points out employees' willingness to pay for pensions at a constant contribution rate, rather than disproportionately at the end of their career when the receipt of real pension obligations is more certain, as evidence of the acceptance among employees of the implicit contract view. Stock market data, which fully value pension liabilities in real terms, are cited as evidence that investors also hold this view.

Yet higher inflation must reduce the expected cost and value of pensions due to terminated workers, who are only paid nominal pensions, and to the after-retirement decline in real benefits. This must be the case unless pensions are portable and ad hoc adjustments are used to make retirees whole, when pension performance allows. Also higher inflation decreases the value (and cost) of defined benefit pensions if the plan is terminated.

Thus, workers should value pensions less and value current wages more at higher inflation rates. Workers may not make this trade-off because they expect real constant pensions in the future due to (1) an anticipated slowdown in inflation, (2) expected job and plan retention and ad hoc adjustments, or (3) money illusion. Alternatively workers may expect a decline in their real pensions after retirement and with early termination. The data Ippolito cites are not robust enough to reject this possibility.

If employees do anticipate a decline in real pensions and wish to adjust pensions to inflation, new instruments are needed. Upon termination or retirement, defined benefit pensions could be converted to defined contribution variable annuity pensions. These would hedge inflation if backed by inflation-hedging assets. In the long run their cost would be borne by pension recipients. The following considers their construction and cost.

Alternative Pension Instruments

Adjusting pensions for inflation prior to and after retirement poses different problems. Defined benefit pensions can be and most have been transformed to final pay plans which adjust to inflation in the working period. With supply shocks, wages may not keep up with inflation. However, since pensions grow with wages, there is little risk to firms of guaranteeing real pensions as a share of final wages when real wage growth is not guaranteed.

Defined contribution pensions also adjust to inflation to the extent that portfolio value does. If inflation risks are understood, defined contribution pensions invested in stocks and bonds may provide a desired risk/return trade-off to workers. The substantial risks involved are the same as those inherent in variable annuities invested in stocks and bonds, discussed in Chapter 4.

Nominal pensions after retirement can be hedged at no risk to the sponsor if funded with long-term bonds. There would be no risk to the retiree of deterioration in the expected value of the pension if there were no serial correlation in inflation. But as Parts One and Two show, serially correlated money supply growth and inflation does occur (especially since World War II) and nominal pension values deteriorate in real terms.

Pension instruments can be constructed to provide inflation protection to retirees without risk to firms. These instruments can also be used to maintain expected real pension value for terminated employees prior to retirement, if pensions are portable. The remainder of this section will address their construction.

The expected real value of nominal pensions declines at the expected inflation rate. Variable annuities (VAs) can be constructed to yield a constant expected real income stream. To do so requires that the interest rate or valuation rate, which is used to determine the VAs' initial value, be set equal to the expected real rate. The VA payment then increases whenever the nominal rate of return on the underlying portfolio investments exceeds this. The rate of increase equals the difference between the portfolio's nominal yield and the valuation rate.

Thus, VAs can provide an income stream that adjusts with inflation. However, the adjustment cannot be perfect. Full indexation to inflation would require three conditions to be fulfilled. First, as before, the valuation rate must be set equal to the expected real rate; second, this rate must be constant over the annuity period; third, inflation must be neutral, so that inflation raises the actual holding period return by the inflation rate. If these hold, the result is that nominal annuity payments increase at the inflation rate. Given the likelihood of changes in the expected real rate and the nonneutrality of inflation, annuity payments may lag or exceed increases in inflation, but the former is more likely.

The portfolio's expected nominal yield equals the expected real rate of return and expected inflation rate. If the valuation rate equals the expected real rate of return, this means that the expected rate of increase equals the expected inflation rate. Thus, the expected value of real annuity payments remains constant. However, actual payments vary. For example, assume the expected real return equals 3 percent; the portfolio's nominal return may equal 7 percent, when actual inflation equals 5 percent. While the annuity payment increases 4 percent, the increase does not keep pace with the 5 percent inflation rate. Moreover, the nominal annuity payment will decline if the nominal rate of return falls beneath the assumed 3 percent real return.

The extent to which real annuity payments vary over time depends on the valuation rate and the asset composition of the portfolio. The valuation rate determines the expected real annuity stream. If the valuation rate chosen exceeds the expected real rate, the expected value of the annuity payment declines over time and, at a given initial payment, the total cost of the VA is lowered.

The variability of the portfolio's asset values and their covariance with inflation determines the extent to which actual annuity payments hedge inflation. The lower the variability in the assets' expected real return and the greater their covariance with inflation, the greater the likelihood that the VAs based on these assets will hedge inflation. The theory and empirical evidence, discussed in Chapter 4, show that because bonds are nominal instruments, long-term bond returns vary inversely with inflation. Stock values were shown to vary inversely with changes in inflation because current and expected equity returns decline with supply shocks and increased risk accompanies increased inflation. Moreover, returns on both stocks and long-term bonds vary more than short-term bond returns. The work of Bodie and Pesando demonstrates the implications of the portfolio's asset composition using these instruments for an annuity's expected value and standard deviation.

Bodie and Pesando explore the real income streams provided by theoretical VAs with alternative asset bases, using historical data from 1953 to 1980.[26] Table 7–1 reproduces their results for VAs backed by one-month Treasury bills, long-term government bonds, common stocks, and a mixed portfolio, based on a combination of bonds, bills, and stocks, which over this period provides the same expected return as a long-term bond portfolio with minimum variance. They base their asset returns and covariances on the historical data for the period for 1953–80, except for bonds whose annual return is assumed to be 3 percent rather than the negative return experienced in that period. Thus, mean annual real returns for bills, bonds, and stocks are assumed to be 0 percent, 3 percent, and 7.5 percent, respectively, with their continuous time equivalent as shown on Table 7–1. Real returns are assumed to be log normally distributed, with historically based standard deviations of 1.52 percent, 7.64 percent, and 18.61 percent, respectively. Because the historical data indicate that real bill returns (unlike those of stocks and bonds) are serially correlated, an additional VA based on bills is examined assuming serial correlation.

It is assumed that VAs are purchased for $100,000 and are paid with certainty for 15 years. As Table 7–1 shows, base annuity

TABLE 7–1
Variable Annuities with Alternative Asset Bases: Theoretical Distributions

Portfolio	Expected Real Return* (percent)	Standard Deviation (percent)	Annuity Valuation Rate (percent)	Base Annuity Payment†	Annuity Payment in Year 5			Annuity Payment in Year 10			Annuity Payment in Year 15		
					Median	Mean	S.D.	Median	Mean	S.D.	Median	Mean	S.D.
Bills	0	1.52	0	$6,667	$6,667	$6,670	$227	$6,667	$6,674	$321	$6,667	$6,678	$393
Bills (serial correlation)‡	0	1.04	0	6,667	6,667	6,677	361	6,667	6,701	679	6,667	6,731	933
Bonds	2.956	7.64	3	8,377	8,377	8,500	1,463	8,377	8,625	2,115	8,377	8,752	2,647
Stocks	7.232	18.61	7.5	11,329	11,329	12,354	5,372	11,329	13,471	8,666	11,329	14,689	12,974
Mixed portfolio§	2.956	6.08	3	8,377	8,377	8,455	1,155	8,377	8,533	1,656	8,377	8,613	2,056
Graduated payment," nominal annuity (graduation rate = 8%)	2.956	—	3	8,377	8,377	8,445	1,080	8,377	8,723	2,531	8,377	9,219	4,236

*Mean of the logarithm of the real annual wealth relative. Annuity valuation rate in column 4 is the equivalent annual rate.

†Initial capital is $100,000; annual payments are made with certainty for 15 years and are reported in constant dollars.

‡Based on the following autoregression for the annual real return on bills: $r_t = .76r_{t-1} + e_t$ with $\sigma_e = 1.04\%$ per year and $r_0 = 0$.

§Mixed portfolio, consisting of bonds (52 percent), bills (29 percent), and stocks (19 percent), minimizes the variance of the annual real return for the given mean.

"Uncertainty regarding the real annuity payments stems solely from uncertainty regarding the price level, which is assumed to be log normally distributed. The continuously compounded rate of inflation (π) follows the following autoregressive process: $\pi_t = .77 + .9\pi_{t-1} + U_t$ with $\sigma_U = 2.00\%$ per year and $\pi_0 = 7.7\%$. The steady-state inflation rate of 7.7 percent is equivalent to the annual graduation rate of 8 percent. The graduated-payment nominal annuity assumes an expected real return equal to that of bonds (i.e., 2.956 percent).

SOURCE: *Statistical Abstract of the United States*, various years. Compiled by Michael D. Hurd and John B. Shoven, "The Economic Status of the Elderly," in *Financial Aspects of the United States Pension System*, ed. Zvi Bodie and John B. Shoven (Chicago: National Bureau of Economic Research, University of Chicago Press, 1985), pp. 359–97.

payments vary inversely with assumed annual mean returns, which are used as the annuity valuation rates, to determine the initial annuity payment which remains the median annuity payment. Using the standard deviations of the underlying assets, Bodie and Pesando calculate the standard deviations for the VAs after 5, 10, and 15 years.

The data show the extreme variability of real payment streams provided by stock- and bond-based VAs. More than 20 percent of the time, real annuities would decline in year 15 by approximately 25 percent for bonds and the mixed portfolio and by more than 80 percent for stocks. Longer annuities are likely to experience even greater losses.

Variable annuities (VAs) based on short-term bonds are shown to have the capacity to provide an income stream which protects against unanticipated as well as anticipated inflation. Even taking into account serial correlation of bill returns, the variability of the payment stream provided by this asset is minimal, as indicated by the standard deviation of the year 15 payment of $933, which is less than one sixth of the mean payment of $6,371. The data also show the costliness of a Treasury bill–based VA. If such a VA was bought to provide the same mean payment offered by bond ($8,752) or stock ($14,685) VAs in year 15 with the bill standard deviation, it would cost not $100,000, but $131,000 or $220,000, respectively.

Bodie and Pesando also show that a graduated payment nominal annuity (GPA) has considerable risk. They illustrate this with a GPA which is graduated at 8 percent annual rate which is equivalent to a steady-state inflation rate of 7.7 percent. The GPA is backed with long-term government bonds that are assumed to yield a 3 percent annual return. The median real payment does not change over the 15 years of the annuity, since the GPA is graduated at the anticipated steady-state inflation rate. However, because actual inflation may be greater or less than this, actual real payments may differ. Indeed, because inflation follows an autoregressive process, the rate of graduation may be significantly greater or less than actual inflation. Based on statistical probabilities, by year 15 real payments more than 40 percent of the time may be greater or less than the actual inflation rate by about 50 percent. This has an obvious cost when actual inflation exceeds the graduation rate, although the risk in this case is lower than under a nominal flat annuity. Less obvious is the cost that occurs when inflation is less than the graduation rate, in terms of too little early real payments and too great late real payments. This aspect of GPAs raises their risk relative to nominal flat annuities.

Alternative GPAs are possible. For example, Modigliani[27] suggests "the annuitant could elect to invest in, say, a three-year nominal instrument, choosing simultaneously a lower value for RV [rate of valuation] with the difference reflecting the expected inflation over the next three years. This instrument produces, for the initial three years, a sure nominal stream with a fixed graduation at a rate equal to the difference between the nominal rate and RV, and hence related to expected inflation. At the end of three years, the annuitant would have an opportunity of choosing another intermediate-term graduation consistent with inflation expected then, but he could also switch to some other form of contract." However, an additional benefit risk is added due to possible decreases in the real rate of return on long-term bonds, which would then lower the real annuity over the next contractual period.

Excess investment return plans are an important class of alternatives to VAs and GPAs. To implement these plans requires specifying a base rate of return (or valuation rate). If this is chosen as the anticipated real rate of return of the underlying portfolio, the resulting plans will be identical to the VAs so far discussed.

VAs based on various assets are the equivalent of excess return plans invested in these assets with the average annual return chosen as the valuation rate. For example, the base annuity payment of an excess return plan invested in Treasury bills would be determined by a zero evaluation rate. The actual annuity payments would then adjust with the Treasury-bill rate. If Treasury bills were available at a higher than zero, say a 3 percent real rate, the base annuity payment could be higher. If the valuation rate were chosen at 3 percent and the actual real return was zero, the annuity payment would decline at 3 percent rate. Excess returns over the anticipated real rate may be positive or negative. If the underlying portfolio is composed of inflation-hedging assets, the annuity will move closely with inflation, as desired. A substantial risk of real and nominal annuity payment decreases occurs, however, if a portfolio of stocks or bonds is chosen.

Excess investment plans, as usually discussed, include a nominal floor, thus precluding a nominal decline in a pension increase once granted. In this case, the sponsor bears the risk that the floor will become binding and the returns on the underlying portfolio will be insufficient to cover the contracted pension costs, thus requiring an increase in contributions to the fund. To avoid this, firms that offer such plans could choose inflation-hedging portfolios whose value would be unlikely to decline in nominal terms. They could also adjust the valuation rate upwards so that it is above the expected real rate of return of whatever portfolio chosen.

For example, if the expected real rate of return on a short-term portfolio is 3 percent and 6 percent is the base rate, only excess returns over 6 percent would be paid out. This hedges the firm against the need for additional contributions to maintain nominal pension benefits. However, the choice of a base rate over the anticipated real rate results in an anticipated decline in the real pension.

The few excess investment plans in operation (such as the Rockefeller Plan) combine a valuation rate above which excess investment returns are paid with a nominal floor. As indicated by Bodie and Pesando, this is equivalent to guaranteeing that the portfolio will earn at least the nominal valuation return. If this rate is chosen above the expected real rate of return, the expected real value of the annuity payments declines over time, as noted above. However, the nominal guarantee provides a floor so that payments cannot decline in nominal terms. The value of this option to retirees depends, first, on the variability of the value of the portfolio's assets and, second, on the valuation rate chosen. The higher the valuation rate chosen, the less likely excess returns will be paid and the faster the expected real decline in pension value.

Excess investment plans with floors expose firms to the risk that the floor will be binding, obligating the firm to a higher annuity than the portfolio can fund. Sponsors could choose low-variance assets as well as a high valuation rate. Assuming that employees can understand the implications of the nominal floors and the valuation rate and the portfolio chosen, it is possible that such plans would be desirable for some. However, in their obvious inflation-hedging use, VAs with floors may not have much purpose.

If the valuation rate is chosen at or near to the expected real rate to prevent a decline in the real annuity and if the portfolio is in inflation-hedging assets, the floor will bind only when nominal rates are low. Using the previous example, the nominal floor will come into play only if the nominal return falls below 3 percent. This is likely to happen only if inflation falls beneath 3 percent, at which point inflation protection is less valuable. Historically experienced real short-term rates are sufficiently low that this is likely to be generally true.

Another modification of excess investment plans would include a cumulative ceiling as well as a floor. The ceiling would prevent increases beyond those necessary for maintaining the real initial postretirement pension. Thus, any investment return above the change in the CPI would be "banked." Although not without some risk to the sponsor, such plans make excess investment plans less risky. The sponsor banks increases in portfolio value above the inflation rate when they occur to compensate for losses in portfolio value. The potential advantage of such plans is that they may allow the retiree to participate in the higher expected rate of return of stock and long-term bond portfolios while providing a smoother income flow than possible from a similarly backed VA without a ceiling or floor.

Pesando and Bodie illustrate such plans for stocks, bonds, and mixed portfolios. The resulting real annuity stream still includes substantial risk to the retiree. Such plans would be identical to similarly backed plans, if ad hoc increases were granted by firms to match inflation when portfolio value increases paid for them. Thus, the evidence is that nominal plans with ad hoc adjustments that are related to portfolio performance through implicit contracts do not hedge inflation nearly as well as VAs or excess investment plans based on inflation-hedging assets. There is a danger that nonknowledgeable or myopic retirees would choose them without understanding their risk.

The bill-based VA remains the only VA that can accomplish inflation hedging with limited risk, and thus in an inflationary environment substitutes for a nominal pension. The cost of inflation hedging is a significantly higher cost pension. Whether the trade-off is worthwhile for most retirees is considered in the following section.

The Optimal Choice of a Pension under Inflation with Indexed Social Security

If available, pension recipients could choose pensions that are designed to hedge inflation. To fund such pensions with minimum risk requires the use of inflation-hedging assets, such as short-term bills. Such pensions would of necessity have a lower rate of return. In the long run, this would result in lower lifetime remuneration since, as discussed above, in the long run employees pay for pensions. Such pensions would be capable of producing a nearly constant real income stream, thus reproducing the result of defined benefit pensions in a world of long-term price stability. Would rational employees choose such a pension in response to inflation?

The previous sections indicated that motives for pension demand on the part of employees include life-cycle income smoothing and the sheltering of savings from income taxes. Pure life-cycle income smoothing is obviously better served by the more certain real income that an inflation-indexed pension provides, while tax-sheltering may be accomplished as well through a nominal pension that is expected to decline in real terms. Liquidity preferences and bequest motives are better served by nominal pensions. Thus, if tax advantages are the primary source of pension demand, nominal pensions may be demanded even with inflation. Moreover, an inflation-hedging portfolio costs more and lowers total remuneration.

Relatively risk-averse individuals may choose an inflation-hedging pension even though it is a higher cost pension with lower expected lifetime remuneration, lower return, and lower risk, while the less risk averse may choose a lower cost nominal pension with a higher expected lifetime remuneration, greater return, and greater risk. Nonetheless, most individuals will trade off somewhat less security for some increase in return. Starting from a point of no risk, an increased return will induce at least an acceptance of a small degree of risk, with the amount of risk accepted depending on how risk averse the individual is. More precisely, it can be shown that all but the infinitely risk averse will accept some increase in risk for a higher return.[28] Thus, retirement income that is *fully hedged* against inflation because it is made up entirely of income from a fully indexed pension is not optimal except for the most risk averse.

Indexed Social Security benefits further decrease the demand for indexed pension benefits since they are substitutes. Together with indexed Medicare benefits and widespread debt-free homeownership at the time of retirement, indexed Social Security benefits may provide adequate replacement of after-tax preretirement income for many. Thus, at current levels of indexed social transfer benefits, there may be little or no demand for indexed pensions.

In spite of the availability of substitutes and the cost of inflation hedging, increased inflation risk may induce some individuals to choose a greater degree of inflation indexing of their previously chosen pension income. Implicit promises to pay ad hoc pensions may fulfill this demand, if kept. Alternatively, the knowledgeable with fungible assets may choose to shift these assets toward shorter-term debt and other hedging investments, while other risk-averse rational individuals whose wealth is predominantly in their pensions may chose variable pensions, if available.

The greater cost of such pensions may lead to less overall pension demand on the part of the relatively risk averse. Those who demand less pensions may choose to consume less in retirement, to retire later, to rely more on self-insurance through greater precautionary savings, and to change other investments to hedging assets. In addition, some individuals are likely to accept greater risk expecting to be compensated by a higher rate of return.

While rational life-cycle planners can deal with increased inflation uncertainty by choosing new forms of indexed annuities and making other optimal adjustments, the myopic and those deceived by money illusion are not likely to choose more indexation, given the higher cost or the requisite decrease in initial pension levels relative to nominal pensions under inflation. For them, the expected decline in the real level of pension benefits and any unexpected decline in the real level of pensions due to unanticipated inflation may be worrisome. This is reinforced if longevity increases, if social transfers are scaled back in the future, and if inflation accelerates. Indeed, the automatic indexation of Social Security and the increased level of Social Security and Medicare benefits initiated in the 1970s may have occurred in part as a response to greater inflation and inflation uncertainty and concerns for old age income security. However, full reliance on indexed Medicare and Social Security benefits may not be optimal, given increased tax rates that may be necessary to accomplish them.

Optional indexation may be the right policy for rational employees, but it may be precisely the wrong policy for myopic employees. Moreover even quite "rational" workers may not be aware beforehand of the impact of a sustained inflation increase on pension income and the likelihood of that increase. Evidence of capital markets supports slow rather than immediate recognition and response to sustained increases in inflation. We do not know how many workers may choose nominal pensions out of ignorance and money illusion, if optional.

Firms may gain in the short run from such money illusion and, thus, may lack the incentive to inform workers of the risks. Even if workers have money illusion, in the long run inflation should not negatively affect lifetime remuneration because, under competition, firms can afford to pay more with lower valued pensions. They can then bid workers away with upgraded current wages until the decline in expected pension value is reflected in an increase in current wages funded by a lower contribution rate. The long run, however, may be very long indeed. In any case, if workers do suffer from money illusion, the result will be a decline in the expected real value of pensions. Moreover, even if fully informed, some workers may be myopic and choose declining pensions although their later retirement income may be inadequate as a result.

Thus, while the optimal public policy response to increased inflation may be to leave adjustments in pensions to individual firms and their employees, assuming rational workers, this response may be inappropriate if most or many workers are not fully informed or myopic. This poses a dilemma. Requiring indexed pensions may be an appropriate solution for some, but it is a costly solution to rational employees who would optimally choose greater risk along with other adjustments.

Without inflation, nominal pensions can contribute to a secure retirement income for all workers whether they have high or low preretirement income levels and whether they are rational or myopic. Inflation results in a public policy dilemma due to the conflicting optimal public policy response depending on whether employees are rational and well-informed or myopic and ill-informed. These public policy issues are examined further in the following chapter.

Notes

[1] IRA accounts are established by individuals; employer-sponsored pension plans are not.

[2] Social Security benefits are indexed if inflation exceeds 3 percent. While wages have increased more than benefits in most years, the opposite has been true in some recent years. A delayed adjustment in COLA indexing, adopted in 1983, is discussed below.

[3] See Paul Taubman, "Pensions and Mortality," NBER Working Paper, July 13, 1981.

[4] Money illusion and inflation's positive impact on the value of housing wealth may also have slowed the development of inflation-linked variable instruments. New institutional developments also take time in both the innovation and implementation phases.

[5] The pension data in this section are taken from Laurence J. Kotlikoff and Daniel E. Smith, *Pensions in the American Economy*, NBER (Chicago: University of Chicago Press, 1982).

[6] More generally, there would be no demand for pensions in a world of perfect capital markets, with actuarially fair pensions, with certainty over retirement and death, and with no separate employer demand factors. Under these conditions of "pension neutrality," the only effect of pensions encouraged by tax exemption is a one-for-one decrease in private savings. Increasing expected income over time, together with imperfect capital markets (which prevent borrowing against future income), actuarially unfair pensions, and separate employer demand factors, can create a demand for pensions as does an uncertain lifetime. Under these conditions, pensions displace savings somewhat but not completely. See Vincent P. Crawford and David M. Lilien, "Social Security and the Retirement Decision," *Quarterly Journal of Economics*, August 1981.

[7] See Kotlikoff and Smith. The privately contracted, actuarially fair annuity allows individvuals the same constant consumption stream with uncertain lifetimes as would occur with certainty. See M. Yari, "Uncertain Lifetime, Insurance, Life Insurance, and the Theory of the Consumer," *Review of Economic Studies*, April 1965.

[8] See Chapter 8 for further discussion.

[9] The life-cycle motive explains the demand for individual annuity contracts, but not for pensions. Several factors explain the far greater prevalence of pensions. First, to avoid adverse selection, annuities need to be provided for

a group, such as a group of employees. Second, pensions receive more favorable tax treatment. Third, pensions can be used by firms to increase productivity.

[10] See Richard Ippolito, *Pensions, Economics and Public Policy* (Homewood, Ill.: Dow Jones-Irwin, 1986).

[11] IRC, Sec. 404.

[12] Sec. 503 (B) of 1954 IRC as amended through 1973. Pensions are distinguishable from other types of benefit plans primarily because of their "defined" nature. The benefits that employees receive under a pension plan must be systematically received and of a definitely determinable nature. The plan instrument specifies according to a formula the benefits that all employees will receive upon retirement. These formulas may be classified by whether the benefit is related to years of service and whether the benefit is related to compensation and, if so, what compensation (e.g., five-year final average pay, career average pay).

Variable benefits represent an attempt to adjust pension income for inflation by tying it to the market value of trust assets or to the CPI. Although such plans do not have definitely determinable benefits, the IRS considers them as meeting the definitely determinable requirement for plan qualification.

Defined contribution plans also may qualify. Profit-sharing plans, for example, are of the "defined contribution" type. Under such a plan, the employer may make defined contributions, but the benefits that employees will receive are uncertain, varying with the yield of the portfolio.

While the basic benefits of a pension plan must be definitely determinable if it is to qualify with the IRS, a qualified plan may contain other "incidental" benefits that are not definitely determinable so long as the retirement-oriented nature of the plan is preserved. Such benefits may include early retirement, disability retirement, health and accident benefits, and death benefits.

If the trust under a plan is to be exempt from federal income tax, the plan and the trust must "qualify" with the IRS. Qualifying the plan is a detailed and complicated process, but there are some basic guidelines that a plan must meet if it is to qualify: (1) the plan instruments (plan and trust) must be written; (2) the plan must be permanent and continuing; (3) the existence of the plan must be communicated to the employees; (4) if the plan is trusteed, the plan instrument must prohibit the use of the trust assets for anything other than the benefit of the employees or their beneficiaries; (5) the plan itself must be for the exclusive benefit of the employees and their beneficiaries; (6) the plan must pass one of several tests to ensure that coverage is nondiscriminatory; (7) more than one plan may be financed through a single trust without affecting the tax-exempt status of the trust; (8) the plan must implement established statutory minimum vesting schedules; (9) if a pension plan is terminated, all accrued benefits must become fully vested.

[13] In particular, in firms where the manager is the owner, there is strong incentive to take pay in tax-favored forms, since marginal tax rates are so high. Similarly, it is not uncommon for pension plans to be initiated by top employees, who are in the highest tax brackets and therefore stand to gain the most.

Furthermore, the ability to vary contributions to pension plans can be used to reduce tax liabilities in especially profitable years. See Dan M. McGill, *Fundamentals of Private Pensions*, 5th ed. (Homewood, Ill.: Richard D. Irwin, 1984).

Other tax rules are complex and beyond the scope of this work, but they are nevertheless a factor in pension demand. The following illustration of tax treatment may serve as an example. If death benefits are payable, the portion attributable to employer plan contributions escapes estate tax unless an employee's estate is his beneficiary and may receive special income tax treatment if paid in a single sum to his beneficiary.

[14] Even if an option exists to cash out at retirement, this is discouraged by the tax advantages granted to the annuity form of pensions, since lump sum distributions are taxed as income in the year received. While pensions are the optimal form of savings for those who save to smooth consumption over working and retirement years, it is not known what proportion of households in fact wish to save for this life-cycle consumption smoothing, as opposed to precautionary altruistic, or other wealth-accumulating motives. Empirical evidence on this, cited in the previous chapter, indicates that some life-cycle saving does occur, but how much is not known.

[15] The second group is constrained to save in the form of pensions if they choose employment in sectors that provide group pensions. Tax law enforces pensions for these employees if the higher income employees are to have their income sheltered by pensions.

[16] See Edward P. Lazear, "Pensions and Severance Pay," NBER Working Paper No. 944, July 1982; and McGill, *Fundamentals of Private Pensions*.

[17] According to J. H. Schultz in *Economics of Aging* (Belmont, Calif.: Wadsworth Publishing, 1980), p. 127, the large differences in pension coverage between large and small firms indicate that firm size is also a factor in employer demand for pensions. For example, in 1980, 81 percent of firms with 500 or more employees had pension plans, while only 42 percent of firms with fewer than 500 employees had them. Schultz offers several reasons for this phenomenon, including: (1) the high costs per employee of establishing and maintaining a private plan (in small firms); (2) the fact that small business firms are often relatively young and, on average, short-lived; (3) the often unstable and insecure financial status of many small businesses; and (4) the lack of effective pressure in some companies from employees or unions.

Unions have historically pushed for the implementation of pension plans for a number of reasons. First, they view pensions as a good supplement to often inadequate Social Security income. Second, they found that they could sometimes get pensions from employers who refused to grant any more wage increases, given the deferred nature of the expense. A 1948 NLRB decision described the obligation of employers to bargain over pension plans, and since then unions have been instrumental in expanding pension plans.

[18] Also, pension receipt depends, in part, on the firm's viability, although this risk has been reduced by ERISA. Pension receipt also depends on the employee's decision to leave the firm before vesting or after vesting in terms of the erosion of real benefits.

[19] See Zvi Bodie, "Purchasing-Power Annuities: Financial Innovation for Stable Real Retirement Income in an Inflationary Environment," NBER Working Paper No. 442, February 1980.

[20] Another common actuarial cost method is known as the "accrued benefit cost method," or "step-rate method."

[21] See Howard E. Winklevoss, *Pension Mathematics* (Homewood, Ill.: Richard D. Irwin, 1977).

[22] Unions in an industry with market power may be able to pass cost increase on to consumers. However this occurs as a result of an increase in the union's

market power, not due to an increase in costs. Thus, even unionized firms cannot in the long run pass on an increase in pensions costs.

[23] Under special circumstances, even long-run costs may be shared by the consumer. Although, for the most part, costs cannot be passed on to the consumer in whole or in part, there is one exception: This may occur if a pension cost increase is mandated by government policy and if labor supply is elastic.

If an increase in pensions (or costs associated with pensions) above the competitively determined equilibrium is universally imposed by government mandate, the extra costs are likely to be reflected in part by higher prices. The increase in costs is in the long run, in part, passed on in higher prices because consumers have few replacement substitutes. However, some decrease in wages is also likely in the long run, since capital and raw materials can be substituted for labor, and those firms that do so will have smaller price increases and will grow relative to others. To remain competitive, firms that are heavy users of labor will have to reduce wages. The extent to which the burden is on the consumer depends on substitutes available and the elasticity of the supply of labor. Social Security changes are more likely to be passed on in the form of price changes than are mandated pension cost increases, since fewer substitute goods are available (that are not produced with laborers who must pay Social Security taxes). Even if mandatory, if labor supply is inelastic, the cost of pensions is borne by workers.

[24] In spite of the required trade-off between current wages and pensions, pension increases, in fact, are not likely to be associated with decreased current wages. In a growing economy, a pension increase is more likely to be reflected in a decrease in the rate of growth of wages than in an actual decrease in wages. Moreover, as the discussion of the previous chapter suggests, pensions, like other savings, are more likely to be demanded when the rate of earnings growth is higher than anticipated. Thus, the required wage/pension trade-off is unlikely to show up in the data as an actual wage decrease.

[25] See Ippolito, *Pensions, Economics and Public Policy.*

[26] See Zvi Bodie and James Pesando, "Retirement Annuity Design in an Inflationary Climate," in *Financial Aspects of the United States Pension System*, ed. Zvi Bodie and John B. Shoven (Chicago: NBER, University of Chicago Press, 1985).

[27] See Franco Modigliani, "Comment on Bodie and Pesando," in *Financial Aspects of the United States Pension System*, ed. Zvi Bodie and John B. Shoven (Chicago: NBER, University of Chicago Press, 1985).

[28] See Martin Feldstein, "Should Private Pensions Be Indexed?" in *Financial Aspects of the United States Pension System*, ed. Zvi Bodie and John B. Shoven (Chicago: NBER, University of Chicago Press, 1985).

Bibliography

BODIE, ZVI. "Purchasing Power Annuities: Financial Innovation for Stable Real Retirement Income in an Inflationary Environment." Cambridge, Mass.: National Bureau of Economic Research Working Paper No. 442, February 1980.

BODIE, ZVI, and JAMES PESANDO. "Retirement Annuity Design in an Inflationary Climate." In *Financial Aspects of the United States Pension System,* ed. Zvi Bodie and John B. Shoven. Chicago: National Bureau of Economic Research, University of Chicago Press, 1985.

CRAWFORD, VINCENT P., and DAVID M. LILIEN. "Social Security and the Retirement Decision." *Quarterly Journal of Economics,* August 1981.

FELDSTEIN, MARTIN. "Should Private Pensions Be Indexed?" In *Financial Aspects of the United States Pension System,* ed. Zvi Bodie and John B. Shoven. Chicago: National Bureau of Economic Research, University of Chicago Press, 1985.

IPPOLITO, RICHARD. *Pensions, Economics and Public Policy.* Homewood, Ill.: Dow Jones-Irwin, 1986.

KOTLIKOFF, LAURENCE J., and DAVID E. SMITH. *Pensions in the American Economy.* Chicago: National Bureau of Economic Research, University of Chicago Press, 1982.

LAZEAR, EDWARD P. "Pensions and Severence Pay." Cambridge, Mass.: National Bureau of Economic Research Working Paper No. 944, July 1982.

MCGILL, DAN M. *Fundamentals of Private Pensions,* 5th ed. Homewood, Ill.: Richard D. Irwin, 1984.

_______. *Social Security and Private Pension Plans: Competitive or Complementary?* Homewood, Ill.: Richard D. Irwin, 1977.

MODIGILANI, FRANCO. "Comment on Bodie and Pesando." In *Financial Aspects of the United States Pension System,* ed. Zvi Bodie and John B. Shoven. Chicago: National Bureau of Economic Research, University of Chicago Press, 1985.

TAUBMAN, PAUL. "Pensions and Mortality." Cambridge, Mass.: National Bureau of Economic Research Working Paper, July 13, 1981.

WINKLEVOSS, HOWARD E. *Pension Mathematics.* Homewood, Ill.: Richard D. Irwin, 1977.

YARI, M. "Uncertain Lifetime, Insurance, Life Insurance, and the Theory of the Consumer." *Review of Economic Studies,* April 1965.

PART FOUR

Public Policy and Inflation's Impact on Pensions

Part Four discusses the nature of pension policy goals and the appropriate government role in the provision of inflation-protected retirement savings and income. Most individuals derive retirement income from a combination of Social Security benefits, private pensions, and their own savings (in addition to housing services and Medicare benefits). The appropriate government role in the provision of these may be changed by inflation. Thus, the principal question addressed in Part Four is: What should be the public policy response to inflation's impact on retirement income?

Public provision of Social Security and tax advantages and regulation of private pensions yield public benefits; they also increase taxes, decrease tax revenues, and impose regulatory costs.[1] Pensions and Social Security create public as well as private benefits and costs.

While the concepts of private benefits and costs are used in their familiar sense, the term *public benefit* and the related economic concepts of market failure, efficiency, and government policy failure may require some discussion. In any policy area, the efficient role for government is defined by the concept of market failure. Markets fail when goods (or services) that individuals wish to consume must be produced, by their nature, in the collective. Government production and/or regulation and encouragement of private production through subsidies or tax advantages are then justified to yield the optimum consumption of the collective or public good, paid for by taxes.

Market failure (due to what economists term *externalities*) occurs when public benefits are created along with private benefits by private action. The quantity of a product or service is optimal when the cost of the last unit produced equals its benefits, public and private.[2] Private individuals pay the cost and thus cause the optimal production of private benefits. But public collective benefits, by definition, are consumed by everyone. There is no way to limit their consumption only to those who pay for them, nor to get private individuals to pay for them, as individuals. There is too little production of goods that yield public benefits by private markets. Since their cost (i.e., the amount of resources used up to produce the last unit) is less than their private and public benefits, production of more units yields society a benefit in excess of the cost.

Public intervention to increase production of the goods or services that yield public benefits can take the form of direct government production or of incentives (with or without regulation) to private industry to produce more. Direct government production or the regulation of private production is appropriate if, due to economies of scale, the goods or services cannot be efficiently produced or delivered by competitive firms. However, regulation or government production may be inefficient, so that they do not counter the inefficiencies of unregulated private production. Taxes may also cause inefficiencies.

Government's tax burden on society must be increased either to pay for the direct production or to give incentives to private industry. Taxes impose two kinds of cost burdens. The first is the amount of the tax itself, which is used for production or for incentives. This direct burden is worthwhile, if, due to market failure, the resources generate net private and public benefits when used in this way. The second is the excess burden of taxes due to the distortion of incentives: For example, work may be discouraged by high after-tax wage rates. All taxes but lump sum taxes create distorted incentives. This is a burden beyond the required shift of resources to the government to finance expenditures. Both burdens need to be compared to the benefits, public and private, created from the tax expenditure. The benefits produced through public policy may not equal the costs, resulting in a decrease in society's welfare and what may be identified as government policy failure.

Thus, government spending or regulatory programs to deal with inflation's erosion of retirement benefits, while possibly valuable in themselves, may or may not be worth the additional cost they may impose on society. To determine whether they are worth the additional cost, the first question that needs to be asked is why the private market does not offer the alternatives the government seeks. Is it because they are not worth their cost to the consumer? Or is it that the collective nature of the good makes it impossible for private competitive markets to respond to the demand? Only in the latter case of market failure should the government intervene.

Several sources of market failure justify a role for government in the provision of retirement income. Chapter 8 discusses the implications of the intergenerational transfer problem, the adverse selection problem, myopia, money illusion, and socially acceptable minimum living standards for the provision of private and public pensions under inflation. Chapter 9 summarizes the impact of inflation on pensions and the alternative public policy responses.

Notes

[1] Regulatory costs include the administrative costs of running the program and checking compliance and the actual cost of compliance. These costs are reflected in higher taxes and higher product costs.

[2] Optimal in the sense that everyone is as well off as can be, given society's resources and income distribution. This concept of Pareto optimality is discussed in microeconomic texts.

8 Retirement Income Security with Inflation

Introduction and Summary

The government encourages individuals to accumulate savings and private pensions, through the tax exemption of income set aside for pensions (and for other retirement savings) and of the interest on that income. To help assure that private pensions serve the public interest, the government also regulates private pensions, primarily through the Internal Revenue Code and the Employee Retirement Income Security Act (ERISA), enacted in 1974.

Tax advantages granted to pensions may be justified by public goals served by pensions. Efficiency objectives may be advanced by encouraging individuals to demand and pay for pensions that provide an adequate retirement income, if myopic behavior or money illusion would otherwise prevent them from doing so. Further, government has the social obligation to provide inflation-protected retirement income up to the socially acceptable minimum standard of living, if individuals do not do so on their own. Avoiding this by encouraging private savings decreases the tax burden on the rest of society. Also, privately accumulated savings raise the capital stock and the amount of capital available per laborer, thus raising labor's productivity and decreasing the tax rate necessary to support safety net income transfers.

Social Security directly serves some of the same purposes advanced by private pensions and can substitute for, as well as complement, private pensions and savings. The wealth diversification need for human as well as physical capital holdings and the adverse selection problem justify Social Security and private pensions rather than incentives for individual savings only. This chapter examines the impact of inflation on the public and private provision of retirement income. In particular, the chapter considers whether the public goals of tax-advantaged pensions and mandatory tax-supported Social Security require indexed retirement benefits.

The first section discusses market failure rationales for the provision and indexation of social transfer payments. These rationales may include equity concerns and myopia and money illusion together with wealth diversification and the adverse selection problem. The optimal level of indexed social transfers depends on the rationality of household savings behavior. Misinformed and myopic households may benefit from funded forced savings, which provide indexed retirement benefits that fully replace preretirement income, while rational savers lose, with the potential loss greater with higher mandatory replacement rates.

The second section describes the current extent of inflation-protected retirement income provided by Social Security and Medicare benefits and their probable cost. Indexed replacement rates of preretirement income are currently relatively high. However, increased taxation of benefits for many and possible future reductions in Medicare benefits may lower effective replacement rates significantly. Lower replacement rates will result in greater dependence on private savings and nominal pensions.

Finally, the third section considers adjustments in pension and savings policies to deal with inflation, assuming both rational and myopic savings behavior. Rational households can adjust to sustained and uncertain inflation by saving a higher proportion of their income (before and after retirement), by postponing retirement, and by diversifying a portion of their wealth holdings into inflation-hedging assets, even with nominal pensions. In addition, they can choose variable annuities, if available. There are a number of government policy initiatives that can assist rational savers in these responses. These include removing impediments to saving more and to working longer. Such policies also have the advantage of raising the total wage bill and allowing lower tax rates to support social transfers than otherwise. Pension-specific policies that can facilitate rational adjustments to inflation include revised tax laws to allow pension sponsors to credit ad hoc payments and to allow retirees to reinvest a portion of their nominal pensions, without taxing interest. In addition, some provisions may have to be made for those who switch jobs, to transfer funded vested pensions to individual retirement accounts. Also, it may be necessary to require pension sponsors to provide an inflation-tracking variable annuity as an optional alternative to nominal pensions.

A substantial proportion of households who display myopia and money illusion may not be able to adjust to inflation, even with these changes. For these households, high sustained inflation may cause significant financial hardship, especially with decreased social transfers and increased longevity. As a result, mandatory performance indexing may be necessary if inflation is not brought under control, although there is a cost to such regulation, borne by rational savers in terms of higher cost pensions, and by the economy as a whole in terms of lowered growth potential. Finally, high levels of uncertain inflation may justify indexed government bonds or rate change insurance, which would allow indexed private pensions.

Market Failure: Rationales for Social Transfer Indexation

Under certain restrictive assumptions, the optimal government role in the provision of retirement savings is limited to assuring price stability. To arrive at this conclusion, it must be assumed that individuals have the foresight to plan for their retirement and the financial ability to save accordingly. In addition, it must be assumed that no adverse selection market failure interferes with the private provision of annuities and that human capital is tradable so that there is no wealth diversification problem. The rationales for government policy provided by the removal of each of these assumptions is discussed in the following.

Wealth Diversification

A central difficulty in providing for retirement income is that retirees must have the "baskets of goods" necessary to live on or claims to these baskets after they themselves can no longer produce these goods. This is not a simple problem. Beyond storage difficulties, some consumption needs involve services that cannot be stored at any cost. Thus, retirees cannot preserve without cost the actual goods and services that their income can purchase in their working years for future use. If they could, the rate of trade-off between consumption today and consumption in retirement years would never be less than one, and the implicit interest rate on such savings would never be less than zero.

The alternative is to invest in those goods that are durable along with financial instruments that can be traded for the needed consumption goods and services. But individuals cannot invest in labor (human capital) or in financial instruments that are denominated in units of labor. Therefore, using instruments available in private markets alone exposes individuals to the risk that the terms of trade between capital and labor will deteriorate. It is possible that due to labor scarcity the rate of return on human capital will increase relative to physical capital. If so, the claim to a share of physical capital will not purchase as much human capital output as otherwise. As a result, savings invested in physical capital may not suffice to purchase the desired retirement mix of goods and services.

What is necessary to avoid this risk is savings in the form of human and physical capital. Trading in human capital is not possible, although family intergenerational transfers can serve this function for those who can rely on their children. While, except for trades within family units, private markets cannot accomplish intergenerational transfers of human capital, the government can.

Thus, one rationale for government involvement in the provision of retirement savings is that the private market cannot supply retirement consumption loans across generations efficiently while society at large can.

Appendix 8.A explains why the efficient trading of human

capital across generations is precluded in private markets. That discussion can be summarized here. Basically, the older working generation must use a part of its income to pay the younger working generation in advance for its support in retirement and, at the same time, must use another part of its income to support the retired generation. The result is disproportionately little income available for consumption in later working years.

The solution to this intergenerational transfer of human wealth problem is a social contract between generations which can substitute for within-family trades. All workers, younger and older, contribute a fixed proportion of their income to the retired. In return, when retired, they receive from the current younger and older workers the same fixed proportion of their income. Such agreements are enforced by the government through its taxing power. Thus, the need to diversify wealth to include human capital holdings provides a rationale for a Social Security–type tax and transfer system.

Aggregate retirement benefits in this social contract are a proportion of aggregate wage income, with the proportion determined by the share the retired generation paid of its own income. This can be viewed as the share of human capital bought. If households plan to spend, say, one fourth of their adult years in retirement, they would save 25 percent of their income, as shown in Chapter 6, with some proportion of this in the form of current contributions (i.e., taxes) to fund benefits to current retirees. With two thirds of their planned retirement income deriving from human capital, the wage tax would equal approximately 16.7 percent of their income.[1]

Aggregate retirement benefits in this wealth diversification system equal the share of aggregate wages contributed multiplied by the current workers' aggregate wage income. Individual benefits equal the share of aggregate wage income divided by the number of retirees. If the aggregate real wage bill declines (e.g., due to a recession) with a constant number of retirees or if a constant real wage bill is divided among a greater number of retirees (e.g., due to a population decline), real benefit levels must decline. Similarly, a population boom may be followed by a bust, and real wage growth may be insufficient to maintain real benefit levels per retiree. These possibilities preclude indexation of a constant real benefit level.

Assuming monetary and fiscal policy consistent with price

stability, inflation only arises out of supply shocks. The wealth diversification rationale does not justify indexing supply shock inflation. Since the productivity of all inputs is lower than otherwise, indexation requires income redistribution away from current workers and a higher tax rate than the rate "agreed to" in the risk-diversifying social contract.

Assuming money or demand shock inflation, the nominal aggregate wage bill and benefit levels eventually rise to match the price level increases. However, indexation before wage adjustments raise tax rates, albeit temporarily.

Indexation of these payments (as of others) also has the potential of destabilizing the economy. Pervasive indexation slows the relative price changes that are necessary to lessen supply shocks' negative output effect and speeds money and demand-shock inflation through the economy. Thus, indexation can be accomplished without harmful effects only if there is no decline in the real wage bill per retiree and if inflation is anticipated.

With human capital nontradable, the government should provide wage-tax-financed transfers to retirees to improve the efficiency of risk bearing in the economy. To accomplish the human capital wealth diversification goal, these transfers must be paid for by the pay-as-you-go collection of wage taxes. But there is no market failure justification for the linkage of these transfers to a price index.[2]

Equity Concerns

We have assumed that people can plan for retirement and have sufficient preretirement income to do so. Many individuals, however, have neither the foresight nor the requisite information to accumulate savings that in retrospect they view as adequate. These individuals can be defined as myopic. Others are too poor to save on their own for a retirement income level that society views as adequate. If society is concerned about the equity of income distribution and the effects of individuals' myopia, a tax-financed mandatory retirement benefit system that is indexed to the price level may be justified on market failure grounds.

Because the income distribution created by the workings of private markets may be viewed as unjust, society may choose to redistribute income and, in particular, to assure a minimum standard of living to serve as a safety net,[3] through taxes and transfers in income and kind. However, a safety net minimum income, guaranteed by means-tested welfare payments, discourages work and the accumulation of savings and can be degrading. Thus, equity concerns can justify a forced savings program for those individuals who cannot or will not save to preclude their future dependency on welfare, with its concomitant work and savings disincentive effects. A forced savings system, with a higher "second tier" level, above the means-tested minimum benefit level, will encourage work to qualify for higher benefits and will not discourage work and savings as much as a means-tested welfare program alone. Such a two-tier program dissuades those who can save and work from joining the truly needy.

Since the minimum benefit forced savings level program is for those who would save little or nothing on their own, the savings rate needs to yield a retirement income that society views as adequate. But forcing an adequate savings rate, in effect, disproportionately taxes the poor (especially those who work intermittently), since the poor choose to save less than the nonpoor. Thus, subsidies are required to obviate the need for a uniformly high tax rate and to maintain the desired minimum safety net. In addition, a subsidy beyond the minimum level is desirable both to avoid a payment decline (with its consequent disincentive effects), if hours worked and benefits exceed the minimum qualification and safety net level, and to have the payment schedule satisfy more general equity goals. Because of these subsidies, the savings program must be mandatory.[4]

Thus, an argument based on equity concerns can be made for publicly financed, fully funded mandatory retirement benefits, with a minimum payment and with a tilt on benefits in excess of the minimum, to preserve work incentives and to produce the desired income distribution outcome. Minimum retirement income standards are socially determined, and social views on adequacy and affordability change over time. If all income levels decline, these may decline also. However, except for such circumstances, which are unlikely to prevail over the long run, these benefit levels should be increased with inflation.

The Adverse Selection Problem

A third rationale for mandatory public pensions, besides equity concerns and wealth diversification, derives from the difficulties that private markets face in providing individual annuities. We have seen above that, in the absence of within-family insurance, the savings rate necessary to assure retirement income security can be significantly lowered if annuities are available. Given an uncertain lifetime and the resulting uncertain retirement income needs, a rational, risk-averse individual may wish to purchase an annuity. However, the price of the annuity will exceed that of annuities that are provided without choice to a group. This is the result of what is termed the *adverse selection problem*.

The insurance company that supplies individual annuity contracts knows that many people never purchase an annuity, yet that a particular individual does want one. The suppliers must rightfully conclude that this individual has higher expected benefits than those who do not wish to buy the annuity, and they therefore set a higher price than for a group annuity. From the suppliers' point of view, the individuals who prefer annuities are adversely selected, since their preference may reflect expected longevity. As a result, the cost of individual annuities is higher than for mandatory annuities provided for a group.

This higher cost of individual annuities poses no difficulty for those who belong to employment or other groups which supply mandatory annuities as an ancillary benefit to the major activity of the group. However, individuals may not belong to such groups or the mandatory group annuity may not be as large as desired. This may be an additional rationale for funded mandatory public pensions, at least at levels viewed by society as minimally adequate.

Like the risk-diversifying rationale and unlike the equity rationale, this does not imply that public or private annuities should be fully indexed. Nonetheless, if individuals tailor their own annuity design, the adverse selection problem may recur. A uniform annuity income stream keeps costs down. Since the purpose is to provide retirement income security, it would be reasonable to choose an income stream that is not expected to decline in real terms during retirement.

Myopia and Money Illusion

The myopia—or the lack of foresightedness—argument, apart from equity concerns, may also justify public intervention in the provision of retirement income, including the encouragement of at least partial indexation or "tilting" of private retirement benefits. Myopia or money illusion may result in too little savings during one's working years.[5] Inefficiently high consumption levels during working years may be due to lack of information or to distorted time preference rates. (They may be too high because the young do not identify with their older selves.) In either case, myopia and money illusion in themselves do not necessarily require an obligatory system such as Social Security in which individuals must put aside a certain proportion of their income.

Rather, such lack of foresightedness may be dealt with by a combination of subsidies and regulations. Subsidies through tax advantages[6] can increase the incentive to save for retirement in the form of pensions and other vehicles that embody safeguards.[7] This assumes, however, that tax advantages and regulations induce employers, together with informed and nonmyopic employees who are near retirement, to impose an adequate level of pensions on younger, myopic workers who would not otherwise choose them. If so, tax-advantaged private pensions may encourage adequate levels of retirement income, deriving from physical capital. Money illusion and myopia may require pension regulations to assure adequate pension savings across income and age groups. For diversity and equity, participation in the Social Security system (mandatory because of the subsidies provided to some) can be used to supply minimum retirement benefits and wage-tax-linked transfers, to complement physical capital savings.

Myopia may also distort after-retirement consumption, so that too little income remains for one's later retirement years. This may justify indexation of Social Security benefits after retirement provided in response to equity and risk-diversification objectives. After-retirement myopia combined with money illusion also may justify public regulation of private pensions to ensure performance-indexed, although not fully indexed, payment streams. Requiring private firms to provide fully indexed pensions would impose substantial risks on firms' stockholders. Private firms could not offer such pensions without substantially increased risk, unless they could purchase instruments that would guarantee a real rate of return. Only the government could provide such instruments, and it has been argued that the government should use its taxing power to do so. However, the government itself cannot in fact insure against money risk. All it can do is transfer this risk to taxpayers. Equity concerns justify the transfer of this risk for those who cannot save enough to provide what society views as a minimally adequate income. But equity concerns alone cannot justify such a transfer for those whose income is not viewed as inadequate.

Nor does after-retirement myopia necessarily justify fully indexed Social Security benefits, which guarantee full replacement of preretirement income for all income groups.

Paternalism

What is required to rationalize such guarantees is a stronger argument, one that is based on a notion of paternalism.[8] Some have argued that Social Security benefits should serve as a general substitute for private saving for retirement, especially given the potential erosion of private nominal pensions by inflation.[9] If so, a substantial proportion of preretirement income should be guaranteed upon retirement, and these benefits should be fully indexed to the price level so that they do not deteriorate over time. This is a policy of paternalism and one that may require tax rate increases, with possible declines in capital and labor productivity and increases in the dependency ratio. Income transfers between generations result. In particular, as the current working generation ages, higher dependency ratios are likely to necessitate the imposition of higher tax rates (to finance projected Social Security and Medicare benefits) on the generation that follows. This implies either that they accept a lower rate of return on the taxes that they pay as tax rates on future generations return to "normal," or that tax rates remain high, with the increased cost of higher tax rates imposed on future generations as well.

Even if it is assumed that dependency ratios and output growth rates are such that tax rates need not rise to guarantee a given replacement rate, the required participation in a national retirement savings fund involves cost to the participants. In establishing and obligating universal participation in such a fund, society substitutes its judgment about what an individual needs (for example, it is assuming that a higher income individual needs a higher retirement income) for the individual's own choices. This prevents an individual from choosing more consumption and less retirement savings, or more investment in one's own or one's children's human capital. It also eliminates the competition between savings funds that can encourage investment efficiency. In addition, social insurance based on a pay-as-you-go system may inhibit greater investment in physical capital investment which may yield a higher expected rate of return for equal risk. According to some forecasts, most of the young workers entering the labor force in the 1980s will receive a real rate of return from their Social Security payments of about 1 percent, while many will receive less. In particular, savers with relatively low risk aversion may be harmed by not being able to choose investments with higher risk/return trade-off.

In the presence of sustained and uncertain inflation, society may choose to rely on Social Security rather than private pensions and savings. Uncertain inflation places an additional burden on those who wish to save for their retirement since indexed savings instruments do not exist and inflation-hedging instruments require higher savings rates due to their lower expected return. But the gain to the currently working of a contract in which their real preretirement income is substantially guaranteed may be less than the cost to them and to future generations.

Indexed Social Transfers: Benefits and Costs

Although a mandatory income source that is invulnerable to inflation is valuable, its value is likely to decline with the percentage of wealth that is indexed, except for the most risk averse. That is, the marginal value of indexation declines as the proportion of income that is indexed increases. On the other hand, the cost to society of indexation varies directly with the degree of indexation. The following sections discuss current and probable future levels of protection and their cost.

Levels of Inflation Protection through Social Transfers

Indexation schemes can range from no indexation to a universal guarantee of a constant real retirement income at approximately after-tax preretirement income levels.[10] There is evidence that policies adopted in the 1970s in fact effectively insulated almost all retirees from the impact of inflation in this period and increased replacement rates.[11] Indeed, during the 1970s, Social Security benefits rose at a faster rate than inflation.[12]

The growth in social transfer payments is reflected in Table 6–8, introduced above, which shows that over the period 1963 to 1978 Social Security's share of the elderly's income increased from 27 percent to 30 percent and Medicaid/Medicare from 2 percent to 16 percent (while earnings declined from 29 percent to 18 percent of total income over the same period), with the result that social transfer payments at the end of the 1970s were the source of 54 percent of the income of the elderly.

Table 8–1 presents data on replacement rates of final earnings for low, average, and high income (maximum income), steady workers, retiring at age 65. The data are derived from the 1985 Trustees Report under alternative II-B intermediate economic assumptions.[13] As shown, the replacement rates for aged 65 low, average, and maximum income steady workers are, respectively, 64 percent, 51.1 percent, and 32.5 percent. As indicated by Table 8–2, these percentages do not differ substantially from those prevailing in Europe.

Replacement rates of preretirement income need to be adjusted by tax differentials to determine the equivalence of after-retirement to preretirement income. Table 8–3 presents data collected by the President's Commission on Pension Policy, which indicate that after adjusting for pre- and postretirement taxes and subtracting savings and work-related expenses, replacement rates needed to maintain preretirement spendable income range from .51 to .79 of gross preretirement income for single persons and .55 to .86 for married couples, with replacement rates varying inversely with income level. Dan McGill concludes that after taking into account the progressive federal and state income tax structures, the replacement rate from all sources necessary to maintain preretirement before tax income levels ranges from 50 to 75 percent.[14]

Using these results and the evidence of Table 8–1, coverages for low- and average-income workers seem to support postretirement maintenance of living standards. Boskin and Shoven estimate that indexed career average (rather than peak) replacement rates exceed one after adjusting for taxes, the lack of dependents, and the greater certainty of Social Security income.[15]

Although the increases in indexed social transfer payments protected the elderly from inflation through the 1970s, planned long-run changes to be gradually phased in until 2030 will decrease inflation protection. To deal with projected short- and long-run Social Security funding crises, a bipartisan National Commission on Social Security Reform was appointed, chaired by Alan Greenspan, in December 1981. Many of this commission's recommendations became embodied in the Social Security Amendments of 1983.

This legislation will result in benefit reductions for those who retire at age 65 and tax increases in the decades to come. The amendments include a permanent six-month delay in the effective date of cost-of-living adjustments (COLA) from July to January, inclusion of up to half of Social Security benefits in taxable income for federal income tax purposes, and, on the positive side, a change in the $1 for $2 reduction in benefits for earnings after 65, to $1 for $3 beginning in 2009, along with an extension of coverage. In addition, there will be a phase-in to a higher normal retirement age of 67 rather than 65 beginning in 2003. The early retirement age was left at 62, although there is a phased-in decline in the percentage of full benefits payable at that age from 80 to 70 percent. The increase in benefits for delaying retirement will rise from 3 to 8 percent per year beginning in 2009.

A study by Gary Fields and Olivia Mitchell,[16] estimates that the likely combined effects of these provisions on the average future retirement age will be small, with an average delay in retirement of approximately one and one half months. The study finds that the mean retirement income will be reduced by 10 to 22 percent. These results are confirmed in a study by Storey, Michel, and Zedlewski,[17] which also finds only a small labor force response and a far more significant benefit decline.

Benefit losses due to the increase in normal retirement age will be phased in over time, and income tax provisions will also grow in importance as the fixed-dollar income tax threshold applies to a greater proportion of recipients.

As shown by the projections of Table 8–4, the combined long-run loss in income due to these provisions in 2030 will vary with the recipient's income, sex, and marital status. On average,

TABLE 8–1

A. Historical Replacement Rates for Steady Workers

	Replacement Rate				Replacement Rate		
Year	*Low*	*Average*	*Maximum*	*Year*	*Low*	*Average*	*Maximum*
1940	39.8	26.3	16.5	1963	39.6	30.8	30.5
1941	36.2	25.5	16.6	1964	39.0	30.3	30.8
1942	38.1	24.4	16.8	1965	40.0	31.4	32.9
1943	38.5	21.9	17.0	1966	40.0	31.4	33.2
1944	39.6	19.2	17.1	1967	40.5	29.9	24.7
1945	40.0	17.6	17.3	1968	41.4	32.3	28.1
1946	39.0	17.5	17.4	1969	37.0	30.8	24.7
1947	32.0	19.1	17.6	1970	42.7	34.3	29.2
1948	32.6	17.0	17.8	1971	47.5	36.6	32.8
1949	33.0	16.2	17.9	1972	51.2	37.7	35.5
1950	33.4	15.8	18.1	1973	61.3*	39.2	35.5
1951	35.5	27.3	27.4	1974	61.3*	40.9	33.0
1952	36.4	25.8	23.4	1975	59.5	42.3	30.1
1953	45.8	30.7	28.3	1976	57.9	43.7	32.1
1954	47.1	30.5	28.9	1977	57.2	44.8	33.5
1955	49.6	34.6	32.8	1978	62.7	46.7	34.7
1956	49.6	33.3	29.1	1979	60.4	48.1	36.1
1957	39.9	31.6	29.6	1980	64.0	51.1	32.5
1958	41.7	32.3	31.0	1981	68.5	54.4	33.4
1959	45.0	34.6	33.1	1982	63.8†	48.7†	28.6†
1960	45.0	33.3	29.8	1983	63.7‡	45.8‡	26.4‡
1961	45.0	32.3	30.0	1984	62.4‡	42.9‡	23.7‡
1962	42.9	32.0	30.3				

NOTE: Age at retirement is 65.

*Special minimum applies.

†Dec 1978 table applies.

‡Decoupled formula applied.

B. Projection of Replacement Rates for Steady Workers (1985 Trustees Report Alternative II-B Economic Assumptions)

	1984	*1985*	*1986*	*1987*	*1988*	*1989*	*1990*	*1991*	*1992*	*1993*	*1994*	*1995*	*1996*
Wage income (%)	4.94	3.77	5.40	6.29	6.05	6.22	5.70	5.43	5.64	5.62	5.60	5.49	5.48
Benefit income (%)	3.50	3.70	5.00	5.30	5.00	4.60	4.10	4.00	4.00	4.00	4.00	4.00	4.00

	1997	*1998*	*1999*	*2000*	*2001*	*2002*	*2003*	*2004*	*2005*	*2006*	*2007*	*2008*	*Ultimate*
Wage income (%)	5.48	5.48	5.48	5.48	5.48	5.48	5.48	5.48	5.48	5.48	5.48	5.48	5.48
Benefit income (%)	4.00	4.00	4.00	4.00	4.00	4.00	4.00	4.00	4.00	4.00	4.00	4.00	4.00

	Replacement Rate				*Replacement Rate*		
Year	*Low*	*Average*	*Maximum*	*Year*	*Low*	*Average*	*Maximum*
1985	63.8*	41.3	22.8	2001	62.8	41.3	25.6
1986	66.2*	42.1	23.3	2002	62.5	41.3	25.8
1987	67.0	42.6	23.8	2003	62.3	41.3	26.0
1988	67.1	42.8	24.6	2004	62.1	41.3	26.2
1989	67.1	42.9	24.9	2005	61.9	41.3	26.3
1990	65.2	41.8	24.3	2006	61.6	41.3	26.5
1991	64.2	41.2	24.0	2007	61.3	41.3	26.7
1992	64.0	41.1	23.8	2008	61.0	41.3	26.9
1993	63.7	41.0	23.9	2009	60.7	41.3	27.0
1994	63.8	41.1	24.2	2010	60.5	41.3	27.1
1995	63.7	41.2	24.5	2011	60.3	41.3	27.2
1996	63.5	41.2	24.6	2012	59.9	41.3	27.3
1997	63.5	41.2	24.8	2013	59.6	41.3	27.4
1998	63.4	41.3	25.0	2014	59.4	41.3	27.5
1999	63.4	41.3	25.2	2015	59.2	41.3	27.6
2000	63.1	41.3	25.4	2016	59.1	41.3	27.7

TABLE 8–1 *(concluded)*

	Replacement Rate				*Replacement Rate*		
Year	*Low*	*Average*	*Maximum*	*Year*	*Low*	*Average*	*Maximum*
2017	59.1	41.3	27.7	2039	57.5	41.3	27.7
2018	59.0	41.3	27.7	2040	57.5	41.3	27.7
2019	58.8	41.3	27.7	2041	57.5	41.3	27.7
2020	58.6	41.3	27.7	2042	57.5	41.3	27.7
2021	58.5	41.3	27.7	2043	57.5	41.3	27.7
2022	58.3	41.3	27.7	2044	57.5	41.3	27.7
2023	58.0	41.3	27.7	2045	57.5	41.3	27.7
2024	57.9	41.3	27.7	2046	57.5	41.3	27.7
2025	57.7	41.3	27.7	2047	57.5	41.3	27.7
2026	57.6	41.3	27.7	2048	57.5	41.3	27.7
2027	57.5	41.3	27.8	2049	57.5	41.3	27.7
2028	57.5	41.3	27.7	2050	57.5	41.3	27.7
2029	57.5	41.3	27.7	2051	57.5	41.3	27.7
2030	57.5	41.3	27.7	2052	57.5	41.3	27.7
2031	57.5	41.3	27.7	2053	57.5	41.3	27.7
2032	57.5	41.3	27.7	2054	57.5	41.3	27.7
2033	57.5	41.3	27.7	2055	57.5	41.3	27.7
2034	57.5	41.3	27.7	2056	57.5	41.3	27.7
2035	57.5	41.3	27.7	2057	57.5	41.3	27.7
2036	57.5	41.3	27.7	2058	57.5	41.3	27.7
2037	57.5	41.3	27.7	2059	57.5	41.3	27.7
2038	57.5	41.3	27.7	2060	57.5	41.3	27.7

NOTE: Age at retirement is 65. Replacement rate is based on 100 percent PIA.

*Old law applies.

TABLE 8–2
Estimated Social Security Retirement Pension as a Percentage of Final Salary

Country	*Range: Lower Paid Employee to Middle Manager*
Spain	90 %
Sweden	73–37
Italy	66
Netherlands	66–29
Portugal	50
Belgium	60–43
United Kingdom	60–45
Switzerland	56–31
Germany	55–40
France	50–27
Denmark	45–22

SOURCE: International Pension Consultants GmbH.

losses are projected to be in the 8–11 percent range. These results are supported by Table 8–1, which shows before-tax replacement rates declining somewhat from their 1980 highs to 57.5 percent, 41.3 percent, and 27.7 percent. While the maximum and average replacement rates do not drop significantly after 1984, low replacement rates drop steadily until they stabilize around 2030. The Fields and Mitchell finding of a decline in retirement income for average and high-income workers reflects the inclusion of up to half of Social Security benefits in taxable income, which does not affect the before-tax replacement rates given in Table 8–1.

Costs of Transfer Payment Indexation

This section evaluates the current and future costs of indexed social transfer benefits. Two different kinds of costs are imposed. First, social transfers distort the labor/leisure trade-off. Second, they distort savings decisions. The impact of these distortions is considered separately below. These effects are in addition to the direct cost of the revenues collected by the government.

Tax rates may increase with future upward shifts in the dependency ratio. Evidence on these shifts from U.S. Social Security projections indicates that an increase in projected life expec-

TABLE 8–3

Retirement Income Equivalent to Preretirement Income for Single Persons and Married Couples Retiring in 1980 (selected income levels)

Gross Preretirement Income	Preretirement Taxes		Disposable Income	Work-Related Expenses‡	Savings	Investments	Net Preretirement Income	Post Retirement Taxes§		Equivalent Retirement Income	
	Federal*	State and Local†						Federal Income	State and Local	Dollars	Ratio
Single persons											
$ 6,500	$ 906	$ 97	$ 5,497	$ 330	0%	$ 0	$ 5,167	$ 0	$ 0	$ 5,167	.79
10,000	1,785	223	7,992	480	3	240	7,272	0	0	7,272	.73
15,000	3,259	444	11,297	677	6	678	9,941	0	0	9,941	.66
20,000	4,055	728	14,217	853	9	1,280	12,064	166	32	12,282	.61
30,000	8,926	1,429	19,645	1,170	12	2,357	16,109	1,077	205	17,391	.58
50,000	18,921	3,328	27,751	1,665	15	4,163	21,923	3,153	599	25,675	.51
Married couples											
$ 6,500	$ 549	$ 29	$ 5,922	$ 355	0%	$ 0	$ 5,587	$ 0	$ 0	$ 5,576	.86
10,000	1,311	133	8,556	513	3	251	7,786	0	0	7,786	.78
15,000	2,550	310	12,140	728	6	728	10,684	0	0	10,684	.71
20,000	3,968	520	15,512	931	9	1,396	13,185	0	0	13,185	.66
30,000	6,986	1,061	21,950	1,317	12	2,634	17,999	53	10	18,062	.60
50,000	15,202	2,622	32,176	1,931	15	4,828	25,419	1,651	314	27,384	.55

*Federal income and Social Security (OASDHI) taxes.

†Based on state and local 1978 income tax receipts which were 19 percent of federal income tax receipts. Does not include property tax.

‡Estimated as 6 percent of disposable income.

§Postretirement taxes are on income in excess of Social Security benefits which are nontaxable. Retirees without Social Security benefits would need higher replacement ratios.

SOURCE: Preston C. Bassett, consulting actuary, President's Commission on Pension Policy, 1980.

TABLE 8–4

Effect of Amendments on the Income of Social Security Beneficiary Families Headed by a Person Age 62–69 in 2030, by Marital Status and Income Category

Married Couples, Living Alone

Pretax Income Pre-1983 Amendments (1980 dollars)	*Percent of Families in Income Class*	*Gross Income Loss*		*Disposable Income Loss*	
		Dollars	*Percent*	*Dollars*	*Percent*
Less than $ 5,000	*	*	*	*	*
5,000– 9,999	3.2	−192	−2.4	−231	−2.9
10,000–14,999	10.3	−686	−5.4	−852	−6.7
15,000–24,999	39.3	−1,119	−5.1	−1,703	−8.9
25,000–34,999	22.2	−1,409	−4.9	−2,581	−9.8
35,000+	24.6	−799	−1.3	−2,574	−6.1

Single Males, Living Alone

Pretax Income Prior to the 1983 Amendments (1980 dollars)	*Percent of Families in Income Class*	*Gross Income Loss*		*Disposable Income Loss*	
		Dollars	*Percent*	*Dollars*	*Percent*
Less than $ 5,000	7.5	−384	−8.4	−384	−8.4
5,000– 9,999	30.5	−708	−9.0	−748	−9.6
10,000–14,999	32.3	−980	−8.1	−1,242	−10.4
15,000–24,999	24.8	−1,101	−6.0	−1,960	−11.1
25,000–34,999	4.2	−1,015	−3.6	−2,730	−10.5
35,000+	*				

Single Females, Living Alone

Pretax Income Prior to the 1983 Amendments (1980 dollars)	*Percent of Families in Income Class*	*Gross Income Loss*		*Disposable Income Loss*	
		Dollars	*Percent*	*Dollars*	*Percent*
Less than $ 5,000	15.8	−397	−8.8	−397	−8.8
5,000– 9,999	48.5	−546	−7.4	−606	−8.3
10,000–14,999	25.6	−671	−5.6	−954	−8.1
15,000–24,999	9.7	−646	−3.5	−1,431	−9.1
25,000–34,999	*	*	*	*	*
35,000+	*	*	*	*	*

*Data not available.

tancy, together with a large drop in fertility after the height of the baby boom in 1955, will combine to increase the ratio of Social Security beneficiaries to workers by 60 percent by 2030.[18] As the baby boom starts to retire in 2020, the ratio of workers to beneficiaries, which is now somewhat over 3 to 1, will begin to decline and reach somewhat over 2 to 1. Planned tax increases from the current level of combined employer and employee payroll taxes of 11.4 percent in 1985 to 12.4 percent by 1990 are projected to enable the funds to pay the projected benefits despite the demographic shift, based on the intermediate "II-B" assumptions. On these assumptions the tax income will exceed the benefit payment each year through 2020, after which there will be an annual deficit. These projections indicate that the trust funds will increase until they amount to approximately 65 months of future benefits. Thus, the Social Security fund will enable the accumulation of financial resources to avoid large negative trust fund balances as the baby boom generation retires. Under pessimistic assumptions regarding economic growth and other factors, the combined payroll tax would have to increase further than scheduled.[19]

The 1983 changes to protect the solvency of the Social Security trust fund did not deal with the projected Medicare funding crisis. The Medicare trust fund is projected to run out of money in 1990, with a necessary 32 percent decrease in program outlays or 48 percent payroll tax increase to maintain solvency over the next 25 years.[20]

Labor Supply and Welfare. It is well accepted that the substantial increase in Social Security benefits since 1950 has had a negative impact on the labor supply of elderly men. Economic theory indicates that, due to income and substitution effects, Social Security benefits increase the incentive to retire. With eligibility for Social Security benefits, income and wealth at retirement are increased. Greater income increases the demand for all "normal" goods, including leisure. Thus, even if Social Security recipients do not have to stop working to be eligible for benefits (as is true after age 70), the greater wealth now available to them will cause most to choose more leisure. Empirical evidence that retirees value a 1 percent increase in leisure more than a 1 percent increase in income supports this conclusion.[21] In addition, the substitution effect which reduces the cost of not working by replacing a large proportion of preretirement income encourages retirement.

Table 8–5 (compiled by Richard V. Burkhauser and John A. Turner)[22] shows labor force participation rates of men for various years between 1950 and 1980, together with the growth of social welfare expenditures and OASDHI expenditures as a proportion to GNP. The table shows the correlation between the decline in work effort and increase in social transfers in retirement. Although this correlation may be due to a variety of factors, including increased private pensions, empirical evidence of econometric studies indicates that retirement is advanced by Social Security benefits. The size of the retirement incentive is unknown. Although its range can be estimated, there is still considerable uncertainty over these estimates due to data imperfections.[23] For example, a study by Pellechio finds that decreasing Social Security benefits to zero would raise the probability of labor force participation by over 34 percent for most 65-year-old men.[24] Thus, almost all the decline shown in Table 8–5 would be ascribed to Social Security benefits. Other studies, however, have found less of an impact.[25] As noted above, the impact of the changes of the 1983 Social Security amendments on retirement have been particularly well studied, and they seem small, although as Storey, Michel, and Zedlewski conclude, this may be because "the most important early retirement incentives (such as eligibility for Social Security and private pensions) were not altered by the amendments."[26]

Female retirement behavior and the response of younger workers to the Social Security system have not received as much attention. Several studies have surmised that the effect on the nonelderly worker labor supply may be positive because younger workers compensate for the anticipated later disincentive effects. However, studies by Jerry A. Hausman show that payroll taxes at current levels may reduce the labor supply of husbands by about 8 percent and that of wives by about 30 percent.[27] The labor supply decline results in an output decline. In addition, there is a welfare loss to workers because income is less than otherwise.

Labor supply and welfare may be decreased because the value workers place on wage tax payments to the Social Security fund

TABLE 8–5

Labor Force Participation Rates and Government Transfer Programs

Year	Social Welfare Expenditures† (billions)	Social Welfare Expenditures GNP	OASDHI Expenditures (billions)	OASDHI GNP	Age (labor force participation rates)					
					55	60	63	65	68	70
1950	$ 14.1	5.3	0.8	0.03	90.7*	84.7*	79.8*	71.7*	57.7*	50.0*
1960	34.3	6.9	11.0	2.2	92.8*	85.9*	77.8*	56.8*	42.0*	37.3*
1968	70.9	8.6	28.7	3.5	91.9	84.8	71.9	53.4	37.5	30.2
1970	94.0	9.8	36.8	3.8	91.8	83.9	69.4	49.9	37.7	30.2
1972	129.9	11.8	48.2	4.4	90.7	82.1	66.5	45.2	33.8	27.1
1974	165.5	12.2	66.3	4.9	88.1	79.0	59.3	39.8	27.7	23.5
1976	239.7	14.7	90.4	5.5	87.1	75.5	55.7	36.6	26.7	22.4
1978	289.9	14.2	117.4	5.8	85.8	74.4	52.2	36.3	28.7	21.7
1980	317.3‡	13.9‡	154.0	5.9	84.9	74.0	52.3	35.2	24.1	21.3

*Based on adjusted U.S. Bureau of the Census labor force participation data. The adjustment is based on the ratio of CPS and census figures for 1970.

†Social welfare expenditures include all social insurance, public aid, health and medical, veteran (except education), housing, and other social welfare programs. These figures are based on data from social welfare expenditures under public programs (U.S. Dept. of HHS).

‡Preliminary unpublished 1979 figures (U.S. Department of HHS).

SOURCE: Compiled by Richard V. Burkhauser and John A. Turner in "Labor-Market Experience of the Almost Old and the Implications for Income Support," presented at the American Economic Association annual meetings, Washington, D.C., December 28, 1981. Labor force participation figures are based on unpublished data from the Current Population Survey (CPS).

are greater than the present value of future benefits. Benefits may be valued less than taxes for several reasons. First, as discussed above, individuals may be constrained to "save" for retirement and to consume less than they would otherwise choose, or they may be able to save at higher expected yields in the form of physical capital on their own or their children's human capital. Second, the savings created by Social Security taxes are not owned, and the value of holdings is not known as certainly as individual savings and may be discounted for this reason.

Capital Formation. In addition to the effects of Social Security on labor force participation, Social Security may adversely affect capital formation, as indicated in Chapter 6.

To summarize that discussion briefly, currently available empirical results cannot indicate the extent to which Social Security decreases savings or even if it does decrease savings. Nonetheless, it is clear that different aspects of Social Security have opposing effects. While the increased incentive to retire early has been shown to increase savings, expected Social Security benefits substitute for the need to save for a given retirement age (assuming that not all families are altruistic, so that all do not integrate the financial well-being of future generations fully into their own welfare).

Depending on the magnitude of these two opposing reactions of life-cycle savers, Social Security benefits will either add to or subtract from the accumulation of savings during working life. There is considerable uncertainty over the impact of Social Security due to these theoretically conflicting factors and to the lack of adequate data to determine the net effect.

Nonetheless, the potential impact on savings may be large. Assuming compensatory public policy to raise the retirement age so that there is no additional savings through a positive impact on retirement age, Social Security benefits may reduce household saving significantly.[28]

Summary of Costs. There is room for considerable disagreement on the costs of Social Security beyond the actual dollars collected, given the lack of knowledge on household labor choice and savings behavior. Policy formation must proceed within this state of considerable ignorance. Conflicting equity and efficiency goals have been balanced in the 1983 Social Security amendments legislation. Nonetheless, equity concerns for low-income benefit recipients,[29] plus efficiency concerns for savings and labor disincentives remain. In addition, the Medicare funding crisis is yet to be resolved. In the coming years, complementary private pension policies to deal with inflation may have to be structured, with possible declines in social transfer payments in mind. In the following section we examine these policies.

Private Pensions and Savings: Alternative Responses to Inflation

Introduction

Indexed social transfer benefits have protected retirees from the inflation of the past two decades. However, with the 1983 amendments, and with possible future Social Security and Medicare cutbacks, after-tax replacement rates of preretirement income through social transfers will decline in the future. As a result, retirees will have to rely more on private pensions, which are expected to grow, as a proportion of retirement income, and savings. However, nominal pensions may impose hardships on myopic savers with high sustained inflation.

Pension plans could use government-issued, indexed long-term debt to supply indexed pensions, if they were available. Unfortunately, as indicated below, under moderate inflation such bonds are necessarily more burdensome to taxpayers than nominally denominated debt. With indexed debt, during unavoidable supply-shock inflationary episodes, when both real income and tax revenue growth decline, the required constant real interest expenditures necessitate either tax increases (at a time of decreased real income growth) or inflationary deficit increases (at a time of increased inflation).[30] The cost of indexed debt relative to nominal debt depends on the degree of inflation uncertainty. Thus, at some point, it may be more efficient for taxpayers to offer indexed debt, in spite of its destabilizing impact during supply-shock episodes. Indexed debt can then be used as a backing for real annuities without imposing additional costs on taxpayers.

In the absence of indexed debt, with serially correlated inflation, nominal pensions can no longer serve as de facto (on the average) real annuities, and it is not feasible for private firms to replace these with contractual real annuities. While full indexation cannot be guaranteed, performance-indexed variable annuities can be supplied which, if invested in short-term securities, can closely track inflation. Nonetheless it may not be efficient to require inflation-hedging pensions. Even if the physical capital portion of retirement savings is not fully or partially indexed to inflation, other private and public adjustments are possible in response to inflation.

The following section discusses the rationales for investment in physical capital. The second section examines rational private retirement and savings adjustments to increased inflation uncertainty. These responses may include increased physical capital accumulation, delayed retirement, and new forms of performance-indexed private pensions.

The third and fourth sections examine appropriate public savings and retirement policies, respectively, in removing impediments to these private adjustments. To summarize these here, moderately risk-averse rational savers might not demand variable annuity payments that track inflation (due to their cost in terms of lost yield and due to the extent of homeownership and indexed social transfer benefits). Thus, new forms of performance-indexed private pensions might not be optimally demanded by all retirees. Under these conditions, requiring various forms of indexation would reduce the value of pensions. Nonetheless, changed tax laws to allow reinvestment of "tilted" nominal pension benefits would be useful for those risk-averse savers who would wish to choose greater income certainty. Also, regulatory changes to facilitate rollovers of vested pensions to IRAs after job changes would be desirable. Increased information on expected real retirement benefits and provision of inflation-tracking variable annuities as an alternative to a nominal pension would also be useful.

Assuming myopic savings behavior or money illusion, mandatory forms of inflation-hedged variable private pensions might be necessary (depending on the levels of inflation and the proportionate shares of guaranteed indexed social transfer payments and pensions in retirement income), in spite of their cost to rational savers. The last section examines the appropriate public policy in the provision of indexed government debt or rate change insurance, assuming substantial inflation uncertainty.

The Role of Physical Capital in Providing Retirement Income Security

Although private pensions cannot provide fully indexed benefits, the alternative of relying on Social Security for full replacement of preretirement consumption is not optimal. As discussed in the preceding section, full reliance on Social Security or wage tax receipts exposes retirees and/or workers to the risk of wage bill decreases due to population or productivity changes and consequent benefit decreases and/or tax increases. Such vulnerability might be justified if the rate of growth of the total wage bill were expected to exceed the rate of return on capital investment, but the reverse is more likely to be true. An anticipated bulge in the number of retirees relative to the working population is likely to lower the growth rate of the total wage bill. Unfortunately, the resulting rise in the dependency ratio also increases the risk of investing in physical assets.

In a closed economy, financial claims have to be sold to the younger working generation. If their savings rate is independent or a negative function of the real rate of interest, the diversification of retirement income sources is less helpful in solving the problem of the expected increase in the dependency ratio. In order to maintain their preretirement consumption levels, retirees must dissave. This holds for all but those who can live off the real interest on their assets. For others, the dissaving may be done directly by those who sell their own financial claims, such as equity or bonds, or indirectly by their agents (i.e. pension funds, which sell securities to maintain the pension income flow). But it is exactly this selling of securities which is likely to lower their value and raise interest rates when the working population is small relative to the retired. The amount of dissavings may exceed the demand for savings on the part of working generations. Under these circumstances, the price of capital plunges and interest rates rise. Indeed, the price of capital will have to fall until the value of capital sold equals the desired fixed-savings rate, if this is unaffected by interest rates. If so, the full brunt of the increased number of retirees is borne by a decrease in retirees' consumption.

However, the assumptions behind the illustrated results are unnecessarily extreme. First, higher yields (i.e., lower prices) on capital may induce a greater savings rate due to less borrowing by income-constrained households and to increased savings by those life-cycle, or altruistic, households whose savings rates are interest elastic. If so, although there will be some decline in the value of capital accumulated, total desired consumption will decrease and savings will increase on the part of working generations. As a result, retirees will be able to consume more. Second, in any case, the increased capital formation that occurs in the years prior to retirement will raise the income of the working generation. Therefore, the tax revenue that they can provide to the elderly at the existing tax rate will increase.

Third, economies are not closed. The overall worldwide supply of savings may be unaffected (or negatively affected) by worldwide rates of return on capital, but the supply of capital to any one country is interest elastic.

If interest rates rise in the United States, savings are attracted from elsewhere in the world until U.S. interest rates are brought into closer alignment with those found elsewhere. The consumption of the U.S. retired can be funded by an increased savings inflow from other economies. Such an inflow can occur even in the context of worldwide dissaving. However, world demographics and economic growth may enable the retired generation of the already industrialized world to respond to an increased worldwide demand for savings vehicles. In part, this new demand may derive from newly middle-class workers in the developing world, whose rising per capita income may allow them to plan for and to demand savings for their own retirement income.

Rational Responses to Inflation

Monetary authorities may pursue an inflationary course, for example, to attain the political-economic benefits of money shocks or to avoid economic downturns. If so, the nominal annuity can no longer be a de facto (on the average) real annuity. The risk of an unanticipated increase in anticipated inflation (i.e., that the annuity's value will decine at a faster than anticipated rate) rests on the retiree. Greater inflation uncertainty increases that risk and decreases the nominal annuity's effectiveness as a source of a secure retirement income. But the substitutes, provided directly by the retiree or indirectly by the pension sponsor, cannot produce a similar steady real income except at an increase in cost. For retirees, the effect of uncertain inflation is the increased cost of a relatively certain real retirement income.

A public good, price stability, has been lost, and this affects both the demanders and suppliers of financial instruments that depend on this good. The loss of price stability directly impedes the financing of long-term capital projects. As discussed above, the borrowing firm has no perfect substitutes for long-term nominal debt financing under price stability. Short-term financing increases the risk that real rates will rise, as does variable rate debt. Indexed long-term debt is not a perfect substitute for nominal long-term debt because, with indexation, firms must guarantee debt payments fixed in real terms. To do so means taking on the burden of guaranteeing debt payments fixed in real terms, even when revenues decline, due to supply-shock inflation. The additional risk this imposes on a firm is unknown and, therefore, cannot be planned for, nor can a "price" easily be set in terms of additional liquid savings needed to cover this risk. Because firms do not offer indexed debt, pension sponsors cannot offer fully indexed pensions.

Inflation has an impact on the tilt and the variance of the real income stream provided by nominal pensions. Due to the tilt effect, the real income derived from a constant nominal income stream decreases at the inflation rate. This may be offset with a portfolio of financial instruments that guarantee a gradually increasing nominal payment stream, set in advance at the level of the anticipated inflation rate. Indeed, graduated payment mortgages do just this. Pensions can then be offered which increase at the anticipated rate and which are backed by such financial instruments.

If higher rates of inflation had no effect on the uncertainty of inflation, then the only impact of inflation would be the tilt effect, which pensions could adjust for. But higher rates of inflation are accompanied by increased uncertainty over what future inflation rates will be (i.e., increased uncertainty about the anticipated inflation rate). In theory, higher inflation rates may be accompanied by greater uncertainty over future inflation rates, because the range of possible inflation rates is expanded (the range still includes the zero point) and because the increase in inflation demonstrates the monetary authority's proclivity to surprising increases in the rate of monetary growth. Empirically, the evidence is that higher rates of inflation are accompanied by an increased variance in the rate of inflation.

A tilted payment stream cannot provide the same security that a nominal payment stream provides, given greater inflation uncertainty. If actual inflation exceeds the anticipated rate, a tilted income flow better preserves real benefits than does a constant flow; however, a decline in actual inflation reduces real benefits in early years and raises real benefits in later years. In the absence of inflation-indexed government debt, a substitute that can provide a relatively steady real retirement income under inflation uncertainty exists in the form of a portfolio of Treasury bills or other short-term debt, combined with commodity futures. Although the expected rate of return on such a portfolio is lower than that of a portfolio composed of long-run nominal debt and equity, historical evidence indicates that it can be used to provide a performance-indexed annuity that will closely track inflation. Because the rate of return on the underlying portfolio will be lower than otherwise, rational employees might not prefer inflation-hedging pensions over nominal pensions.

Among the reasons that rational employees may prefer nominal pensions are the following. First, in retirement, time preference rates may be positive, with a preference for more income in early than in late retirement. Second, individuals who anticipate that they will not be long-lived are likely to prefer annuities whose value declines over time. Third, individuals with sufficient within-family insurance arrangements may prefer to have diminishing wealth in pensions over time, especially since pension wealth is not bequeathed to children. Fourth, retirees who are moderately risk averse may choose the higher rate of return/risk trade-off that nominal pensions provide, especially given indexed Social Security and Medicare benefits.

Moreover, faced with a nominal pension, which is expected to decline over time (thus, lowering overall pension wealth), and increased inflation risk, there are a number of adjustments that retirees can make to increase their retirement income security, short of choosing an inflation-hedging variable annuity. First, more wealth can be accumulated as a buffer against an unanticipated increase in inflation for retirement consumption, or as a planned bequest. Second, the composition of nonpension wealth can be shifted to include more short-term bonds, variable rate debt, real estate, and commodity futures, which are likely to hedge inflation. Third, individuals may choose to respond to the increased uncertainty of a retirement income and increased cost of a relatively certain real income stream by deciding to postpone retirement or to work part-time during retirement, especially given increased longevity. Fourth, a portion of the income stream from nominal pensions and annuities can be reinvested to provide a more inflation-proof income stream. Fifth, retirees can choose to absorb an increased risk that their real retirement income will deviate from the level that they had anticipated.

The optimal responses to increased inflation uncertainty and lower expected pension wealth will vary with the individual. Among the factors that should determine an individual's optimal responses are tastes (which include risk aversion, rate of time preference, and utility of leisure versus consumption) and the level and vulnerability to inflation of expected income (which includes earnings from employment, capital income, owned housing, expected Social Security and Medicare benefits, and within-family insurance arrangements). Health, expected longevity, and desired bequests also must enter portfolio composition, consumption versus saving, and work versus retirement adjustments. Thus, whether the rational individual adjusts to greater inflation and inflation uncertainty by choosing a variable annuity (if available), or by planning to work longer to save more, or by altering the composition of his or her nonpension wealth portfolio will depend on all of these factors.

The alternative to these individual adjustments is to have the government require mandatory performance-indexed pensions. If individuals can maximize their welfare through their own decisions, mandatory indexing of any sort will impose costs on those whose actions are constrained. Moreover, even if most individuals are myopic, it does not necessarily follow that inflation-hedging variable annuities should be mandatory. For many, the lower rate of return resulting from performance-indexed pensions may not be worth the lower resulting inflation risk. This is especially so since Social Security, Medicare, and housing provide a large portion of preretirement income, which is not vulnerable to inflation. Nonetheless, if there are many myopic households who will suffer financial hardship in retirement due to sustained inflation and a declining role for indexed social transfer payments, mandatory indexed private pensions may become socially desirable.

Hence, at the minimum, government should remove the existing impediments to rational private adjustments. In addition, given the anticipated population bulge and increased inflation uncertainty, the costs and benefits of those public policies which discourage savings and encourage early retirement should be reevaluated. As the value to the individual of private savings increases with the possible decline in social transfer retirement income, the costs of policies that effectively tax private savings increases. Similarly, policies that encourage early retirement become more costly if individuals push their desired retirement years further beyond the mandated or subsidized retirement year under current policy.

For myopic households, these public policy responses may be insufficient. If inflation levels are sufficiently high and myopia sufficiently widespread, government regulation of pensions to assure some form of indexing may be necessary. The following sections consider optimal savings and retirement policies in response to inflation, respectively.

Public Savings and Pension Policy with Inflation

Household savings for future consumption are discouraged by the current tax system in the United States, which is not neutral to the future/current consumption trade-off, but rather encourages current consumption. To deal with this, liberalized limits on tax-exempt savings earmarked for retirement, such as IRAs, or tax exemption for general savings accounts would be helpful. Assuming that a consumption tax in place of an income tax (or, to the same end, the removal of taxes on interest with an increase in other taxes) left lifetime disposable income unchanged, this would raise wealth accumulation and the savings rate.[31] More critically, fiscal policies that decrease government deficits and increase government investment raise capital accumulation.[32]

Should policy changes that increase the savings rate and quantity of physical capital accumulated be implemented? There are costs involved in their implementation. For example, decreasing taxes on savings raises the after-tax rate of return on capital and, therefore, may make the distribution of income less equal. This is especially so if tax exemption is allowed for all savings accounts, without limit.[33] Similarly, decreasing government spending may harm the poor disproportionately. An increase in income tax rates (or corporate tax rates) to reduce the deficit does not suffer from these effects but is likely to decrease labor supply (or investment).

Nonetheless, the large deficits of the 1980s have had a significant negative impact on the savings rate in the United States. There is evidence that accompanying high real interest rates have reduced capital formation and productivity growth in the United States even though an inflow of foreign funds has allowed more investment than otherwise. In the long run, reliance on foreign investment to fund the deficit reduces real income growth due to the outflow of interest payments. Moreover, if the deficit is not reduced, interest payments will grow and become a larger share of an increasing deficit over time. Unless steps to reduce the deficit are taken now, when the baby boom generation retires in the first quarter of the next century, still larger deficits, together with unfunded Medicare liabilities, will require significant tax increases.[34]

The other long-run alternative to dealing with the deficit is to inflate our way out of it. Resurgent inflation would somewhat reduce the real cost of fixed nominal interest payments and, temporarily, the real interest rate, as well as the real capital outflow to foreign dollar debt holders. For nominal pension holders, however, inflation is not the solution, but rather the problem.

Pension-specific policy changes could help to deal with inflation. Several reforms could make it easier for individuals to deal with moderate inflation. First, regulatory changes to facilitate rollovers of vested pensions to IRAs after job changes would be desirable. Second, tax laws could be changed to allow pension sponsors to credit ad hoc pension payments, thereby encouraging such payments. Third, retirees could be allowed to reinvest a portion of their constant nominal pensions, without taxing returns, to provide a constant real pension. Fourth, pension sponsors could be required to provide information on the expected real income stream that a nominal pension will provide, in constant dollars, for the course of the retirement period, under assumed inflation rates. Fifth, pension sponsors could be required to offer an inflation-hedged variable annuity as an optional alternative to the nominal pension. While helpful, these reforms would not be sufficient to deal with resurgent chronic double-digit inflation if myopia and money illusion were prevalent.

Tax advantages granted to private pensions are justified because they encourage workers to save more for retirement than otherwise. Some workers (perhaps mostly younger and lower income) may not wish to trade off current for future income but do so in the form of pensions, because desired long-term jobs are available in firms that provide pensions. Firms may offer such pensions because others (especially the higher income and older workers) wish them in any case, and because they reduce after-tax wage costs.

If, due to money illusion, inflation confuses workers as to the low savings the plans provide, they may neither demand higher real wages to compensate for the expected loss in retirement income nor demand increased expected real pension benefits. The result might be that tax advantages increase firms' profits without providing sufficient retirement income security. The justification for the decline in tax revenues that pension tax advantages cause might then be lost.

Even without money illusion, myopia implies that workers and retirees may not mind the erosion of their expected retirement benefits resulting in too low retirement income, especially if the higher nominal rate of return that accompanies inflation reduces funding costs and raises current wages. With sufficiently severe myopia and high inflation, some retirees may be pleased to have the tax subsidized pension benefits and not mind or even welcome their negative tilt. Myopia, which justifies tax-advantaged pensions in the first place, may make nominal pensions unserviceable in a time of high inflation if the goal is to preserve a constant real retirement income.

An unavoidable policy dilemma emerges. While performance-indexed pensions may be necessary for some, especially the myopic, the effect of their mandatory implementation will be to raise pension costs to all, even those who would continue to be well served by nominal pensions. The incentives provided to savings through tax advantages are considerably diminished if low-yield, inflation-hedging assets are legislatively required. Thus, pensions would be less desired relative to IRAs and other vehicles of wealth accumulation. Moreover, the dilemma can be expected to be heightened by the high nominal returns available in a period of resurgent inflation, relative to the yields available in inflation-hedging assets. The problem is that the relative need for and the relative cost of variable pensions grow with the level of inflation, since higher levels of inflation are accompanied by increased inflation uncertainty and higher real and nominal interest rates on long-term bonds.

Thus, optional indexation may not be a sufficient policy response. Requiring retirees to accept mandatory inflation-hedging variable annuities might become necessary if severe inflation recurs in the coming decades. If the economy returns to the double-digit inflation of the late 1970s, myopic savings decisions (of households who do not, but should, choose inflation-hedging variable annuities) may result in late-retirement financial hardships. If private pension tax advantages are rationalized by myopia, pensions should be performance indexed, in spite of the cost, if inflation threatens old age income security through the erosion of nominal pensions. The avoidance of this erosion requires mandatory performance indexation of private pensions or high guaranteed preretirement real income replacement rates through indexed Social Security and Medicare benefits.

Private and Public Retirement Policies with Inflation

One response to the increased cost of a de facto (on the average) real pension due to increased inflation uncertainty is the advancement of the desired retirement age. For the risk averse, increased uncertainty of the real amount of retirement income also advances the desired retirement age.

Firms can mandate or encourage earlier or later retirement than desired, but have to compensate workers if they do so. Firms may wish to delay (or advance) workers' retirement since the cohort of retirees may be more (or less) productive for their average wage, determined by the market, than the cohorts that follow.

Expected shifts in demography and longevity may advance the firms' and the workers' desired retirement age in the coming decades. Medical advances that extend longevity and the quality of life may postpone the workers' desired retirement age. Moreover, as the baby boom generation ages and becomes eligible for retirement, the cohort of workers behind them will be smaller.[36] Smaller future cohorts will have higher wages relative to the larger baby boom cohort. Thus, firms may wish to extend the working period beyond the current retirement age in the decades to come.

In the current period, however, firms and society as a whole seem to have opted for the encouragement of early retirement, perhaps in part as a mechanism to deal with low wage growth and high unemployment rates among the baby boom generation. Thus, industry,[37] as well as the government, has adopted regulations that actively encourage relatively early retirement in historical terms.

These regulations will lose their usefulness and, indeed, become pernicious when the large baby boom generation begins to retire. This will be especially so if sustained and uncertain inflation makes retirement income sources more insecure.

Various policies can be implemented in the coming period to neutralize public policy that causes workers to retire earlier than otherwise. Among these, of course, is raising or removing the mandatory retirement age. Changes in pension and Social Security regulations to encourage work after retirement or not to discourage postponed retirement may be useful. Empirical studies of the likely impact of incentives embodied in the 1983 Social Security amendments suggest that they will have little effect on desired retirement age. Thus, additional changes in Social Security rules to encourage later retirement may also be desirable. For example, it has been estimated that a 15 percent penalty for early retirement (which was under consideration before the 1983 Social Security amendments were adopted) could raise the average retirement age by three months.[38] Raising the eligibility age for Social Security and Medicare, along with a cutback in benefits would be likely to have far greater effects on the average desired retirement age.

Government Indexation of Bonds

As a substitute or supplement to indexed social transfer payments, the government can supply bonds with coupons and principal indexed to inflation. These instruments can be made available directly to private individuals or to pension funds. In either case, they may be used as a portfolio to support a guaranteed real retirement income. Alternatively, the government could supply rate change insurance to pension funds to guarantee a given real interest rate.

If inflation is sufficiently uncertain, the use of indexed debt will be less burdensome to the taxpayer than alternative government methods of debt finance. However, the supply of these bonds transfers the risk of uncertain inflation to the taxpayer. They also make it more difficult for the government not to inflate the economy. With low or moderate inflation uncertainty, these disadvantages are likely to outweigh the benefits to the taxpayers. In any case, the provision of index bonds should not necessarily be used to require private pensions to fully index pensions. To do so would impose a low risk/low return trade-off on the rational saver, who might choose more risk. However, with high sustained inflation, uncertain inflation, and myopic savings behavior, indexed government bonds (or rate change insurance) and mandatory indexed pensions may be optimal.

For indexed bonds not to be costly to the taxpayer, their guaranteed real rate of return would have to be lower than short-term debt. But even if the government could sell these bonds at a lower real rate of interest, they still would make taxpayers worse off than in the situation where there is zero long-term inflation because taxpayers must bear an additional risk. The risk occurs when unanticipated accelerations of inflation are correlated with depressed real income.

As Table 5–7 indicates, the burden to the taxpayer of financing debt with alternative instruments varies with the source of inflation. The real cost of indexed debt does not vary, while the cost of nominal long-term debt varies inversely with the inflation rate. Accelerations of inflation due to supply shocks lead to lower real debt costs at a time of reduced income; decelerations raise real costs as real income increases. Under these circumstances, long-term nominal debt reduces the tax burden when such reductions are most helpful. Thus, long-term nominal debt is beneficial.

On the other hand, if money supply accelerations and long-term inflation uncertainty cannot be limited, the use of indexed debt becomes cost efficient and such use further destabilizes the economy. As real income growth and government tax revenues decline with supply-shock inflation, the Treasury must either increase taxes to fund the constant real cost of indexed debt or allow the deficit to grow. The latter is inflationary, the more so if increased debt is monetized. Thus, the use of indexed debt further destabilizes the economy either by decreasing already slowly growing income or by increasing already high inflation.

Because of these effects, it is harmful to resort to the use of indexed debt. However, if inflation is sufficiently uncertain, even short-term debt must carry a large risk premium. Indeed, at some point, indexed debt becomes the only salable debt. Paradoxically, if inflation is sufficiently uncertain, there is no extra burden to society in providing the indexed debt that can help assure retirement income security.

APPENDIX 8.A
The Intergenerational Human Capital Transfer Problem and Its Solutions

The Problem Defined

The reason that consumption loans based on human capital cannot be provided across generations efficiently is explained by Paul Samuelson.[39] Samuelson assumes a constant population size and no output growth. Nature is assumed to be so parsimonious that investment in either human or physical capital does not generate a positive yield. He then demonstrates that the socially optimal trade-off between current and retirement consumption financed by consumption loans is one and that the implicit optimal interest rate is zero. But the marketplace will result in a less advantageous trade-off for retirees, one in which future consumption costs more than current consumption and the interest rate is negative.

TABLE 8–6
Lifetime Consumption Patterns through Intergenerational Loans with No Population or Income Growth

Lifetime Consumption with Private Trading of Consumption Loans: An Example

Consumed in Period		
A	B	C
⅓ ⅓ ⅓ ⅓	⅓	⅓

A and B are working periods; C is retirement period.
Total output over lifetime is two units.

Constant Lifetime Consumption through Government Taxes and Transfers: An Example

Earned in Period		
A	B	C
⅓ ⅓ ⅓	⅓ ⅓ ⅓	0

Consumed in Period		
A	B	C
⅓ ⅓	⅓ ⅓	⅓ ⅓

Saved in Period		
A	B	C
⅓	⅓	0

Deals can be made between the retired and working to support the retired, but only ones that are costly for retirees. To illustrate, assume there are three groups (which is all that is necessary to generalize to the *n* group case), younger workers (group A), older workers (group B), and retirees (group C), and that all workers earn the same income. The terms of such a deal would be that group B would give up some of their current income to younger workers of group A now, in exchange for their promised support when group B retires.

In a world where goods can be saved, assuming a retirement period that is one third of working and retired years, a savings rate of one third would yield a constant lifetime consumption pattern. To achieve this, groups A and B need to save one third of their income. This is illustrated in Table 8–6, assuming that per capita real output is one unit each for groups A and B, two units in total. The resulting desired consumption in each period would be constant at two thirds of a unit.

But without a vehicle to store savings, a constant consumption pattern is impossible. As shown in Table 8–6, with no store of value group B's members are required to give two thirds of their one unit of production in total to groups A and C (one third to finance group C's retirement and one third to pay group A in advance). While group B is put into a difficult position, group A consumes one unit of its own production plus one third of a unit lent by group B. Lifetime consumption is disproportionately distributed. Although other patterns are possible, all will involve too little consumption in periods B and C and too much in period A. Thus, the rate of trade-off between consumption while working in period A to period B and retirement consumption is costly; as a result, less is consumed during retirement years, although all wish a constant consumption stream.

Three Solutions: Assuming Constant Population and Real Income

There are three possible solutions to this social problem and paradox, but all require introducing social norms or government.

Intergenerational Taxes and Transfers

One possible solution is for the government to guarantee the following Social Security–type tax and transfer arrangement: Group A contributes a fixed proportion of its current income to group C, as does group B. In return, when members of group A retire and become group C, they receive from the current group A and B the same proportion of their income. The intergenerational agreement is enforced by the taxing power of the government.[40] After the start-up period, this achieves a constant lifetime consumption pattern and an interest rate of zero. At the program's beginning, the initial group C gets a gift equal to their retirement income since they have not saved anything on their own. But, thereafter, all generations but the last receive what they put in, thus smoothing their lifetime consumption patterns. As a result, constant consumption is maintained and the trade-off between consumption when working and retired is one, even though nature offers no mechanism in which to save for retirement.

The last generation to participate in this agreement loses, since it has paid in but has no one to pay for them. This result underlies the extent to which the solution depends on population constancy or growth, as discussed further below. For the last, as for the start-up generation, the rate of return differs from zero. For all others, the rate of return is zero.

In the illustrative example, it is assumed that the savings rate and the tax rate used to transfer the savings equal one third of income or one half of consumption, and years spent in retirement are one half of working years. This example can be generalized. Any length of retirement can be chosen as long as the following equation is satisfied.

(8.1) $$CRR = \frac{S}{Y - S}\left(\frac{W}{R}\right)$$

or, equivalently,

(8.2) $$CRR = \frac{S}{C}\left(\frac{W}{R}\right)$$

CRR is the consumption replacement rate of preretirement consumption (or, equivalently, in a tax and transfer system, the "after-tax" replacement rate). Y is the amount of income per active worker prior to the savings or transfer; S is the savings or transfer for each active worker; and C (equal to $Y - S$) is the amount of consumption for each. R is the number of years in retirement, and W is the number of working years.[41] Because the population is constant, R/W gives the ratio of retired to workers. It is this ratio that determines the feasible set of replacement rates and savings rates. This illustration does not reflect differing income tax rates before and after retirement.

If a replacement rate of one is chosen,

(8.3) $$1 = \frac{S}{Y - S}\left(\frac{W}{R}\right)$$

The savings over consumption ratio must equal the proportion of retired to working years. In symbols,

(8.4)
$$\frac{S}{C} = \frac{R}{W}$$

If, for example, due to the need to support children during working years, retirement consumption needs are lower than preretirement, a replacement rate lower than one may be desired. But for any *CRR* chosen, Equation 8.1 must be satisfied.

The tax rate, expressed as a ratio of savings to consumption, equals the consumption replacement rate multiplied by the ratio of retirees to active workers:

(8.5)
$$TRC = \frac{S}{C} = CRR\left(\frac{R}{W}\right)$$

Table 8–7 indicates, assuming no population growth, the tax rates as a percent of gross income consistent with desired average lengths of retirement, with consumption replacement rates of 100 percent and 50 percent. To derive retirement ages consistent with various tax rates, it is assumed that work begins at age 20. Then it is possible to calculate retirement ages and lengths of retirement under various longevity assumptions. For example, if average lifetime is 70 years, of which after the first 20 years 40 are spent working and 10 retired, the tax rate has to equal 20 percent for a replacement rate of 100 percent and 11.11 percent for a replacement rate of 50 percent.

Even if time preferences are such that individuals wish to consume less in their retirement years, the constant population and real output assumption result in a constant trade-off between consumption today and tomorrow. This is by nature of the agreement which entitles all members of society to a given proportion of the output of those that follow, a proportion equal to that which they gave.

For example, if there are 1,000 active worker members of society and each contributes 1/1,000 of the total contribution, during retirement they each are entitled to 1/1,000 of the total contributions made by active workers each year. If future contributions are the same (and they will be with a constant tax rate, population, and output), whatever is saved results in the same income in retirement.

Thus, no matter what the retirement consumption pattern chosen, the production transformation possibilities between current

TABLE 8–7

Tax (Savings) Rates Consistent with Retirement Periods of Varying Lengths with Zero or Steady Population Growth

		Desired Retirement Age and Number of Retirement Years Based on Given Average Lifetime							
		Average Lifetime 70		*Average Lifetime 75*		*Average Lifetime 80*		*Average Lifetime 85*	
Percent Tax Rates on Gross Income	*Ratio of Working Years to Retirement Years*	*Retirement Age*	*Retirement Years*	*Retirement Age*	*Retirement Years*	*Retirement Age*	*Retirement Years*	*Retirement Age*	*Retirement Years*
Assuming after-tax replacement ratio (CRR) = 1.0									
50%	1.00	45.0	25.0	47.5	27.5	50.0	30.0	52.5	32.5
33⅓	2.00	53.3	16.7	56.7	18.3	60.0	20.0	63.3	21.7
25	3.00	57.5	12.5	61.2	13.8	65.0	15.0	68.7	16.3
20	4.00	60.0	10.0	64.0	11.0	68.0	12.0	72.0	13.0
15	5.67	62.5	7.5	66.7	8.3	71.0	9.0	75.2	9.8
10	9.00	65.0	5.0	69.5	5.5	74.0	6.0	78.5	6.5
5	19.00	67.5	2.5	72.2	2.8	77.0	3.0	81.7	3.3
Assuming after-tax replacement ratio (CRR) = .50									
20%	2.00	53.3	16.7	56.7	18.3	60.0	20.0	63.3	21.7
14.29	3.00	57.5	12.5	61.3	13.7	65.0	15.0	68.8	16.2
11.11	4.00	60.0	10.0	64.0	11.0	68.0	12.0	72.0	13.0
9.09	5.00	61.7	8.3	65.8	9.2	70.0	10.0	74.2	10.8
6.98	6.67	63.5	6.5	67.8	7.2	72.2	7.8	76.5	8.5
4.76	10.00	65.5	4.5	70.0	5.0	74.5	5.5	79.1	5.9
2.44	20.00	67.6	2.4	72.4	2.6	77.1	2.9	81.9	3.1

NOTE: It is assumed that work begins at age 20.

and future consumption, inherent in the fact that each member of society leaves one member (i.e., that same amount of resources) to follow, imply a rate of return on savings of zero. In equilibrium, individuals will adjust their savings rate so that their rate of time preference equals the given zero interest rate. If, at a constant stream of income, future income is worth less to individuals than current income, less will be saved, until consumption during retirement is worth the consumption given up during working years. This will mean in this case that individuals will consume less after than prior to retirement, but the resulting zero rate of interest and saving pattern are optimal, reflecting consumers' preferences and the technological possibilities.

In general, all combinations of retirement income level and age of retirement that are consistent with the savings rate and the zero rate of return possible on those savings can be chosen, as indicated by Equation 8.1. For optimal welfare, these variables should be chosen so that resulting rate of time preference is equal to one which, with no population or real income growth, represents the trade-off possible between consumption while working and in retirement.

Interfamily Transfers

The second solution is to rely on intergenerational transfers within the family. Retired workers may rely on their children to provide for them in their old age with the expectation that in return their offspring will provide for them. Social norms then substitute for government-enforced agreements.

Indeed, intergenerational consumption loans through taxes and transfers can be thought of as a socialization of such private transfers through the family. The two systems are substitutes. Given the uncertainties involved, society may opt for an impersonal form of transfer that relies on all of society's children rather than one's own. Within-family transfers require parents that are more dependent on their children and children that feel they must live up to the social norms of filial loyalty. In addition, there are transition problems at the inception or at any change in the consumption replacement rate, number of working and retirement years, and the like.

Of course, in this solution, if some are childless they will not be provided for and, conversely, if couples have more than two children surviving when they are elderly, they will receive more than they have put in.[42] This result can be generalized, as will be seen in the following section.

Constant Money Supply

The third solution is for the government to insure a constant money supply. Individuals can then save in the form of dollars in their working years and spend the dollars saved in retirement. Assuming as before a constant population size and constant real output, the rate of trade-off between current and future consumptions remains at one. To illustrate, assume as before that with such a trade-off, individuals choose a constant consumption stream and a retirement period equal to one third of their working and retired years. In their working periods A and B, individuals accumulate one third of their income in the form of dollar holdings. They then use these dollars to finance their retirement consumption.

With output constant, the dollars that are disbursed during group C's retirement will finance the purchase of one third each of group A's and B's income. They, in turn, will have accumulated the requisite dollars to finance their retirement.

This approach, however, has major transition problems since, if the approach has not always been in effect, at its inception neither retired nor active worker have saved in prior years, as well as other problems discussed below.

The Three Systems Compared

With the constant money solution, individuals could vary their claims on future income by varying their savings. The tax and transfer system could also allow for variations in savings. To accomplish this, individuals would be given "bonds" equivalent to their desired savings. The bonds then would be presented to the government for repayment during retirement.

If the working generations then "purchase" the bonds, or are taxed to do so, the solution is identical to the above, and indeed the bonds serve the store of value function of a stable money supply. If all individuals are identical, this modification is, of course, irrelevant. If not, a policy that lacks individual choice imposes a burden on those whose savings preferences differ from the rate mandated for all.[43] Some may find that their preferences do not agree with those of society as a whole and, therefore, that they are worse off than before. In addition, it has been implicitly assumed that labor supply is inelastic so that it is not affected by tax rates. But more realistically, labor supply is likely to be decreased by a tax and transfer program that reduces real income, as discussed below. The two other solutions of within-family transfers and money stability do not suffer from these two problems because they allow individual decisions on the desired amount of consumption loans, retirement income, and labor supply (although they do suffer from other problems).

In particular, a savings rate chosen by one generation may impose burdens on all future generations if implemented through a tax and transfer solution, but not through the other systems. There is an asymmetry in how this can happen. If the current working generation wishes an increase in the savings rate, the increase is likely to be passed into law since it will have the approval of current working generations, along with that of the retired who are getting a free gift. A decrease in the savings rate by the current generation, if desired, is more difficult to implement since the current retired will be solidly opposed, and a substantial proportion of workers, those who have already paid in at the higher tax rate, are also likely to be opposed. Moreover, the current retired generation may be able to get a permanently higher tax rate passed to benefit itself even if it would not willingly have saved more and even if the current working generations' time preference rates have not decreased. They may be able to impose such an increase for their own personal gain, again because the increase will have their political support and also the support of those in the working generations who will gain at the expense of younger workers.

The stable money supply and family transfer solutions do not share this bias. With these solutions, if the desired preretirement savings rate is to be translated into retirement consumption, the working generations must agree to adhere to the same savings rate. In other words, in both of these solutions the current and future generations must agree on the total amount that is to be saved if the equilibrium consumption pattern is to be continued. On the other hand, if it is decided that the present income level of those already retired is inadequate, the tax and transfer system can immediately increase the amount of tax and transfer to solve the problem, while the stable money supply system is impotent to respond.

Interfamily and stable money systems also are vulnerable to their reliance on the young. With interfamily transfers, the young may choose not to support the elderly to the extent anticipated. The power to make this decision is in the hands of the young. If future generations desire to save less for retirement, they could do so in the money savings system by spending rather than saving the money transferred to them by current retirees. If the dollars received are respent rather than saved, their purchasing power will decline. If bonds are used to store value until retirement and the working generations desire to save less, demand for bonds will fall as they are sold to finance retirement consumption. Their value in terms of output would then be decreased, and the current retired could not purchase the amounts desired.

A decision by the young to save a lower proportion of their output may reflect an optimal adjustment to a change in time preference rates or possible rates of return. On the other hand, the young may be myopic. If so, the systems that rely on individual choice will not produce sufficient savings.

In addition, a constant money supply is likely to destabilize the economy when the rate of growth of potential output increases. A higher rate of growth of real output with a constant money supply necessitates, in equilibrium, an increase in the rate of decline of prices and wages. In an advanced manufacturing and service economy, where prices and wages are set by managers and unions and not by auction markets, prices do not immediately decline in response to a decline in demand. Decreased demand then results in declines in purchases. A fall-off in purchases may induce decreases in production. In addition, firms may interpret the resistance to their old prices (that derives from tight money due to increased overall growth) as a signal of lack of demand for their product and, for this reason as well, may decrease their production. Declines in production and employment may then result in further output and employment decreases through a Keynesian multiplier effect. Substantial production and employment decreases may be necessary before prices and wages fall sufficiently to allow a return to full employment. Because such adjustments take time, misperceived increases in real potential output may cause recessions.

Moreover, adherence to a constant money supply interferes with the use of both monetary and fiscal policies to dampen recessions. For example, faced with a decrease in foreign demand for U.S. output, precipitated perhaps by a trade war as in the events that preceded the Great Depression, the government could neither ease credit nor increase spending without increasing taxes. The decrease in aggregate demand could not be offset by domestic policy and would result in a spiraling downward of output. Nor would the moderating influence of "built-in stabilizers" be as powerful, since they would be accompanied by higher interest rates.

It is true that the economy may return eventually to full employment on its own, as prices drop due to the excess supply conditions. And the price decline and real output increase will restore the value of retirees' cash reserves. But there is no guarantee that this process will be an expeditious one, or even that it will happen at all, since investors may respond to a climate of uncertainty by refusing to invest while consumers decrease their own spending due to the decline in income.[44] Indeed, it was only the successful deficit spending of World War II, funded by printing dollars, which reemployed idle workers and factories and ended the 1930s depression. Retirees, as well as others, are harmed by resulting recessions since workers save less as their income declines.

Given these problems, the only alternative in a world that requires human capital transfers to assure retirement income security is the tax and transfer solution. The bias in this system must be guarded against, especially as discussed in the following section, when temporary increases in the dependency ratio lower replacement rates and rates of return.

The Impact of Output and Population Changes on Intergenerational Consumption Loans

All of these solutions, as described, result in a real interest rate of zero or cost of future consumption of one. This outcome depends on the assumptions that there is no real growth of per capita income and that the ratio of active workers to retirees is steady.

Per Capita Output Changes

If output per capita increases (decreases), the real interest rate on these consumption loans increases (decreases) with constant replacement rates. To illustrate why this is so, the intergenerational consumption loan can be conceived of as the loan of the product of a given proportion of hours worked, with repayment in terms of the product of the same proportion of hours worked. For example, let us assume again that group A promises to give one third of its working hours' product per year, say 700 hours, to group C in return for the same promise of the output of one third of future group A's hours worked. The savings to consumption ratio is then 700/1,400 or one half.

If output per hour increases, with number of hours worked constant, real income received in retirement will exceed the amount saved by retirees when they worked, by the amount of the productivity increase. Therefore, the rate of return earned on savings will exceed one.[45]

Population Changes

The ratio of retired to workers may change over time, although a constant population growth rate could eventually result in a constant dependency ratio. Equation 8.2 may be modified to indicate that *W*, *R*, and *CRR* vary with time *t* so that

$$CRR_t = \frac{S}{C}\left(\frac{W_t}{R_t}\right) \tag{8.6}$$

In fact, the ratio of workers to retirees is expected to decline significantly in the next three decades if the average retirement use does not increase. Table 8–8 illustrates the predicament facing retired and working generations if the ratio of workers to retirees decreases. In the example shown, with population constant two individuals in A and B support one retired individual in C. Both A and B contribute one third of their time and output produced to C's retirement for a total of 1,400 hours of produce

TABLE 8–8
Alternative Responses to a Decline in Population Growth or Output When Retirees' Consumption Equals Workers' Savings

		Generation		
		Working Generations		*Retired*
		A	*B*	*C*
1. Constant population (ratio of workers to retired equals 2):	Total	2,100	2,100	
	Save	700	700	0
	Consume	1,400	1,400	1,400
2. Population decreased in half (ratio of workers to retired equals 1):		A and B		C
a. Alternative 1:	Save	700		
	Consume	1,400		700
b. Alternative 2:	Save	1,400		
	Consume	700		1,400
c. Alternative 3:	Save	1,050		
	Consume	1,050		1,050
d. Alternative 4:	Save	900		
	Consume	1,200		900

Units are output per year per person in each group. It is assumed that output per hour is fixed at one unit and that number of hours worked per year are fixed at 2,100. Production of 2,100 units per working person is available to be distributed.

and themselves consume the remaining two thirds (i.e., 1,400 hours worth of produce).

The result of the halving of the working population as shown in Table 8–8 is that one member each of A and B must now support one member of C. If working population halves so that one worker supports one retiree, the individual who consumed 1,400 hours' worth of output per year while working and saved the remaining 700 will have only 700 hours' worth of product during retirement. The result in terms of Equation 8.5 is shown as follows:

$$CRR = \frac{1}{2} \cdot \frac{1}{1} = \frac{1}{2}$$

The savings and consumption pattern is now in disequilibrium. Retirees and workers face several alternatives. Alternative

1 is, as already indicated, to maintain the agreement to tax and transfer one third of workers' output to retirees. As a result, retirees' consumption drops to half of the preretirement level they had planned to maintain. Conversely, in alternative 2, retirees consume in retirement what they saved by doubling taxation rates and halving workers' consumption. In alternative 3, retirees and workers both decrease their living standards by 25 percent with a 50 percent tax rate.

In a more realistic model, hourly output and the number of hours worked can be changed and might respond negatively to higher tax rates. Considerations of this sort might motivate retirees to prefer a lower tax rate, such as shown by alternative 4. In any case, retirees may very well react to the temporary increase in the dependency ratio and the consequent decrease in their transfer benefits by attempting to raise tax rates. The shift in the dependency ratio also increases the political power of retirees. Thus, they may be able to exert their political power over government to coerce the current working generation to go along with their desired tax rate. But it may not be optimal for the current retired to impose their desired tax rate on those to come. If the retired do succeed in increasing existing tax rates in spite of constant preferences of the working generations, once the taxes are paid in and they retire, they too will have an interest in maintaining the high savings and tax rates. Depending on the constellation of political power, the result may be a too large equilibrium intergenerational transfer of savings.[46]

Inflation and the Use of Intergenerational Consumption Loans for Efficient Wealth Diversification

In the real world, society need not rely on intergenerational consumption loans as the sole source of retirement income. Nature is not as parsimonious as has been assumed. What purpose do loans of the output of a given proportion of labor serve in a world with alternative real interest earning investment vehicles? Since most goods are produced by both labor and capital, and some services in retirement are provided almost entirely by labor, efficient risk-bearing requires holdings of both. Otherwise, retirees are exposed to the risk of changing factor shares. An efficient portfolio of investments is a diversified one. Factor-share risk could be diversified away if human capital were tradable. In the absence of the possibility of such trades, a system of consumption loans in which current workers purchase a share of future workers' output by transferring that same share to current retirees allows investment in human capital.[47] This investment in human capital complements investment in physical capital.

A stable money supply can be used to invest in both forms of capital. Relying on this solution, however, increases the problems discussed above. On the other hand, inflation caused by an increase in the money supply, or the threat of such inflation, would be inconsistent with the use of money as a means of storing a claim to a constant share of output produced by labor and capital.

In the absence of price stability (or of family intergenerational transfers), a pay-as-you-go wage tax with a transfer of the proceeds to retirees can be used to accumulate claims to human wealth to accomplish the diversification purpose. The system must be pay-as-you-go and financed by current wages rather than funded to provide the requisite diversity of retirement income sources.

Although wage taxes for retirement benefits provide a means of efficient risk-bearing, they may have costs. Tax levels may be decided on collectively, imposing a burden on some individuals with differing preferences. In addition, the retired and older working generations may have the power to impose heavier taxes on the younger and all following generations than is optimal for the health of the economy.

A wage tax transfer to retirees can coexist with inflation and, indeed, can be viewed as a substitute for money in the presence of money-shock inflation. However, it may not be possible for benefits to serve their risk-reducing function optimally and at the same time be indexed to inflation. Aggregate benefits in the optimal system will be perfectly correlated with changes in aggregate wage income. Therefore, individual benefits in the optimal system are indexed to aggregate wage income divided by the number of retirees. If the ratio of aggregate real wage bill per retiree declines, individual real benefit levels must decline.

As discussed below, uncertain inflation raises the cost and/or risk of providing retirement income through financial instruments. Thus, there is an increased incentive to use a tax-based intergenerational transfer system to provide the indexed annuities that private markets cannot provide. But the use of the system in this way to protect the elderly from uncertain inflation, while possible, may burden future generations. In general, efficient human wealth transfers cannot be indexed to inflation under the maintained assumptions. Shares of the output of human labor should be transferred across generations, but these do not necessarily allow constant real retirement income. They do so only if labor income across generations is constant (or growing).

Notes

[1] This may be regarded as a maximum since parents give bequests to children and children are concerned for the welfare of their parents. For some evidence on within-family insurance and intergenerational transfers, see L. J. Kotlikoff and A. Spivak, "The Family as an Incomplete Annuities Market," *Journal of Political Economy*, April 1981.

[2] Under these assumptions, in the optimal system individual benefits are indexed to aggregate wage income divided by the number of retirees, as discussed in the previous chapter.

[3] The establishment of a safety-net minimum income level, as well as other more general income redistribution, may be a response to an identification and concern for the poor or to a perceived need for insurance against uncontrollable shifts in fortune to which everyone is vulnerable.

[4] A mandatory universal pension system (MUPS) could be used to require workers to save. However, an obligatory Social Security system has the advantage of not inflicting small businesses with administrative costs that are higher than those borne by large businesses. Since these costs would vary with the nature of the business, especially its labor-intensity, government grants could not be used to compensate for the higher costs without subsidizing some. In addition, the desired equity tilt would have to be preserved through tax-financed subsidies to individual workers who qualify. Thus, government transfers (supported by taxes) would still have to be distributed to subsidize minimum payments, to support the desired equity tilt, and to compensate small businesses for the extra burden of administrative costs. Given the necessity of these public transfers, the economies of scale of centralizing the administration of the program into a Social Security benefit system are likely to be significant. The subsidized retirement benefits can then be added to the wage-tax-financed transfers used to diversify factor shares risk (although the subsidized portion of retirement benefits need not be paid for through the pay-as-you-go collection of wage taxes).

[5] It is difficult to find direct evidence on the existence or extent of myopia.

Positive time preference and interest rates do not indicate myopia, but merely a rational adaptation to positive interest rates generated by the usefulness of capital goods. See Mancur Olson and Martin J. Bailey, "Positive Time Preference," *Journal of Political Economy*, February 1981. Clearly, most families in the United States are currently able to save, as evidenced by the majority who at retirement own homes and the use of housing as an investment vehicle. The insignificance of personal savings for all but the well-off may be the effect of current relatively high Social Security benefit levels. Using very rough calculations on savings of 50-year-olds in the 1950s when Social Security benefits were significantly lower than they are now, Peter Diamond, in "A Framework for Social Security Analysis," *Journal of Public Economics* 8 (1977), p. 212, estimates that perhaps only 20 to 30 percent of the population was saving too little. On the other hand, young and middle-aged workers know very little about their pension benefits. See Laurence J. Kotlikoff and David E. Smith, *Pensions in the American Economy*. (Chicago: National Bureau of Economic Research, University of Chicago Press, 1985).

[6] The tax advantages currently used to subsidize pensions and other savings are discussed in Chapter 7. In general, approved pensions and IRA accounts are encouraged by exempting the funds put aside and interest on the funds in future years from income taxes. Given proportional income taxes, subsidies that derive from tax exemption aid the wealthy more than the poor; thus, an income distribution bias is introduced. This is an additional rationale for a progressive Social Security system. On the other hand, the regressive tilt of tax exemptions can help to compensate for labor disincentive effects created by a progressive income tax system.

[7] The Employee Retirement Income Security Act (ERISA), enacted in 1974, sets minimum standards to qualify pensions for tax advantages. The regulations, for example, those that rule out self-dealing and that require minimum vesting periods, seek to prevent managers and owners from exploiting workers' lack of information. They also seek to prevent the establishment of pensions merely as a means of avoiding taxes without encouraging additional retirement savings. IRA legislation set minimum qualifying standards for individual savings vehicles.

[8] In the discussion thus far, the only market failure justification for an unfunded Social Security system other than equity concerns is the provision of benefits tied to labor's output share for efficient risk-bearing. This requires the indexing of benefits to the total wage bill divided by the number of retirees. A higher dependency ratio and/or output slowdowns may decrease wage-tax revenues per retiree and necessitate a decrease in real benefits, unless Social Security tax rates are increased as a solution. This decrease can be implemented with a planned decrease in retirement benefits and/or increase in eligibility age to deal with anticipated dependency ratio increases (with the date at which the benefit and/or eligibility age changes are to go into effect announced sufficiently before retirement to allow adjustments in private savings), together with a link of after-retirement payments to a wage or price index, whichever is lower (to deal with unanticipated wage declines). Whatever the method chosen, real benefits would have to decline under these circumstances, and this is inconsistent with the indexation of a particular level of real Social Security payments to the price level.

[9] This follows from the diversification argument presented earlier in this

section. Depending on the amount of social transfers to be financed, the requisite funding might exceed the national debt, in which case critical issues of public lending to private firms would arise. See Alan J. Auerbach and Laurence J. Kotlikoff, "Simulating Alternative Social Security Responses to the Demographic Transition," NBER Working Paper No. 1308, March 1984.

[10] A possible goal of government Social Security policy is to guarantee each generation of retirees the same proportion of preretirement earnings. The 1974 adoption of automatic annual adjustments to match increases in the CPI and the 1977 amendments to correct for overindexing could be interpreted as having this goal. To quote a Joint Economic Committee Congressional report, "[These] were aimed at maintaining the ratio of Social Security benefits to preretirement earnings at roughly constant levels through time, regardless of inflation." The principle is that each generation of future retirees should have roughly the same proportion of preretirement earnings replaced by Social Security benefits. See "Social Security and Pensions: Programs of Equity and Security," Joint Economic Committee, Special Study on Economic Change, a Staff Study, October 1980, p. 7.

[11] Two different kinds of data are presented in a paper by Michael Hurd and John Shoven to support this conclusion. The results, which were presented above in Tables 6–2 and 6–4, indicate that on the average, retirement income and wealth were not being significantly eroded by inflation in spite of the lack of indexation of private pension benefits in the 1970s. The source of this result was the growing importance of Social Security and Medicaid/Medicare in the budgets of the elderly and the guaranteeing of the benefits of these programs against inflation.

The reported data on relative per capita income show that elderly households had on average 56 percent as much disposable income as the average household in 1970 and that by 1978 this had grown to 63 percent. Per capita elderly income was 116 percent of nonelderly income in 1970 and grew to 121 percent in 1978 (the difference between the two groups is affected significantly by family size). Annual data on the relative position of the elderly, given in Table 6–2, indicate steady gains in this period. While wage earners and investors suffered from stagflation and tax bracket creep, the growing importance and the indexation of social transfer payments, primarily Social Security and Medicaid/Medicare, to inflation protected the elderly. See Michael Hurd and John B. Shoven, "The Economic Status of the Elderly," in *Financial Aspects of the United States Pension System*, ed. Zvi Bodie and John B. Shoven (Chicago: National Bureau of Economic Research, University of Chicago Press, 1985).

[12] The substantial increase in the importance of social transfer payments relative to other income sources occurred with the introduction of Medicare in 1965, ad hoc increases in Social Security followed by automatic indexation of Social Security benefits along with over-indexation, which began in 1975 and ended in 1977.

[13] The data of Table 8–1 have been provided by Orlo R. Nichols of the Social Security Administration.

[14] See Dan M. McGill, "Formulating National Retirement Policy," Committee for Economic Development, February 4, 1981, pp. 85–86.

[15] See Michael Boskin and John Shoven, "Concepts and Measures of Earnings Replacement during Retirement," NBER Working Paper No. 1360, June 1984.

[16] See Gary Fields and Olivia Mitchell, "The Effects of Social Security Reforms on Retirement Ages and Retirement Incomes," NBER Working Paper No. 1348, May 1984.

[17] See James R. Storey, Richard C. Michel, and Sheila R. Zedlewski, "Saving Social Security: The Short- and Long-Run Effects of the 1983 Amendments," Urban Institute, September 1983.

[18] See Alicia H. Munnell, "The Social Security Solution, Continued: Navigating a Few Rough Spots Ahead," *New York Times*, August 12, 1984. Also see "Financing Options for Social Security," prepared for the Conference on Policy Issues in Work and Retirement, Institute of Management and Labor Relations, Rutgers University, October 14–15, 1982.

[19] Ibid.

[20] See John J. Fialka, "Candidates Avoid Medicare Cure," *The Wall Street Journal*, September 12, 1984, p. 64.

[21] See Fields and Mitchell, "The Effects of Social Security Reforms on Retirement Ages and Retirement Incomes," p. 15.

[22] Compiled by Richard V. Burkhauser and John A. Turner in "Labor-Market Experience of the Almost Old and the Implications for Income Support," presented at the American Economic Association annual meetings, Washington, D.C., December 28, 1981.

[23] See Sheldon Danziger, "How Income Transfer Programs Affect Work, Savings, and the Income Distribution: A Critical Review," *Journal of Economic Literature* 19, no. 3 (September 1981).

[24] See Anthony Pellechio, "The Effect of Social Security on Retirement," National Bureau of Economic Research Working Paper No. 260, July 1978.

[25] See Richard V. Burkhauser and Joseph Quinn, "The Effect of Changes in Mandatory Retirement Rules on the Labor Supply of Older Workers," presented at NBER Conference on the Economics of Compensation, Cambridge, Mass., November 1980.

[26] See Storey, Michel, and Zedlewski, "Saving Social Security: The Short- and Long-Run Effects of the 1983 Amendments," p. 17.

[27] See Jerry A. Hausman, "Income and Payroll Tax Policy and Labor Supply," in National Bureau of Economic Research Working Paper No. 610, December 1980; and "The Effect of Taxes on Labor Supply," in *How Taxes Affect Economic Behavior*, H. Aaron and J. Pechmen eds. (Washington, D.C.: Brookings Institution, 1981).

[28] Assuming that Social Security and Medicare wealth are somewhat less than half of overall wealth and that they cause somewhat less than a 50-cent loss of savings per dollar, the overall savings rate would be approximately 25 percent lower. For the former estimate see Table 6–3; for the latter estimate, see note 38 of Chapter 6 and Michael J. Boskin, "Theoretical and Empirical Issues in the Measurement, Evaluation, and Interpretation of Post-War U.S. Saving," in *Savings and Capital Formation: The Policy Options*, ed. F. Gerard Adams and Susan M. Wachter (Lexington, Mass.: D. C. Heath, 1985). As a result, GNP could be lowered by 10 percent. (This halves Martin Feldstein's estimate discussed in note 38 of Chapter 6.) Econometric estimates of the impact of a decline in savings on the average productivity of labor suggest that a decline of this magnitude could reduce a 1.5 percent growth rate in average productivity

of labor by approximately one third. See Marshall E. Blume, Jean A. Crockett, and Irwin Friend, "Stimulation of Capital Formulation: Ends and Means," *Toward a New U.S. Industrial Policy?* ed. Michael L. Wachter and Susan M. Wachter (Philadelphia, Pa.: University of Pennsylvania Press, 1981), pp. 41–94.

[29] Improvements in social transfers have reduced the percentage of the elderly who are poor (from one in four in 1965 to one in seven in 1980) to a rate that equals the percentage of poor in the population as a whole. However, cutbacks in Medicare/Medicaid and in Social Security benefits, together with increased longevity, may threaten these gains. Lower income workers are less well covered by pensions and have less of a tax incentive to use retirement savings vehicles. Thus, modification of across-the-board social transfer decreases may be necessary to protect low-income workers' standard of living, especially if Medicare/Medicaid cutbacks are severe.

[30] Indexed debt is not burdensome during demand-pull-caused accelerations in inflation, because real income and tax revenues increase. The cost of nominal debt declines during such episodes, but increases during the corrective contraction (as inflation drops beneath its anticipated rate and real interest rates rise). During demand-pull cycles, indexed debt can be helpful to smooth out real interest costs. Indeed, if demand-pull-caused accelerations cannot be controlled, a money risk premium will be built into long-term debt and, with sufficient uncertainty, into short-term debt as well.

[31] A transition of this sort, however, would create an inequity for those near retirement age at the date of change who paid income taxes during their working years and now face consumption taxes during retirement.

[32] To increase the quantity of savings available for private investment, the government can also reduce the deficit by reducing government spending or by increasing taxes, while maintaining expenditures unchanged. The latter will decrease the amount of disposable income consumers have available for consumption and savings, but will decrease consumption more than savings. Of the two methods of reducing the deficit, a decrease in government spending generates a greater increase in the quantity of savings. But both methods make more resources available for investment. The resulting lower interest rate will also increase the demand for investment, as more projects pass the interest rate cost hurdle. The government can also reduce the portion of government expenditures that is used for consumption and increase the portion used for investment. Public spending can be for social infrastructure investment such as roads, bridges, or schools or for consumption expenses and for human capital investment through education.

[33] While increased savings earmarked for retirement and general savings both increase the productivity of workers, they have differing effects. Earmarked funds, especially annuities or pensions, represent claims of retired people on current production that can substitute for Social Security benefits. Other savings can be used for retirement spending or bequeathed. Public policy to stimulate the former is a useful way of encouraging an alternative source of retirement income if Social Security and Medicare benefits are decreased. However, there is a rationale to encouraging other savings as well: Precisely because they are less likely to be used in the retirement period, they will increase the productivity of workers, without being an additional drain on resources in the period of high dependency ratios when the dissaving of retirees may drive down the value of capital. Thus, it may be desirable for the govern-

ment to generate increased accumulation of physical capital through exempting (from federal income taxation) general savings as well as retirement savings.

[34] See F. Gerard Adams and Susan M. Wachter, eds., *Savings and Capital Formation: The Policy Options* (Lexington, Mass.: D.C. Heath, 1985).

[35] Other factors include the worker's expected state of health and expected longevity, taste for leisure relative to taste for work, nature of work and expected change in it, level of relative risk aversion, and rate of time preference, income, and wealth.

[36] The impact of the cohort size on average wages of the cohort has been empirically documented.

[37] The relationship of the baby boom generation to the older and smaller near-retirement cohorts causes firms to prefer early retirement policies in the current period. The baby boom generation provides a ready supply of relatively inexpensive labor. Technological advances that increase the skills of the newly maturing labor force relative to older workers may also induce firms to prefer early retirement, currently. Moreover, the increased labor force participation of women has raised female employment rates among the baby boom generation, while raising unemployment rates in general. The evidence of pension benefits for early retirement indicates that firms have encouraged retirement at and before age 65.

[38] See Fields and Mitchell, "The Effects of Social Security Reforms on Retirement Ages and Retirement Incomes."

[39] See Paul A. Samuelson, "An Exact Consumption-Loan Model of Interest with or without the Social Contrivance of Money," *Journal of Political Economy*, December 1958.

This theory has been extended by Merton as a rationale for Social Security, as discussed below. See Robert C. Merton, "On the Role of Social Security as a Means for Efficient Risk Sharing in an Economy Where Human Capital Is Not Tradeable," in *Financial Aspects of the United States Pension System*, ed. Zvi Bodie and John B. Shoven (Chicago: National Bureau of Economic Research, University of Chicago Press, 1985).

[40] A nearly equivalent solution is to rely on government-guaranteed intergenerational transfers within the workplace. For example, current workers may agree to pay one third of their income to current retirees with the firm contractually arguing to "tax" future workers to pay future retirees. Government or government-regulated firm-wide insurance would have to be required to provide pension benefits for retirees of firms that fail.

[41] Workers transfer to the retired what they do not consume. Thus the absolute amount transferred is the amount of annual income (Y) not consumed, $Y - C$ multiplied by the number of workers, or $W(Y - C)$, which equals $W(Y)\left(1 - \frac{C}{Y}\right)$. If the retired each wish to consume the same amount that workers consume (or that they consumed when they were workers), then retirees' desired total income will be equal to $R\frac{C}{Y}(Y)$. Thus, if these are to be equal

$$W(Y)\left(1 - \frac{C}{Y}\right) = R\frac{C}{Y}(Y)$$

Since, by definition,

$$\frac{S}{Y} = 1 - \frac{C}{Y}$$

The equation can be rewritten, substituting $\frac{S}{Y}$ for $1 - \frac{C}{Y}$, as follows:

$$W(Y)\,\frac{S}{Y} = R\,\frac{C}{Y}\,(Y)$$

or, equivalently,

$$\frac{W}{R} = \frac{\frac{C}{Y}}{\frac{S}{Y}} = \frac{C}{S}$$

If retirees choose to consume a fraction $CRR < 1$ of workers' consumption, then the following must hold:

$$W(Y)\,\frac{S}{Y} = R\,\frac{C}{Y}\,(Y)\,CRR$$

or, equivalently,

$$\frac{W}{R} = \frac{C}{S}\,CRR$$

In general, then,

$$\left(\frac{W}{R}\right)\left(\frac{S}{C}\right) = CRR$$

or the fraction of workers' income desired in retirement.

[42] See Kotlikoff and Spivak, "The Family as an Incomplete Annuities Market."

[43] There is a second potential difference, as well, which does not arise in the model as described so far. The money holdings can be used as a claim against privately held physical capital as well as human capital. This is discussed below.

[44] Due to the decreased output and income and to the increased unemployment, individuals have less income with which to purchase goods, so prices decline. In terms of the quantity theory of money, actual output is less than full-employment output, so that the ratio of money output to money holdings (i.e., velocity) decreases as spending and real income decline. Individuals' desired money balances relative to output are higher because the decline in real income decreases desired consumption and investment, even though monetary wealth has not diminished. Indeed, the value of cash increases with the decline in prices. Thus, holders of money find that their money wealth has increased due to the shortfall in aggregate demand, although they may suffer from the recession itself.

[45] The initial replacement rate is not changed by uniform productivity growth. Nor is the after-retirement replacement rate of average per capita in-

come affected. As seen in Table 8–8, with constant population, output per hour changes do not affect the ratio of retirees' to workers' consumption. The income of the retired increases with that of the general population, and the replacement ratio remains at one. Conversely, productivity losses induce lowered rates of return but, again, with replacement ratios of current per capita income unaffected.

[46] For a model describing the circumstances under which such an equilibrium is likely, see Kriss A. Sjoblom, "Voting for Social Security," Fels Discussion Paper No. 154, School of Public and Urban Policy, University of Pennsylvania, November 1981.

[47] See Merton, "On the Role of Social Security as a Means for Efficient Risk-Bearing in an Economy Where Human Capital Is Not Tradeable."

Bibliography

BAILEY, MARTIN J., and MANCUR OLSUN. "Positive Time Preference." *Journal of Political Economy,* February 1981.

BLUME, MARSHALL E.; JEAN A. CROCKETT; and IRWIN FRIEND. "Stimulation of Capital Formulation: Ends and Means." In *Toward a New U.S. Industrial Policy?* ed. Michael L. Wachter and Susan M. Wachter. Philadelphia, Pa.: University of Pennsylvania Press, 1981.

BOSKIN, MICHAEL J. "Theoretical and Empirical Issues in the Measurement, Evaluation, and Interpretation of Post-War U.S. Savings." In *Savings and Capital Formations: The Policy Options,* ed. Gerald Adams and Susan M. Wachter. Lexington, Mass.: D. C. Heath, 1985.

BOSKIN, MICHAEL J., and JOHN SHOVEN. "Concepts and Measures of Earnings Replacement." National Bureau of Economic Research Working Paper No. 1348, May 1984.

BURKHAUSER, RICHARD V., and JOSEPH QUINN. "The Effect of Changes in Mandatory Retirement Rules on the Labor Supply of Older Workers." NBER Conference on the Economics of Compensation, Cambridge, Mass., November 1980.

BURKHAUSER, RICHARD V., and JOHN A. TURNER. "Labor Market Experience of the Almost Old and the Implications for Income Support." Washington D. C., December 28, 1981.

DANZIGER, SHELDON, et al. "How Income Transfer Programs Affect Work, Savings, and the Income Distribution: A Critical Review." *Journal of Economic Welfare* 19, No. 3 (September 1981).

DIAMOND, PETER. "A Framework for Social Security Analysis." *Journal of Public Economics* 8 (1977).

FIALKA, JOHN J. "Candidates Avoid Medicare Cure." *The Wall Street Journal,* September 12, 1984.

FIELDS, GARY, and OLIVIA MITCHELL. "The Effects of Social Security Reforms on Retirement Ages and Retirement Incomes." National Bureau of Economic Research Working Paper No. 1348, May 1984.

HAUSMAN, JERRY A. "Income and Payroll Tax Policy and Labor Supply." National Bureau of Economic Research Working Paper No. 610, December 1980.

HURD, MICHAEL, and JOHN B. SHOVEN. "The Economic Status of the Elderly." In *Financial Aspects of the United States Pension System,* ed. Zvi Bodie and John B. Shoven. Chicago: National Bureau of Economic Research, University of Chicago Press, 1985.

KOTLIKOFF, L. J., and A. SPIVAK. "The Family as an Incomplete Annuities Market." *Journal of Political Economy,* April 1981.

MCGILL, DAN M. "Formulating National Retirement Policy." Committee for Economic Development, February 4, 1981.

MERTON, ROBERT C. "On the Role of Social Security as a Means for Efficient Risk-Bearing in an Economy Where Human Capital Is Not Tradeable." Massachusetts Institute of Technology, August 1981.

MICHEL, RICHARD C.; JAMES R. STOREY; and SHEILA R. ZEDLEWSKI. "Saving Social Security: The Short- and Long-Run Effects of the 1983 Amendments." Urban Institute, September 1983.

MUNNEL, ALICIA H. "The Social Security Solution, Continued: Navigating a Few Rough Spots Ahead." *New York Times,* August 12, 1984.

PELLECHIO, ANTHONY. "The Effect of Social Security on Retirement." National Bureau of Economic Research Working Paper No. 260, July 1978.

SAMUELSON, PAUL A. "An Exact Consumption Loan Model of Interest with or without the Social Contrivance of Money." *Journal of Political Economy,* December 1958.

SJOBLOM, KRISS A. "Voting for Social Security." Fels Discussion Paper No. 154, School of Public and Urban Policy, University of Pennsylvania, November 1981.

9 Summary: Inflation's Impact on Pensions and Policy Conclusions

Chronic inflation, even at a moderate level such as 5 percent a year, rapidly erodes the value of nominal pensions. An average inflation rate of 5 percent will decrease the real value of a pension by approximately 50 percent in 15 years. Inflation poses a serious problem for retirees who rely on nominal private pensions to maintain preretirement standards of living.

Inflation has decreased from its double-digit highs of the late 1970s. Monetary policy of the early to mid-1980s supported moderate underlying inflation in the 4 to 5 percent range. Even if the anti-inflation monetary policies adopted by the Federal Reserve Board in October 1979 were maintained, it would be years before inflation subsides completely. Moreover, there is a possibility that monetary policies that moderate inflation will be discontinued in favor of resurgent inflation, especially if the costs of inflation are not well understood.

The problem of inflation's impact on pensions does not exist for those who rely entirely or substantially on expected indexed Social Security and Medicare benefits. Demographic shifts, however, will increase the proportion of old to young in this country, which will raise the long-term cost of existing benefit levels. The plan that has been adopted to solve Social Security's long-term financial problems increases payroll taxes and effectively decreases the after-tax percentage of preretirement income replaced by benefit levels for those retiring at age 65. Moreover, Medicare benefits may have to be scaled back to assure long-term solvency. Thus, we cannot look to an expansion of social transfers as a solution to inflation's erosion of private retirement benefits.

A solution to this problem would be relatively straightforward if private pensions could be fully or even partially indexed to a measure of inflation. This book addresses the questions of, first, to what extent it is economically feasible and desirable to provide full or partial indexing and, second, in the absence of such indexing, what other changes can help to minimize the impact of inflation. The first question can be posed somewhat differently. If it is feasible and desirable in a world of no inflation to have benefits defined in nominal terms, is it not also feasible and desirable in a world of inflation to have defined benefits indexed to a measure of inflation?

The answer to this question depends on the value and cost of indexed pensions. If we can assume that inflation has no real effects; that is, if we can assume that we live in a world of what economists term *neutral inflation*, the cost of indexing pension benefits can be calculated relatively easily. Indeed, the extra cost of fully indexing a new plan to neutral inflation is zero. That is, the cost of a new fully indexed plan would be the same as the cost of a new nominal plan in a world without inflation.

Assuming neutral inflation and nominal benefits, the cost of existing pensions is, of course, lower than without inflation. In this kind of a world, changing from pensions defined in nominal terms to fully indexed pensions requires either a decrease in the initial value of pensions (by approximately 50 percent assuming 5 percent inflation) or a decrease in current wages (by approximately 5 percent) to pay for indexation.

In essence, *neutral* inflation reduces the cost of a nominal defined benefits plan by the same amount that it reduces the real value of the pension. In the inflationary experience of 1960 to 1980, however, pension sponsors' costs did not decrease as much as retirees' real benefits because inflation was not neutral.

For inflation to be neutral it must be due solely to anticipated excessive growth in the money supply. Neutral inflation has no real effects on relative prices (the ratios of prices) because the excessive money supply growth is anticipated. When an increase in prices is fully anticipated all contracts can be easily adjusted so that they include the anticipated general price increase and in real terms remain unchanged. In addition, anticipated inflation must occur in a world where tax effects are neutralized. Under neutral inflation, money is a veil, and increases in the money supply have no real effects other than to change the value of the currency.

In the short run, real shocks, such as an unanticipated decline in output growth, cause inflation, even with a noninflationary growth in the money supply, simply because these growth declines cannot be predicted. If output growth declines beneath predicted levels, inflation results until money supply growth declines.

Because short-run inflation is unanticipated and correlated with real output changes and relative price changes, it cannot be neutral. Sustained long-run inflation must be accompanied by money supply growth. Rational investors will predict such inflation and, accordingly, require higher nominal yields. Thus, in theory, long-run inflation can be anticipated and neutral.

With relative price changes, the measurement of inflation is affected by the cost-of-living (COL) index used. The consumer price index (CPI) is an example of a Laspeyres index. Such an index assumes people cannot adjust their expenditure patterns to reflect changing relative prices. This could bias the CPI upward, although the available empirical evidence indicates that this bias is generally small. As a market-based COL index, the CPI also may suffer from not measuring changes in the cost of living that result from the public goods or home production sectors. In addition, adjustments for quality changes and the use of an average index, rather than indexes tailored to individual or group consumption patterns (such as that of the elderly), result in a less than perfect measurement of inflation, although any bias of using a general price index to reflect price changes experienced by the elderly appears to be inconsequential.

Even if we could resolve the problem of determining the correct inflation index, there remains the more serious and difficult issue of whether everything in the economy can be indexed to the measured inflation rate to provide a costless solution to the inflation problem. In particular, is it costless to index pensions to inflation? If inflation is neutral, real rates of return are not affected, and the cost of indexing new pensions is zero.

Needless to say, the inflation of the 1960 to 1980 period was not neutral. As a result, historical rates of return on most asset portfolios were low and in real terms negative. However, we cannot conclude that future inflation will be associated with negative real rates of return. Inflation was not neutral, first, because its sources also had negative effects on rates of growth; second, because it occurred in a nonneutral tax environment; and, third, because it was not anticipated. In order to separate out those effects on real rates of return associated with past inflation from those likely to prevail in the future, each of these factors must be considered.

First, over these two decades inflation was caused at various times by both demand-pull and supply-shock factors, with money supply erratically expanding at excessive rates. The initial inflationary spurt in the mid- and late-1960s was due to demand-side pressure arising out of the attempt to run a war in Vietnam and a war on poverty at the same time without increasing taxes. The second inflationary spurt of 1973 and 1974 was due to the worldwide OPEC increase in oil prices as well as to worldwide food shortages; OPEC oil price increases also induced the third 1979 inflationary spurt. And over this entire period, on average, monetary policy ratified demand and supply shocks and pushed the economy to expand at rates that exceeded the economy's potential.

In the 1970s, demand-pull and supply-shock factors redistributed income away from more productive to less productive uses. OPEC increases in oil prices had negative effects on labor and capital productivity and real rates of return. In addition, the decline in labor productivity and real rates of return can be attributed to a large youth cohort in the labor force. The OPEC-induced energy price rises directly resulted in higher inflation together with lower growth rates. Also, lower labor and capital productivity, indirectly induced inflation because monetary and fiscal authorities did not adjust for the lower growth potential of the economy.

The declines in productivity and the real rates of return that were due to energy shocks have been turned around. In addition, the unskilled youth cohort has moved on and become more skilled so that the decline in labor productivity and rates of return on capital due to this factor have been mitigated. Disinflation has resulted. But the economy remains vulnerable to supply shocks and renewed inflation. Reinflation could be the response to persistently high interest rates and large federal deficits financed, in part, by foreign capital inflow. Supply shocks that both decrease output and increase inflation could arise in the newly vulnerable international trade sector with a crisis of confidence causing an outflow of international capital and a devalued exchange rate.

Second, inflation of the 1960s and 1970s interacted with a tax system that was and still is not neutral. As nominal interest rates rise with increased anticipated inflation, the effective tax rate on nominal returns increases since they are taxed as though they were real returns. Other nonneutralities result from the full deductibility of nominal interest payments. In addition, depreciation deductions are allowed only on historical rather than real values. These and other nonneutralities are well known and well understood. What is less well known is their impact on after-tax rates of returns of holding different assets. It is often said that the tax system's interaction with inflation hurt profits over these decades, but it is by no means clear that overall it did so. It is true that the inability to depreciate in real terms increased effective tax rates. On the other hand, the real returns on and the cost of debt were negative due to the combined effects of inflation and the deductibility of interest payments. Thus, effective corporate tax rates may have been unchanged. Pensions, highly leveraged real estate, and other tax-sheltered investment vehicles were more in demand as a result of higher inflation and higher effective federal income taxes on taxable interest earnings, but the net impact on before-tax rates of return probably was small. In any case, tax reform legislation of 1986 lessened the tax advantages of debt-financed shelters in an inflationary environment.

Third, inflation was caused by erratic and excessive growth in the money supply that could not be anticipated. With uncertain growth in the money supply and uncertain inflation, relative prices are distorted. Capital markets in particular suffer because of the importance of long-term nominally fixed contracts. Long-term inflation uncertainty interferes with lenders and borrowers coming to terms on nominally fixed interest rates on nominal noncallable long-term debt.

Even if inflation is substantially mitigated over the coming years, the threat of renewed inflation in the future will have continuing effects on long-term bond markets. Only a continuing experience of steadily declining inflation rates and eventual price stability will remove the uncertainty with which our past experience has left us. The largest effect of an unanticipated resurgence of inflation will then, as before, be a decline in the value of long-term noncallable nominal bonds.

The inflation of the 1960s and 1970s was not neutral and was accompanied by lower real rates of return on traditional capital market assets. An unanticipated resurgence of inflation, if set off by supply shocks or by money shocks, could have similarly negative effects on capital markets. In general, real returns on stocks and long-term bonds decrease with unanticipated increases in inflation and inflation uncertainty.

In a world without sustained money supply increases or the resulting sustained inflation, it is possible to fund a de facto average real annuity with long-term bonds without risk to the sponsor. However, neither long-term bonds nor equities can be used to fund indexed pensions without additional risk to sponsors. Because of the nonneutrality of inflation in the short run, the real cost of pensions indexed to measured inflation exceeds that of nominal pensions.

Firms may find that the terms on which they can offer indexed contracts to suppliers are so unfavorable due to the increased risk borne by the firms' owners, that nominal contracts are preferred. Few pensions are indexed. The widespread lack of indexation may be due to a rational preference for nominal contracts. Variable-rate pensions could closely track inflation if invested in inflation-hedging assets without risk to firms, but such pensions would be more costly to recipients because of their necessarily lower rate of return.

Supply shocks are the root cause of the impossibility of indexing pensions without additional risk or cost to the sponsoring firm. Nominal payment contracts (such as nominal debt and nominal pensions) are useful to the firm, precisely because their real decline cushions the real earnings loss of a supply shock, since unanticipated inflation occurs at the same time and proportionately to the severity of the supply shock.

Short-term debt can closely but not perfectly track serially correlated inflation. It is precisely the unpredictable supply shocks that such instruments miss. Thus, they offer a very close substitute to an indexed security that still allows some risk sharing. Necessarily, the expected returns on such instruments are less than on long-term debt. Long-term debt allows lenders to bear the risk of long-term interest rate changes. This diminishes risk to long-term investors, who are consequently willing to pay a higher expected yield than on short-term debt which does not reduce long-term investment risk.

Interest rates on short-term bonds do move more or less in tandem with inflation, and they could be used to fund performance-indexed, inflation-hedging variable annuities. But, as Zvi Bodie has shown, historically the return on a risk-free minimal variance portfolio, that is, a portfolio made up predominantly of Treasury bills hedged against unanticipated inflation by a small position in a diversified portfolio of commodity futures, has been approximately zero.

The cost of choosing a portfolio of short-term bonds and commodities, relative to the long-term bond portfolio that could yield nearly constant real payments, in the absence of uncertain inflation can be measured as the difference in the real yield on long- and short-term bond portfolios, a historical difference of approximately 2 percentage points annually.

If this is the case, financing performance-indexed pensions with an inflation-hedging portfolio may raise the cost of new indexed pensions relative to nominal pensions, in a world of no inflation, by 50 percent. Thus, future retirees may face a trade-off of a 5 percent current wage decrease if they wish performance-indexed pensions. This is in addition to the 5 percent current wage decrease needed to move to a constant real pension in a world of 5 percent inflation. Overall, the cost of existing pension plans may increase by 100 percent if initial real pension levels were to be maintained in a world of sustained and uncertain inflation.

In response to inflation, retirees could convert final pay defined benefit pensions to defined contribution plans upon retirement so that annuity income would vary with returns on inflation hedging assets. Alternatively, pension recipients might choose to maintain nominal pensions.

The benefits and risks to retirees of these alternatives differ. With possible ad hoc payment augmented nominal defined benefit pensions, pension costs continue to be low, with retirees bearing considerable inflation risk. Moreover, retirees must rely on the investment decisions of those managing the funds, on the continuing profitability of the firm, on their continued attachment to the firm, and on the firm's recognition of implicit contractual obligations to retirees.

With payments that vary with underlying asset returns, there is no need to rely on any sense of obligation on the part of the firm or its profitability. On the other hand, although benefits may increase with inflation, there is no guarantee that they will or that rates of return will be positive. With this alternative, the retiree may have the option to choose the type of asset portfolio to be used. This allows knowledgeable retirees to tailor investments to their own risk/return trade-offs, but it increases the risk to naive or myopic retirees of not choosing appropriately.

In a variant of this, excess investment returns above a minimum rate of return are returned to the retiree. If the minimum rate of return equals the real rate of return, this option provides the retiree with real benefits that are the same under neutral inflation as under zero inflation. With nonneutral inflation that has a negative impact on overall rates of return, correspondingly, real earnings are lowered. They are also affected by the sponsor's choice of minimum rate of return and of underlying assets.

The closer the underlying portfolio is to the minimum-variance inflation-hedging portfolio and the closer the rate of return is to the short-run real rate of return, the more inflation protection is provided by this plan design. But moving to a low assumed rate of return would reduce initial retirement benefits, or raise benefits costs as a percentage of wage income, considerably. Thus, rational workers may prefer the lack of an explicit inflation-tied contract.

Private plans have the capacity to adjust initial pensions to keep up with inflation's impact on wages. During the working years, firms can keep wages, and pension obligations that depend on wages, in line with productivity since wage contracts, implicit and explicit, are renegotiated in the light of the firm's and overall economy's productivity. Hence, defined benefit plans increasingly are in the form of final pay plans which deal with inflation's impact on pensions during the working period due to the increased cost of inflation hedging pensions. The problem is heightened because workers differ in their abilities to plan rationally for their retirement.

Some workers may rationally prefer nominal pensions. Others may be misled by myopia and money illusion to focus only on high initial pension levels. Myopia, which justifies tax-advantaged pensions in the first place, may make nominal pensions unserviceable in a time of high inflation, especially for those who change jobs and for surviving spouses who rely on a pension of the primary worker.

Uncertain inflation causes an unavoidable policy dilemma. While inflation-hedging pensions may be necessary for some, especially the myopic, the effect of their mandatory implementation will be to raise pension costs to all, even those who would continue to be well served by nominal pensions. The incentives provided to savings through tax advantages are considerably diminished if high-cost inflation-hedging assets are effectively required. Thus, pensions would be less desired relative to IRAs and other vehicles of wealth accumulation. Moreover, the dilemma can be expected to be heightened by the high nominal and real returns available in a period of resurgent inflation, relative to the yields available in inflation-hedging assets. The problem is that the relative need for and the relative cost of variable pensions grow with the level of inflation since higher levels of inflation are accompanied by increased inflation uncertainty and higher real and nominal interest rates on long-term bonds.

The problem ultimately rests with government policies that create uncertainty over the long-term value of the dollar. In response to high and uncertain inflation, changes in public policy would be called for, although no public policy adjustment could eliminate the negative effects of uncertain inflation except by halting inflation itself.

The potential need to decrease retirees' reliance on fully indexed Social Security and Medicare benefits and to increase their reliance on private pensions in the future might require a stronger private pension inflation linkage than retirees would choose or than private firms would provide. Myopia combined with money illusion may induce employees to accept nominal pensions, even though there is substantial risk of resulting real pensions that are too low to support minimal retirement living standards. Current levels of Social Security and Medicare benefits, together with housing services provided by occupant-owned housing, provide substantial protection against inflation-eroded retirement income. However, in the future, nominal private pensions and private savings may provide a far higher proportion of expected real retirement income.

As a result, high or even moderate inflation, together with increased longevity, may cause a substantial decline in living standards among the long-lived, especially for those with relatively low Social Security replacement rates. Thus, if inflation worsened, government intervention to require performance indexing with inflation-hedging portfolios might become necessary, in spite of the high cost in terms of lost expected yield. In addition, some public or cooperative arrangement to facilitate the transfer of vested benefits would be necessary to deal with the problem of the preretirement erosion of nominal pensions of those who change jobs.

Other regulatory changes could deal with moderate to high inflation if indexed social transfers assured a safety net. These include government policy changes to facilitate the private provision of a constant real retirement income stream. Tax laws could be changed to allow for crediting ad hoc payments and to allow retirees to themselves reinvest their constant nominal pensions without taxing returns to provide a constant real pension. In addition, policies that encourage later retirement and private savings and the option of inflation-hedging variable annuities would be desirable. Depending on the levels of inflation protection provided by indexed social transfers, these policy changes may be sufficient if inflation remains moderate. If accelerated inflation threatens the public goal of retirement income security, at some point mandatory inflation-hedging pensions, along with their transfer upon reemployment, may become socially optimal, in spite of their costs, as a "second-best" response to the inability to achieve the first-best solution of price stability.

If inflation became chronic and highly uncertain, other interventions that ensure real rates of return on pension portfolios while requiring fully indexed pensions would have to be considered. Indexed bonds or rate change insurance are not costless responses to inflation uncertainty, although their cost declines as the money risk premium on nominal debt rises. They require increased tax rates or deficits when real income growth rates decline with supply shocks. Nonetheless, serious attention to these alternatives may be necessary in the United States in the future if the moderation of inflation proves to be an elusive goal.

SOLOMON R. BAKER LIBRARY
3 1725 00363 1038